# GCSE
# GERMAN

**John Davies**
**Former Headteacher, Beauchamps**
**G.M. School**

**Joan Low**
**Head of Modern Languages, Ferryhill Comprehensive**

*Letts*
EDUCATIONAL

Letts Educational
Aldine Place
London W12 8AW
Tel: 020 8740 2266
Fax: 020 8743 8451
e-mail: mail@lettsed.co.uk

First published 1983
Revised 1987, 1990,1993, 1994, 1997
Reprinted 1988, 1991, 1995, 1996, 1998 (twice), 1999 (twice)

Text: © John Davies and Joan Low 1997
Design and illustrations: © BPP (Letts Educational) Ltd 1997

**British Library Cataloguing in Publication Data**
A CIP record for this book is available from the British Library.

ISBN 1 85805 429X (with CD)
ISBN 1 85805 430 3 (book only)

**Acknowledgments**
The useful IT vocabulary on page 107 is taken from *Modern Languages, Information File No. 1* published in 1990 by the National Council for Educational Technology (NCET) and is reproduced here with the permission of the publishers.

Printed in Great Britain by Bath Press Colourbooks, Glasgow

Letts Educational Ltd, a division of Granada Learning Ltd. Part of the Granada Media Group.

# Contents

# Examination practice

# Introduction

This book has been written to help you revise for your GCSE examinations in German. The key to your success in these examinations depends on your ability to convince the examiners that you have mastered the four basic skills which all the examining groups test in one form or another. These skills are based on the requirements of the Attainment Targets as detailed in the National Curriculum Orders for Key Stage 4 and are:

- Listening, understanding and responding (Attainment Target 1)
- Speaking German (Attainment Target 2)
- Reading, understanding and responding (Attainment Target 3)
- Writing German (Attainment Target 4)

## How to use this book

The first thing you need to find out before you plan your revision programme is exactly what will be expected of you in the examination itself. The analysis of the syllabuses of each of the examining groups on pages 9–19. will help you to do this. If you are a mature student it can be used to give you guidance on which group's examination will suit you best. It tells you about the types of question which will be set and you should concentrate on the types of question set by your chosen group, and ensure that you are given the fullest possible information about the grammar, vocabulary and areas of experience which you are expected to have studied. If you cannot obtain this information from your teacher, you can always write to the examining group for your own copy of their syllabus and any other information you require about your chosen examination. The addresses of the examining groups are listed on pages 9–19.

Success at GCSE in German means having a good knowledge of vocabulary and the grammar of the language. This is not a course book or a vocabulary book, but if you use it wisely as an aid to your revision and in conjunction with your course books and any specimen examination materials you have access to, there should be no difficulty for you in achieving success in your examinations.

This book assumes that you have studied German for at least two years. You should use it to help you plan your revision programme over the last twelve months or so leading up to your examinations. You should work systematically through the grammar section and follow the advice and examiner's tips on how to tackle the questions you will be expected to answer in your examinations. Finally you can practise the sorts of question which you will have to do.

Remember there is a lot of distilled experience and advice contained in the hints on examination technique in this book. So if you learn your vocabulary properly, if you know your grammar and you follow the advice on how to tackle the various types of question you should find that the reward for your efforts will be the success you are anxious to achieve. Enjoy your revision and good luck in your German examinations.

# About the exam

- In England, Wales and Northern Ireland you will have four examinations to do, Listening, Speaking, Reading and Writing, each of which will be worth 25% of the marks.
- In Scotland there are only three examinations, Speaking, Listening and Reading. Speaking is worth 50% of the total marks, while Listening and Reading are given 25% each. Writing is an *optional* examination at either General or Credit Level in Scotland.
- Your oral examination will be conducted by your teacher and externally moderated.
- Some examination groups give you an option of *coursework* instead of a terminal examination for the writing and the speaking examinations. You should make sure you know whether you are doing any coursework option and the date by when your work has to be completed.
- If your examination is for the Southern Examining Group (SEG), then you will be doing a *modular course* and different rules apply. See the Analysis in detail of the examination syllabuses later in this section for more information.
- Nearly all the questions and the rubrics will be in German and you will be expected to answer in German. You should therefore make sure that you study carefully the rubrics given later in this section. Remember that if you make a mistake in your German when answering a question in the Listening or Reading Examinations, you will not lose marks unless your meaning is unclear to a native German speaker.
- About 20% of the questions in the Listening and Reading examinations will be in English to be answered in English.
- In some parts of the examinations you are allowed to use a dictionary. Make sure you know in which examinations you are allowed to do this and that you study the section on *Using a dictionary* in this book to help you make the most of this opportunity. Check the rules for your examining group in the *Analysis* section of this book and remember electronic dictionaries are *not* allowed.
- In your examinations there are two levels of entry known as tiers, called Foundation Tier and Higher Tier. For each examination there is what is called *overlapping material*. This means that the harder questions at the end of the Foundation Tier are *exactly the same* as the easier questions at the beginning of the Higher Tier.
- In Scotland there are three levels of entry known as Foundation, General and Credit Levels. It is quite normal for you to attempt the papers at two adjacent levels. They will be graded separately and you will be awarded the better of the two sets of grades.
- Under the present National Curriculum Orders it is possible for you to do either the *short course* or the *full course*. You need to know which you are being entered for as the requirements are different. You can also combine a *short course* with another short course in a different subject like Business Studies. Basically in German if you study the short course, you only have to study two of the five *Areas of Experience* (see page 19). In Scotland there is no short course option.

## Grading

You will be graded on the eight-point scale of A*, A, B, C, D, E, F, G.

After your answers are marked, your work will be awarded a number of points depending on how good your work was. There are eight points available for each skill or component. The points you score for each component are added up and the total number of points decides what grade you get.

This is the scale that all Boards use:

| Points per component | Grade | Scale |
|:---:|:---:|:---:|
| 8 | A* | 30–32 |
| 7 | A | 26–29 |
| 6 | B | 22–25 |
| 5 | C | 18–21 |
| 4 | D | 14–17 |
| 3 | E | 10–13 |
| 2 | F | 6–9 |
| 1 | G | 2–5 |
| 0 | U | 0–1 |

In Scotland there are six grades, numbered 1 to 6, with grade 7 being reserved for those who complete the course but fail to meet the grade criteria for any level.

## Tiering

- For each skill (listening, speaking, reading and writing) there are two possible levels of entry.
- These levels of entry are called the Foundation Tier and the Higher Tier.
- Foundation Tier will assess Grades C–G.
- Higher Tier will assess Grades A★–D.
- If you enter for the Higher Tier in all the skills (listening, speaking, reading and writing) and you get less than the minimum mark for Grade D, then you will be given a Grade U (ungraded).
- You must enter for all four skills (listening, speaking, reading and writing).
- You may enter either the same tier for all four skills or you may mix your tiers.
- You cannot enter for both Foundation Tier and Higher Tier for the same skill.
- In Scotland there are three entry levels and two grades are assessed at each level.

| | | |
|---|---|---|
| **Foundation Level** | (in any of the three areas of assessment) – grades assessed 6 and 5 |
| **General Level** | (in any of the three areas of assessment) – grades assessed 4 and 3 |
| **Credit Level** | (in any of the three areas of assessment) – grades assessed 2 and 1 |

If you are entered for the optional Writing examination in either of the two upper levels the grades assessed are the same as shown above. The following table is a helpful guide to the papers which you are advised to attempt:

| Expected External Grade | Papers/Levels | Grades Assessed |
|---|---|---|
| 7, 6 | Foundation | 6, 5 |
| 5, 4 | Foundation and General | 6, 5, 4, 3 |
| 3, 2, 1 | General and Credit | 4, 3, 2, 1 |

## Areas of Experience

These are the topic areas which you will be expected to study for your GCSE examinations as laid down by the National Curriculum Orders, and all the exam boards have to follow them. There are five of them listed below as Areas A–E.

If you do the *full course* you have to cover *all five*. If you do the *short course* in years 10 and 11, then you must choose *one* of the Areas A, B or C together with *one* of Areas D or E, making a total of *two* to be studied for the *short course*.

**A Everyday activities**
- Life at home
- Food and drink
- Health and fitness
- Life at school

**B Personal and social life**
- Myself, family and personal relationships
- Free time and social activities
- Holidays and special occasions

**C The world around us**
- Home town and local area
- The natural and man–made environment
- People, places and customs

**D The world of work**
- Further education and training
- Careers and employment
- Language and communication in the workplace

**E The international world**
- Travel at home and abroad
- Life in other communities and countries
- World events and issues

You will find more detail about these areas of experience in the syllabus for your particular examining group's examinations. All skills will be tested by use of these topic areas and the vocabulary related to them.

The *Topic Areas* in Scotland are very similar and include:

| | | |
|---|---|---|
| Self | Environment, places and | Accidents and emergencies |
| Home | facilities | Time/Dates |
| Family/Daily routine | Food and drink | Events (past, present, future) |
| School | Goods and services | Weather |
| Work | Personal belongings/Pets/ | Clothes and fashion |
| Leisure | Money | Morale (happy, bored etc) |
| Holidays and travel | Places | People |
| | Immediate plans | Physical state (hungry, ill etc) |

## Examination rubrics

Rubrics are the instructions at the beginning of a question in any of the papers which tell you what you are expected to do. They will mostly be in German and depending on which Examination group's papers you are taking they will either be in the 'du' (familiar) form or the 'Sie' (polite) form of the imperative. In the list which follows both alternatives are given, as in this example:

      Lies/Lesen Sie die Liste... *Read the list...*

You will need to learn carefully the form which is being used by your examining group and check with the syllabus which form it is. For a full explanation of the forms of the imperative in German see page 54 in Chapter 1.

●    Firstly here are some general words which could be used in almost any kind of rubric/ instruction in any paper:

| | |
|---|---|
| Zuerst... | *first...* |
| Hier ist ein Beispiel | *here is an example* |
| Was? | *what?* |
| Jetzt... | *now...* |
| Die folgenden Antworten | *the following answers* |
| Wo? | *where?* |
| Auf deutsch | *in German* |
| Einige Fragen | *some questions* |
| Wer? | *who?* |
| In Ziffern | *in numbers* |
| Für jede Frage/Person | *for each question/person* |
| Wann? | *when?* |
| Richtig | *true* |
| Er/sie spricht/schreibt über... | *he/she is speaking/writing about...* |
| Falsch | *false* |
| Lies/Lesen Sie die Fragen. | *Read the questions.* |
| Warum? | *why?* |
| Antworte/Antworten Sie auf deutsch oder kreuze/kreuzen Sie die Kästchen an. | *Answer in German or tick the boxes.* |
| Beantworte/Beantworten Sie die Fragen auf deutsch/englisch. | *Answer the questions in German/English.* |
| Du brauchst/Sie brauchen nicht alle Buchstaben. | *You will not need all the letters.* |
| Finde/Finden Sie die Wörter/Sätze. | *Find the words/sentences.* |
| Fülle/Füllen Sie die Tabelle/das Formular/ den Fragebogen aus. | *Fill in the table/form/questionaire.* |
| Fülle/Füllen Sie die Lücken aus. | *Fill in the blanks, gaps or spaces.* |
| Kreuze/Kreuzen Sie das entsprechende Kästchen an. | *Tick the corresponding box.* |
| Kreuze/Kreuzen Sie nur 5 Kästchen/ Buchstaben an. | *Tick only 5 boxes/letters.* |
| Für jede Frage hast du/haben Sie vier Antworten zur Auswahl. | *For each question you have a choice of four answers.* |
| Mach/Machen Sie Notizen. | *Make notes.* |
| Mach/Machen Sie einen Kreis um Ja oder Nein. | *Circle yes or no.* |
| Schreib/Schreiben Sie die Antworten. | *Write the answers.* |
| Schreib/Schreiben Sie den Buchstaben/ die Nummer. | *Write the letter/number.* |
| Schreib/Schreiben Sie den Buchstaben, der am besten paßt. | *Write the letter which best corresponds.* |
| Schreib/Schreiben Sie..., die am besten paßt. | *Match up...* |
| Sieh/Sehen Sie die Notizen/die Zeichnungen/ die Tabelle an. | *Look at the notes/drawings/grid.* |
| Wähle/Wählen Sie die Beschreibung, die am besten paßt. | *Choose the description that best fits.* |
| Wenn die Aussage/der Satz richtig ist, kreuze/ kreuzen Sie das Kästchen RICHTIG an. | *If the statement/sentence is true, tick the box TRUE.* |

● The following could be used as rubrics in *listening tasks*:

| | |
|---|---|
| Sie besprechen… | *They are discussing…* |
| Bevor du/Sie das Gespräch anhörst/anhören… | *Before listening to the conversation…* |
| Hör/Hören Sie gut zu. | *Listen carefully.* |
| Jetzt hörst du/hören Sie (zweimal) ein Gespräch/ einen Dialog/einen Monolog/einen Bericht/ eine Sendung/ein Interview/einige Bemerkungen. | *Now you will hear (twice) a conversation/dialogue/monologue/ report/programme/interview/some remarks.* |
| Jetzt spricht… über… | *Now… is speaking about…* |
| Notiere/Notieren Sie die Preise/Uhrzeiten in Zahlen. | *Note down the prices/times in figures.* |
| Wo findet dieses Gespräch/diese Szene statt? | *Where does this conversation/scene take place?* |
| Zwei Personen reden über… | *Two people are talking about…* |

● The following could be used as rubrics in *speaking tasks*:

| | |
|---|---|
| Äußere/Äußern Sie dich/sich dazu… | *Respond to…* |
| Beantworte/Beantworten Sie die Frage. | *Answer the question.* |
| Begrüße/Begrüßen Sie… | *Greet…* |
| Du/Sie beginnst/beginnen… | *You begin…* |
| Dank/Danken Sie… | *Thank…* |
| Erkläre/Eklären Sie… | *Explain…* |
| Frag/Fragen Sie nach… | *Ask about…* |
| Gib/Geben Sie folgende Information… | *Give the following information…* |
| Gib/Geben Sie deine/Ihre Meinung… | *Give your opinion…* |
| Kannst/Können Sie das buchstabieren? | *Can you spell that?* |
| Dein/Ihr Lehrer beginnt. | *Your teacher begins.* |
| Dein/Ihr Lehrer wird die Rolle des/der… spielen. | *Your teacher will play the role of the…* |
| Melde/Melden Sie dich/sich… | *Say who you are (on the phone).* |
| Nenne/Nennen Sie zwei Dinge… | *Name two things…* |
| Sag/Sagen Sie… | *Say…* |
| Stell/Stellen Sie die Frage… | *Put/Ask the question…* |
| Stell/Stellen dir/sich vor. | *Introduce yourself.* |
| Was meinst/meinen du/Sie? | *What do you mean?* |
| Welche Zahl ist das? | *Which figure/number is that?* |
| Wiederhol/Wiederholen Sie bitte… | *Please repeat…* |
| Zeig/Zeigen Sie mir… | *Show me…* |

● The following could be used as rubrics in *reading tasks*:

| | |
|---|---|
| Finde/Finden Sie die Entsprechungen im Text. | *Find the equivalents in the text.* |
| Hak/Haken Sie… ab. | *Tick or cross off…* |
| Lies/Lesen Sie die Anzeige(n)/den Artikel/den Brief/ die Fragen/die Schilder/die Sätze/ den Text. | *Read the small ad(s)/the article/the letter/the questions/the signs/the sentences/the text.* |
| Lies/Lesen Sie die Beschreibung/Broschüre/ Postkarte. | *Read the description/brochure/postcard.* |
| Lies/Lesen Sie den Text und füll/füllen Sie die Lücken in den folgenden Sätze aus. | *Read the text and fill in the gaps in the following sentences.* |
| Numeriere/Numerieren Sie sie in der richtigen Reihenfolge. | *Number them in the right sequence.* |
| Ordne/Ordnen Sie die Bilder/die Sätze/ den Dialog. | *Put the pictures/sentences/dialogue in order.* |
| Die Sätze sind durcheinander. | *The sentences are all jumbled up.* |
| Schau/Schauen Sie… an. | *Look at…* |
| Schau/Schauen Sie/Schlag/Schlagen Sie das Wort nach. | *Look up the word…* |
| Streich/Streichen Sie die falschen Aussagen durch. | *Cross out the wrong statements.* |
| Trag/Tragen Sie in die Tabelle ein. | *Make an entry in the table/chart.* |

| | |
|---|---|
| Unterstreich/Unterstreichen Sie.... | *Underline…* |
| Was bedeutet dieses Symbol? | *What does this symbol mean?* |
| Welches Wort fehlt? | *Which word is missing?* |
| Die fehlenden Wörter sind unten. | *The missing words are below.* |
| Welche Wörter gehören zusammen? | *Which words go together?* |
| Zeichne/Zeichnen Sie mit einem X… | *Mark with an X…* |
| In einer deutschen Zeitung liest/lesen du/ Sie die persönlichen Anzeigen. | *In a German newspaper you are reading the personal adverts* |

● The following could be used as rubrics in *writing tasks*:

| | |
|---|---|
| Beantworte/Beantworten Sie alle Fragen. | *Answer all questions.* |
| Beschreib/Beschreiben Sie… | *Describe…* |
| Dein/Ihr Brief/Bericht/deine/Ihre Erzählung soll folgende Punkte abdecken. | *Your letter/report/account should cover the following points.* |
| entweder… oder… | *either… or…* |
| Erfinde/Erfinden Sie… | *Make up…* |
| Ergänze/Ergänzen Sie die Sätze mit den passenden Worten. | *Complete the sentences with suitable words.* |
| Erklär/Erklären Sie… | *Explain…* |
| Ersetze/Ersetzen Sie… | *Replace…* |
| Erzähle/Erzählen Sie eine Geschichte… | *Tell a story…* |
| Erzähle/Erzählen Sie ihm von… | *Tell him about…* |
| Füll/Füllen Sie das Formular aus. | *Fill in the form.* |
| Gib/Geben Sie Information über… | *Give information about…* |
| Kopiere/Kopieren Sie… | *Copy…* |
| Mach/Machen Sie eine Liste. | *Make a list.* |
| Du/Sie schickst/schicken… | *You are sending…* |
| Schreib/Schreiben Sie einen Bericht über… | *Write a report about…* |
| Schreib/Schreiben Sie einen Brief/eine Postkarte an… | *Write a letter/postcard to…* |
| Schreib/Schreiben Sie an deine(n)/Ihre(n) Brieffreund(in). | *Write to your penfriend (m/f).* |
| Schreib/Schreiben Sie in das Tagebuch. | *Write in the diary* |
| Schreib/Schreiben Sie die richtige Nummer (auf den Plan). | *Write the right number (on the plan).* |
| Schreib/Schreiben Sie deine/Ihre Meinung zu… | *Write your opinion about…* |
| Schreib/Schreiben Sie positive/negative Sätze. | *Write positive/negative sentences.* |
| Du/Sie sollst/sollen etwa… Worte schreiben. | *You should write about… words.* |
| Verbinde/Verbinden Sie (die Satzteile). | *Join together (the parts of the sentence).* |
| Vergleiche/Vergleichen Sie den Text mit der Nacherzählung. | *Compare the text with the retelling of story.* |
| Wähl/Wählen Sie eines der folgenden Themen. | *Choose one of the following themes.* |

This is not an exhaustive list but it gives you a good idea of what to expect from the rubrics of the questions in your examination.

## Question types

For the Listening and Responding and the Reading and Responding, there are a number of question types that you need to understand.

There may be:

1 Multiple-choice questions. An example is question 1 on page 148.
2 True/false questions. An example is question 6 on page 114.
3 Grid completion. An example is question 5 on page 114.
4 Responses in German. An example is question 10 on page 150.
5 Matching (you have to tick correct box or write appropriate letter). An example is question 9 on page 115.
6 Sequencing (you have to re-arrange jumbled sentences). An example is question 14 on page 152.

## Using a dictionary

Having the opportunity to use a dictionary in some parts of your examinations should in theory make things easier for you, but in practice this may not be the case, especially if you mis-use your dictionary.

● Mis-use of a dictionary can lead to mistakes.

● Over-use of a dictionary can lead to a serious loss of time.

Choosing the right dictionary is important. You need a bi-lingual German–English, English–German version with around 40,000 plus references in it. You also need to understand the entries and what they tell you when you look up a word in either the German or the English sections.

Here are some simple rules for you to follow:

1   Get to know your dictionary, the way it is laid out and what the entries are telling you.

2   Use the words in **bold** at the top of the page to help you find an entry more quickly.

3   Remember that nearly all words will have more than one entry and that the most common meaning will usually be the first one listed. There will be others and you will have to decide which one is the most appropriate in the context.

4   All dictionaries use abbreviations, you must learn the ones which appear in your dictionary, they are usually listed at the beginning of the book.

5   Do not bother looking up words which you do not need to know to answer the question. Look up the *key* words only.

6   Do your examinations where dictionaries are allowed with little or no help from your dictionary and then towards the end of the time allocated for the completion of the examination concerned use your dictionary for the rest of the time available as a tool to help you with the words you are not sure about.

7   Work out how long it takes you on average in seconds to find a word, then work out for yourself for each of your examinations how many words you will *realistically* have time to look up in the time without spoiling your chances of getting the answers down properly.

8   When doing Speaking or Writing examinations use language you know to be correct rather than trying to create something new with the help of a dictionary. You won't have time!

Dictionaries will be allowed by most Examination groups in your Reading and responding, Writing German and in the preparation time of your Speaking examinations only. For the precise details of your examining group's rules about dictionaries refer to the Analysis of the Examination Syllabuses on pages 9–19.

Here are some of the most commonly used abbreviations taken from an actual dictionary:

Relating to nouns: *n* – noun, *m* – masculine, *f* – feminine, *nt* – neuter, *pl* – plural

Relating to verbs: *vi* – intransitive, *vt* – transitive, *vr* – reflexive

Relating to other parts of speech: *adj* – adjective, *adv* – adverb, *prep* – preposition

Relating to cases: *nom* – nominative, *acc* – accusative, *gen* – genitive, *dat* – dative

By studying your dictionary and using the Grammar section of this book, you will be able to use your dictionary effectively in your examinations.

Below are examples of what you will find in a bilingual dictionary, make sure you know how yours works.

### English–German section

● author[1] ['ɔ:θər] [2]*n* [3](*profession*) [4]Schriftsteller ([5]in *f*) [6]*m*, [4]Autor ([5]in *f*) [6]*m*; [3](*of document*)[4] Verfasser ([5]in *f*) [6]*m*

> [1] in the brackets is the phonetic spelling of the word which tells you how to say it in English
>
> [2] *n* shows this is a *noun*
>
> [3] the entries in brackets tell you which words in German correspond to the use of the word *author* when it refers to a *profession* or *author of a document/report etc.*
>
> [4] these are the three possible German words to translate *author* in the given contexts
>
> [5] these indicate the *feminine* forms of the three possible translations Schriftstellerin, Autorin, Verfasserin
>
> [6] *m* is the gender of these three nouns which are *masculine*.

Look at the entries here:

● volume[1] ['vɒlju:m] [2]*n* [5](*of book*) [3]Band [4]*m*, [5](*space occupied*) [3]Volumen [4]*nt*, [5](*size, amount*) [3]Umfang [4]*m*, [5](*large amount*) [3]Massen [4]*f pl*, [5](*sound*)[3] Lautstärke[4].

Here there are five different meanings[5] of the word *volume* given with their German equivalents [3]and genders[4]. The phonetic spelling is also there[1] plus the fact that this is a noun[2].

**German–English section**

- bedeuten [1]*vt* [2](haben) [3]*mean*

   This is a simple entry which tells you [1]this is a transitive verb, [2]the past perfect tenses are formed with **haben** and [3]the meaning in English.

- Buch [1]*nt* [2]–(e)s, [3]"er, [4]*book*

   This is another simple entry with the gender[1], the genitive singular[2], the plural[3] and the meaning[4].

   Check carefully how your dictionary presents its entries on each part of speech in both English and German and ensure that you cross–check that you have the translation that fits the context. It is obvious from these few examples that the structure of German does not allow a word for word translation. To use a dictionary properly you need to know what kind of word you are looking for (noun, verb, adjective etc.) and what part it plays in the sentence in conveying the meaning. You need to practise using your dictionary properly so that you can make the best use of it in the examinations where it is allowed.

# Syllabus analysis

The following table lists all of the topics you will need to revise for your German GCSE course, no matter which syllabus you are studying. It has spaces for you to write notes in and fill in work dates, and a tick column for indicating finished topics so that you can easily see what you still have to do.

| Topic | Covered in Unit No | Target finish date | Notes | ✔ |
|---|---|---|---|---|
| **Foundation Tier** | | | | |
| Grammar | 1.1–3.8 | | | |
| Vocabulary | 4.1–4.8 | | | |
| Listening and responding | 5.1–5.5, 5.7–5.8 | | | |
| Speaking | 6.1–6.5, 6.7–6.8 | | | |
| Reading | 7.1–7.5, 7.7 | | | |
| Writing | 8.1–8.3, 8.5–8.6 | | | |
| **Higher Tier** | | | | |
| Grammar | 1.1–3.8 | | | |
| Vocabulary | 4.1–4.8 | | | |
| Listening and responding | 5.1–5.8 | | | |
| Speaking | 6.1–6.9 | | | |
| Reading | 7.1–7.7 | | | |
| Writing | 8.1–8.6 | | | |

Specific details for each syllabus are given on the following pages.

# Edexcel Foundation (incorporating London Examinations)

Address: Stewart House, 32 Russell Square, London, WC1B 5DN        Tel: 0171 331 4000

## Listening and responding

- Dictionaries are *not* allowed.
- You have to listen to a cassette recorded by native speakers. You will hear everything at least *twice*.
- Your teacher will stop the cassette to allow you time to write your answers.
- The questions will require non-verbal responses (i.e. ticking boxes), target-language answers or answers in English.
- About 20% of the questions will be answered in English. These will usually be at the end of the tests.

*Foundation Tier*
The test will last approximately 25 minutes.

- You will have to understand instructions, announcements, telephone messages, short narratives, advertisements, news items.

- For Grades E, F and G you will have to identify main points and extract specific details.
- For Grades C and D you will have to identify points of view and understand references to the past, present and future.

*Higher Tier*

The test will last approximately 35 minutes.

- You will have to do some of the harder Foundation Tier questions.
- You will hear radio broadcasts, discussions, presentations and interviews.
- You will have to identify points of view, understand references to the past, present and future, recognise attitudes and emotions and be able to draw conclusions.

## Speaking

You must choose between the Coursework Option and the Terminal Exam Option.

### Terminal Exam Option

The test will be recorded by your teacher.

- You may use a dictionary during the preparation time.
- Whether you do Foundation or Higher Tier, you do two role-plays and two conversations.
- The role-plays will either be in the form of instructions in English with pictures to guide you, or prompts in the target language.
- The two conversations will be chosen from this list. You choose the first one; your teacher chooses the second one: shopping; school/college and future plans; friends; food and meals; leisure and entertainment; the world of work; holidays; local area; home and family; daily routine at home, school and work; special occasions; pocket money.

*Foundation Tier*

The test will last 8–9 minutes

- Role-play A will be simple. Role-play B will have some unpredictability.
- In the conversations, if you want to get Grades C or D you will have to be able to refer to the past, present and the future and be able to express personal opinions.

*Higher Tier*

The test will last 11–12 minutes

- Role-play B will have some unpredictability. Role-play C will have even more unpredictability. It will be marked for communication *and* quality of language.
- In the conversations you will have to produce longer sequences of speech and use a variety of structures and vocabulary in order to express ideas and justify points of view.

### Coursework Option

Your teacher has details of what you must do.

- You must submit three units of work.
- Each unit must have a transaction and a conversation element.
- One of the units must be from Areas of Experience D or E.
- The work must be completed by the end of the first week in May of Year 11.
- Your work will be marked by the teacher and moderated by the Board.

## Reading and Responding

- You may use a dictionary.
- 20% of the questions will be in English and require an answer in English.
- The English questions will usually come at the end of the tests.

*Foundation Tier*

The test will last 30 minutes

- The materials will be signs, notices, adverts, messages, letters, leaflets, newspaper and magazine extracts.
- You will have to identify main points and extract specific detail.
- For Grades C and D you will have to identify points of view, understand unfamiliar language and understand references to past, present and future events.

*Higher Tier*

The test will last 50 minutes

- You will do the harder questions from the Foundation Tier.
- The texts will be longer than in the Foundation Tier.
- You will have to identify points of view, understand unfamiliar language, understand references to past, present and future events, recognise attitudes and emotions, and be able to draw inferences and conclusions.

## Writing

You must choose between the Coursework Option and the Terminal Exam Option.

### Terminal Exam Option

You will have the use of a dictionary throughout.

*Foundation Tier*

The test will last 30 minutes. You have to do *three* tasks:
1  Write a list, e.g. a shopping list.
2  Write a message or a postcard of about 30 words.
3  Write about 70 words, e.g. a letter.

*Higher Tier*

The test will last 50 minutes. You have to do *two* tasks:
1  Task 3 from the Foundation Tier
2  Write about 150 words, e.g. a narrative or a letter.

### Coursework Option

You have to submit three pieces of work. Your teacher has full details of how to approach these.

- They must be from three different Areas of Experience – one must be from Areas of Experience C or D.
- They can be a collection of short pieces or a single piece of writing.
- For Grades D–G submit at least 250–350 words in total.
- For Grades A*–C submit at least 500–600 words.
- Your teacher may guide you but cannot correct your work in detail before it is submitted.
- Coursework must be submitted by the end of the first week in May of Year 11.
- Your teacher will mark your work and it will be moderated by the Board.

# Midland Examining Group (MEG)

Address: 1 Hills Road, Cambridge, CB1 2EU                    Tel: 01223 553311

## Listening and Responding

The test will last approximately 40 minutes.
- Dictionaries are not allowed.
- You will listen to a cassette recorded by native speakers. You will hear everything at least twice.
- The questions will require non-verbal responses (i.e. ticking boxes), target-language answers or answers in English.
- About 20% of the questions will be answered in English. These will be the first one in the Foundation Tier and one of the last ones in the Higher Tier.

*Foundation Tier*
- You attempt Sections 1 and 2 of the paper.
- You will have to understand instructions, announcements, telephone messages, short narratives, advertisements, news items.
- For Grades E, F and G you will have to identify main points and extract specific details.
- For Grades C and D you will have to identify points of view and understand references to the past, present and future.

*Higher Tier*
- You will have to do some of the harder Foundation Tier questions, i.e. you attempt Sections 2 and 3 of the paper.
- You will hear radio broadcasts, discussions, presentations and interviews.
- You will have to identify points of view, understand references to the past, present and future, recognise attitudes and emotions and be able to draw conclusions.

## Speaking

The test will last 10–12 minutes. It will be recorded by your teacher.
- You may use a dictionary during the preparation period.
- Whether you do Foundation or Higher Tier, you have to do two role-plays, make a presentation and take part in a conversation.

- The role-plays will either be in the form of instructions in English with pictures to guide you, or prompts in the target language.
- The Presentation means that you have to prepare a topic of your choice chosen from the Areas of Experience. In the exam you talk for one minute on your topic and then you discuss your topic more freely with the teacher. You may bring a cue-card with up to five short headings into the exam to help you remember what to say. You may use illustrative materials for your presentation. You must not use written notes.
- General Conversation means that the examiner (your teacher) will lead you into a conversation on *three* topics, drawn from the Areas of Experience, such as life at home and at school, holidays, friends, opinions. You will not know the titles of the topics before the exam. You cannot use the same topic for your presentation and your conversation. Your teacher will ensure that this does not happen. The more you say, the more accurate your language is, the more complex your language is, the higher your score.
- Your exam will be recorded on cassette. Either your teacher will mark it and send it away to the Board for moderation or he/she will send it off for external marking.

*Foundation Tier*
- Role-play A will be simple. Role-play B will have some unpredictability.
- In the Presentation and Conversation, if you want to get Grade C you will have to be able to refer to the past, present and the future and be able to express personal opinions.

*Higher Tier*
- Role-play B will have some unpredictability. Role-play C will require you to act as a story-teller, relating an incident that happened in the past. You must develop the incident in your own way. It will be marked for communication *and* quality of language.
- In the Presentation and Conversation you will have to produce longer sequences of speech and use a greater variety of structures and vocabulary to express ideas and justify points of view.

## Reading and Responding

The test will last 50 minutes.
- You may use a dictionary.
- 20% of the questions will be in English and require an answer in English. These will be at the beginning of the Foundation Tier and near the end of the Higher Tier.

*Foundation Tier*
- The materials will be signs, adverts, messages, letters, leaflets, newspaper and magazine extracts.
- You will have to identify main points and extract specific detail.
- For Grades C and D you will have to identify points of view, understand unfamiliar language and understand references to past, present and future events.

*Higher Tier*
- You will do the harder questions from the Foundation Tier.
- The texts will be longer than at Foundation Tier.
- You will have to identify points of view, understand unfamiliar language, understand references to past, present and future events, recognise attitudes and emotions, and be able to draw inferences and conclusions.

## Writing

You must choose between the Coursework Option and the Terminal Exam Option.

### Terminal Exam Option
The test will last 50 minutes. You will have the use of a dictionary throughout.

*Foundation Tier*
You have to do *four* tasks:
1–2 Single-word tasks, e.g. form-filling, writing a list.
3 A message or postcard of about 40 words.
4 A text of about 100 words, e.g. a letter. You will have a choice of two.

*Higher Tier*
You have to do *two* tasks:
1 Task 4 from the Foundation Tier.
2 Write a composition of about 150 words. It could be a report on something you have experienced. You will have a choice of two.

**Coursework Option**

You have to submit three pieces of work. Your teacher has full details of how to approach these.

- For Grades E, F and G the pieces should be about 40 words, e.g. design a poster, complete a booking form.
- For Grades C and D the pieces should be about 100 words, e.g. an article or a letter.
- For Grades A★ to C the pieces should be about 150 words, e.g. tell the story of a film, an account of an adventure or an experience.

# Northern Examinations and Assessment Board (NEAB)

Address: 12 Harter Street, Manchester, M1 6HL                                           Tel: 0161 953 1180

## Listening and Responding

- Dictionaries are only allowed during the five-minute reading time at the beginning and the five-minute checking time at the end.
- You have to listen to a cassette recorded by native speakers. You will hear everything twice.
- Your teacher will stop the cassette to allow you time to write your answers.
- The questions will require non-verbal responses (i.e. ticking boxes), target-language answers or answers in English.
- About 20% of the questions will be answered in English.

*Foundation Tier*

The test will last approximately 30 minutes

- You will have to understand instructions, announcements, telephone messages, short narratives, advertisements, news items.
- For Grades E, F and G you will have to identify main points and extract specific details.
- For Grades C and D you will have to identify points of view and understand references to the past, present and future.

*Higher Tier*

The test will last approximately 40 minutes

- You will have to do some of the harder Foundation Tier questions.
- You will hear radio broadcasts, discussions, presentations and interviews.
- You will have to identify points of view, understand references to the past, present and future, recognise attitudes and emotions and be able to draw conclusions.

## Speaking

The test will be recorded by your teacher.

- You will be given ten minutes preparation time during which you can use a dictionary. You can also make notes. You can take the notes with you into the exam but not the dictionary.
- Whether you do Foundation or Higher Tier, you do two role-plays, a presentation followed by a discussion, and then a general conversation.
- The role plays will either be in the form of instructions in English with pictures to guide you, or prompts in the target language
- You prepare your presentation before the exam. You have to provide a stimulus, e.g. a book, an article, a poster. Then you talk about your stimulus and your teacher will ask you questions.
- You will have a conversation on at least two, or at most three of the following topics: education and career; self and others; home and abroad; home and daily routine; leisure; holidays and travel.
- You will not know which of the topics you will have to talk about until the day of the exam.

*Foundation Tier*

The test will last 8–10 minutes.

- Role-play A will be simple. Role-play B will have some unpredictability.
- In the conversations, if you want to get Grades C or D you will have to be able to refer to the past, present and the future and to be able to express personal opinions.

*Higher Tier*

The test will last 10–12 minutes.

- Role-play B will have some unpredictability. Role-play C will have even more unpredictability. It will be marked for communication *and* quality of language

- In the conversations you will have to produce longer sequences of speech and use a variety of structures and vocabulary in order to express ideas and justify points of view.

## Reading and Responding

- You may use a dictionary.
- 20% of the questions will be in English and require an answer in English. These will be at the beginning of the Foundation Tier and near the end of the Higher Tier.

*Foundation Tier*

The test will last 30 minutes.

- The materials will be signs, notices, advertisements, messages, letters, leaflets, newspaper and magazine extracts.
- You will have to identify main points and extract specific detail.
- For Grades C and D you will have to identify points of view, understand unfamiliar language and understand references to past, present and future events.

*Higher Tier*

The test will last 50 minutes.

- You will do the harder questions from the Foundation Tier.
- The texts will be longer than at Foundation Tier.
- You will have to identify points of view, understand unfamiliar language, understand references to past, present and future events, recognise attitudes and emotions, and be able to draw inferences and conclusions.

## Writing

You must choose between the Coursework Option and the Terminal Exam Option.

### Terminal Exam Option

- You can use a dictionary throughout.
- Provided the tasks are completed the number of words is not important. The Board, however, does suggest numbers of words for the more difficult questions.

*Foundation Tier*

The test will last 40 minutes. You have to do *three* tasks:

1 A short list or a form to be completed.
2 A message or postcard or text for a poster. (**1** and **2** should require a total of about 40 words.)
3 A letter (approximately 90 words) in which you must use different tenses if you want to get a Grade C.

*Higher Tier*

The test will last 60 minutes. You have to do *two* tasks:

1 Task 3 from the Foundation Tier.
2 A text of about 120 words, e.g. an article, a letter, publicity material.

### Coursework Option

- You must submit three assignments drawn from a list of about 60: your teacher has a copy of the list.
- Your assignments must cover at least three of the Areas of Experience.
- If you are a Foundation Tier candidate your assignments should total 200–300 words.
- If you are a Higher Tier candidate your assignments should total 300–500 words.
- To get a C or above you must use past, present and future tenses and express personal opinions.

# Northern Ireland Council for the Curriculum Examinations and Assessment (NICCEA)

Address: Clarendon Dock, 29 Clarendon Road, Belfast, BT1 3BG          Tel: 01232 261200

## Listening and Responding

The test will last 30 minutes.

- Dictionaries are not allowed.
- You have to listen to a cassette recorded by native speakers. You will hear everything twice.
- The questions will require non-verbal responses (i.e. ticking boxes), target-language answers or answers in English.

- About 20% of the questions will be answered in English.

*Foundation Tier*
- You will have to understand instructions, announcements, telephone messages, short narratives, advertisements, news items.
- For Grades E, F and G you will have to identify main points and extract specific details.
- For Grades C and D you will have to identify points of view and understand references to the past, present and future.

*Higher Tier*
- You will have to do some of the harder Foundation Tier questions.
- You will hear radio broadcasts, discussions, presentations and interviews.
- You will have to identify points of view, understand references to the past, present and future, recognise attitudes and emotions and be able to draw conclusions.

## Speaking

The test will last 30 minutes. It will be recorded by your teacher.
- You can use a dictionary only in the ten-minute preparation time.
- Whether you do Foundation or Higher Tier, you will do role-plays and a general conversation.
- The role-plays will either be in the form of instructions in English with pictures to guide you, or prompts in the target language.

*Foundation Tier*
- Role-play A will be simple. Role-play B will have some unpredictability.
- In the conversations, if you want to get Grades C or D you will have to be able to refer to the past, present and the future and be able to express personal opinions.

*Higher Tier*
- Role-play B will have some unpredictability. Role-play C will have even more unpredictability. It will be marked for communication *and* quality of language.
- In the conversations you will have to produce longer sequences of speech and use a variety of structures and vocabulary in order to express ideas and justify points of view.

## Reading and Responding

The test will last 40 minutes.
- You may use a dictionary.
- 20% of the questions will be in English and require an answer in English. These will be at the beginning of the Foundation Tier and near the end of the Higher Tier.

*Foundation Tier*
- The materials will be signs, notices, advertisements, messages, letters, leaflets, newspaper and magazine extracts.
- You will have to identify main points and extract specific detail.
- For Grades C and D you will have to identify points of view, understand unfamiliar language and understand references to past, present and future events.

*Higher Tier*
- You will do the harder questions from the Foundation Tier.
- The texts will be longer than at Foundation Tier.
- You will have to identify points of view, understand unfamiliar language, understand references to past, present and future events, recognise attitudes and emotions, and be able to draw inferences and conclusions.

## Writing

The test will last 45 minutes.
- You can use a dictionary throughout.
- Provided the tasks are completed the number of words is not important. The Board however does suggest numbers of words for the more difficult questions.

*Foundation Tier*
- You may have to complete forms, produce lists, write notes or cards.
- You will have to write a text, such as a letter.
- There will be about 120 words in total.

*Higher Tier*
You have to do two tasks:
- The text or letter from the Foundation Tier.
- A longer text, e.g. a letter, report or account.

---

## Scottish Qualifications Authority (formerly SEB)

---

Address: Ironmills Road, Dalkeith, Midlothian, EH22 1LE          Tel: 0131 663 6601

In Scotland the exam is called Standard Grade. In England there are two Tiers; in Scotland there are three Levels: Foundation, General and Credit. Candidates may attempt Listening and Reading papers in two adjacent levels: Foundation and General or General and Credit.

### Listening

This counts for 25% of your mark.
- Dictionaries are not allowed.
- There will be three separate papers, one at each level.
- Material will be presented on tape and heard twice.
- Questions will be set in English, to be answered in English.
- There will be a progression in difficulty across the three levels.
- The items in each paper will be connected thematically, the theme will be stated in English.
- Responses expected from candidates will vary from a few words to a detailed answer. No long answers will be expected at Foundation Level.

### Speaking

This counts for 50% of your mark.
- Dictionaries are not allowed.
- There will be no end of course examination – assessments will be made throughout your course and recorded on tape.
- These assessments will be made by your teacher, but in March each year a Moderator will visit the school to assess the candidates' performance based on a Speaking activity set by the Board.
- Speaking activities can be wide ranging – a sample will be used for moderation purposes and these will involve a face-to-face conversation with your teacher lasting ten minutes.

### Reading

This counts for 25% of your mark.
- You may use a dictionary in all three levels.
- Questions will be set in English to be answered in English at all three levels.
- Questions will require general or detailed responses and there will be a progression in difficulty and in length from Foundation to Credit Level.
- Responses expected will vary from a few words to a detailed answer across the levels.
- Items within each paper will be connected by a thematic development which will be stated in English.

### Writing

- This is an optional paper and can only be taken at General or Credit Level. Success in this paper will be recorded on the certificate but will not contribute to the overall grade awarded.
- Dictionaries are allowed at both levels.
- At General Level you will be asked to write a number of short simple messages in German.
- At Credit Level you will be required to respond to a passage, or passages in German by writing an answer of about 200 words in German, expressing your views coherently.

---

## Southern Examining Group (SEG) Modular

---

Address: Stag Hill House, Guildford, GU2 5XJ          Tel: 01483 506506

This course is divided into four modules. Each module will last about 15 weeks.

**Module 1**
**Title**: Contact with a German-speaking country.

**When assessed**: February of Year 10.
**The three tests**: Listening, Speaking and Reading. Each counts for 5% of your final mark.
**Listening**: You listen to a cassette recorded by native speakers. You will hear the material up to three times. You answer questions mostly in the target language, but some of the questions will be non-verbal (e.g. box-ticking) or in English. Dictionaries are not allowed.
**Speaking**: You must produce a short tape-recorded monologue. Your teacher will help you with choosing a title. You can use a dictionary when preparing it, but not when actually recording it. You can use prompts, but you cannot read aloud from a prepared script.
**Reading**. You have to do a variety of reading tests and you may use a dictionary.

### Module 2
**Title**: Organising a visit to a German-speaking country.
**When assessed**: June of Year 10.
**The two tests**: Listening and Reading. Each counts for 10% of your final mark.
**Listening**: You listen to a cassette recorded by native speakers and answer the questions in an examination booklet. You may not use a dictionary. You will hear each item twice.
**Reading**: You have to do a variety of reading tests and you may use a dictionary.

### Module 3
**Title**: Holidays and travel.
**When assessed**: Through coursework during the autumn term of Year 11.
There are two skills tested: Speaking (5%) and Writing (10%).
**Speaking**: As for Module 1.
**Writing**: You have to produce two pieces of written work as coursework. It is not a test. You are allowed to draft and re-draft. Use IT if you want.
*Foundation Tier*
(a) One piece of writing of about 30 words, for example a postcard, message or form.
(b) One piece of writing of 100–120 words, for example a letter or a response to a questionnaire.
*Higher Tier*
Two pieces of writing, of different types, of 100–120 words. They may be for example formal or informal letters, articles or reports.

### Module 4: External exam
This takes place in the normal summer examination period of Year 11. There are four exams:
**Speaking** (15%)
One role-play and one conversation. You have five minutes (*Foundation*) or eight minutes (*Higher*) preparation time during which you can use a dictionary, but you may not make notes.
**Listening** (10%)
As for Module 2.
**Reading** (10%)
As for Module 2.
**Writing** (15%)
You have to produce one piece of written work. You may use a dictionary.
*Foundation Tier*
One piece of writing of about 80 words, e.g. a response to a questionnaire or a letter.
*Higher Tier*
One piece of writing of about 120 words, e.g. a response to a letter, an article or a report.

# Welsh Joint Education Committee (WJEC)

Address: 245 Western Avenue, Cardiff, CF5 2YX                    Tel: 01222 265000

## Listening and Responding

The test will last 45 minutes.
- Dictionaries are only allowed during the ten-minute reading time at the beginning and the ten-minute checking time at the end.
- You have to listen to a cassette recorded by native speakers. You will hear everything three times.
- The questions will require non-verbal responses (i.e. ticking boxes), target-language answers or answers in English/Welsh.

- About 20% of the questions will be answered in English/Welsh.

*Foundation Tier*

- You will have to understand instructions, announcements, telephone messages, short narratives, advertisements, news items.
- For Grades E, F and G you will have to identify main points and extract specific details
- For Grades C and D you will have to identify points of view and understand references to the past, present and future.

*Higher Tier*

- You will have to do some of the harder Foundation Tier questions.
- You will hear radio broadcasts, discussions, presentations and interviews.
- You will have to identify points of view, understand references to the past, present and future, recognise attitudes and emotions and be able to draw conclusions.

## Speaking

The test will be recorded by your teacher.

- You can use a dictionary only during the preparation time.
- Whether you do Foundation or Higher Tier, you do two role-plays and a conversation.
- The role-plays will either be in the form of instructions in English/Welsh with pictures to guide you, or prompts in the target language.

*Foundation Tier*

The test will last 10 minutes.

- Role-play A will be simple. Role-play B will have some unpredictability.
- In the conversation, if you want to get Grades C or D you will have to be able to refer to the past, present and the future and be able to express personal opinions.

*Higher Tier*

The test will last 12 minutes.

- Role-play B will have some unpredictability. Role-play C will have even more unpredictability. It will be marked for communication and quality of language.
- In the conversation you will have to produce longer sequences of speech and use a variety of structures, tenses and vocabulary in order to express ideas and justify points of view.

## Reading and Responding

The test will last 40 minutes.

- You may use a dictionary.
- 20% of the questions will be in English/Welsh and require an answer in English/Welsh.

*Foundation Tier*

- The materials will be signs, notices, advertisements, messages, letters, leaflets, newspaper and magazine extracts.
- You will have to identify main points and extract specific detail.
- For Grades C and D you will have to identify points of view, understand unfamiliar language and understand references to past, present and future events.

*Higher Tier*

- You will do the harder questions from the Foundation Tier.
- The texts will be longer than at Foundation Tier.
- You will have to identify points of view, understand unfamiliar language, understand references to past, present and future events, recognise attitudes and emotions, and be able to draw inferences and conclusions.

## Writing

You must choose between the Coursework Option and the Terminal Exam Option.

### Terminal Exam Option

You may use a dictionary throughout.

*Foundation Tier*

The exam lasts 45 minutes. You will be expected to:

- elicit and provide information
- describe events in the past, present and future
- express opinions, emotions and ideas

*Higher Tier*

The exam lasts 60 minutes. You will be expected to:

- write in different ways to suit the audience and the context
- justify any ideas and points of view expressed
- write with increased accuracy and an increasingly wide range of language

**Coursework Option**

Five pieces of work may be submitted in the coursework option. These will be pieces of work done in class under teacher supervision. A dictionary may be used. Further details are given in the WJEC syllabus.

# Short course

This is what you need to know if you are taking a short course.

- The exam boards do not mark your papers more leniently because you are taking a short course. The same level of competence is expected for, say, a grade A* in the short course as for a grade A* in the full course.
- The main difference between a full course and a short course is that the full course tests knowledge of all five Areas of Experience (see page 3), whereas the short course tests only two.
- In theory you could be studying one Area from either A, B or C and one Area from D and E. In practice you are likely to be doing Areas B and D – but do check with your teacher.
- When learning vocabulary concentrate on the words that deal with Areas of Experience B and D (see pages 90–98 and 105–107). However, you should also learn as much vocabulary as you can from the other Areas of Experience.

## Speaking

Make sure that you can talk about family, free time, holidays and your future career.

## Listening

Again the topics of family, free time, holidays and your future career will be tested. Make sure you know the vocabulary.

## Reading

You may well have a lot of questions set on texts to do with the world of work. Make sure you know the words for unemployment, salary, working times, boss, lunch break, training, tax, etc. See the Area D vocabulary section on pages 105–107.

## Writing

It is absolutely essential that you know how to write a letter applying for a job. It could be a temporary summer job or a permanent post. Study the letters in Chapter 8.

# Devising a revision programme

It is assumed that you are studying the *full course* and that you have five–and–a–half term's work before taking your final examinations in the June of year 11. We can also assume that you have already completed two years studying German. You will probably have between 2 and 3 hours of lessons plus 3 hours of homework each week designated to German. School years are about 38 weeks long, so you will only have a total of 60 weeks maximum apart from holidays to complete your course. (It is not 76 weeks because you only have five full terms in which to do any realistic work and in most instances you will have end of year examinations in year 10 and some kind of Mock Examination around Christmas in year 11.) We suggest that you complete your course and all aspects of the syllabus by Easter in year 11 having started in the September of your year 10.

This revision programme is therefore divided into five terms, totalling 60 weeks. What is suggested is a list of priorities for each term starting with the Autumn Term of year 10 and assuming that you are not doing a modular course. It is tempting to say as far as the Areas of Experience are concerned that you should cover one per term. This makes some sense as there is a kind of progression from the personal experiences of home and school to the wider aspects of society and the world around us, including further education, the world of work and travel, but it is unrealistic to confine oneself to any one Area of Experience in the first year of this period. It is probably better to plan your programme to ensure that all five areas are completed in terms of vocabulary learned and the relevant structures absorbed by the end of the Spring Term in year 11.

## Autumn Term Year 10

Maximum totals: 14 weeks, 42 hours tuition plus 42 hours homework

### Priorities
1   Build up the level of your listening, speaking and reading skills.
2   Learn all the vocabulary and list words under Areas of Experience, concentrating at this stage on Areas A and B.
3   Grammar – concentrate this term on learning and understanding:
   **(a)**   nouns – their genders and plurals
   **(b)**   the articles and the four cases
   **(c)**   verbs – present tense, simple past tense, strong and weak formations
   **(d)**   co-ordinating conjunctions and
   **(e)**   word order in main clauses
   **(f)**   numerals, dates, time.

Use the summary of Grammar in Chapter 1 to check that you fully understand what is expected. All the grammatical terms are explained there in detail and there is a section on 'testing yourself' once you have learned a structure.

## Spring Term Year 10

Maximum totals: 10 weeks, 30 hours tuition plus 30 hours homework

### Priorities
1   Continue to practise your listening, speaking and reading skills and begin simple writing tasks.
2   Continue to list and learn all vocabulary and add Area C to the Areas of Experience to which you are paying particular attention.
3   Grammar – concentrate this term on
   **(a)**   adjectives and their endings
   **(b)**   possessive adjectives
   **(c)**   adverbs
   **(d)**   personal pronouns

**(e)** verbs – future tense, perfect tense with **haben** or **sein**, uses of the infinitive

**(f)** subordinating conjunctions

**(g)** word order in subordinate clauses.

## Summer Term Year 10

Maximum totals: 12 weeks, 36 hours tuition plus 36 hours homework

**Priorities**

1 There will probably be some kind of end of year examination during this term, so remember to leave time to revise the work completed so far.

2 Continue to practise all four skill areas using all the hints and opportunities for practice in this book.

3 Continue to learn and list all vocabulary and include Area D in the Areas of Experience on which you are now building up a store of useful words and phrases.

4 Coursework assignments are likely to be chosen during this term, if you are entered for a coursework option. In most cases a total of three assignments must be completed and research, choice of topics etc. should be completed by the end of this term.

5 Grammar – concentrate this term on:

**(a)** demonstrative adjectives

**(b)** comparative and superlative forms of adjectives and adverbs

**(c)** indefinite and reflexive pronouns

**(d)** prepositions with the accusative and/or dative and abbreviated forms

**(e)** verbs – imperative forms, modal verbs

**(f)** asking questions (interrogatives) – word order, adverbs, pronouns.

## Autumn Term Year 11

Maximum totals: 14 weeks, 42 hours tuition plus 42 hours homework

**Priorities**

1 There could be a 'Mock Exam' towards the end of this term, so remember to leave time to revise for it.

2 If you are doing a coursework option, then at least one of your major assignments should be completed before the end of this term.

3 Continue to practise all four skill areas progressing towards the more demanding tasks and testing your ability to complete them under the time restrictions of examination conditions.

4 Continue to list and learn all vocabulary, pigeon-holing words and phrases in the appropriate Area of Experience and concentrating this term on Area E.

5 Grammar – concentrate this term on:

**(a)** interrogative adjectives

**(b)** **hin** and **her** used as prefixes

**(c)** relative pronouns

**(d)** prepositions with the genitive

**(e)** verbs – impersonal, separable and inseparable, pluperfect and conditional tenses.

## Spring Term Year 11

Maximum totals: 10 weeks, 30 hours tuition plus 30 hours homework

**Priorities**

1 If you are doing a coursework option, all assignments will have to be completed before the end of this term so that they can be assessed and sent to the examining group for moderation.

2 Continue to practise all four skill areas concentrating on doing past papers/specimen questions using examination timings.

3 Make sure you are skilled at using a dictionary in examination conditions, devising your own method for looking up and checking words and their meanings quickly.

4 Consolidate your knowledge of all vocabulary continuing to add to the lists of words and phrases within the Areas of Experience and revising all five thoroughly.

5 Grammar – most of the linguistic structures listed in the examination groups' syllabuses should have been covered by this stage. Revise them thoroughly and add:

**(a)** verbs – the subjunctive and its uses

**(b)** the passive

**(c)** the use of **lassen** as a modal verb.

## Summer Term Year 11

These are the last crucial few weeks before your GCSE examinations in all subjects begin for real. As far as German is concerned this is a particularly important time, as you cannot expect to remember all the grammar and vocabulary that you have learned over a perod of three to four years unless you are prepared to revise carefully. You need to be able to recall the vocabulary and rules of grammar from your memory during any part of the examination. You need therefore to organize your revision by making a timetable. Choose a time when you are at your most receptive. It might be best to revise early in the evening before you get too tired, or early in the morning after a good night's sleep. Having decided when to revise, put the times on your revision timetable.

You also need a suitable place to revise. Find a quiet, or relatively quiet room away from distractions like TV or loud music. You need a table, a chair, adequate light (a table lamp will often help you to concentrate) and a comfortable temperature. It is better to revise sitting at a table than lying down. It is more effective to revise inside the house rather than basking in the sun.

## Some practical tips for revising German

- When revising vocabulary do not keep reading the words and their meanings through aimlessly. Try to learn the words in context. Remember you need to know the gender and the plural of all nouns and whether a verb is strong (irregular) or weak (regular).
- Learn lists of words in short spells at a time and always give yourself a written test. In other words you must review the words you have learned. Without this review you will forget what you have learned very quickly.
- When revising grammar points, make notes on postcards, which will then help you to do some quick revision on the night before your German examinations. Look for the important key facts about German grammar and make notes on them as you revise. Use the 'Test yourself' section of this book to check what you have revised. If you have not understood and are still getting it wrong, go back to the relevant grammar section and look at it again.
- The reviewing of what you have revised and learned is very important. You should try to carry out this testing and retesting of what you have learned during a revision session after 24 hours, then after a week and maybe again after a month. You should keep your summary notes for use just before the examinations.
- Plan all your revision in short bursts, depending on your span of concentration.
- Remember you learn most efficiently by studying for 20–40 minutes and then testing yourself to see how much you have retained.
- When you are revising, take regular breaks. On your timetable you could split a two–hour session into four shorter periods, like this: revise for 25 minutes; have a break for 10 minutes; work for another 25 minutes; then take a longer break (20–30 minutes) and then work for another 30–40 minutes. Give yourself a reward at the end of the revision period, e.g. watch TV, read a book, listen to a record, tape, CD or the radio, or go and see a friend.
- Have a definite start and finish time. Learning efficiency tends to fluctuate as the session progresses, but you are more likely to remember what you revised at the end of the session than at the beginning.
- Allow two hours each day for revision at the beginning of your programme and build it up to at least three hours a day during the last three or so weeks of revision before the examinations start. Make sure German has a weekly session in your revision programme.
- Don't waste revision time. Recognise when your mind is beginning to wander and do something about it.
- If you have things on your mind deal with them first, make a list of the things you need to do and then go back to your revision afterwards.
- Get up and move around – do something different, make a cup of tea, etc.
- Change your revision subject – move to another subject for a while, then come back to German revision.
- Work with a friend, if you can. This is good for learning vocabulary; you can test one another.
- Practise talking German with a friend. Listen to German radio broadcasts together.
- Make sure you understand what you are doing. Learning grammar 'parrot fashion' does not help you to understand it. You will therefore have lower recall. Remember the pattern: work, test, rest, reward.
- Do not give up even if you feel irritable or depressed, others will be experiencing the same problems.

- Use 'tricks' like mnemonics to help you remember important facts. For example BUD GO FEW gives you the initial letters of the prepositions which take the accusative only: **bis, um, durch, gegen**, **ohne, für, entlang** and **wider**.

Here is the 'Ladder to Success', study it carefully, it will help you to understand how to prepare properly not only for your German examinations but other examinations as well.

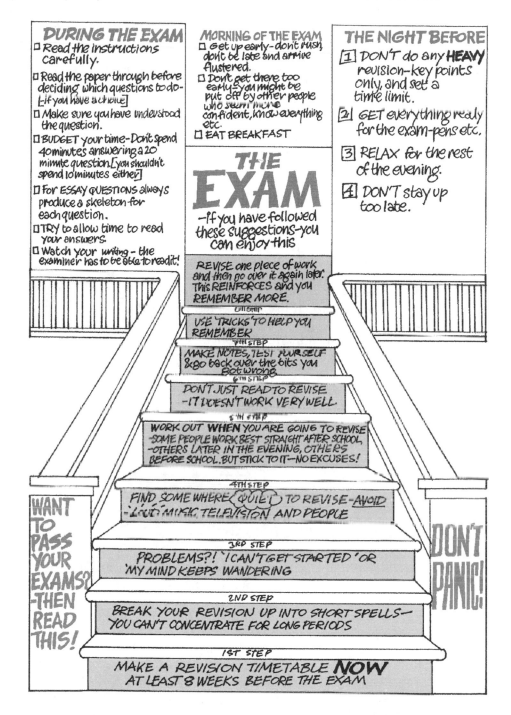

# Chapter 1
# *Grammar revision*

## 1.1 Introduction

The aim of this chapter is to set out in simple terms the essential details of German grammar which every GCSE candidate is expected to know, as listed in the syllabuses of the examining groups. At the head of each section there is a brief explanation of the equivalent English grammatical terms so that you will be able to understand the terms being used to explain the structure of the German language.

At first sight German, with its formal sentence construction, seems difficult to understand, but it need not be. What you have to do is make a determined effort to learn certain fundamental rules and then apply them carefully and conscientiously. Once these basics have been absorbed and understood, you will have much more confidence in your own ability to understand both spoken and written German and be able to speak and write clear accurate German yourself. What we have tried to do here is make German grammar easy to understand.

## 1.2 Nouns

Nouns are words that are used for the names of things, ideas and living creatures, including human beings. The rules you need to know about nouns in German are:
- All nouns are written with a capital letter. They are easy to spot therefore in the middle of a sentence.
- All nouns have one of three genders – masculine, feminine or neuter. This is not the same as in English where gender is decided by sex or 'natural gender'. In German inanimate objects (things) can be masculine or feminine as well as neuter.
- When listing vocabulary you should always list and learn nouns with their gender and where appropriate their plural form.

### Gender

To show the gender you use the definite article 'the' as follows:

| *Masculine* | *Feminine* | *Neuter* |
|---|---|---|
| **der Mann** (¨er) *man* | **die Frau** (-en) *woman* | **das Kind** (-er) *child* |

but note the following names of things:

| | | |
|---|---|---|
| **der Stuhl** (¨e) *chair* | **die Schule** (-n) *school* | **das Buch** (¨er) *book* |

Here are a few hints which will help you to learn the gender of nouns:

#### Masculine
The following groups of nouns are masculine:
- all nouns referring to male gender including animals:
  **der Hund** (¨e) *dog*, **der Lehrer** (-) *teacher (male)*, **der Onkel** (-) *uncle*
- seasons, months, days of the week, points of the compass
  **der Frühling** (-e) *spring*, **der Februar** *February*, **der Montag** *Monday*, **der Norden** *north*
- persons carrying out a profession or trade who are male

**der Kellner (-)** *waiter,* **der Sänger (-)** *singer,* **der Schauspieler (-)** *actor*
- most nouns formed from the stem of a verb
  **der Besuch (-e)** *visit* from **besuchen** *to visit*

### Feminine
The following groups of nouns are feminine:
- all nouns referring to the female gender including animals
  **die Katze (-n)** *cat,* **die Lehrerin (-nen)** *teacher (female),* **die Tante (-n)** *aunt*
- most nouns ending in the following:

  | | | |
  |---|---|---|
  | -ei | **die Konditorei (-en)** | *cakeshop* |
  | -in | **die Studentin (-nen)** | *female student* |
  | -schaft | **die Landschaft** | *(no pl) scenery* |
  | -heit | **die Krankheit (-en)** | *illness* |
  | -keit | **die Sehenswürdigkeit (-en)** | *sight* |
  | -ung | **die Kleidung** | *(no pl) clothing* |

  There are many more which belong to this group.

### Neuter
The following groups of nouns are neuter:
- the infinitive of a verb used as a noun
  **das Singen** *(no pl) singing,* **das Trinken** *(no pl) drinking*
- the young of persons and animals
  **das Kind (-er)** *child,* **das Baby (-s)** *baby,* **das Lamm (¨er)** *lamb*
- nouns ending in **-chen** and **-lein**
  **das Mädchen (-)** *girl,* **das Fräulein (-)** *young lady (unmarried)*
- the names of most countries and all towns are neuter in German
  **das Deutschland** *Germany,* **das London der Nachkriegszeit** *postwar London*
- a small number of countries are feminine
  **die Schweiz** *Switzerland,* **die Türkei** *Turkey*

### Two genders
A small number of nouns have two genders with different meanings. The list below contains those which are important for you to know for GCSE.

| | | | | |
|---|---|---|---|---|
| **der Band (¨e)** | *volume* | **das Band (¨er)** | *ribbon* |
| **der Golf (-e)** | *gulf* | **das Golf** *(no pl)* | *golf* |
| **der Leiter (-)** | *leader* | **die Leiter (-n)** | *ladder* |
| **der Messer (-)** | *measurer, meter* | **das Messer (-)** | *knife* |
| **der See (-n)** | *lake* | **die See (-n)** | *sea* |

### Compounds
Many words in German are formed by joining two or more smaller words together to form a compound. The gender of the compound word is always the gender of the last part.
  **der** Fahr**plan (¨e)** *timetable,* **die** Bushalte**stelle (-n)** *bus stop*

## The formation of noun plurals

In English, making a noun plural nearly always means simply adding an 's' – *one boy, six boys.*
  In German there are seven ways of forming the plural of nouns.

### Group 1
Nouns which do not change in the plural: most of these are **masculine** and **neuter nouns** ending in **-el, -en, -er,** plus **neuters** ending in **-lein, -chen** and beginning with **Ge-** and ending with **-e.**
  Example: **der Onkel** *uncle*

| | Singular | Plural |
|---|---|---|
| *Nom* | der Onkel | die Onkel |
| *Acc* | den Onkel | die Onkel |
| *Gen* | des Onkels | der Onkel |
| *Dat* | dem Onkel | den Onkeln |

Other examples: **der Nebel (-)** *mist, fog,* **der Briefkasten (-)** *letter box, post box,* **der Pullover (-)** *pullover,* **das Viertel (-)** *quarter,* **das Kissen (-)** *cushion,* **das Fenster (-)** *window,* **das Häuschen (-)** *cottage,* **das Fräulein (-)** *young lady (unmarried),* **das Gebirge ( )** *mountain range*

### Group 2

Nouns which do not have an ending in the plural, but an Umlaut is added to the vowels **a, o, u, au** when they are stressed in pronunciation. An Umlaut in German is written as two dots over the vowel (**ä, äu, ö, ü**) and it changes the sound. These are nearly all **masculine nouns** ending in **-el, -en, -er.**

Example: **der Apfel** *apple*

|     | Singular | Plural |
| --- | --- | --- |
| *Nom* | der Apfel | die Äpfel |
| *Acc* | den Apfel | die Äpfel |
| *Gen* | des Apfels | der Äpfel |
| *Dat* | dem Apfel | den Äpfeln |

Other examples: **der Mantel** (¨) *coat,* **der Bruder** (¨) *brother,* **der Garten** (¨) *garden*

Two very common **feminine nouns** are in this group: **die Mutter** (¨) *mother,* **die Tochter** (¨) *daughter*

One **neuter noun** is in this group: **das Kloster** (¨) *monastery*

### Group 3

Nouns forming their plural by adding **-e.**

Example: **das Jahr** *year*

|     | Singular | Plural |
| --- | --- | --- |
| *Nom* | das Jahr | die Jahr**e** |
| *Acc* | das Jahr | die Jahr**e** |
| *Gen* | des Jahres | der Jahr**e** |
| *Dat* | dem Jahr | den Jahr**en** |

To this group belong most **neuter nouns** of one syllable with the exception of those belonging to groups 1 and 4 and those ending in **-tum** or **-um.**

Here is a list of the commonest **neuter nouns** belonging to this group:

| | | | | | |
| --- | --- | --- | --- | --- | --- |
| **Bein** | *leg* | **Kinn** | *chin* | **Recht** | *right* |
| **Bier** | *beer* | **Mal** | *time* | **Salz**\* | *salt* |
| **Boot** | *boat* | **Meer** | *sea* | **Schaf** | *sheep* |
| **Brot**\* | *bread* | **Netz** | *net* | **Schiff** | *ship* |
| **Ding** | *thing* | **Öl**\* | *oil* | **Schwein** | *pig* |
| **Gas** | *gas* | **Paar** | *pair* | **Spiel** | *game* |
| **Fest** | *festival* | **Pferd** | *horse* | **Stück** | *piece* |
| **Haar** | *hair* | **Pfund** | *pound* | **Tier** | *animal* |
| **Heft** | *exercise book* | **Pult** | *desk* | **Zelt** | *tent* |

Note those marked with \* are rarely used in the plural.

Most **neuter nouns** of more than one syllable also form their plural this way by adding **-e.** Here are a few of them:

| | | | | | |
| --- | --- | --- | --- | --- | --- |
| **Alphabet** | *alphabet* | **Problem** | *problem* | **Talent** | *talent* |
| **Dutzend** | *dozen* | **Programm** | *programme* | **Telegramm** | *telegram* |
| **Konzert** | *concert* | **Prozent** | *percentage* | **Telefon** | *telephone* |
| **Paket** | *parcel* | **System** | *system* | | |

Most **masculine nouns** of more than one syllable (not listed so far) belong to this group plus a number of one-syllable **masculine nouns** which do not have an Umlaut in the plural as in Group 4 below. Here are some examples:

| | | | | | |
| --- | --- | --- | --- | --- | --- |
| **Abend** | *evening* | **Fahrschein** | *ticket* | **Monat** | *month* |
| **Apparat** | *phone* | **Fotoapparat** | *camera* | **Urlaub** | *holiday* |
| **Besuch** | *visit* | **Frühling** | *spring* | **Versuch** | *attempt* |
| **Bleistift** | *pencil* | **Lehrling** | *apprentice* | **Zwilling** | *twin* |

Single syllable **masculine nouns** which do not take an Umlaut in the plural.

| | | | | | |
| --- | --- | --- | --- | --- | --- |
| **Arm** | *arm* | **Laut** | *sound* | **Ruf** | *call* |
| **Dom** | *cathedral* | **Mond** | *moon* | **Schuh** | *shoe* |
| **Hund** | *dog* | **Ort** | *place* | **Stoff** | *stuff, material* |
| **Kurs** | *course* | **Punkt** | *point* | **Tag** | *day* |

### Group 4

Nouns forming their plural by adding **-e** with an Umlaut on the vowels **a, o, u, au** when stressed in pronunciation. Most of these are **masculine nouns** with one syllable not listed elsewhere.

Example: **der Sohn** *son*

|     | Singular | Plural |
| --- | --- | --- |
| Nom | der Sohn | die Söhne |
| Acc | den Sohn | die Söhne |
| Gen | des Sohnes | der Söhne |
| Dat | dem Sohn | den Söhnen |

This is a very large group of **masculine nouns** e.g. **der Arzt ("e)** *doctor*, **der Stuhl ("e)** *chair* and many more.

An important group of **feminine nouns** form their plural this way. Here are the most common:

| **Hand** | *hand* | **Maus** | *mouse* | **Stadt** | *town* |
| --- | --- | --- | --- | --- | --- |
| **Kuh** | *cow* | **Nacht** | *night* | **Wand** | *wall* |
| **Kunst** | *art* | **Nuß ("sse)** | *nut* | **Wurst** | *sausage* |

N.B. This group of **feminine nouns** does not follow the normal pattern in the formation of the plural of **feminine nouns** (see group 6), so learn them carefully.

### Group 5

Nouns forming their plural by adding **-er** with an Umlaut on the stressed vowel where possible.

Example: **das Dorf** *village*

|     | Singular | Plural |
| --- | --- | --- |
| Nom | das Dorf | die Dörfer |
| Acc | das Dorf | die Dörfer |
| Gen | des Dorfes | der Dörfer |
| Dat | dem Dorf | den Dörfern |

About a quarter of all **neuter nouns** belong to this group, most of them have one syllable. Remember that an Umlaut can only be used on the vowels **a, o, u, au,** e.g. **das Bad ("er)** *bath*, **das Haus ("er)** *house* **das Schloß ("sser)** *castle*, **das Buch ("er)** *book*, **das Kind (-er)** *child*

A small number of **masculine nouns** also belong to this group: **der Gott ("er)** *God*, **der Mann ("er)** *man*, **der Wald ("er)** *wood, forest*.

### Group 6

Nouns forming their plural by adding **-n** or **-en**. These are the endings of the plural of virtually all **feminine nouns**.

Example: **die Bluse** *blouse*

|     | Singular | Plural |
| --- | --- | --- |
| Nom | die Bluse | die Blusen |
| Acc | die Bluse | die Blusen |
| Gen | der Bluse | der Blusen |
| Dat | der Bluse | den Blusen |

Note that **feminine nouns** ending in **-in** double the '**n**' before adding the **-en**, so the plural of **die Lehrerin** (*teacher female*) is **die Lehrerinnen.**

Note that the -n is added to **feminine nouns** ending in -e, -l, -r in this group. e.g. **die Ecke (-n)** *corner*, **die Gabel (-n)** *fork*, **die Mauer (-n)** *wall (outside)*

A small group of **neuter nouns** have plurals ending in **-n** or **-en**. These include: **das Auge** *eye*, **das Bett** *bed*, **das Ende** *end*, **das Hemd** *shirt*, **das Interesse** *interest*, **das Ohr** *ear*.

**Masculine nouns** ending in -e belong to this group and add **-n** to form their plural. There is also a group of **masculine nouns** which add **-en** to form their plural. These nouns have **-n** or **-en** in every case except the nominative singular. This is explained later on page 28.

Examples:

| **der Junge** *boy* | | **der Mensch** *human being* | |
| --- | --- | --- | --- |
|     | Singular | Plural | Singular | Plural |
| Nom | der Junge | die Jungen | der Mensch | die Menschen |
| Acc | den Jungen | die Jungen | den Menschen | die Menschen |
| Gen | des Jungen | der Jungen | des Menschen | der Menschen |
| Dat | dem Jungen | den Jungen | dem Menschen | den Menschen |

- Other examples:

  Masculine nouns ending in **-e** with **-n** in the plural: **der Beamte (-n)** *official*, **der Franzose (-n)** *Frenchman*, **der Löwe (-n)** *lion*, **der Matrose (-n)** *sailor*, **der Neffe (-n)** *nephew*, **der Russe (-n)** *Russian*, **der Schotte (-n)** *Scotsman*.

Masculine nouns like **Mensch** adding **-en** in the plural **der Elefant (-en)** *elephant,* \*der Herr (-en) *gentleman,* **der Spatz (-en)** *sparrow,* **der Student (-en)** *student,* (N.B. \*der Herr only has an **-n** in the singular – **den Herrn, des Herrn, dem Herrn.**).

### Group 7

Nouns which add **-s** in the plural. These are nearly all words from other languages:

Example: **das Auto** *car*

|      | Singular  | Plural    |
|------|-----------|-----------|
| *Nom* | das Auto  | die Auto**s** |
| *Acc* | das Auto  | die Auto**s** |
| *Gen* | des Auto**s** | der Auto**s** |
| *Dat* | dem Auto  | den Auto**s** |

Note there is no **-n** in the dative plural and this ending is also used for the plural of family names: **die Brauns** *the Browns.*

Here is a short list of some of these words which are in different genders:

| **das Hobby** | *hobby* | **das Restaurant** | *restaurant* |
|---------------|---------|--------------------|--------------|
| **der Klub**  | *club*  | **die Kamera**     | *camera*     |
| **das Hotel** | *hotel* | **der Tunnel**     | *tunnel*     |

### How to use nouns and proper nouns

When we use a noun in a sentence in German we need to know what case it is in and whether it has any other endings. Have a careful look at the pattern illustrated below, paying particular attention to the endings of the nouns shown in **bold**. The pattern shows three nouns in each of the three genders in the four cases and in the singular and plural. The definite article *'the'* is used in the pattern to show the case endings.

*Singular*      *Plural*

|      | *M* | *F* | *N* | *M* | *F* | *N* |
|------|-----|-----|-----|-----|-----|-----|
| *Nom* | der Mann | die Mutter | das Kind | die Männer | die Mütter | die Kinder |
| *Acc* | den Mann | die Mutter | das Kind | die Männer | die Mütter | die Kinder |
| *Gen* | des Mann**es** | der Mutter | des Kind**es** | der Männer | der Mütter | der Kinder |
| *Dat* | dem Mann | der Mutter | dem Kind | den Männer**n** | den Mütter**n** | den Kinder**n** |

Points to note:

- The four cases which are explained later are:
  Nom = Nominative, Acc = Accusative, Gen = Genitive, Dat = Dative.

- Nouns change very little in the different cases. The only changes are to masculine and neuter nouns in the genitive singular, where **-es** is normally added to a one syllable noun or **-s** is added if there is more than one syllable. In the dative plural of all nouns **-en** or **-n** is added except where the plural ends in **-s** or already ends in **-n**.

- There are two groups of nouns which have a different pattern. They are illustrated below. One group **(a)** has **-en** or **-n** endings in all cases except the nominative singular. The other group **(b)** is virtually the same except that they have **-ens** or **-ns** in the genitive singular.

  Examples:

| | **(a) der Prinz** *prince* | | **(b) der Name** *name* | |
|------|-----------|-----------|-----------|-----------|
| | *Singular* | *Plural* | *Singular* | *Plural* |
| *Nom* | der Prinz | die Prinz**en** | der Name | die Name**n** |
| *Acc* | den Prinz**en** | die Prinz**en** | den Name**n** | die Name**n** |
| *Gen* | des Prinz**en** | der Prinz**en** | des Name**ns** | der Name**n** |
| *Dat* | dem Prinz**en** | den Prinz**en** | dem Name**n** | den Name**n** |

- Other examples of nouns in group a) are given in Group 6 on page 27.

- There are a small number of **masculine nouns** which have the group **(b)** pattern like **Name**, they are:

| **Buchstabe** | *letter of the alphabet* | **Glaube** | *faith* |
|---------------|--------------------------|------------|---------|
| **Friede**    | *peace*                  | **Same**   | *seed*  |
| **Gedanke**   | *thought*                | **Wille**  | *will*  |

One neuter noun **das Herz** *heart* has a similar pattern:

Nom – **das Herz**, Acc – das Herz, Gen – des Herz**ens**, Dat – dem Herz**en**

# 1.3 The cases

To succeed in your German studies you must know what the four cases are and how to use them. We have already given examples of nouns and articles showing how they change in German by using different endings to show the case, the gender and the plural. In English we do not often show the cases by changing the shape of the words except when we are using personal pronouns. For example *I* sometimes becomes *me*, *he* becomes *him*, *we* becomes *us*, *she* becomes *her* and *they* becomes *them*. These changes in pronouns show how we use cases in English. The change depends on the role of the pronoun in the sentence. This is really what cases are – they show the role of the word in the sentence. Look at these examples in English:

**(a)** *I saw him, but he did not see me.*

**(b)** *We saw them, but they did not see us.*

These two sentences both contain two **subjects**, the verb *to see* in two forms of the past tense and two **direct objects**. After you have read the next few paragraghs you should be able to say which words are the subjects and which are the direct objects.

Let us look at this in a little more detail. First of all we need to understand the structure of a sentence. The simplest sentences contain just a subject and a finite verb, e.g. *He dreamed. We left. The doorbell rang.* The subject of a verb can be either a noun or a pronoun and its role is to tell us who or what did the action. The action is explained by the verb. *He, we* and *The doorbell* are the subjects, *dreamed, left* and *rang* are the finite verbs.

Here is a slightly more complicated sentence, but it is still simple because it only contains one verb: *The girl stayed at home with her brother.*

This sentence has a subject – *the girl*, a finite verb – *stayed* and two phrases with small words called prepositions, one of which tells us *where* she stayed – *at home* and the other *how* she stayed – *with her brother.* They are called prepositional phrases of place and manner.

Now let us look at four sentences which show the main use of each of the four cases in German:

**(a)** The father gives the son the brother's pencil. (The German words here are all masculine.)

**(b)** The mother gives the sister the daughter's handbag. (The German words here are all feminine.)

**(c)** The child gives the girl the young lady's book. (The German words here are all neuter.)

**(d)** The parents give the friends the children's toys. (The German words here are all plural.)

Each of these sentences has the same five elements:

- a subject
- a verb
- a direct object
- an indirect object
- a phrase which shows possession or ownership.

It is important for you to be able to recognise these five elements and the role they play in each sentence. If you can recognise the role of each element you will know which case to use in German and you can then use the right case endings.

The four cases in German are the **Nominative**, **Accusative**, **Genitive** and **Dative** – **Nom**, **Acc**, **Gen**, **Dat** for short.

Here are the four sentences again, this time with the German underneath and the cases and elements made clear:

| | | | | | |
|---|---|---|---|---|---|
| **(a)** | The father | gives | the son | the pencil | of the brother. |
| | **Der Vater** | **gibt** | **dem Sohn** | **den Bleistift** | **des Bruders**. |
| | **(Nom)** | **(verb)** | **(Dat)** | **(Acc)** | **(Gen)** |
| **(b)** | The mother | gives | the sister | the handbag | of the daughter. |
| | **Die Mutter** | **gibt** | **der Schwester** | **die Handtasche** | **der Tochter**. |
| | **(Nom)** | **(verb)** | **(Dat)** | **(Acc)** | **(Gen)** |
| **(c)** | The child | gives | the girl | the book | of the young lady. |
| | **Das Kind** | **gibt** | **dem Mädchen** | **das Buch** | **des Fräuleins**. |
| | **(Nom)** | **(verb)** | **(Dat)** | **(Acc)** | **(Gen)** |
| **(d)** | The parents | give | the friends | the toys | of the children. |
| | **Die Eltern** | **geben** | **den Freunden** | **die Spielzeuge** | **der Kinder**. |
| | **(Nom)** | **(verb)** | **(Dat)** | **(Acc)** | **(Gen)** |

The four nouns in these sentences each show one of the four cases in German and represent the main use of that case. In most instances it is the article word for *the* which shows the case endings. You should learn these sentences off by heart and then you will always be able to remember the case endings and the role each case plays in a sentence.

Let us now summarise the main uses of each case:

**Nom**: The **nominative** case is used for the **subject** of a verb, i.e. the person or thing doing the action.

**Acc**: The **accusative** case is used for the **direct object** of the verb. The direct object is the noun or pronoun, thing or person, receiving the action of the verb directly. In our four sentences **what is given** is the direct object, i.e. *the pencil, the handbag, the book* and *the toys*.

**Gen**: The **genitive** case is the one which shows **possession** or **ownership**. It means in English *of the, of a, of my* etc although it is often shown by '**s** or **s**'. In our four examples the **genitives** are *the brother's/of the brother, the daughter's/of the daughter, the young lady's/of the young lady* and *the children's/of the children*.

**Dat**: The **dative** case is used for the **indirect object** of the verb. Indirect objects only occur with certain types of verb like give, show, buy for example. The indirect object is the person or thing to whom or to which the action of the verb is done. In our four examples we could have written the sentences a different way, changing the word order and using the word **to** before the indirect objects:

**(a)** The father gives the brother's pencil **to** *the son.*
**(b)** The mother gives the daughter's handbag **to** *the sister.*
**(c)** The child gives the young lady's book **to** *the girl.*
**(d)** The parents give the children's toys **to** *the friends.*

This is the best way to check for an indirect object in English. Insert the word *to* and change the word order. If this does not change the meaning of the sentence, the noun or pronoun with the *to* in front of it is the **indirect object** and therefore in German will be in the dative case.

N.B. The other uses of the cases (e.g. with prepositions) are explained later in this chapter.

## Revision tip

Make yourself a series of postcards, each with an essential point of German grammar on them. You will always then have an easy grammar aid to help you when writing in class or at home. You will also be able to memorise the details more easily and quickly, because the information is on a small card. You should also be able to visualise each card in the examination which will help you to be accurate in all tasks.

## Proper nouns

Proper nouns include actual names like George, Henry, Jason and Mary along with the names of rivers, towns and countries. In German as in English they have a capital letter.

● Note that they do not normally change in German except in the genitive case where they add an **-s** as in English, but without the apostrophe: *George's book* **Georgs Buch** *Mary's pencil* **Maries Bleistift** *Mr Smith's car* **Herrn Schmidts Auto.**

● Geographical names usually add **-s** in the genitive if they are masculine or neuter, remaining unchanged if they are feminine: **die Ufer des Rheins** (m) *the banks of the Rhine,* **die Geschichte Deutschlands** (n) *the history of Germany,* but **die Ufer der Donau** (f) *the banks of the Danube.*

# 1.4 Articles

There are two articles known in English as the **definite article** and the **indefinite article**.

## The definite article

In English the definite article is *the* and is always the same. In German the word for *the* has a pattern of endings which show the gender of the noun, whether it is singular or plural and which case it is in. Here is the full pattern of the words for *the* in German. Learn it thoroughly!

|  | *Masculine* | *Feminine* | *Neuter* | *Plural* |  |
|---|---|---|---|---|---|
| *Nom* | der | die | das | die | *the* |
| *Acc* | den | die | das | die | *the* |
| *Gen* | des | der | des | der | *of the* |
| *Dat* | dem | der | dem | den | *to the* |

Points to note:

- these words for *the* are used with nouns, showing the gender, the case and whether the noun is singular or plural
- the following words in German have the same endings as **der** in the pattern above: **dieser** *this*, **jener** *that*, **jeder** *each*, **welcher** *which* and **alle** (plural) *all*. Examples: **dieser Mann** *this man*, **alle Kinder** *all children*, **welches Buch** *which book*
- make yourself a revision card with the pattern of the endings of the definite article on it
- sometimes **das, der** and **dem** are not written in full but are contracted with certain prepositions as follows:

| | | | | | | |
|---|---|---|---|---|---|---|
| **an das** | becomes | **ans** | | **in das** | becomes | **ins** |
| **an dem** | becomes | **am** | | **in dem** | becomes | **im** |
| **auf das** | becomes | **aufs** | | **um das** | becomes | **ums** |
| **bei dem** | becomes | **beim** | | **von dem** | becomes | **vom** |
| **durch das** | becomes | **durchs** | | **zu dem** | becomes | **zum** |
| **für das** | becomes | **fürs** | | **zu der** | becomes | **zur** |

### Special uses of the definite article in German

Generally the definite article in German is used in the same way as it is in English. There are, however, some special uses which you should learn.

- It is used with names of the days, months and seasons, in English we usually leave it out. Learn the following phrases:

| | | | | |
|---|---|---|---|---|
| **am** Montag | *on Monday* | | **im** Januar | *in January* |
| **am** Dienstag | *on Tuesday* | | **im** Sommer | *in summer* |
| **im** August | *in August* | | **im** Frühling | *in spring* |

  N.B. These are the contracted forms of **dem**.

- It is always used with the names of countries, rivers and streets which are masculine or feminine, in English we often miss it out. Look at these examples and learn them:

| | |
|---|---|
| Wir fahren in **die** Schweiz. | *We are going to Switzerland.* |
| Er wohnt in **der** Friedrichstraße. | *He lives in Friedrich street.* |
| Er steht auf **dem** Potsdamer Platz. | *He is standing in Potsdam Square.* |
| **Der** Rhein fließt durch Köln. | *The Rhine flows through Cologne.* |
| London liegt an **der** Themse. | *London is on the Thames.* |

- It is used with a proper name when there is an adjective included, again we miss it out in English. Look at these examples and learn them:

| | |
|---|---|
| *little Peter* | **der** kleine Peter |
| *present-day Germany* | **das** heutige Deutschland |

- It is used in phrases with parts of the body and clothes, where in English we would usually say *my, his, her*, etc. Look at these examples and learn them:

| | |
|---|---|
| Er hob **den** Arm. | *He raised **his** arm.* |
| Sie zog **den** Mantel aus. | *She took off **her** coat.* |
| Er hielt **den** Hut in **der** Hand. | *He held **his** hat in **his** hand.* |
| Vati wusch ihr **die** Hände. | *Dad washed **her** hands.* |

- It is used in phrases containing a reflexive verb, again instead of 'my', 'his', 'our' etc. Look at these examples and learn them:

| | |
|---|---|
| Er wusch sich **die** Hände. | *He washed **his** hands.* |
| Ich wasche mir **die** Haare. | *I wash **my** hair.* |

- It is used in common phrases about transport and meals. In English we leave it out. Look at these examples and learn them:

| | |
|---|---|
| *at breakfast* | **beim** Frühstück |
| *after lunch* | nach **dem** Mittagessen |
| *by train* | mit **dem** Zug |
| *by air* | mit **dem** Flugzeug |

- It also occurs in some phrases of place 'where to' where it is missed out in English:

| | |
|---|---|
| in **die** Stadt gehen | *to go to town* |
| in **die** Kirche gehen | *to go to church* |
| in **die** Schule gehen | *to go to school* |

- It replaces *a* and *an* in English in these phrases which you should learn:

| | |
|---|---|
| zwei Mark **das** Kilo | *two marks **a** kilo* |
| Er kommt zweimal in **der** Woche. | *He comes twice **a** week.* |
| Wir fuhren 80 Kilometer **die** Stunde. | *We were doing 80 kilometres **an** hour.* |

**Omission of the definite article**
- As in English it is left out in German in pairs of nouns which are linked and when **weder... noch...** are used. Look at these examples and learn them carefully:

| | |
|---|---|
| Hand in Hand | *hand in hand* |
| Tag und Nacht | *day and night* |
| Lesen und Schreiben | *reading and writing* |
| Er hat **weder** Vater **noch** Mutter. | *He has **neither** father **nor** mother.* |

- *Christmas, Easter* and *Whitsuntide* are **Weihnachten, Ostern** und **Pfingsten** in German, also without the definite article.
- Names of countries which are neuter and the names of towns, when used on their own also have no article. Learn these examples:

| | |
|---|---|
| Wir wohnen in Deutschland. | *We live in Germany.* |
| Die Hauptstadt von Rußland ist Moskau. | *The capital of Russia is Moscow.* |

# The indefinite article

The indefinite article is used with nouns in a similar way to the definite article. It means *a* or *an* in English and indicates that no particular one is meant. There is no plural form of the indefinite article, **ein Buch** – *a book* becomes **Bücher** – *books*. Here is the pattern in full, showing the case endings of the words for *a* or *an*. Learn it carefully:

| | *Masculine* | *Feminine* | *Neuter* | |
|---|---|---|---|---|
| *Nom* | ein | eine | ein | *a(n)* |
| *Acc* | einen | eine | ein | *a(n)* |
| *Gen* | eines | einer | eines | *of a(n)* |
| *Dat* | einem | einer | einem | *to a(n)* |

Points to note:
- In German the indefinite article is left out when we would expect to use it in English referring to nationalities and professions:

| | |
|---|---|
| Er ist Arzt. | *He is **a** doctor.* |
| Sie ist Französin. | *She is **a** Frenchwoman.* |

- You also miss it out after **als** (*as*):

| | |
|---|---|
| Er sprach als Freund. | *He spoke as **a** friend.* |

- You miss it out in some phrases with prepositions. Look at these and learn them:

| | |
|---|---|
| ein Land ohne König | *a country without **a** king* |
| mit schwerem Herzen | *with **a** heavy heart* |
| mit lauter Stimme | *in **a** loud voice* |

# Kein

**Kein** means *not a* or *not any*. It does not mean *not one*, which is **nicht ein** in German. **Kein** has the same endings as **ein** and also has a plural form meaning *not any*.

Here is the full pattern of **kein** – *not a, no, not any*. Learn it carefully:

| | *Masculine* | *Feminine* | *Neuter* | *Plural* |
|---|---|---|---|---|
| *Nom* | kein | keine | kein | keine |
| *Acc* | keinen | keine | kein | keine |
| *Gen* | keines | keiner | keines | keiner |
| *Dat* | keinem | keiner | keinem | keinen |

Points to note:
- The following have the same endings as **kein** in the four cases:
  **mein** *my*, **dein** *your*, **sein** *his*, **ihr** *her*, **unser** *our*, **euer** *your*, **Ihr** *your* (polite form), **ihr** *their*.
  Examples:

| | |
|---|---|
| Er kann **sein** Buch nicht finden. | *He cannot find his book.* |
| **Unsere** Mutter ißt keine Tomaten. | *Our mother does not eat any tomatoes.* |
| **Mein** Bruder hat keine Lust nach Hause zu gehen. | *My brother has no desire to go home.* |

- Pay careful attention to the similarities and differences of the patterns of the endings of **der** *(the)* and **kein** *(not a)*. The differences are really very few in number and therefore important. They are simply that in the **kein** pattern the masculine and neuter singular of the nominative case and the neuter accusative singular are the same because they do not have an ending. All the other endings of both patterns are exactly the same. What this means is that the **ein** or **kein** pattern does not tell you in the nominative singular whether the noun is masculine or neuter because there is no ending. **Ein Vogel** *(a bird)* could be either a masculine or neuter noun, the **ein** does not tell us which it is. That is why when we list vocabulary in our vocabulary book we use the definite article (**der, die** or **das**) which tells us the gender. In fact it is **der Vogel**, so it is masculine. This becomes even more important when we look at the endings of adjectives used in front of nouns (see below).

- Learn these two patterns very carefully so that you can recognise the endings which go with each case in all three genders and in both the singular and the plural.

# 1.5 Adjectives

An adjective is a word used to describe a noun or a pronoun. Here are some examples of adjectives in English: a *small* chair, the *long* journey, an *old* friend, or clothes are *expensive*, she is *fat*, the road is *clear*. The words in italics are adjectives and straight away you can see that there are two ways in which adjectives are used, either **before** the noun they are describing as *small, long, old* in the examples given, or **after** the verb as in *expensive, fat* and *clear*.

The same two ways of using adjectives exist in German. When they are used *after* verbs, they do not change and work the same way as they do in English. Look at these examples:

Sie ist **schlank**. *She is **slim**.* Der Mann ist **hungrig**. *The man is **hungry**.*

## Adjective endings

When an adjective is used **before a noun** in German, it must agree with that noun in three ways: in **number** (i.e. whether it is *singular or plural*), in **gender** (i.e. whether it is *masculine, feminine* or *neuter*) and in **case** (i.e. whether it is in the *nominative, accusative, genitive* or *dative*). There are three patterns of adjective endings to choose from in German and you need to know all three for GCSE. They cause problems for students of German because there is nothing similar in English to help you.

Fortunately the number of different case endings for adjectives is small, there are only five altogether and the most frequently used ending is **-en**. The others are **-er, -e, -es, -em,** the problem is which one to use where. Let us now look at the three patterns of adjective endings in turn.

### Pattern 1

The 'easy-to-remember' pattern, there are only two endings **-e,** and **-en**

|     | Masculine | Feminine | Neuter | Plural |
|-----|-----------|----------|--------|--------|
| Nom | dieser gut**e** Mann | diese gut**e** Frau | dieses gut**e** Kind | diese gut**en** Eltern |
| Acc | diesen gut**en** Mann | diese gut**e** Frau | dieses gut**e** Kind | diese gut**en** Eltern |
| Gen | dieses gut**en** Mannes | dieser gut**en** Frau | dieses gut**en** Kindes | dieser gut**en** Eltern |
| Dat | diesem gut**en** Mann | dieser gut**en** Frau | diesem gut**en** Kind | diesen gut**en** Eltern |
|     | *(this good man)* | *(this good woman)* | *(this good child)* | *(these good parents)* |

These endings are used after the words **der** (*the*), **dieser** (*this*), **jeder** (*each, every*), **jener** (*that*), **solcher** (*such*), **welcher** (*which*) and **alle** (*all*). These words all have the same case endings themselves.

Examples:

Diese schön**e** Rose wächst in diesem klein**en** Blumenbeet.
*This beautiful rose is growing in this small flowerbed.*

Jedes klein**e** Kind hatte diese grün**en** Bonbons. *Every small child had these green sweets.*

Points to note:

- The **-en** endings are those below the line drawn through the pattern above.
- Two adjectives used together before a noun will have the same endings:
  diese schön**e**, rot**e** Rose *this beautiful red rose*.

### Pattern 2

This pattern has four endings **-er, -e, -es** and **-en**, the first three showing the gender of the noun they are describing in the nominative and accusative singular, where the gender is not shown by another word.

|     | Masculine | Feminine | Neuter | Plural |
|-----|-----------|----------|--------|--------|
| Nom | kein gut**er** Wein | keine warm**e** Milch | kein kalt**es** Bier | keine frisch**en** Eier |
| Acc | keinen gut**en** Wein | keine warm**e** Milch | kein kalt**es** Bier | keine frisch**en** Eier |
| Gen | keines gut**en** Weines | keiner warm**en** Milch | keines kalt**en** Bier(e)s | keiner frisch**en** Eier |
| Dat | keinem gut**en** Wein | keiner warm**en** Milch | keinem kalt**en** Bier | keinen frisch**en** Eiern |
|     | *(no good wine)* | *(no warm milk)* | *(no cold beer)* | *(no fresh eggs)* |

These endings are used after **ein** (*a, an*), **kein** (*not a, not any, no*), **mein** (*my*), **dein** (*your*), **sein** (*his*), **ihr** (*her*), **unser** (*our*), **euer** (*your*), **lhr** (*your* formal form), **ihr** (*their*).

Most of the endings are still **-en** (below the line). The other endings (**-er, -e, -es**) are used in the nominative singular showing the gender of the noun being described and in the accusative singular with feminine and neuter nouns only.

**Pattern 3**

This is the pattern of case endings which is used for an adjective in front of a noun when there is no other word before that adjective. This pattern is the least common and uses all five endings. If you look at the endings of **dieser** in pattern 1, you will find that the endings of the adjectives in pattern 3 are almost the same. Here is the pattern in full:

|  | *Masculine* | *Feminine* | *Neuter* | *Plural* |
|---|---|---|---|---|
| *Nom* | gut**er** Wein | warm**e** Milch | kalt**es** Bier | frisch**e** Eier |
| *Acc* | gut**en** Wein | warm**e** Milch | kalt**es** Bier | frisch**e** Eier |
| *Gen* | gut**en**★ Weines | warm**er** Milch | kalt**en**★ Bier(e)s | frisch**er** Eier |
| *Dat* | gut**em** Wein | warm**er** Milch | kalt**em** Bier | frisch**en** Eiern |
|  | *(good wine)* | *(warm milk)* | *(cold beer)* | *(fresh eggs)* |

Points to note:

- The only endings in pattern 3 which are not the same as the endings of **dieser** on page 33 are the **-en** endings in the genitive★ of the masculine and neuter singular.
- These adjective endings show the gender, number and case of the noun they are describing.
- These adjective endings are used after the numbers with the exception of **eins**, e.g. zwei gut**e** Bücher *two good books*. These adjective endings are used after the words **viele** (*many*), **wenige** (*a few*), **einige** (*some*) and **mehrere** (*several*)

  viele klein**e** Kinder      *many small children,*
  wenige frisch**e** Eier      *a few fresh eggs,*
  ein Haus mit einigen groß**en** Zimmern      *a house with some large rooms,*
  mehrere englisch**e** Touristen      *several English tourists.*

**To sum up**

- In pattern 1 there are only two endings **-e** and **-en**, the case is shown by the article word.
- In pattern 2 the adjective endings are **-er, -e, es** and **-en**. They show the gender in the nominative and accusative singular where the determining words **ein, kein, mein** etc do not have any endings.
- In pattern 3 the adjective takes the place of a word like **der** or **dieser** and has the same endings as **dieser** except in the masculine and neuter genitive singular.
- Once you have grasped fully how the cases work in German and which endings are used with each case, the adjective endings in each pattern are not difficult to learn or memorise. Remember correct use of adjective case endings is rewarded in the Higher Tier writing papers.
- Make yourself three revision cards about adjective endings, one for each pattern.

# Other points about adjectives

- Almost all adjectives can be used as nouns. To make an adjective into a noun simply write it with a capital letter and add the ending according to the patterns above:
  Der **Blinde** sitzt im Gras.    *The blind man is sitting on the grass.* (pattern 1 ending)
  Ein **Blinder** kam ins Hotel.   *A blind man came into the hotel.* (pattern 2 ending)
- A few adjectives change their form when they have endings:
  **dunkel** (*dark*) loses the **e**: **ein dunkles Haus** *a dark house*
  **hoch** (*high*) loses the **c**: **ein hoher Berg** *a high mountain*
- When the name of a town is used as an adjective you simply add **-er** in German to the name of the town. There are no other endings:
  die **Berliner** Kaufhäuser    *the Berlin department stores*
  der **Hamburger** Hafen    *the port of Hamburg.*

# The comparative and superlative forms of adjectives

A comparative is used when two items are being compared, the superlative is used when more than two items are being compared.

In English the comparative and superlative of adjectives can be formed in two ways:

| *Basic* | *Comparative* | *Superlative* |
|---|---|---|
| small | smaller | smallest |
| beautiful | more beautiful | most beautiful |

The **-er/-est** endings are used on short adjectives but long adjectives of more than one syllable require **more** and **most** to be used. In German adjectives only add **-er** or **-st**. The other form is not used. Look at these examples:

| Basic | Comparative | Superlative |
|---|---|---|
| klein (*small*) | kleiner (*smaller*) | der/die/das kleinste (*smallest*) |
| intelligent (*intelligent*) | intelligenter (*more intelligent*) | der/die/das intelligenteste (*most intelligent*) |

Comparative: Die **kleinere** der beiden Schwestern heißt Maria.
*The **smaller** of the two sisters is called Maria*

Superlative: Heute habe ich den **intelligentesten** Schüler in meiner Klasse nicht gesehen.
*I have not seen the **most intelligent** schoolboy in my class today.*

Points to note:

- The comparative and superlative forms of adjectives have to have the right case endings when they are used before nouns. The patterns of the endings are as above.
- Adjectives ending in **-t, -d, -sch, -s, -ß, -z** have an **-est** ending in the superlative to make them easier to pronounce:
  intelligent, intelligenter, der/die/das intelligent**este**   *intelligent, more intelligent, most intelligent*
  heiß, heißer, der/die/das heiß**este**   *hot, hotter, hottest.*
- Adjectives ending in **-e** only add **-r** in the comparative:
  weis**e**, weise**r**, der/die/das weiseste   *wise, wiser, wisest.*
- Adjectives ending in **-el, -en, -er** sometimes drop this **-e** in the comparative:
  dunkel, **dunkler**, der/die/das dunkelste   *dark, darker, darkest*
  trocken, **trockner**, der/die/das trockenste   *dry, drier, driest*
  sicher, **sichrer**, der/die/das sicherste   *safe, safer, safest.*
- Some adjectives have an Umlaut in the comparative and superlative forms. Remember an Umlaut can only be used on the vowels **a, au, o** and **u**
  For example: arm *poor*, ärmer *poorer*, der/die/das ärmste *poorest.*
  The following is a list of the adjectives which have the Umlaut in the comparative and superlative and should be known for GCSE.

| | | | | | |
|---|---|---|---|---|---|
| **alt** | *old* | **klug** | *clever* | **schwach** | *weak* |
| **dumm** | *stupid* | **krank** | *ill* | **schwarz** | *black* |
| **gesund** | *healthy* | **kurz** | *short* | **stark** | *strong* |
| **jung** | *young* | **lang** | *long* | **warm** | *warm* |
| **kalt** | *cold* | **scharf** | *sharp* | | |

- There is also a small group which are irregular and need to be learned carefully:

| | | | |
|---|---|---|---|
| **groß** | **größer** | **der/die/das größte** | *big, bigger, biggest* |
| **gut** | **besser** | **der/die/das beste** | *good, better, best* |
| **hoch** | **höher** | **der/die/das höchste** | *high, higher, highest* |
| **nah** | **näher** | **der/die/das nächste** | *near, nearer, nearest* |
| **viel** | **mehr** | **der/die/das meiste** | *much, more, the most* |

- Be careful about the superlative, it must be a true comparison. Look at these examples:
  **Der kälteste Monat ist Februar.**
  *The coldest month is February.* (This is a true comparison.)
  **Dieses Buch ist gut, aber jenes Buch ist das interessanteste.**
  *This book is good but that book is the most interesting.* (This is a true comparison.)
  *but* **Das ist ein sehr interessantes Buch.**
  *That is a most interesting book.* (This is not a comparison, it implies this is a **very** interesting book not **the most** interesting book.)
- Other phrases involving comparisons need to be learned carefully:
  (a) The repeated comparative is **immer ..** in German: Die Ferien werden **immer kürzer.**
      *The holidays are getting **shorter and shorter.***
  (b) **(Eben) so... wie** is used for comparisons of equals:
      Hans ist **(eben) so** groß **wie** Fritz.   *Hans is **(just) as** tall **as** Fritz.*
  (c) **als** means *than* in a comparison of unequals:
      Hans ist größer **als** Fritz.   *Hans is taller **than** Fritz.*
  (d) **weniger... als** is used for comparisons of inferiority:
      Hans ist **weniger** klug **als** Fritz.   *Hans is **less** clever **than** Fritz.*
      (Hans ist **nicht so** klug **wie** Fritz.   *Hans is **not so** clever **as** Fritz* is also possible)
  (e) **Je... desto** (or **umso**) are used with comparatives as in this example:
      **Je** früher die Sonne aufgeht, **desto** (or **umso**) später geht sie unter.
      *The earlier the sun rises the later it sets*

## Possessive adjectives

Adjectives which tell us about the 'belonging to' or possession of something/someone are known as the **possessive adjectives.** They have the same endings as **ein** and **kein** as shown in Pattern 2 and are listed on page 34. They are linked with the personal pronouns. Here is the list again showing the link with the personal pronouns:

|  | Singular Pronoun | Possessive Adjective | Plural Pronoun | Possessive Adjective |
|---|---|---|---|---|
| 1st Person | ich, *I* | **mein**, *my* | wir, *we* | **unser**, *our* |
| 2nd Person | *du, *you* | **dein**, *your* | *ihr, *you* | **euer**, *your* |
| 3rd Person | er, *he* | **sein**, *his* |  |  |
|  | sie, *she* | **ihr**, *her* | sie, *they* | **ihr**, *their* |
|  | es, *it* | **sein**, *its* |  |  |
|  | *Sie, *you* | **Ihr**, *your* | *Sie, *you* | **Ihr**, *your* |

*Note that there are three ways of saying *you* and *your* in German. **Du** and **dein** should be used when addressing one person who is well known to the speaker or the writer, usually a member of the family, a close friend, a child or an animal. In the same way **ihr** and **euer** should be used when addressing more than one member of the family, close friends, children or animals. **Sie** and **Ihr** are the words for *you* and *your* when addressing any other person or persons who are not known to you or who are older than you. They are the 'polite' or 'formal' forms of *you* and *your* in German either in the singular or the plural and always have a capital letter. The others **du, dein, ihr** and **euer** are the 'friendly' or 'familiar' forms of *you* and *your*. When you are speaking or writing in your examinations it is very important to decide which forms you should be using and stick to your choice without **mixing** the two. It is equally important always to link the correct pairs of words for *you* and *your* – **du** with **dein** and so on.

Here is the pattern of the case endings of the possessive adjectives:

|  | Masculine | Feminine | Neuter | Plural |
|---|---|---|---|---|
| Nom | mein | mein**e** | mein | mein**e** |
| Acc | mein**en** | mein**e** | mein | mein**e** |
| Gen | mein**es** | mein**er** | mein**es** | mein**er** |
| Dat | mein**em** | mein**er** | mein**em** | mein**en** |

Points to note:
- These endings are exactly the same as the endings of **ein** and **kein.** (See page 32.)
- All the possessive adjectives take their number, gender and case from the noun they are describing and the role that that noun plays in the sentence.
- Be careful **unser** (*our*) and **euer** (*your*) look like **dieser** (*this*) but are not, they are words which have the same endings as **mein, kein** and **ein.**
- Other adjectives used with the possessive adjectives have the Pattern 2 case endings (see page 33) and the examples below.
- Here are some examples of possessive adjectives in use:
  Jeden Tag fährt **mein** Vater mit **seinem** kleinen Auto in die Stadt.
  *Every day **my** father drives to town in **his** small car.*
  Wo wohnst du, Hans? **Dein** Onkel ist Arzt, nicht wahr?
  *Where do you live, Hans? **Your** uncle is a doctor, isn't he?*
  Lotte, Uschi, kommt herunter! **Euer** Frühstück ist auf dem Tisch.
  *Lotte, Uschi, come down! **Your** breakfast is on the table.*
  Guten Morgen, Herr Braun! **Ihr** Kaffee ist fertig.
  *Good morning Mr. Brown! **Your** coffee is ready.*
  Wir sehen **unseren** alten Großvater nicht sehr oft.
  *We do not see **our** old grandfather very often*
  Anna hat **ihren** roten Bleistift vergessen, und Alfred liest **sein** neues Buch.
  *Anna has forgotten **her** red pencil and Alfred is reading **his** new book.*

Points to note:
- In the last example **ihren** is masculine accusative singular not *feminine* even though it refers to Anna and means *her*. It is actually describing *the pencil* which is a masculine word in the accusative because it is the direct object of the verb *has forgotten*. Similarly **sein** is neuter accusative singular because *the book* is a neuter word in the accusative, the direct object of the verb *is reading*.
- Remember the rule 'all kinds of adjective used *before* nouns must agree in number, gender and case with the noun they are describing'.

## Demonstrative adjectives

These are the words in English for *this, that* and *such*. In German they are **dieser** (*this*), **jener** (*that*) and there are several ways of translating *such* – **solcher, solch ein, so ein, ein so** (see the examples below). **Dieser** and **jener** have the same pattern of case endings as **der** (*the*) (see page 30).

|     | Masculine | Feminine | Neuter | Plural |
|-----|-----------|----------|--------|--------|
| Nom | dies**er** Mann | dies**e** Frau | dies**es** Kind | dies**e** Eltern |
| Acc | dies**en** Mann | dies**e** Frau | dies**es** Kind | dies**e** Eltern |
| Gen | dies**es** Mannes | dies**er** Frau | dies**es** Kindes | dies**er** Eltern |
| Dat | dies**em** Mann(e) | dies**er** Frau | dies**em** Kind(e) | dies**en** Eltern |
|     | (*this man*) | (*this woman*) | (*this child*) | (*these parents*) |

Points to note:
- **Jener** is usually used in contrast to **dieser** and is much less common in German.
  **Diese** Frage ist schwer, **jene** Frage ist aber ganz leicht zu beantworten.
  ***This*** *question is difficult, but **that** question is very easy to answer.*
- Here are some ways of translating *such*:
  **(a)** Einen **solchen** Wagen möchte ich nicht kaufen. *I would not like to buy **such a** car.*
  In this example **solch ...** has the Pattern 2 case endings and behaves like an adjective.
  **(b)** **Solche** Männer verdienen nicht viel. ***Such** men do not earn much.*
  In this example **solch ...** has the same endings as **dieser** (*this*) see pattern above.
  **(c)** **Solch ein** hübsches Mädchen wohnt hier. ***Such a** pretty girl lives here.*
  This is a slightly more emphatic way of saying *such a* than *so ein* **hübsches Mädchen** or even *ein so* **hübsches Mädchen wohnt hier**.
  In the three examples in **(c) solch** does not have any endings, **ein** and **hübsch** have the normal endings of Pattern 2 according to number, gender and case and **so** does not change.

## Interrogative adjectives

These are adjectives used in asking questions. There are basically two of them in German – **welcher** (*which*) and **was für** (*what sort of*). **Welcher** has the same endings as **dieser** (see above) and like **dieser** takes its number, gender and case from the noun it is describing in the usual way. Look carefully at these examples:

**Welches** Buch ist das? / ***Which*** *book is that?*
**Welchen** Bleistift hält er in der Hand? / ***Which*** *pencil is he holding in his hand?*
Mit **welchem** Zug fährt er nach Köln? / *By **which** train is he travelling to Cologne?*
**Was für** Blumen sind das? / ***What sort of*** *flowers are those?* (with a plural noun)
**Was für ein** Hund ist das? / ***What sort of (a)*** *dog is that?* (with a singular noun)
Mit **was für einem** Kugelschreiber schreibt er? / ***What sort of (a)*** *ballpoint pen is he writing with?*

Note that **was für** does not change, it has no endings; with a singular noun you must use **ein** in the appropriate case with the ending which agrees with the noun it describes.

# 1.6 Adverbs

Adverbs are words which describe the action of a verb. They are mainly in three groups which describe *when, where* or *how* things happen i.e. adverbs of **time, place** and **manner** – e.g. *always, upstairs, quickly*. There are also adverbs which are used with adjectives or other adverbs. These are known as **adverbs of degree**, e.g. He arrived ***very*** late. He did it ***extremely*** badly. He worked ***surprisingly*** long hours. You can usually recognise an adverb in English because it ends in –**ly**. In German adverbs are much the same as in English except that they do not have a special ending. Adverbs in German do not have any endings.

## Adverbs of time

| | | | | | |
|---|---|---|---|---|---|
| **bald** | *soon* | **gestern** | *yesterday* | **immer** | *always* |
| **damals** | *then* | **gleich** | *at once* | **jetzt** | *now* |
| **danach** | *afterwards* | **gleichzeitig** | *at the same time* | **lange** | *(for) a long time* |
| **dann** | *then* | **heute** | *today* | **manchmal** | *sometimes* |
| **früh** | *early* | **heutzutage** | *nowadays* | **morgen** | *tomorrow* |

| | | | | | |
|---|---|---|---|---|---|
| **nachher** | *afterwards* | **selten** | *seldom, rarely* | **vorher** | *beforehand* |
| **neulich** | *recently* | **sofort** | *immediately* | **zeitweise** | *at times* |
| **nun** | *now* | **sogleich** | *immediately* | **zuerst** | *at first* |
| **oft** | *often* | **spät** | *late* | **zugleich** | *at the same time* |
| **rechtzeitig** | *in good time* | **stets** | *always* | **zuletzt** | *at last* |
| **seither** | *since then* | **täglich** | *daily* | | |

## Adverbs of manner

| | | | |
|---|---|---|---|
| **eben** | *even, just* | **plötzlich** | *suddenly* |
| **gern** | *gladly, willingly* | **sonst** | *otherwise* |
| **gleichfalls** | *likewise* | **vielleicht** | *perhaps* |
| **hoffentlich** | *hopefully* | **wahrscheinlich** | *probably* |
| **leider** | *unfortunately* | **wirklich** | *really* |

N.B. **gern** is used with verbs to show 'liking' e.g. Er trinkt **gern** Milch. *He **likes drinking** milk*

## Adverbs of place

| | | | |
|---|---|---|---|
| **hier** | *here* | **mitten** | (plus preposition) *in the middle of* |
| **dort** | *there* | **oben** | *above, upstairs* |
| **da** | *there* | **unten** | *below, downstairs* |
| **irgendwo** | *somewhere* | **überall** | *everywhere* |
| **nirgendwo** | *nowhere* | **anderswo** | *elsewhere* |

**Hin** and **her** as adverbial expressions need special mention, **hin** implies motion away from the speaker, **her** implies motion towards the speaker. They are mostly used with verbs as in these examples:

Er ging die Treppe **hin**unter.     *He went downstairs.*
Er kam die Treppe **her**unter.     *He came downstairs.*

But, Sie fuhren mit dem Zug dort**hin**. *They went there by train* and, Wo**her** kommen Sie? *Where do you come from?* show how they can be used in other ways.

## Adverbs of degree

| | | | |
|---|---|---|---|
| **besonders** | *especially* | **kaum** | *scarcely, hardly* |
| **etwas** | *a little, somewhat* | **sehr** | *very* |
| **fast** | *almost* | **völlig** | *completely* |
| **ganz** | *quite* | **ziemlich** | *rather* |
| **genug** | *enough* | **zu** | *too* |
| **höchst** | *extremely, highly* | | |

Most of these are used with adjectives or other adverbs to emphasise or tone down the meaning of the word they are qualifying:

Sie ist **sehr** schön.     *She is **very** beautiful.*
Das ist **zu**viel.     *That is **too** much.*
Er schlief **fast** ein.     *He **almost** fell asleep.*
Er konnte **kaum** sehen.     *He could **hardly** see.*

## Adverbs which ask a question

| | | | |
|---|---|---|---|
| **wo** | *where* | **Wo** liegt sein Buch? | *Where is his book?* |
| **wann** | *when* | **Wann** beginnt die Schule? | *When does school begin?* |
| **wie** | *how* | **Wie** alt ist sie? | *How old is she?* |
| **warum** | *why* | **Warum** spielt er Fußball? | *Why does he play football?* |

**Wie** can be combined with other words to form adverbs which introduce a question:

| | | | |
|---|---|---|---|
| **wie lange** | *how long* | **Wie lange** dauert dieses Spiel? | *How long does this game last?* |
| **wie oft** | *how often* | **Wie oft** fährt ein Bus nach Bonn | *How often does a bus go to Bonn?* |
| **wieviel** | *how much* | **Wieviel** Geld hat er? | *How much money has he got?* |
| **wie viele** | *how many* | **Wie viele** Geschenke kauft sie? | *How many presents is she buying?* |

**Wo** can be combined with **hin** and **her** to form adverbs which introduce a question:

| | | | |
|---|---|---|---|
| **wohin** | *where (to)* | **Wohin** fahren wir heute? | *Where are we going **to** today?* |
| **woher** | *where from* | **Woher** kommt der Zug? | *Where is the train **from**?* |

Points to note:
- Many adjectives can be used as adverbs. When used as adverbs they have no endings and sometimes have a slightly different meaning: e.g.

  **gut** *good* (adjective)     Das ist ein **gutes** Buch.     *That is a **good** book.*
  **gut** *well* (adverb)     Dieses Buch ist **gut** geschrieben.     *This book is **well** written.*
- The position of adverbs needs care. They are usually placed next to the word they affect in German, but the other rules of word order must be applied first. (See page 63.)

  Er lief **schnell** die Straße entlang.     *He ran **quickly** along the street.*
  Er mußte den Brief seiner Tante **schnell** lesen.     *He had to read his aunt's letter **quickly**.*
- You can also form an adverb by adding **–erweise** to certain adjectives as in these two useful examples:

  glücklich**erweise**   *fortunately*     unglücklich**erweise**   *unfortunately*

## The comparative and superlative of adverbs

These are similar to the comparison of adjectives (see page 34). The difference is that the superlative of the adverbs is formed with **am ... sten**. Look at these examples:

| | | |
|---|---|---|
| **scharf** (*sharply*) | **schärfer** (*more sharply*) | **am schärfsten** (*most sharply*) |
| **klar** (*clearly*) | **klarer** (*more clearly*) | **am klarsten** (*most clearly*) |
| **schnell** (*quickly*) | **schneller** (*more quickly*) | **am schnellsten** (*most quickly*) |

Points to note:
- As with adjectives the superlative must be one on its own.

  **Der Schüler spricht sehr klar** means *The schoolboy speaks most/very clearly.*
  But **der Schüler spricht am klarsten in der Klasse** means *The schoolboy speaks the clearest in the class.* i.e. he speaks the most clearly of all.
- Note these words which are adverbs and have the **–st** ending without anything else: **höchst** and **äußerst** (*extremely*), **möglichst schnell** (*as quickly as possible*), **längst** (*long since*).
- By adding **–ens** to certain superlative forms you make some more useful adverbs like **höchstens** (*at the most*), **meistens** (*for the most part*), **spätestens** (*at the latest*), **mindestens** and **wenigstens** (*at least*).
- Be careful with the irregular patterns of the comparison of adverbs. Here are a few you ought to make sure you know:

| | | | | | |
|---|---|---|---|---|---|
| **bald** | *soon* | **eher** | *sooner* | **am ehesten** | *soonest* |
| **gern** | *willingly* | **lieber** | *more willingly* | **am liebsten** | *most willingly* |
| **hoch** | *high* | **höher** | *higher* | **am höchsten** | *highest* |

  The second example **gern** is important because it can be used with the verb **haben** to mean *like*.

  Ich habe Mathematik **gern**.     *I **like** maths.*
  Ich habe Deutsch **lieber**.     *I **prefer** German.* (like better)
  Ich habe Englisch **am liebsten**.     *I **like** English **best**.*

  It can of course be used with other verbs meaning *like (doing)* e.g. Ich singe **gern**, *I like singing.*

## Negatives

Most of the following negatives are used adverbially:

| | | | |
|---|---|---|---|
| **nicht** | *not* | **nirgendwo** | *nowhere* |
| **gar nicht** | *not at all* | **nie** | *never* |
| **nicht mehr** | *no more, no longer* | **nichts** | *nothing* |
| **nicht einmal** | *not even* | **gar nichts** | *nothing at all* |
| **noch nicht** | *not yet* | **nicht..., sondern...** | *not..., but...* |
| **nein** | *no* | **weder... noch...** | *neither... nor...* |
| **niemand** | *nobody* | **noch nie** | *never yet* |
| **nichts als** | *nothing but* | **nicht wahr** | *isn't it, etc* |

Examples:

| | |
|---|---|
| Ich habe ihn **nicht** gesehen. | *I have **not** seen him.* |
| Ich habe **gar nichts** gegessen. | *I have eaten **nothing at all**.* |
| Er ist **noch nicht** angekommen. | *He has **not yet** arrived.* |
| Er spricht **nichts als** die Wahrheit. | *He speaks **nothing but** the truth.* |
| Er schrieb den Brief, **nicht wahr**? | *He wrote the letter, **didn't he**?* |
| Wir können **nicht mehr** ins Kino gehen. | *We cannot go to the cinema **any more**.* |
| Er ist **nicht** klein, **sondern** groß. | *He is **not** small **but** tall.* |
| Sie kann **weder** singen **noch** tanzen. | *She can **neither** sing **nor** dance.* |

## Other words which are like adverbs

**also** *so, thus, then* (it does not mean *also*)

| | |
|---|---|
| Er blieb **also** in der Schule. | *So he stayed at school.* |
| Du wirst mir **also** helfen können. | *You are going to help me **then**.* |

**denn** *then, well then, so*

| | |
|---|---|
| Geht der Junge **denn** heute nicht in die Schule? | *Isn't the boy going to school today, **then**?* |
| Was ist **denn** hier los? | *What **on earth** is going on here?* |

**doch** can be used in a number of different ways often contradicting, emphasising or disagreeing with what has just been said. Look at these examples:

| | |
|---|---|
| Gestern hat es **doch** geregnet. | *It **did** rain yesterday.* (emphasising) |
| Er ist **doch** nicht gekommen. | *He has not come **after all*** (disagreeing) |
| Öffne **doch** das Paket! | ***Do** open the parcel!* (emphasising urgency) |
| Hast du ihn nicht gesehen? | *Haven't you seen him?* |
| **Doch,** ich habe ihn gestern gesehen. | ***Oh yes,** I saw him yesterday.* |
| (contradicting, answering yes to a negative question) | |

**eben** *just*

| | |
|---|---|
| Er hat den Zug verpaßt, also essen wir **eben** eine halbe Stunde später. | *He has missed the train, so we'll **just** have to eat half an hour later.* |

**erst** *not until, only*

| | |
|---|---|
| Sie kam **erst** um vier Uhr an. | *She did **not** arrive **until** four o'clock.* |
| Er ist **erst** sechzehn Jahre alt. | *He is **only** sixteen years old.* |

**mal** *just used to reduce emphasis in a command*

| | |
|---|---|
| Sagen Sie mir **mal,** was geschah! | ***Just** tell me what happened!* |

**noch** *still, yet*

| | |
|---|---|
| Er schläft **noch.** | *He is **still** asleep.* |
| Sonst **noch** etwas? | ***Anything else?*** |
| **Noch** ein Glas Milch, bitte. | ***Another** glass of milk, please.* |

**nur** *only, just, merely, simply expressing a limitation*

| | |
|---|---|
| Ich wollte **nur** schlafen. | *I **just/only** wanted to sleep.* |

**schon** *already*

| | |
|---|---|
| Es war **schon** 9 Uhr, als er ausging. | *It was **already** 9 o'clock when he went out.* |

**wohl** *I suppose, probably*

| | |
|---|---|
| Sie wissen **wohl,** was passiert. | ***I suppose** you know what is happening.* |

# 1.7 Personal pronouns

A pronoun is a word which is used in place of a noun. The personal pronouns do not all replace nouns as they are in three persons. This is very like English with first, second and third person pronouns existing in both the singular and the plural. Have a look at the chart given here to work out how they all work:

| | | First person singular | | First person plural | |
|---|---|---|---|---|---|
| Nom | (Subject) | **ich** | *I* | **wir** | *we* |
| Acc | (Direct object) | **mich** | *me* | **uns** | *us* |
| Dat | (Indirect object) | **mir** | *to me* | **uns** | *to us* |
| | | Second person singular | | Second person plural | |
| Nom | (Subject) | **du** | *you (familiar form)* | **ihr** | *you (familiar form)* |
| Acc | (Direct object) | **dich** | *you (familiar form)* | **euch** | *you (familiar form)* |
| Dat | (Indirect object) | **dir** | *to you (familiar form)* | **euch** | *to you (familiar form)* |
| | | Second person singular or plural | | | |
| Nom | (Subject) | **Sie** | *you (polite form)* | | |
| Acc | (Direct object) | **Sie** | *you (polite form)* | | |
| Dat | (Indirect object) | **Ihnen** | *to you (polite form)* | | |

| | | Third person singular | | | | Third person plural | |
|---|---|---|---|---|---|---|---|
| | | Masculine | | Feminine | Neuter | | |
| Nom | (Subject) | **er** *he, it* | **sie** *she, it* | | **es** *it* | **sie** *they* | |
| Acc | (Direct object) | **ihn** *him, it* | **sie** *her, it* | | **es** *it* | **sie** *them* | |
| Dat | (Indirect object) | **ihm** *to him, it* | **ihr** *to her, it* | | **ihm** *to it* | **ihnen** *to them* | |

Points to note:

- The chart above shows the forms of the personal pronouns in three cases only. The genitive has been omitted, because it is seldom used in German and you do not need to know it for GCSE
- You must know which case to use according to the role the pronoun has in the sentence
- First and second person pronouns in German work almost the same way as in English, where we see that the pronoun changes from *I* to *me* as in German *ich* becomes *mich* when we change the case from the nominative to the accusative. *To me* is dative and therefore *mir* in German etc. Have a look at these examples:

| | |
|---|---|
| Er sieht **mich** zu Hause. | *He sees **me** at home.* (**me/mich** is direct object – accusative case) |
| Sie gibt **uns** ein Buch. | *She gives **us** a book.* (**us/uns** is *to us* indirect object – dative case) |
| Wir werden **euch** morgen sehen. | *We shall see **you** tomorrow.* (**you/ euch** direct object – accusative case) |
| Er gibt **dir** ein Geschenk. | *He gives **you** a present.* (**you/ dir** is *to you* indirect object – dative case) |

- The third person pronouns need a little more care, because in the singular you need to know the gender of the noun for which they are standing as well as the case. You just need to know the case in the plural. Look at these examples. In the left hand column the nouns are in **bold**. In the right hand column the nouns have been replaced by pronouns, also in **bold**.

| | | | |
|---|---|---|---|
| (a) | **Liesel und Karl** sitzen **auf einer Bank**. | **Sie** sitzen **darauf**. | |
| | *Liesel and Karl are sitting on a bench.* | ***They** are sitting **on it**.* | |
| (b) | Sie sprechen mit **einer Krankenschwester**. | Sie sprechen mit **ihr**. | |
| | *They are talking with a nurse.* | *They are talking with **her**.* | |
| (c) | „Hatte **der Mann** nichts bei sich?" fragte **Liesel**. | „Hatte **er** nichts bei sich?" fragte **sie**. | |
| | *"Had the man nothing with him?" asked Liesel.* | *"Had **he** nothing with him?" **she** asked.* | |
| (d) | Er war **mit seinem neuen Auto** sehr zufrieden. | Er war **damit** sehr zufrieden. | |
| | *He was very pleased with his new car.* | *He was very pleased **with it**.* | |
| (e) | **Liesel** öffnete **die Handtasche**. | **Sie** öffnete **sie**. | |
| | *Liesel opened the handbag.* | ***She** opened **it**.* | |
| (f) | Sie zog **ein kleines Stück Papier** heraus. | Sie zog **es** heraus. | |
| | *She pulled out a small piece of paper.* | *She pulled **it** out.* | |
| (g) | Sie nahm **einen Bleistift** und begann zu schreiben. | Sie nahm **ihn** und begann zu schreiben. | |
| | *She took a pencil and began to write.* | *She took **it** and began to write.* | |

Points to note:

- All third person pronouns must agree in number, gender and case with the nouns they replace.
- Pronouns referring to 'things' used with a preposition are replaced by **da-** or **dar-** plus the preposition as in examples **(a)** *darauf* *on it* and **(d)** *damit* *with it*. **Dar-** is used when the preposition begins with a vowel.
- **Du, ihr** and **Sie** are the words for *you*. Every student must learn the difference between the formal **Sie** and its associated words and the familiar **du** (singular) and **ihr** (plural). This is explained on page 36. When writing informal letters **Du** and **Ihr** (*you*), **Dein** and **Euer** (*your*) should be used and written with capital letters. A letter to a friend might start like this:

Liebe Lotte!

Wie geht's **Dir**? Danke für **Deinen** Brief, den ich gestern gelesen habe ...

## Revision tip

Make a revision card giving yourself the essential details about the Personal Pronouns:

## Uses of 'es'

**(a)** In the phrase *It is I* you change it round in German and say **'Ich bin es'**.

**(b)** **Es** is used for the English word *there* in phrases like:

| | |
|---|---|
| **Es** gibt Bücher in einer Buchhandlung. | *There are books in a bookshop.* (this is a general statement) |
| **Es** ist ein Buch auf dem Tisch. | *There is one book on the table.* (this is a specific statement) |
| **Es sind** zwei Bücher auf dem Tisch. | *There are two books on the table.* (a specific statement, plural) |

## Indefinite pronouns

**man** (*one*), **jemand** (*someone*), **jedermann** (*everyone*), **niemand** (*no-one, nobody*), **nichts** (*nothing*)

All of these pronouns are third person and are used with the third person singular of the tenses of verbs:

| | |
|---|---|
| **Man** muß arbeiten, um Geld zu verdienen. | **One** has to work to earn money. |
| **Jemand** hat ihm einen Brief geschrieben. | **Someone** has written him a letter. |
| **Jedermann** sah das Mädchen. | **Everybody** saw the girl. |
| Ich habe **niemanden** gesehen. | I have seen **no-one**. |

**Nichts** can be used with an adjective which must have a capital letter.

| | |
|---|---|
| Ich habe **nichts Neues** gesehen. | I have seen **nothing new**. |

## Indefinite pronouns or adjectives

**all** (*all*), **ander** (*other*), **beide** (*both*), **ein bißchen** (*a little*), **ein paar** (*a few*)
**etwas** (*something, some*), **viel** (*much*), **wenig** (*little*).
Examples

**all, alles, alle** *all, everything*

| | |
|---|---|
| Ist **alles** da? | *Is everything there?* |
| **all** diese Leute | *all these people* |
| **Alle** sind angekommen. | *All have arrived.* |
| **alle** zwei Wochen | *Every other week, every second week.* |

**beide** *both*

| | |
|---|---|
| **Beide** sind schon weg | *Both have gone already* |
| Meine **beiden** Schwestern... | *My two sisters... Both my sisters...* |

**ein bißchen** *a little,* **ein paar** *a few,* **etwas** *something, some*

| | |
|---|---|
| **ein bißchen** Brot | *a little bread, a bit of bread* |
| **ein paar** Blumen | *a few flowers* (i.e. very few) |
| Ich will dir **etwas Gutes** sagen. | *I want to say something good to you.* (compare **nichts Neues** above) |

**viel** and **wenig**

These two tend to be used without any endings in the singular but have the endings of **dieser** in the plural.

| | |
|---|---|
| **Viel** Glück! | *Good luck!* |
| Er arbeitet **viel**. | *He works a lot.* |
| Er hatte noch ein **wenig** Geld. | *He still had a little money.* |
| **Viele** sind angekommen. | *Many arrived.* |
| Er hat **wenige** Freunde. | *He has few friends.* |

Both of them have the pattern 1 adjective endings when used after the definite article:

| | |
|---|---|
| Ich staunte über das **viele** Geld, das er ausgab. | *I was amazed at the large amount of money he spent.* |
| Das **wenige** Geld, das er verdiente... | *The little money that he earned...* |

## Reflexive pronouns

(a) These are used mostly with reflexive verbs. Nearly always the reflexive pronoun is the direct object of a reflexive verb in the accusative. The action of a reflexive verb relates back to the subject. Here is an example, learn it off by heart:

| | |
|---|---|
| **sich** waschen | *to wash **oneself*** |
| ich wasche **mich** | *I wash **myself*** |
| du wäschst **dich** | *you wash **yourself*** |
| er/sie/es wäscht **sich** | *he/she/it washes **himself/herself/itself*** |
| wir waschen **uns** | *we wash **ourselves*** |
| ihr wascht **euch** | *you wash **yourselves*** |
| sie waschen **sich** | *they wash **themselves*** |
| (Sie waschen **sich** | *you wash **yourself/yourselves***) (polite form) |

(b) For Higher Tier candidates only: Sometimes the reflexive pronoun is in the dative case. Only two of the reflexive pronouns change in the dative, they are **mich** and **dich** which become **mir** and **dir** respectively. Look at these examples and learn them carefully. In each of these sentences the reflexive pronoun is in the dative:

| | |
|---|---|
| ich wasche **mir** die Hände | *I wash my hands* (i.e. *to myself the hands*) |
| du wäschst **dir** die Hände | *you wash your hands* |
| Sie waschen **sich** die Hände | *you wash your hands* (polite form singular) |

| er wäscht **sich** die Hände | *he washes his hands* |
| sie wäscht **sich** die Hände | *she washes her hands* |
| wir waschen **uns** die Hände | *we wash our hands* |
| ihr wascht **euch** die Hände | *you wash your hands* |
| Sie waschen **sich** die Hände | *you wash your hands* (polite form plural) |
| sie waschen **sich** die Hände | *they wash their hands* |

Another example of the reflexive pronouns in the dative: **sich vorstellen** *to imagine*. This is a weak verb with a separable prefix and the reflexive pronouns are in the dative, (see page 49ff for details about weak and separable verbs).

| ich | stelle **mir** vor | *I imagine* | wir stellen **uns** vor | *we imagine* |
| du | stellt **dir** vor | *you imagine* | ihr stellt **euch** vor | *you imagine* |
| er/sie/es | stellt **sich** vor | *he/she/it imagines* | sie stellen **sich** vor | *they imagine* |
| Sie | stellen **sich** vor | *you imagine* | | |

For a list of other reflexive verbs see pages 58 and 59.

## Pronouns which introduce questions

There are two kinds of pronouns which introduce questions, those which refer to people and those referring to things. This is the same in English as it is in German. As you have probably guessed the words in German have to be in the appropriate case, but the endings are familiar. There is no plural form.

| | Referring to people (m. and f.) | | Referring to things (n.) | |
|---|---|---|---|---|
| *Nom* | wer | *who* | was | *what* |
| *Acc* | wen | *whom* | was | *what* |
| *Gen* | wessen | *whose* | (wessen) | *(of what)* (rarely used) |
| *Dat* | wem | *to whom* | (wem) | *(to what)* (rarely used) |

Points to note:
- Higher level candidates need to know all four cases.
- When using a preposition to ask a question referring to things **wo-** or **wor-** is used with the preposition in a similar way to **da-** and **dar-** as explained on page 41.
  **Womit** schreibst du? *With what are you writing?*
  **Worauf** steht die Flasche? *On what is the bottle standing?*
  Again **wor-** precedes a preposition beginning with a vowel.
- Here are some more examples showing the different ways of asking questions with these pronouns in the four cases:
  *Referring to people:*

| **Wer** wohnt hier? | **Who** *lives here?* | (nominative) |
| **Wen** sah er gestern abend? | **Whom** *did he see yesterday evening?* | (accusative) |
| **Wessen** Buch ist das? | **Whose** *book is that?* | (genitive) |
| **Wem** gab sie das Heft? | **To whom** *did she give the exercise book?* | (dative) |
| Mit **wem** spricht er? | *With* **whom** *is he speaking?* | (dative after **mit**) |

  **Referring to things:**

| **Was** liegt auf dem Tisch? | **What** *is on the table?* | (nominative) |
| **Was** kann er sehen? | **What** *can he see?* | (accusative) |
| **Wovon** spricht er? | **Of what** *is he speaking?* | (replaces genitive) |
| **Worauf** liegt das Buch? | **On what** *is the book?* | (replaces dative) |

## Relative pronouns

These are only required to be known for the Higher Tier examinations.

In English the relative pronouns when used are *who, whom, whose* referring to people and *which* or *that* referring to things. In English we often omit the relative pronoun, in German it **must** be used. You must also be careful to check that *that* is actually a relative pronoun in English. The way to do this is to replace *that* with *who* or *which* and if the sense is not changed it is a relative pronoun and one of the list below must be used accordingly in German.

Examples:
*Where is the book I bought yesterday?*
The relative pronoun has been omitted and *which* or *that* should be supplied.
*Where is the book **that** I bought yesterday?*
**Wo ist das Buch,** *das* **ich gestern gekauft habe?**
*We believe **that** you bought this book yesterday.*
If you replace *that* in this sentence with *which* it does not make any sense any more, so *that* is not a

relative here. The word for *that* in German is **daß** in this sentence: Wir glauben, **daß** du dieses Buch gestern gekauft hast.

### The forms of the relative pronoun

|  | Masculine | Feminine | Neuter | Plural |  |
|---|---|---|---|---|---|
| Nom | der | die | das | die | *who, which, that* |
| Acc | den | die | das | die | *whom, which, that* |
| Gen | dessen | deren | dessen | deren | *of whom, of which, whose* |
| Dat | dem | der | dem | denen | *to whom, to which* |

The first thing to notice about these case endings is that they are very similar to the endings of **der** the definite article. Only the genitives and the dative plural are different.

The rules for choosing which of these to use in a given sentence are as follows:
- The relative pronoun takes its number and gender from the word for which it stands, its **antecedent.**
- Its case is decided by the role it plays in the clause which it introduces.
- The verb in the relative clause must be placed at the end of the clause.
- The clause must be separated from the rest of the sentence by commas.

Look at these examples where the antecedent, the relative pronoun and the verb have been highlighted:

| Nom. fem. singular | Wo ist **die Frau**, **die** letztes Jahr in diesem Haus **wohnte**? |
|---|---|
|  | *Where is the woman, who lived in this house last year?* |
| Acc. masc. singular | **Der Mann, den** ich gestern **sah,** verließ heute das Hotel. |
|  | *The man (whom) I saw yesterday left the hotel today.* |
| Masc. gen. singular | **Mein Freund, dessen** jüngster Sohn sehr klug **ist,** wohnt in Münster. |
|  | *My friend, whose youngest son is very clever, lives in Münster.* |
| Dative plural | Ich wohne bei **den Eltern** meiner Freundin, mit **denen** ich viel Deutsch **spreche.** |
|  | *I am living with my girl friend's parents with whom I speak a lot of German.* |
| Genitive plural | **Die Freunde**, mit **deren** Bruder ich **arbeite,** wohnen in Bonn. |
|  | *The friends whose brother I work with, live in Bonn.* |

i.e. *with the brother of whom I work* – the *friends* are the antecedent.

# 1.8 Prepositions

Prepositions are small words which normally precede nouns or pronouns and indicate *where, how* or *when* something is happening. In both English and German there are many ways of using prepositions and there is no short cut to mastering how they work except to learn carefully which cases are used with them in German and the most common phrases which contain them. No attempt has been made here to give an exhaustive list of the uses of prepositions in German, but those which you are expected to know for GCSE are covered. Prepositions should be learned in groups according to the case which they govern i.e. the case which follows them.

## Prepositions with the accusative only

| **bis** | *as far as, till* | **gegen** | *against, towards, about* |
|---|---|---|---|
| **durch** | *through* | **ohne** | *without* |
| **entlang**[*] | *along* | **um** | *round, at* |
| **für** | *for, by* |  |  |

Examples:

**bis**

| Er bleibt **bis nächsten Montag** | *He is staying till next Monday* |
|---|---|
| **Bis morgen!** | *See you tomorrow!* |

**durch**

| Er ging **durch den Wald** | *He walked through the wood* |
|---|---|

**entlang**

| Er fuhr **die Straße entlang** | *He drove along the street* |
|---|---|

N.B. *entlang usually follows the word it governs.

**für**

| | |
|---|---|
| Er arbeitet **für sie** | *He works for her* |
| Sie hielt ihn **für einen Freund** | *She considered him a friend* |
| Ich interessiere mich **für Sport** | *I am interested in sport* |

**gegen**

| | |
|---|---|
| Wir laufen **gegen den Wind** | *We are running against the wind* |
| Er fährt **gegen Osten** | *He is driving/travelling eastwards* |
| **Gegen acht Uhr** muß ich abfahren | *I must leave about eight o'clock* |

**ohne**

| | |
|---|---|
| Er kam **ohne mich** | *He came without me* |

**um**

| | |
|---|---|
| Sie saßen **um den Tisch** | *They were sitting round the table* |
| Er kam **um halb acht** an | *He arrived at half past seven* |
| Er bittet **um Hilfe** | *He asks for help* |
| Es handelt sich **um Freiheit** | *It is a question of freedom* |

## Prepositions with the dative only

| | | | | | |
|---|---|---|---|---|---|
| **aus** | *out of* | **gegenüber*** | *opposite* | **seit** | *since, for* |
| **außer** | *except for, out of* | **mit** | *with, by* | **von** | *from, of* |
| **bei** | *by, at, at the house of* | **nach** | *to, after, according to* | **zu** | *to, at* |

Examples:

**aus**

| | |
|---|---|
| Er lief **aus dem Haus** | *He ran out of the house* |
| Er kommt **aus Bonn** | *He comes from Bonn* |
| Es ist **aus Leder** | *It is made (out) of leather* |
| Es besteht **aus Holz** | *It is made of wood* |

**außer**

| | |
|---|---|
| Keiner **außer ihm** kam | *No one except him came* |

**bei**

| | |
|---|---|
| Er stand **beim Fenster** | *He was standing by/at the window* |
| Er wohnt **bei mir** | *He is living at my house (with me)* |
| **beim Frühstück/Mittagessen** | *at breakfast/lunch* |
| Ich habe kein Geld **bei mir** | *I have no money on me* |
| **bei schlechtem Wetter** | *in bad weather* |

**gegenüber** (*often follows the noun)

| | |
|---|---|
| Er wohnt **dem Rathaus gegenüber** | *He lives opposite the town hall* |

**mit**

| | |
|---|---|
| Er kam **mit mir** | *He came with me* |
| Sie winkte **mit der Hand** | *She waved her hand* |
| Sie sprach **mit lauter Stimme** | *She spoke in a loud voice* |

Meaning *by* in phrases to do with transport

| | |
|---|---|
| **mit dem Zug, mit dem Auto, mit dem Bus** | *by train, by car, by bus* |
| **mit dem Dampfer, mit dem Flugzeug** | *by steamer, by plane* |
| **mit der Post, mit der Luftpost** | *by post, by airmail* |

**nach**

Meaning *to* (somewhere)

| | |
|---|---|
| Er fuhr **nach** Berlin, **nach** Italien | *He went to Berlin, to Italy* |
| Er ging **nach** Hause | *He went home* |

Meaning *after*

| | |
|---|---|
| **Nach einer Weile** schlief sie ein | *After a while she fell asleep* |
| Er kam **nach mir** an | *He arrived after me* |

Meaning *according to* when it usually follows the noun it governs

| | |
|---|---|
| **Meiner Meinung nach** ist er zu jung | *In my opinion he is too young* |
| **Dem Gesetz nach** ist er zu jung | *According to the law he is too young* |

Other uses:

| | |
|---|---|
| Wir schickten **nach dem Arzt** | *We sent for the doctor* |
| Das schmeckt **nach Obst** | *That tastes of fruit* |

**seit**

| | |
|---|---|
| **Seit dem Krieg** wohnt er in Bonn | *Since the war he has been living in Bonn* |

Ich wohne **seit vier Jahren** hier                  *I have been living here for four years*
Ich wohnte **seit vier Jahren** hier                 *I had been living here for four years*

**von**

Wir fuhren **von** Paris nach Berlin                 *We travelled from Paris to Berlin*
Er war ein Mann **von zwanzig Jahren**               *He was a man of twenty years of age*
**von Zeit** zu Zeit                                  *from time to time*
Es hängt **vom Wetter** ab                            *It depends on the weather*

**zu**

Meaning *to*

Er ging **zum Arzt**                                  *He went to the doctor*
Er ging **zum Bahnhof**                               *He went to the station*
Er ging **zu Bett**                                   *He went to bed*

Meaning *at*

**zu Ostern, zu Weihnachten**                         *at Easter, at Christmas*
**zu dieser Zeit**                                    *at this time*
**Briefmarken zu 60 Pfennig**                         *60 Pfennig stamps (stamps at ...)*
**zu Hause**                                          *at home*
**zu beiden Seiten**                                  *on either side*
**zum halben Preis**                                  *at half price*

Other phrases to remember:

Er sah **zum Fenster** hinaus                         *He looked out of the window*
Was gibt es heute **zum Frühstück?**                  *What's for breakfast today?*
**zum Beispiel, zum Spaß**                            *for example, for a joke*
**zu Fuß, zu Pferd**                                  *on foot, on horseback*
**zu meinem Erstaunen**                               *to my surprise*
**zu Ende, zum Glück**                                *at an end, fortunately*

## Prepositions with either the dative or the accusative

| **an** | *by, on, at, to* | **hinter** | *behind* | **vor** | *in front of, before* |
|---|---|---|---|---|---|
| **auf** | *on, onto* | **neben** | *beside, near* | **unter** | *under, below* |
| **in** | *in, into* | **über** | *over, above* | **zwischen** | *between* |

These are all prepositions which indicate 'place where' or 'place whereto'. 'Motion towards somewhere' is in the accusative, whereas 'place where' is in the dative.

Look at these examples and learn them:

Er ging **an die See** (accusative)                  *He went to the seaside (whereto)*
Er wohnt **an der See** (dative)                      *He lives at the seaside (where)*
Das Buch liegt **auf dem Tisch** (dative)            *The book is lying on the table (where)*
Er legte das Buch **auf den Tisch** (accusative)     *He put the book onto the table (whereto)*
Sie sitzt **auf einer Bank** (dative)                *She is sittng on a bench (where)*
Sie setzt sich **auf eine Bank** (accusative)        *She sits down on(to) a bench (whereto)*

Here are some more examples for each preposition plus either the accusative or the dative.

**an**

The main meaning of **an** is *on* in the sense of against a vertical surface, as opposed to *on top of* which is **auf** in German. In this way **an** can also mean *at*:

**an** (plus dative)

Das Bild hängt **an der Wand**                        *The picture is hanging on the wall*
Er steht **an der Tür**                               *He is standing at the door*
Er wartet **an der Bushaltestelle**                   *He is waiting at the bus-stop*
Er wohnt **an der Mosel**                             *He is living by/on the Mosel*

'On the underside of' is also **an**:

Die Lampe hängt **an der Decke**                      *The lamp is hanging from the ceiling*
Die Sterne funkeln **am Himmel**                      *The stars are twinkling in the sky*

To be employed at an institution is **an**:

Er ist Lehrer **am Gymnasium**                        *He is a teacher at the grammar school*

In expressions of time **an** is used with days of the week and parts of the day:

**am nächsten Morgen, am Abend**                      *the next morning, in the evening*
**am Wochenende, am Freitag**                         *at the weekend, on Friday*

Other useful phrases:

Er ging/fuhr **am Postamt** vorbei                    *He went past the post office*

| | |
|---|---|
| Er ist **an Bord** | *He is on board* |
| Er kam **an seiner Stelle** | *He came in his place* |
| Er leidet **an der Grippe** | *He is suffering from the flu'* |
| Sie starb **an der Grippe** | *She died of flu'* |
| Er nahm **am Theaterstück** teil | *He took part in the play* |

**an** (plus accusative)

| | |
|---|---|
| Er ging **ans Fenster** | *He went to the window* |
| Wir fuhren **an die Küste** | *We drove to the coast* |
| Er schrieb einen Brief **an mich** | *He wrote a letter to me* |
| Ich denke **an meine Schwester** | *I am thinking of my sister* |
| Ich erinnere mich **an meinen Bruder** | *I remember my brother* |
| Sie kommt **an die Reihe** | *It is her turn* |
| Er gewöhnt sich **an seine neue Schule** | *He is getting used to his new school* |

**auf** (plus dative)

**Auf** literally means *on top of*. It is used in German in a number of phrases where in English we use *in* or *at*:

| | |
|---|---|
| Er war **auf dem Lande** | *He was in the country* |
| Der Junge spielte **auf der Straße** | *The boy was playing in the street* |
| Die Kühe waren **auf der Wiese** | *The cows were in the meadow* |
| Er stand **auf dem Platz** | *He was standing in the square* |
| Sie war **auf dem Markt** | *She was at the market* |
| Wir sind **auf der Bank/auf der Post** | *We are at the bank/at the post office* |
| Er studiert **auf der Universität** | *He is studying at university* |
| Er ist **auf dem Rückweg** nach Köln | *He is on the way back to Cologne* |
| Er wurde **auf frischer Tat** ertappt | *He was caught in the act* |
| **auf der anderen Seite** | *on the other hand* |

**auf** (plus accusative)

Here it means literally *on to*.

| | |
|---|---|
| Er stellte die Flasche **auf den Tisch** | *He put the bottle on (to) the table* |
| Er ging **auf die Bank/auf die Post** | *He went to the bank/to the post office* |
| Er lief **auf die Straße** | *He ran into the street* |
| Er ging **auf die Universität/aufs Land** | *He went to university/into the country* |
| Er fährt **auf eine Woche** an die See | *He is going to the seaside for a week* |
| Sie kam **auf mich** zu | *She came up to me* |
| Sie ging **auf ihn** zu | *She went up to him* |
| Sie sprach **auf deutsch** | *She spoke in German* |
| Er antwortete nicht **auf meine Frage** | *He did not answer my question* |
| Er blickte **auf das hübsche Mädchen** | *He looked at the preetty girl* |
| Wir freuen uns **auf die Sommerferien** | *We are looking forward to the summer holidays* |
| Sie hofft **auf ein neues Kleid** | *She is hoping for a new dress* |
| Wir warten **auf den nächsten Bus** | *We are waiting for the next bus* |
| Sie ist böse **auf ihren Chef** | *She is angry about her boss* |
| Wir sind stolz **auf uns(e)ren Hund** | *We are proud of our dog* |
| **auf jeden Fall** | *in any case* |
| **auf diese Weise** | *in this way* |
| **auf eigene Kosten** | *at one's own expense* |
| **auf eigene Gefahr** | *at one's own risk* |

**in** (plus dative)

Means basically *inside*, within something.

| | |
|---|---|
| Er ist **im Theater/im Kino/im Konzert** | *He is at the theatre/at the cinema/at the concert* |
| Sie ist **in der Stadt/in der Kirche** | *She is in town/at church* |
| Er ist **in der Schule** | *He is at school* |
| Er kam **in der Stadt** an | *He arrived in the town* |
| Er arbeitet **im Freien** | *He is working out of doors/in the open air* |
| Er wohnt **in der Nähe** | *He lives nearby/in the neighbourhood* |
| Er lebt **im Ausland** | *He lives abroad* |
| **im Fernsehen/im Radio** | *on television/on radio* |
| **im ersten Stock** | *on the first floor* |
| **in diesem Augenblick** | *at this moment* |
| heute **in acht Tagen** | *a week today* |

|  |  |
|---|---|
| Ich habe sie **im Stich** gelassen | *I have left her in the lurch* |

**in** (plus accusative)

Conveys the idea of *into* something

|  |  |
|---|---|
| Er fuhr **in die Schweiz** | *He went to Switzerland* |
| Er reiste **ins Ausland** | *He travelled abroad* |
| Er ging **ins Theater/ins Kino/ ins Büro** | *He went to the theatre/to the cinema/ to the office* |
| Er geht **in die Schule/in die Kirche** | *He goes to school/to church* |
| Sie geht **in die Stadt** | *She goes to town* |
| Ich schnitt mich **in den Finger** | *I cut my finger* |
| Das muß ich **ins Deutsche** übersetzen | *I must translate that into German* |
| Sie steigen **in den Zug** ein | *They board the train* |

**hinter** (plus dative)

|  |  |
|---|---|
| Er stand **hinter ihr** | *He stood behind her* (place where) |

**hinter** (plus accusative)

|  |  |
|---|---|
| Er fuhr den Wagen **hinter das Haus** | *He drove the car behind the house* (place, whereto) |

**vor** (plus dative)

Referring to place it means *in front of*

|  |  |
|---|---|
| Er stand **vor der Tür** | *He was standing in front of the door* |
| Ich habe Angst **vor Spinnen** | *I am afraid of spiders* |

Referring to time it means *before, ago*

|  |  |
|---|---|
| **Vor dem Krieg** wohnten wir in Berlin | *Before the war we lived in Berlin* |
| **vor vielen Jahren** | *many years ago* |
| **vor kurzem** | *a short time ago* |

**vor** (plus accusative)

|  |  |
|---|---|
| Er lief **vor das Auto** | *He ran in front of the car* |

**über** (plus dative)

Indicates position where

|  |  |
|---|---|
| Das Bild hängt **über dem Sofa** | *The picture is hanging over the sofa* |
| Er wohnt **über der Grenze** | *He lives across/over the border* |

**über** (plus accusative)

Implying movement it means *above, over, across* or *beyond*

|  |  |
|---|---|
| Er hängte das Bild **über den Tisch** | *He hung the picture above the table* |
| Er schwamm **über den Fluß** | *He swam across the river* |
| Er fuhr **über Ostende** | *He went via Ostend* |
| Er blieb **über Nacht** | *He stayed overnight* |
| Kinder **über acht Jahre** | *children over eight* |

Other phrases to learn:

|  |  |
|---|---|
| Wir freuten uns **über seinen Brief** | *We were pleased about his letter* |
| Er lachte **über seine Fehler** | *He laughed about his mistakes* |

**unter** (plus dative)

Indicates position meaning *below, beneath, underneath*

|  |  |
|---|---|
| Der Hund lag **unter dem Tisch** | *The dog lay under the table* |
| Das Paket wiegt **unter einem Kilo** | *The parcel weighs under (less than) a kilo* |
| 200 Meter **unter dem Gipfel** | *200 metres below the summit* |

Other phrases worth learning:

|  |  |
|---|---|
| **unter Freunden** | *among friends* |
| **unter meinen Sachen** | *among my things* |
| **unter diesen Umständen** | *in these circumstances* |

**unter** (plus accusative)

Indicates position *whereto*

|  |  |
|---|---|
| Er schob den Stuhl **unter den Tisch** | *He pushed the chair under the table* |

## Prepositions followed by the genitive

These are only required for the Higher Tier examinations.

**statt** *instead of*, **trotz** *in spite of*, **während** *during*, **wegen** *on account of, because of*.

Here are some examples:

|  |  |
|---|---|
| **statt meines Bruders** | *instead of my brother* |
| **trotz des schlechten Wetters** | *in spite of the bad weather* |
| **während der Sommerferien** | *during the summer holidays* |
| **Wegen seines Vaters sagte ich nichts** | *Because of his father I said nothing* |

# 1.9 Verbs

Verbs are the most important words in any sentence. They tell us what is happening, who or what is doing the action and the time sequence in which the action is set, i.e. in the past, in the present or the future.

## How to use verbs

A verb will usually have a subject which tells you who or what is doing the action. Look at these short sentences in English which have the subject and the verb highlighted:

|          | First Person | Second Person | Third Person |
|----------|--------------|---------------|--------------|
| Singular | **I live** here | **You live** here | **He lives** here, **she lives** here, **it lives** here |
| Plural   | **We live** here | John and Peter, **you live** here | **They live** here |

This is one form of the present tense in English of the verb *to live*. You can see that it has three persons which can each be used in either the singular or the plural.

## The persons

The **first person** is used when the speaker is performing the action of the verb. In English we use *I* (singular) and *we* (plural), in German they are **ich** and **wir.**

The **second person** is *you* in English. This is the person who is being spoken to, who is performing the action of the verb. In German there are three words to choose from for *you*. They are **du** (sing), **ihr** (plur.), the familiar forms, and **Sie** (sing. or plur.) the polite or formal form. (see the explanation on page 36)

The **third person** is used when someone else is performing the action of the verb, not the speaker nor the person being spoken to. In English we use *he, she, it, one* (singular) or *they* (plural). Remember these are pronouns and the nouns which they are replacing can also be the subject of a verb in the **third person.** In German they are **er** (*he*), **sie** (*she*), **es** (*it*), **man** (*one*) and **sie** (*they*) or any noun replacing them.

## The tenses

The tense tells you when something is happening, it indicates the time of the action of the verb.

For Foundation Tier you must know the present, future, imperfect and perfect tenses.

For Higher Tier you must know in addition the pluperfect and conditional tenses, plus the imperfect subjunctive of *sein* and *haben* in conditional sentences.

## Weak, strong and mixed verbs

In a German dictionary verbs are listed by their **infinitive**, which ends in **-en** or **-n**. This does not tell us whether the verb is a regular 'weak' verb or an irregular 'strong' or 'mixed' verb in German. It is important to know this and the only way of doing this satisfactorily is to learn the list of irregular strong and mixed verbs on pages 67–69 very thoroughly. Fortunately the **weak** verbs are by far the largest group overall. Let us now look at the formation of the tenses of these three types of verb in some detail

### (a) Weak verbs

All weak verbs are regular and follow the same pattern of endings in each tense. Using **wohnen** (*to live*) as an example here are all the tenses of a **weak** verb. **Wohnen** is the infinitive made up of the stem **wohn-** and the ending **-en**.

**Present tense**

|            | Singular | | Plural | |
|------------|----------|--------------|--------|--------|
| 1st person | ich wohn**e** | *I live* | wir wohn**en** | *we live* |
| 2nd person | du wohn**st** | *you live* | ihr wohn**t** | *you live* |
| 3rd person | er/sie/es wohn**t** | *he/she/it lives* | sie wohn**en** | *they live* |

*2nd person (singular or plural)* Sie wohn**en** *you live*

Points to note:
- This is the only form of the present tense in German. There are three forms of this tense in English: *I live*, etc *I am living*, etc and *I do live* etc.
- All weak verbs in German follow a regular pattern forming the present tense by taking the stem of the verb and adding the endings highlighted above: **-e, -st, -t, -en, -t, -en**

**Imperfect tense or simple past tense**

|  | Singular |  | Plural |  |
|---|---|---|---|---|
| 1st person | ich wohn**te** | I lived | wir wohn**ten** | we lived |
| 2nd person | du wohn**test** | you lived | ihr wohn**tet** | you lived |
| 3rd person | er/sie/es wohn**te** | he/she/it lived | sie wohn**ten** | they lived |

2nd person (singular or plural) Sie wohn**ten** *you lived*

Points to note:
- The imperfect endings of all weak verbs are: **–te, –test, –te, –ten, –tet, –ten**. They should be added to the stem of the verb to form this tense.
- This is the only form of the imperfect tense in German, the other two forms in English are: *I was living* etc and *I did live*, etc.

**Future tense**

|  | Singular |  | Plural |  |
|---|---|---|---|---|
| 1st person | ich **werde** | I shall live | wir **werden** | we shall live |
| 2nd person | du **wirst** } wohnen | you will live | ihr **werdet** } wohnen | you will live |
| 3rd person | er/sie/es **wird** | he/she/it will live | sie **werden** | they will live |

2nd person (singular or plural) Sie **werden** wohnen *you will live*

Points to note:
- The future tense is formed with the present tense of the verb **werden** plus the infinitive of the verb concerned. This infinitive must go to the end of the sentence. (See word order page 63.)
- The verb **werden** (*to become*) is one of the three important verbs which are explained in detail on page 51. Make sure you learn them carefully.

**Perfect tense**

|  | Singular |  | Plural |  |
|---|---|---|---|---|
| 1st person | ich **habe** | I have lived | wir **haben** | we have lived |
| 2nd person | du **hast** } gewohnt | you have lived | ihr **habt** } gewohnt | you have lived |
| 3rd person | er/sie/es **hat** | he/she/it has lived | sie **haben** | they have lived |

2nd person (singular or plural) Sie **haben** gewohnt *you have lived*

Points to note:
- The perfect tense is formed with the present tense of **haben** plus the **past participle** of the verb concerned. The past participle of a weak verb is formed with **ge-** before the stem of the verb and the ending -**t.** For **wohnen** it is therefore **ge-wohn-t**.
- The past participle must be placed at the end of the part of the sentence in which it occurs. (See word order page 63.)
- N.B. The perfect/pluperfect tenses of some verbs are formed with the present tense of **sein** (see page 54.)

**Pluperfect tense** (Higher Tier only)

|  | Singular |  | Plural |  |
|---|---|---|---|---|
| 1st person | ich **hatte** | I had lived | wir **hatten** | we had lived |
| 2nd person | du **hattest** } gewohnt | you had lived | ihr **hattet** } gewohnt | you had lived |
| 3rd person | er/sie/es **hatte** | he/she/it had lived | sie **hatten** | they had lived |

2nd person (singular or plural) Sie **hatten** gewohnt *you had lived*

Point to note:
- The pluperfect tense is formed with the imperfect tense of **haben** plus the **past participle** of the verb concerned. The past participle must be placed at the end of the part of the sentence in which it occurs.

**Conditional tense** (Higher Tier only)

|  | Singular |  | Plural |  |
|---|---|---|---|---|
| 1st person | ich **würde** | I should live | wir **würden** | we should live |
| 2nd person | du **würdest** } wohnen | you would live | ihr **würdet** } wohnen | you would live |
| 3rd person | er/sie/es **würde** | he/she/it would live | sie **würden** | they would live |

2nd person (singular or plural) Sie **würden** wohnen *you would live*

Points to note:
- The conditional tense is formed with the imperfect subjunctive of **werden** plus the **infinitive** of the verb concerned. The infinitive must be placed at the end of the part of the sentence in which it occurs.
- The imperfect subjunctive is the same as the imperfect of **werden**, except that it has an Umlaut throughout.

**Imperative or command forms**

Wohn**e** in Bonn!     *Live in Bonn!* This is the familiar form singular, speaking to one friend.

| | |
|---|---|
| Wohn**t** in Bonn! | *Live in Bonn!* This is the familiar form plural, speaking to some friends. |
| Wohn**en** Sie in Bonn! | *Live in Bonn!* This is the polite form singular or plural. |
| Wohn**en** wir in Bonn! | *Let us live in Bonn!* This is the 1st person plural form *Let us...!* |

Points to note:

● Endings of the command forms are -**e**, -**t**, -**en**, -**en**. Except for the first one they are the endings of the corresponding parts of the present tense.

● The -**e** in the 2nd person familiar form is often omitted especially in speech:
**Sag** mir, was geschehen ist! *Tell me what has happened!*

### (b) Strong verbs

Strong verbs are irregular and change the vowel of the stem of the verb in the imperfect tense. Some of them change the stem vowel in other tenses. There are few rules about these changes, so you simply have to learn the list on pages 67–69. This is just like English where an irregular or strong verb does the same sort of thing. Here is an example: *I drink, I drank, I have drunk* in English becomes **ich trinke, ich trank, ich habe getrunken** in German. As you can see the vowel changes in the stem are very like the English changes. Unfortunately they are not all as easy as this example.

Let us use **trinken** *(to drink)* as our example to explain how a **strong verb** works.

| **Present tense** meaning *I drink etc.* | | **Imperfect tense** meaning *I drank etc.* | | **Command** meaning *drink* |
|---|---|---|---|---|
| ich trink**e** | wir trink**en** | ich trank | wir trank**en** | trink**e**! (familiar-sing.) |
| du trink**st** | ihr trink**t** | du trank**st** | ihr trank**t** | trink**t**! (familiar-plur.) |
| er/sie/es trink**t** | sie trink**en** | er/sie/es trank | sie trank**en** | trink**en** Sie! (polite form) |
| Sie trink**en** | | Sie trank**en** | | trink**en** wir! *Let us drink!* |

If we compare these tenses with the weak verb **wohnen** on page 49, we can see the following similarities and differences:

● In the present tense the endings for both **weak** and **strong** verbs are the same: -**e**, -**st**, -**t**, -**en**, -**t**, -**en**. These are added to the stem of the verb.

● The endings of the **imperative/command** forms are the same: -**e**, -**t**, -**en**, -**en**.

● The endings of the **Imperfect tense** are different and the stem vowel changes from -**i**- to -**a**- in this example.

● Remember the endings of **all strong verbs** in the **imperfect** are: -, -**st**, -, -**en**, -**t**, -**en**.

The other tenses of **strong verbs** are formed in the same way as the **weak verbs**. The only difference is in the formation of the past participle in the **perfect** and **pluperfect tenses**. The **past participle** of a **strong verb** begins the same way with **ge-** but ends in -**en**. There is often a change of stem vowel as well (see the list on pages 67–69.) Here are the other tenses of **trinken**, compare them with the weak verb **wohnen** on pages 49 and 50.

**Future tense**
ich **werde** trinken usw.         *I shall drink etc.*

**Perfect tense**
ich habe **getrunken** usw.         *I have drunk etc.*

**Pluperfect tense**
ich hatte **getrunken** usw.         *I had drunk etc.*

**Conditional tense**
ich **würde** trinken usw.         *I should drink etc.*

Points to note:

● usw. is short for **und so weiter** and means *and so on* or *etc.*

● When you learn **strong verbs** you need to know the principal parts of each verb. They are listed on page 67ff and include the following:

| *Infinitive* | *Meaning* | *3rd pers. sing. present* | *3rd pers. sing. imperfect* | *Perfect with haben/sein* |
|---|---|---|---|---|
| trinken | *to drink* | trinkt | trank | hat getrunken |
| fahren | *to drive* | fährt | fuhr | ist gefahren |

### (c) Three important verbs – *haben*, *sein* and *werden*

It is clear from the explanation about the formation of the tenses above that these three verbs are used a lot in German to form the various tenses. They are so important that they are given in full below and you should learn them very carefully. **Haben** or **sein** are used to form the perfect and pluperfect tenses, while **werden** is used to form the future and conditional tenses. They are also slightly irregular. Here they are side by side:

| | | |
|---|---|---|
| Infinitive: **haben** (basically weak) | **sein** (irregular strong) | **werden** (irregular strong) |
| *to have* | *to be* | *to become* |

**Present tense**

| ich | habe | *I have* | bin | *I am* | werde | *I become* |
|---|---|---|---|---|---|---|
| du | hast | *you have* | bist | *you are* | wirst | *you become* |
| er/sie/es | hat | *he/she/it has* | ist | *he/she/it is* | wird | *he/she/it becomes* |
| wir | haben | *we have* | sind | *we are* | werden | *we become* |
| ihr | habt | *you have* | seid | *you are* | werdet | *you become* |
| Sie | haben | *you have* | sind | *you are* | werden | *you become* |
| sie | haben | *they have* | sind | *they are* | werden | *they become* |

**Imperative**

habe! habt! haben Sie! *Have!*    sei! seid! seien Sie! *Be!*    werde! werdet! werden Sie! *Become!*

haben wir! *Let us have!*    seien wir! *Let us be!*    werden wir! *Let us become!*

**Imperfect tense**

| ich | hatte | *I had etc.* | war | *I was etc.* | wurde | *I became etc.* |
|---|---|---|---|---|---|---|
| du | hattest | | warst | | wurdest | |
| er/sie/es | hatte | | war | | wurde | |
| wir | hatten | | waren | *we were etc.* | wurden | |
| ihr | hattet | | wart | | wurdet | |
| Sie | hatten | | waren | | wurden | |
| sie | hatten | | waren | | wurden | |

**Future tense**

| ich | werde haben usw. | werde sein usw. | werde werden usw |
|---|---|---|---|
| *I* | *shall have etc.* | *shall be etc.* | *shall become etc.* |

**Perfect tense**

| ich | habe ⎫ | | *I have had etc* | bin ⎫ | | *I have been etc* | bin ⎫ | | *I have become etc.* |
|---|---|---|---|---|---|---|---|---|---|
| du | hast ⎬ | gehabt | | bist ⎬ | gewesen | | bist ⎬ | geworden | |
| er/sie/es | hat ⎭ | | | ist ⎭ | | | ist ⎭ | | |
| wir | haben ⎫ | | | sind ⎫ | | | sind ⎫ | | |
| ihr | habt ⎬ | gehabt | | seid ⎬ | gewesen | | seid ⎬ | geworden | |
| Sie | haben ⎬ | | | sind ⎬ | | | sind ⎬ | | |
| sie | haben ⎭ | | | sind ⎭ | | | sind ⎭ | | |

**Pluperfect tense**

ich hatte gehabt usw.     ich war gewesen usw.     ich war geworden usw.

*I had had etc.*          *I had been etc.*         *I had become etc.*

   N.B. The perfect tenses of **sein** and **werden** are also formed with the present tense of **sein** (see page 53.)

**Conditional tense**

ich würde haben usw.     ich würde sein usw.     ich würde werden usw.

*I should have etc.*     *I should be etc.*     *I should become etc.*

## Summary of the formation and use of tenses

From the examples above we can draw up some rules for the formation of the tenses of virtually all weak (regular) and strong (irregular) verbs in German. We need to know the important parts of each verb and then we can add the endings to form the tenses:

- Weak verbs do not change their stem.
- Strong verbs always have a change of stem vowel, usually in the imperfect tense, but often elsewhere. The principal parts of all strong verbs are listed on page 67ff.

## The present tense

For both weak and strong verbs the endings are: **–e**, **–st**, **–t**, **–en**, **–t**, **–en**.

These endings are added to the stem of the infinitive:

   wohnen *to live* (ich wohn**e**), trinken *to drink* (ich trink**e**).

   Some **strong verbs** have vowel changes in the 2nd and 3rd person singular of the present tense. For a complete check see the list on page 67ff.

- Stem vowels **a** or **au** change to **ä** or **äu**. Examples are **fallen** *to fall,* **laufen** *to run*:
   ich falle, du f**ä**llst, er/sie/es f**ä**llt, wir fallen, ihr fallt, sie fallen, (Sie fallen)
   ich laufe, du l**äu**fst, er/sie/es l**äu**ft, wir laufen, ihr lauft, sie laufen, (Sie laufen)
- Stem vowel '**e** (short)' or '**e** (long)'. In most of these '**e** (short)' becomes **i** and '**e** (long)' changes to **ie**. Examples are **sprechen** *to speak* ('e' short) and **lesen** *to read* ('e' long):
   ich spreche, du spr**i**chst, er/sie/es spr**i**cht, wir sprechen, ihr sprecht, sie sprechen, (Sie sprechen)
   ich lese, du l**ie**st, er/sie/es l**ie**st, wir lesen, ihr lest, sie lesen, (Sie lesen)

There is only **one** form of the **present tense** in German which indicates what is happening now, in the present. In English we have three versions of each tense. Look at these examples:

**Er spielt Fußball, nicht Tennis**.

In English this can mean:

**(a)** He plays football, not tennis, **(b)** He is playing football, not tennis, **(c)** He does play football, not tennis.

The exact meaning of the English depends on the context:

**(a)** implies something which he always does, **(b)** implies he is doing it now, it is continuous, **(c)** emphasises that it is football that he plays at the moment, not tennis.

The present tense in German can also refer to the immediate future :

**Heute abend spielt er Fußball.**

*He will play football this evening/ is going to play football this evening.*

The present tense is also used with **seit** (+ dat) to indicate an action that is still going on:

Er **wohnt seit** vier Jahren in Frankfurt.

*He **has been living** in Frankfurt **for** four years* (and still is living there).

## The imperfect tense or simple past tense

- Weak verbs add the following endings to the stem of the infinitive:
  **-te, -test, -te, -ten, -tet, -ten**. Example: ich wohn**te** (etc).
- Strong verbs have a change of stem vowel. There are no endings added to the stem in the 1st and 3rd persons singular. The endings added to the stem are therefore:
  **-, -st, -, -en, -t, -en**. Example: ich trank, du trank**st** (etc).
- This tense is easily the most widely used past tense in formal writing and therefore has a lot of importance for your written work. It can be used in a number of ways to convey the English forms of the past tense.
- **Er wohnte in Münster** can mean *he was living in Münster, he used to live in Münster, he lived in Münster, he did live in Münster.*
- The imperfect with **seit** (+dat) expresses what had been going on and still was going on, even though in English the pluperfect is used:
  Er **arbeitete** schon **seit** vier Stunden. *He **had been working for** four hours*

## The future tense

- This tense is formed with the present tense of **werden** plus the **infinitive** which goes to the end of the clause (see page 63 for rules of word order):
  Er **wird** in Köln **wohnen.** He will be living in Cologne.
  Wir **werden** nach Frankreich **fahren.** We shall be going to France.
- As the name implies this tense refers to an event or an intention in the future some time away from the present. So 'next week' *he will be living in Cologne* or 'next year' *we shall be going to France.*
- The 'immediate future' is translated by the present tense in German (see above).

## The perfect tense

This tense is formed with the present tense of **haben** or **sein** plus the past participle.

- The past participle of a weak verb is formed **ge-** stem **-t**.
- The past participle of a strong verb is formed **ge-** stem **-en**.
  Examples:
  Er **hat** Fußball **gespielt.** (weak verb with **haben)** *He has played football.*
  Er **ist** nach England **gereist.** (weak verb with **sein)** *He has travelled to England.*
  Wir **haben** seinen Onkel **gesehen.** (strong verb with **haben)** *We have seen his uncle.*
  Wir **sind** nach Hause **gegangen** (strong verb with **sein)** *We have gone home.*
- Note the position of the past participles at the end of each sentence. See page 63 for the rules of word order.
- This tense is mostly used in spoken language and informal writing such as letters to refer to actions in the past, which are over or completed.
- The four examples above could be translated in a number of different ways: *He has been playing football. He travelled to England. We saw his uncle. We did go home.* In each example the action is over and finished whichever form of the tense you use in English.

## The pluperfect tense

This tense is formed with the imperfect of **haben** or **sein** plus the past participle:

Er **hatte** Fußball **gespielt**.          *He had been playing football.*
Er **war** in die Schweiz **gefahren**.          *He had gone to Switzerland.*

● This tense is usually used as in English in combination with the imperfect or the perfect to describe actions which **had happened** before others in the past:

Bevor er nach Hause kam, hatte er drei Wochen in Deutschland verbracht.
*Before he came home he had spent three weeks in Germany.*

## The conditional tense

This is formed with the imperfect subjunctive of **werden** plus the infinitive:

Er **würde** in Bonn **wohnen**.          *He would live in Bonn.*
Er **würde** Wein **trinken**.          *He would drink wine.*

The imperfect subjunctive of **werden** is the same as the ordinary imperfect, except that there is an **Umlaut** throughout.

The use of this tense is dealt with more fully on page 62 but it is used in sentences which imply a condition:

*He would live in Bonn, if he could find a flat there.*
Er **würde** in Bonn **wohnen**, **wenn** er dort eine Wohnung finden **könnte**.
*He would drink wine, if he liked it better than beer.*
Er **würde** Wein **trinken**, **wenn** er ihn lieber als Bier **hätte**.

Such sentences in German are called '**wenn**' sentences and are explained in detail on page 62.

## The imperative

**wohnen** *to live* – **a weak verb**

Wohn**e** nicht in London! *Don't live in London!*          (2nd person sing. telling a friend, familiar form)
Wohn**t** nicht in London! *Don't live in London!*          (2nd person plur. telling friends, familiar form)
Wohn**en Sie** nicht in London! *Don't live in London!*          (2nd person singular or plural polite form)
Wohn**en wir** in London! *Let us live in London!*          (1st person plural form)

**trinken** *to drink* – **a strong verb**

Trink**e** ein Glas Bier! *Drink a glass of beer!*(2nd person singular familiar form)
Trink**t** ein Glas Bier! *Drink a glass of beer!* (2nd person plural familiar form)
Trink**en Sie** ein Glas Bier! *Drink a glass of beer!*    (2nd person singular or plural polite form)
Trink**en wir** ein Glas Bier!          *Let us drink a glass of beer* (1st person plural form)

● When written all forms require an exclamation mark to show that this is a command.
● The '**e**' ending of the familiar form singular is often omitted in German.

**Gib** deine Meinung! *Give your opinion!*          **Geh** weg!          *Go away!*
**Lies** den Brief! *Read the letter!*          **Komm** schnell!          *Come quickly!*
**Hör** gut zu! *Listen carefully!*          **Füll** das Formular aus! *Fill in the form!*
**Mach** Notizen! *Make notes!*          **Schreib** eine Postkarte! *Write a postcard!*

● The verb **lassen** can be used to say *Let us* (do something)!

**Laß** uns ins Kino gehen!          *Let us go to the cinema!* (talking to a friend)
**Laßt** uns ins Kino gehen!          *Let us go to the cinema!* (talking to more than one friend)
**Lassen** Sie uns ins Kino gehen!          *Let us go to the cinema!* (talking to one or more persons in a formal way)

## 'Haben' or 'sein' in the perfect and pluperfect tenses?

Most verbs form these tenses with **haben**. There are four groups of verbs which form these tenses with **sein**:

**(a) verbs of motion**

**fahren★**     *to go* (by vehicle)     ich bin gefahren (etc)
     plus these compounds of **fahren**: **abfahren** *to depart*, **mitfahren** *to go with* (*someone*), **radfahren** *to cycle*, **vorbeifahren** *to go past*.

**gehen**\*     *to go* (on foot)     ich bin gegangen (etc)
     plus these compounds of **gehen**: **abgehen** *to leave/depart*, **aufgehen** *to rise* (*of sun*), **ausgehen** *to go out*, **spazierengehen** *to go for a walk*, **untergehen** *to set* (*of sun*), **vorbeigehen** *to go past*, **weggehen** *to go away*.

**kommen*** *to come*  ich bin gekommen (etc)

 plus these compounds of kommen: **ankommen** *to arrive,* **mitkommen** *to come along with,* **vorbeikommen** *to come past*

Other verbs of 'motion':

**bummeln** *to stroll,* **eilen** *to rush,* **joggen** *to jog,* **laufen*** *to run,* **rennen*** *to run/race,* **verschwinden*** *to disappear,* **wandern** *to hike,* **fallen*** *to fall,* **ausfallen*** *to fall out,* **fliegen*** *to fly,* **abfliegen*** *to fly away/take off,* **folgen** *to follow,* **fließen*** *to flow,* **schwimmen*** *to swim,* **reisen** *to travel,* **abreisen** *to leave,* **verreisen** *to go away,* **steigen*** *to climb,* **aussteigen*** *to get off (train/bus),* **einsteigen*** *to get on (train),* **umsteigen*** *to change (bus),* **bergsteigen*** *to go mountaineering,* **sinken*** *to sink,* **springen*** *to jump/leap,* **aufstehen*** *to get up*

### (b) verbs expressing a 'change of state'

| | | | |
|---|---|---|---|
| **aufwachen** | *to wake up,* | Ich **bin** um halb acht aufgewacht. | *I woke up at half past seven.* |
| **einschlafen*** | *to fall asleep* | Er **ist** um Viertel elf eingeschlafen. | *He fell asleep at a quarter past ten.* |
| **sterben*** | *to die* | Sie **ist** gestern abend gestorben. | *She died yesterday evening.* |
| **wachsen*** | *to grow* | Die Blumen **sind** gut gewachsen. | *The flowers have grown well.* |

### (c) verbs meaning *meet by chance, happen, succeed*

| | | | |
|---|---|---|---|
| **begegnen** | *to meet* | Wir **sind** uns gestern in der Stadt begegnet. | *Yesterday we met each other in town.* |
| **geschehen*** | *to happen* | Was **ist** heute morgen geschehen? | *What has happened this morning?* |
| **gelingen*** | *to succeed* | Es **war** ihm gelungen. | *He had succeeded.* |

N.B. Verbs marked with an * are strong verbs listed on page 67ff.

### (d) the verbs *bleiben, sein* and *werden*

| | |
|---|---|
| Ich bin in Bonn geblieben. | *I stayed in Bonn.* |
| Sein Sohn war krank gewesen. | *His son had been ill.* |
| Er ist Student geworden. | *He has become a student.* |

## Mixed verbs

There is a group of nine verbs which have the weak verb endings, but change the stem vowel like strong verbs, as shown in this list:

| Infinitive | Meaning | Present | Imperfect | Perfect |
|---|---|---|---|---|
| brennen | *to burn* | brennt | brannte | hat gebrannt |
| bringen | *to bring* | bringt | brachte | hat gebracht*** |
| denken | *to think* | denkt | dachte | hat gedacht |
| kennen* | *to know* | kennt | kannte | hat gekannt |
| nennen | *to name* | nennt | nannte | hat genannt |
| rennen | *to run/race* | rennt | rannte | ist gerannt |
| senden | *to send* | sendet | sandte | hat gesandt |
| wenden | *to turn* | wendet | wandte | hat gewandt |
| wissen** | *to know* | weiß | wußte | hat gewußt |

 *kennen means to know a person, **wissen** means *to know a fact or thing*

 **erkennen** *to recognise* has the same endings as **kennen** e.g. **er erkannte** *he recognised*

 **The present tense of **wissen** is irregular:

 **ich weiß, du weißt, er/sie/es weiß, wir wissen, ihr wißt, sie wissen, (Sie wissen)**

 ***verbringen** *to spend* (of time) has the same endings as *bringen:*

 **Er verbrachte drei Nächte im Hotel.** *He spent three nights in the hotel.*

## Other minor variations in the endings of verbs

### Adding –e

This is done in both weak and strong verbs when the stem ends in **–d** or **–t** as in these examples:

**arbeiten** *to work* (weak verb)

- In the present tense: du arbeit**e**st, er/sie/es arbeit**e**t, ihr arbeit**e**t
- In the command form:  arbeit**e**t! (familiar plural form)
- In the imperfect tense:  ich arbeit**e**te, du arbeit**e**test, er/sie/es arbeit**e**te, wir arbeit**e**ten, ihr arbeit**e**tet, sie arbeit**e**ten, (Sie arbeit**e**ten)
- In the past participle  ich habe gearbeit**e**t

**finden** *to find* (strong verb)

- In the present tense  du find**e**st, er/sie/es find**e**t, ihr find**e**t
- In the command form  find**e**t! (familiar plural form)

Note that when a vowel change occurs in a strong verb the extra 'e' is **not** used,

- e.g. du f**a**ndst (*you found*) **halten** *to hold* is a good example to illustrate this: present tense: ich halte, du **hältst**, er/sie/es **hält,**wir halten, **ihr haltet**, sie halten (Sie halten). There is no extra 'e' in the singular because there is a vowel change **a** to **ä,** but in **ihr haltet** there is no vowel change, so the extra 'e' is inserted.

Other verbs like **atmen** *to breathe* and **rechnen** *to count/calculate* need the extra 'e' in the same way as **arbeiten** above. They are both weak verbs – er atm**e**te (*he breathed*), wir rechn**e**ten (*we counted*). The extra 'e' is to make the words easier to say.

### No ge- in the past participle

The **ge-** is omitted in the past participle of inseparable verbs (see below) and when the infinitive of the verb ends in **–ieren**. e.g.

(weak verb – inseparable) zerstören *to destroy* Ich habe nichts **zerstört.** *I have destroyed nothing.*

(strong verb – inseparable) beginnen *to begin* Er hat gestern **begonnen.** *He began yesterday.*

**studieren** *to study* Er hat dieses Theaterstück **studiert.** *He has studied this play.*

## Separable and inseparable verbs

These are verbs in German which begin with a prefix (often a preposition). As its name implies the prefix is attached to the front of a basic verb. These verbs are either **weak** or **strong** and have the same endings as other weak or strong verbs. In fact they are mostly compounds of other verbs.

### (a) Inseparable verbs

Prefixes which are always inseparable are: **be-**, **emp-**, **ent-**, **er-**, **ge-**, **ver-**, **zer-**.

The only difference between verbs which begin with these prefixes and other verbs is that they do not have a **ge-** in the past participle in the perfect tenses and the prefix is **unstressed** when spoken:

Gestern hat er **begonnen.**                          *He has begun yesterday.*
Die Bombe hatte das Gebäude **zerstört.**       *The bomb had destroyed the building.*

**Beginnen** is a strong inseparable verb pronounced with the emphasis/stress on **-ginn-** not the **be-.**
**Zerstören** is a weak inseparable verb with the stress on the stem **–stör-** when spoken.

### (b) Separable prefixes

Separable prefixes are more of a problem. They are called separable because they can be separated from the rest of the verb in the ways illustrated in the examples of **ankommen** (*to arrive*) below.

Rules regarding separable prefixes are as follows:

- In pronunciation they are always stressed: **an**kommen *to arrive,* the stress is on **an-.**
- In a main clause the prefix is placed at the end:
  Er kam um acht Uhr **an.**                          *He arrived at eight o'clock.*
- In a subordinate clause the prefix is attached to the verb at the end of the clause:
  Als er in Stuttgart **an**kam, regnete es.        *When he arrived in Stuttgart it was raining.*
- The past participle of a separable verb has the prefix attached before the **ge-:**
  Er ist noch nicht **an**gekommen.               *He has not yet arrived.*
- In a phrase using an infinitive requiring **zu:**
  Er mußte früh aufstehen, um pünktlich in der Schule **an**zukommen.
  *He had to get up early, in order to arrive punctually at school.*
- In a sentence using an infinitive without **zu:**
  Er wollte um neun Uhr in Köln **an**kommen.
  *He wanted to arrive in Cologne at nine o'clock.*

N.B. See 1.13 for details about the position of separable prefixes, infinitives etc in sentences and clauses.

- The commonest prefixes which are always **separable** in German are given in the list below, each with an example of a separable verb:

| prefix | infinitive | meaning |
| --- | --- | --- |
| **ab-** | abfahren | *to depart/leave/drive off* |
| **an-** | ankommen | *to arrive* |
| **auf-** | aufhören | *to stop/cease* |
| **aus-** | ausgehen | *to go out* |
| **bei-** | beilegen | *to insert/enclose* |
| **dar-** | darstellen | *to show/portray/represent* |
| **davon-** | davonlaufen | *to run away* |
| **ein-** | einschlafen | *to fall asleep* |
| **entgegen-** | entgegenkommen | *to approach* |

| fern- | fernsehen | *to watch television* |
| fest- | festhalten | *to hold on to* |
| fort- | fortsetzen | *to continue* |
| heim- | heimgehen | *to go home* |
| her- | herstellen | *to produce/manufacture* |
| hin- | hingeben | *to give up* |
| los- | losgehen | *to set out* |
| mit- | mitteilen | *to inform* |
| nach- | nachdenken | *to consider* |
| nieder- | niedersinken | *to sink down* |
| statt- | stattfinden | *to take place* |
| teil- | teilnehmen | *to take part* |
| vor- | vorhaben | *to have in mind* |
| weiter- | weiterkommen | *to progress* |
| zu- | zugeben | *to concede/admit* |
| zusammen- | zusammenstoßen | *to collide* |

N.B. **hin-, her-,** and **vor-** are often used with another preposition to form other separable prefixes, e.g. **hinausgehen** *to go out,* **herunterkommen** *to come down,* **vorbeifahren** *to go/drive past.*

This is not a complete list, but gives you a very good idea of how separable verbs are formed.

### (c) Separable or inseparable prefixes

There is a third group of prefixes which can be either separable or inseparable. These are: **durch-, über-, um-, unter-, voll-, wider-** and **wieder-**.

There is no hard and fast rule as to when a prefix is **separable** or **inseparable** except in the way the verb is pronounced. **All inseparable prefixes are unstressed in pronunciation.** The emphasis is placed on the stem of the verb in spoken German. If the prefix is separable therefore, it will be **stressed** when pronounced.

Here are a few examples which you could find useful in your work for GCSE:

| | | | |
|---|---|---|---|
| **durchfallen** *(sep.)* | *to fail (e.g. an exam)* | **umsteigen** *(sep.)* | *to change (e.g. trains)* |
| **überholen** *(insep.)* | *to overtake* | **umtauschen** *(sep.)* | *to exchange* |
| **übernachten** *(insep.)* | *to stay overnight* | **untergehen** *(sep.)* | *to set (of sun)* |
| **überraschen** *(insep.)* | *to surprise* | **sich unterhalten** *(insep.)* | *to talk* |
| **übersetzen** *(insep.)* | *to translate* | **unterrichten** *(insep.)* | *to teach* |
| **umarmen** *(insep.)* | *to embrace/hug* | **unterschreiben** *(insep.)* | *to sign* |
| **umdrehen** *(sep.)* | *to turn over* | **untersuchen** *(insep.)* | *to examine* |
| **sich umdrehen** *(sep.)* | *to turn round* | **vollpacken** *(sep.)* | *to pack full* |
| **sich umsehen** *(sep.)* | *to look around* | **wiederholen** *(insep.)* | *to repeat* |

### Six important verbs of mood – modal verbs

They are:

| | | | | | |
|---|---|---|---|---|---|
| **dürfen** | *to be allowed to* | **mögen** | *to like to* | **sollen** | *to be supposed to* |
| **können** | *to be able to* | **müssen** | *to have to* | **wollen** | *to wish/want to* |

The present tense of each verb is slightly irregular, as follows:

| | dürfen | können | mögen | müssen | sollen | wollen |
|---|---|---|---|---|---|---|
| ich | darf | kann | mag | muß | soll | will |
| du | darfst | kannst | magst | mußt | sollst | willst |
| er/sie/es | darf | kann | mag | muß | soll | will |
| wir | dürfen | können | mögen | müssen | sollen | wollen |
| ihr | dürft | könnt | mögt | müßt | sollt | wollt |
| sie | dürfen | können | mögen | müssen | sollen | wollen |
| Sie *(you)* | dürfen | können | mögen | müssen | sollen | wollen |

The imperfect tense for all six has the weak verb endings **-te** etc:

ich durfte, konnte, mochte, mußte, sollte, wollte (etc) – note there are no Umlauts used here.

The perfect and pluperfect tenses are formed with haben and the infinitive replaces the past participle:

Er **hat** nicht gehen **können.**   He has not been able to go.
Sie **hatte** ausgehen **wollen.**   She had wanted to go out.

The other tenses are formed as for a weak verb (see page 49).

## Revision tip

Make a revision card with these six verbs on it as set out above.

## How to use modal verbs

- These verbs are usually used with the infinitive of another verb.
- In this kind of sentence there is no **zu** with the infinitive which has to be at the end of the sentence.

| | |
|---|---|
| **Er darf nicht ausgehen**. | *He is not allowed to go out/He must not go out.* |
| **Wir können noch nicht nach Hause gehen**. | |
| *We cannot go home yet/We are not able to go home yet.* | |

**dürfen** denotes permission to do something – when used with **nicht** it means *must not*:

| | |
|---|---|
| Darf ich ins Kino gehen? | *May I go to the cinema?* |
| Er durfte das tun. | *He was allowed to do that.* |
| Wir dürfen hier nicht Fußball spielen. | *We must not play football here.* |

**können** denotes ability, knowledge and possibility:

| | |
|---|---|
| Er kann sehr schnell laufen. | *He can run very quickly.* |
| Sie kann Deutsch. | *She can speak German.* |
| Das könnte sein. | *That could be.* |

**mögen** denotes liking, possibility or probability:

| | |
|---|---|
| Ich möchte gerne in die Schweiz fahren. | *I should like to go to Switzerland.* |
| Sie mag ihn. | *She likes him.* |
| Das mag wohl sein. | *That may well be.* |

**müssen** denotes being obliged to:

| | |
|---|---|
| Das muß schwer sein. | *That must be difficult.* |
| Er muß in die Schule gehen. | *He has to go to school.* |
| Wir mußten lachen. | *We couldn't help laughing/we had to laugh.* |

- Note the difference between:

| | |
|---|---|
| Er muß ein Wörterbuch kaufen. | *He has to buy a dictionary. (needs to…)* |
| Er hat ein Haus zu verkaufen. | *He has a house to sell.* |

- Remember *must not* is usually **dürfen nicht** in German.

**sollen** means to be to, to be supposed to, shall, should, ought:

| | |
|---|---|
| Er soll nach Italien fahren. | *He is to go to Italy.* |
| Der Prinz soll reich sein. | *The prince is supposed to be rich.* |
| Um wieviel Uhr soll ich kommen? | *What time shall I come?* |
| Er sollte das nicht tun, weil es so gefährlich ist. | *He should not do that, because it is so dangerous.* |
| Er sollte das getan haben. | *He ought to have done that.* |

**wollen** denotes wish, willingness, intention:

| | |
|---|---|
| Wollen Sie mitkommen? | *Will you come with me?* |
| Er will alles sehen. | *He wants to see everything.* |
| Wir wollen eben ausgehen. | *We are on the point of going out.* |
| Der Sohn wollte eben aufstehen. | *The son was about to get up.* |

**lassen** is not a modal verb but it works like one. It means *to let, to allow, to leave, to have (something done)*:

| | |
|---|---|
| Laß mich kommen! | *Let me come!* |
| Er ließ sie nicht zur Diskothek gehen. | *He did not allow her to go to the disco.* |
| Ich habe das Buch auf dem Tisch liegenlassen. | *I have left the book lying on the table.* |
| Ich habe mir die Haare schneiden lassen. | *I have had my hair cut.* |
| Er ließ mich warten. | *He made me wait.* |

## Reflexive verbs

A reflexive verb can be either **weak** or **strong** and **separable** or **inseparable**. The reflexive pronouns are explained on page 42. They are usually accusative, but can be dative in certain circumstances. The following is a list of the reflexive verbs you ought to know, where the reflexive pronoun is dative it is indicated:

**(a) Weak reflexive verbs**

| | |
|---|---|
| **sich anmelden** (*sep*) | *to book in, report* |
| **sich hinlegen** (*sep.*) | *to lie down* |
| **sich aufregen** (*sep*) über (+ *acc*) | *to get excited about* |
| **sich hinsetzen** (*sep.*) | *to sit down* |
| **sich ausruhen** (*sep*) | *to relax, have a rest* |
| **sich interessieren für** (+ *acc*) | *to be interested in* |
| **sich beeilen** (*insep.*) | *to hurry* |
| **sich** (*dat.*) **die Haare kämmen** | *to comb one's hair* |

| | |
|---|---|
| sich langweilen | *to get bored* |
| sich (*dat.*) **die Haare bürsten** | *to brush one's hair* |
| sich lohnen (*impers.*) | *to be worthwhile* |
| sich entschuldigen (*insep.*) | *to apologise* |
| sich (*dat.*) **die Zähne putzen** | *to clean one's teeth* |
| sich entspannen (*insep.*) | *to relax* |
| sich rasieren | *to shave* |
| sich erholen (*insep.*) | *to recover/get better* |
| sich schminken | *to put on make-up* |
| sich erinnern (*insep.*) **an** (+ *acc.*) | *to remember* |
| sich setzen | *to sit down* |
| sich erkälten (*insep.*) | *to catch cold* |
| sich sonnen | *to sun oneself* |
| sich erkundigen (*insep.*) | *to enquire* |
| sich umkleiden (*sep.*) | *to get changed (clothes)* |
| sich freuen auf (+ *acc.*) | *to look forward to* |
| sich verabschieden (*insep.*) | *to say goodbye* |
| sich freuen über (+ *acc.*) | *to be pleased about* |
| sich vorstellen (*sep.*) | *to introduce oneself* |
| sich fühlen | *to feel* |
| sich (*dat.*) **vorstellen** | *to imagine* |

**(b) Strong reflexive verbs**

| | |
|---|---|
| sich bewerben (*insep.*) | *to apply for (a job)* |
| sich anziehen (*sep.*) | *to get dressed* |
| sich umsehen (*sep.*) | *to look around* |
| sich auskennen★ (*sep.*) | *to know one's way around* |
| sich umziehen (*sep.*) | *to get changed (clothes)* |
| sich ausschlafen (*sep.*) | *to have a good sleep* |
| sich unterhalten (*insep.*) | *to converse* |
| sich ausziehen (*sep.*) | *to get undressed* |
| sich verfahren (*insep.*) | *to lose one's way* |
| sich befinden (*insep.*) | *to be situated* |
| sich verlassen (*insep.*) **auf** (+ *acc.*) | *to rely on* |
| sich entschließen (*insep.*) | *to decide* |
| sich zurechtfinden (*sep.*) | *to find one's way* |

- **Kennen**★ is a mixed verb see page 55.
- The abbreviations used in lists **(a)** and **(b)** are: *acc.* – accusative; *dat.* – dative; *impers.* – impersonal; *sep.* – separable prefix; *insep.* – inseparable prefix.

## Impersonal verbs

These are only used in the '**es**' form of each tense. There are three different sorts which you should know for GCSE:

**(a) Those describing the weather**

| | | | |
|---|---|---|---|
| **es blitzt** | *there is lightning flashing* | **es hagelt** | *it is hailing* |
| **es donnert** | *it is thundering* | **es regnet** | *it is raining* |
| **es friert** | *it is freezing* | **es schneit** | *it is snowing* |

**(b) Those with a dative construction**

| | | | |
|---|---|---|---|
| **es tut mir leid** | *I am sorry* | **es fällt mir ein** | *it occurs to me* |
| **es gefällt mir** | *I like it (it is pleasing to me)* | **es ist mir warm/kalt** | *I am warm/cold* |
| **es tut ihm weh** | *it hurts him* | **es geht ihr gut** | *she is well* |
| **es gelingt mir** | *I succeed* | **wie geht's dir?** | *how are you?* |
| **es scheint mir** | *it seems to me* | **ihm schmeckt es nicht** | *he is off his food* |

**(c)  Those with a reflexive pronoun**
| | |
|---|---|
| **Es handelt sich ums Verbrechen.** | *It is a question of crime.* |
| **Es lohnt sich, nach Deutschland zu fahren.** | *It is worthwhile going to Germany.* |

## Uses of infinitives

**(a)** An infinitive can be used as a noun. These nouns are always neuter.
**essen** *to eat* – **das Essen (–)** *the meal*

**(b)** In most sentences an infinitive is preceded in German by **zu** and placed at the end of the sentence:

| | |
|---|---|
| Ich habe nichts **zu tun**. | *I have nothing to do.* |
| Wir beginnen **zu verstehen**. | *We begin to understand.* |
| Er versucht, Deutsch **zu lernen**. | *He tries to learn German.* |
| Er hatte keine Lust, ins Kino **zu gehen**. | *He did not want to go to the cinema.* |

(Note that in the last two examples there are other words dependent on the infinitives. They form an infinitive construction in German which is separated from the rest of the sentence by a comma.)

**(c)** Infinitives used with modal verbs do not have **zu**, nor do infinitives used with **sehen, hören** and **lassen**:

| | |
|---|---|
| Er kann nicht **kommen**. | *He cannot come.* |
| Ich sah ihn **kommen**. | *I saw him coming.* |
| Er hörte sie **kommen**. | *He heard her coming.* |
| Er ließ sich die Haare **schneiden**. | *He had his hair cut.* |

**(d)** **Um** (etwas) **zu tun** is *in order to (do something)*. This is a phrase which includes an infinitive and is separated from the rest of the sentence by a comma in German:

Er setzte sich hin, **um** die Zeitung **zu lesen**. *He sat down (in order) to read the newspaper.*
**ohne ...** zu **...** and **(an)statt ...** zu **...** are similar constructions:
Er ging aus, **ohne** ein Wort **zu sagen**. *He went out without saying a word.*
Sie blieb zu Hause, **(an)statt** in die Schule **zu gehen**.
*She stayed at home instead of going to school.*

## Revision tip

Make some revision cards about the formation of tenses and keep them to hand when you are working at home or in class.

# 1.10 The passive

(This is for Higher Tier candidates only.)

Usually we use the active to describe what is going on. However, the passive allows us to describe an activity without necessarily saying who is doing it.

In German we use the verb **werden** to form the tenses of the passive plus the past participle of the other verb concerned. In English we use the verb *to be* plus the past particple. The tenses are basically the same as the active as follows:

| | | |
|---|---|---|
| *Football is (being) played.* | Fußball **wird gespielt.** | (Present) |
| *Football was (being) played.* | Fußball **wurde gespielt.** | (Imperfect) |
| *Football will be played.* | Fußball **wird gespielt werden.** | (Future) |
| *Football has been played.* | Fußball **ist gespielt <u>worden</u>.** | (Perfect) |
| *Football had been played.* | Fußball **war gespielt <u>worden</u>.** | (Pluperfect) |
| *Football would be played.* | Fußball **würde gespielt werden.** | (Conditional) |

Points to note:

- The past participles and the infinitives must be placed at the end of the part of the sentence in which they are used.
- In the perfect and pluperfect tenses of the passive the **ge–** of the past participle of 'werden' is dropped, **worden** is therefore used instead of **geworden** as underlined above.

Here are some notes on how the passive works:

**(a)** A passive can only be used if the verb in the active has a direct object in the accusative case in German.

**(b)** To make an active sentence passive, the direct object in the active has to become the subject in the passive.

**(c)** The tense in the passive is the same as the the tense in the active.

**(d)** The person *by whom* an action *is done* is known as the *agent*, whereas the thing *by which* an action is completed is known as the *means through which* the action is done. In German **von** (+dat) is **by** with an agent (person) and **durch** (+acc) is *by* with the means (thing). Look at these examples:

Active:   Der Mann hat seinen Hund im Garten gesehen.
          *The man has seen his dog in the garden.*
Passive:  Ein Hund ist **vom** Mann im Garten gesehen worden.
          *A dog has been seen by a man in the garden*
Active:   Die Bomben zerstörten die Stadt.
          *The bombs destroyed the town.*
Passive:  Die Stadt wurde **durch** Bomben zerstört.
          *The town was destroyed by bombs.*

**(e)** You can avoid the passive simply by turning the sentence into the active form:
Der Rasen wurde von meiner Mutter gemäht. *The lawn was mown by my mother.* (passive)
Meine Mutter mähte den Rasen. *My mother mowed the lawn.* (active)

**(f)** You can also avoid the passive by supplying the word **man** in German when there is no *agent* in the passive. **Man** means *one, they, you* in a general way:
Jeden Samstag wurde Fußball im Park gespielt.
    *Every Saturday football was played in the park.* (passive)
Jeden Samstag spielte **man** Fußball im Park.
    *Every Saturday one played football in the park.* (active)

**(g)** A very small number of verbs are not used with an accusative direct object, to use these in the passive you have to use an impersonal construction or **man**:
Es wurde mir geholfen *I was helped.* (passive) or Man half mir (active) literally *one helped me.*

**(h)** Be careful about the past participle in English being used with the verb *to be* when it is implying a 'state' not an 'action'. Die Tür **wurde** von mir **geschlossen** (*The door was shut by me*) – this is a real passive referring to the action of closing the door, but *The door is closed* does not imply any action, it merely describes the state of the door which is *shut* not *open*. In German this would be – Die Tür **ist geschlossen** or more simply Die Tür **ist zu** using the verb *sein* not *werden*.

# 1.11 The subjunctive

(This is for Higher Tier candidates only.)

- The endings of the subjunctive in German are: **-e, -est, -e, -en, -et, -en**.
- For the present subjunctive of both weak and strong verbs these endings are added to the stem of the verb:
  **wohnen** (*weak verb*): ich wohn**e**, du wohn**est**, er/sie/es wohn**e**, wir wohn**en**, ihr wohn**et**, sie wohn**en**
  **trinken** (*strong verb*): ich trink**e**, du trink**est**, er/sie/es trink**e**, wir trink**en**, ihr trink**et**, sie trink**en**
- No vowel changes occur in the present subjunctive of strong verbs:
  **werden**: ich werd**e**, du werd**est**, er/sie/es werd**e**, wir werd**en**, ihr werd**et**, sie werd**en**
- **Sein** is the only verb which is irregular in the present subjunctive:
  ich sei, du seiest, er/sie/es sei, wir seien, ihr seiet, sie seien
- The imperfect subjunctive of weak verbs is the same as the imperfect indicative:
  **wohnen**: ich wohnte, du wohntest, er/sie/es wohnte, wir wohnten, ihr wohntet, sie wohnten (see page 50).
  **haben** is slightly irregular, it has an Umlaut all the way through: **ich hätte, du hättest, usw**.
- The imperfect subjunctive of strong verbs has the subjunctive endings added to the stem of the imperfect indicative plus an Umlaut on the stem vowels **a, au, o, u** in most instances. For the list of strong verbs see page 67ff.
  **sein**:     ich wäre, du wärest, er/sie/es wäre, wir wären, ihr wäret, sie wären
  **werden**:  ich würde, du würdest, er/sie/es würde, wir würden, ihr würdet, sie würden
  **trinken**: ich tränke, du tränkest, er/sie/es tränke, wir tränken, ihr tränket, sie tränken

## Using the subjunctive in German

- To express a wish: Es **lebe** die Königin!                    *Long live the queen!*
- In reported speech:
  Er sagte, daß er nicht nach Hause **käme**.           *He said that he was not coming home.*
  Sie fragte, ob er angekommen **wäre**.              *She asked whether he had arrived.*
- In conditional sentences in the past tenses:
  Wenn er Fieber **hätte, wäre** er krank.            *If he had a temperature he would be ill.*
  or **Hätte er** Fieber, **(so) wäre** er krank. (This is the same sentence with the **wenn** omitted.
  This changes the word order and you can sometimes insert the **so**.)
  Wenn er gekommen **wäre, hätte** ich ihn gesehen.     *If he had come I should have seen him.*
  or **Wäre** er gekommen, **(so) hätte** ich ihn gesehen. (The same sentence without **wenn**.)
- After **als ob** meaning *as if*:
  Er sprach, **als ob** er krank **wäre**.            *He spoke as if he was ill.*
  Note the change of word order if the **ob** is omitted: Er sprach, **als wäre er** krank.

# 1.12  Conjunctions

These are small words used to join parts of sentences together to make longer often more complex sentences. In German they are divided into two groups, those which have an effect on word order and those which do not.

## Conjunctions which do not change the word order

These are called coordinating conjunctions. In German they are:

**und**  *and*    **aber**  *but*    **sondern**  *but* (after a negative)
**denn**  *for*    **oder**  *or*

Here are some examples:

Er ging ins Bett **und** schlief ein.            *He went to bed and fell asleep.*
Ich habe davon gehört, **aber** ich glaube es nicht.   *I have heard about it but I do not believe it.*
Er kann heute nicht kommen, **denn** er ist viel zu krank.  *He cannot come today for he is much too ill.*
Günter wollte nicht arbeiten, **sondern** er wollte spielen.  *Günter did not want to work but he did want to play.*

**Und, aber, sondern** and **oder** can link nouns, pronouns, adjectives etc as well as parts of sentences:

Du **und** ich sollten nicht ausgehen.           *You and I ought not to go out.*
Meine Schwester **oder** mein Vater wird kommen.      *My sister or my father will come.*
Sie ist nicht schön, **sondern** häßlich.          *She is not beautiful, but ugly.*
Er ist klug, **aber** faul.                *He is clever but lazy.*

## Conjunctions which do affect word order

These are **subordinating conjuctions**. In German they are:

| **als** | *when, as* | **falls** | *in case that* | **solange** | *as long as* |
|---|---|---|---|---|---|
| **als ob** | *as if* | **indem** | *while, as* | **so daß** | *so that* |
| **bis** | *until* | **nachdem** | *after* | **während** | *while* |
| **bevor** | *before* | **ob** | *whether, if* | **wenn** | *when, if* |
| **da** | *as, since* | **obwohl** | *although* | **wann** | *when* (indirect question) |
| **damit** | *in order that* | **seitdem** | *since* | **weil** | *because* |
| **daß** | *that* | **sobald** | *as soon as* | **wie** | *as* |

These conjunctions *always* send the **main verb** to the end of the clause they introduce in German. For a full explanation of the rules of German word order refer to page 63.

Here are some examples of sentences using subordinating conjunctions:

**Bevor** er zu Bett **ging,** trank er ein Glas Milch.
*Before he went to bed he drank a glass of milk.*

Er konnte nicht ausgehen, **weil** er so krank **war.**
*He could not go out because he was so ill.*
**Als** er in Bonn **ankam,** holten wir ihn vom Bahnhof ab.
*When he arrived in Bonn we met him at the station.*
**Wenn** er krank **ist,** muß er zu Hause bleiben.
*When he is ill, he has to stay at home*
**Wenn** er zum Bahnhof **ging**, pflegte er immer eine Zeitung zu kaufen.
*When(ever) he went to the station he always used to buy a newspaper.*
Er fragte mich, **wann** der Zug **abfahre.**
*He asked me when the train departed.*

# 1.13 Word order

The rules of German word order are very important and must be understood and then learned very carefully. The rules are formal and rarely alter. Unlike English, German does not rely on the order of the words to convey the sense. Reverse the positions of the subject and the direct object of a verb in an English sentence and you change the meaning completely. Look at these simple examples:

- *The boy saw the man in town.*
- *The man saw the boy in town.*

Now look at these two German sentences:

- **Der Junge sah den Mann in der Stadt.**
- **Den Mann sah der Junge in der Stadt.**

In German both these sentences mean exactly the same and both are correct German, even though the word order has been changed apparently in the same way as the two English sentences. By changing the English sentences around we have completely changed the meaning. In German there is no change of meaning because the case endings tell us which words are the subject and which words are the direct object. In both sentences **den Mann** is in the accusative case and therefore is the direct object of the verb **sah** (*saw*). Similarly **der Junge** is in the nominative case and therefore the subject of the verb. From these two simple examples we can see that the sense is not dependent on the order of the words in German as it is in English.

## Rules governing word order in German

The first thing we need to understand is what are the component parts of any sentence. All sentences, however simple must have a main finite verb, that is one which has a subject. The simplest sentences consist of just a subject and a verb:

*The boy sings.* **Der Junge singt.** *The boy* is the subject, *sings* is the verb, in German **der Junge** is nominative case and the subject, **singt** is the verb in the present tense.

This is the simplest form of **main statement**, to which we can add all sorts of other bits to make the sentence more complex:

*The boy sings quietly, because he does not want to disturb his sister who is asleep in the next room.*

This sentence is complex, it has a main clause or statement which can stand on its own and two subordinate clauses, one which tells you why he is singing quietly and the other describes what his sister is doing. Neither of these other two clauses can stand on their own, they depend on each other for us to be able to understand what is being related in this sentence. Let us have a look at the same sentence in German and see what rules of German word order we can find in it.

**Der Junge singt leise, weil er seine Schwester nicht stören will, die im nächsten Zimmer schläft.**
          ❶                     ❷  ❸                  ❸

This sentence illustrates the three main rules of German word order which are:

❶ In a main clause statement the main finite verb must be the second idea.
❷ Infinitives, past participles and separable prefixes go to the end of the clause in which they occur.
❸ In a subordinate clause the main finite verb is placed at the end of the clause in which it occurs.

Let us look at each of these in turn and go into a little more detail about them.

## Main clause statements: Rule 1 verb as the second idea

Here the main finite verb must be the second idea, frequently as in our example above the subject is the first idea:

Der Junge **singt** leise. *The boy sings quietly.*
Der junge Mann **stand** vor dem Rathaus. *The young man was standing in front of the town hall.*

In both these examples the main verb **singt** or **stand** is the second idea and the subject is the first idea.

If the subject is not the first idea then the subject in German must follow the verb in what is known as *inverted word order*. The verb remains the second idea.

Gestern **stand** der junge Mann vor dem Rathaus.
*Yesterday the young man was standing in front of the town hall.*

## Questions and commands

In questions and commands the verb is the first idea in German. In a question the subject follows the verb or there is a question word in front of the verb. Look at these examples:

**Singt der Junge** leise?     *Is the boy singing quietly?*
Warum **singt er** leise?     *Why is he singing quietly?*

In a command the verb is the first idea or element:

**Gib** mir das Buch!     *Give me the book!*
**Öffnen Sie** doch das Paket!     *Do open the parcel!*

## Rule 2: Separable prefixes, past participles, infinitives go to end of clause

The rule is that these three parts of verbs must be placed at the end of the clause in which they are used. Here are some examples:

**Main clause statements:**
Nächste Woche werde ich in Bonn **sein**. *Next week I shall be in Bonn.* (Future – infinitive at the end)
Um neun Uhr kommt er **an**. *He arrives at nine o'clock.* (Separable prefix at the end)
Er mußte früh **aufstehen**. *He had to get up early.* (Separable verb infinitive at the end)
Ich habe ihn nicht **gesehen**. *I have not seen him.* (Past participle at the end)
Er ist spät **angekommen**. *He has arrived late.* (Past participle of separable verb at end)

**Questions and commands:**
Warum konnte er nicht **kommen**? *Why couldn't he come?* (Modal verb with infinitive at the end)
Was hast du in der Zeitung **gelesen**? *What have you read in the newspaper* (Past participle at end)
Warum bist du so spät **angekommen**? *Why did you arrive so late?* (Past participle separable verb)
Um wieviel Uhr stehst du **auf**? *At what time do you get up?* (Separable prefix at end)
Laß uns Tennis **spielen**! *Let's play tennis!* (Infinitive – command)
Steh **auf**! *Get up!* (Separable prefix – command)

## Rule 3: Verb at the end of a subordinate clause

In a subordinate clause the verb is placed at the end. This is called *transposed word order*. Look at these examples:

(a) Der Junge singt leise**, weil** er seine Schwester nicht **stören will**.
    *The boy sings quietly because he does not want to disturb his sister.*
    The subordinate clause begins with **weil** and ends with **will**. It is separated from the main statement by a comma. This example also has the infinitive **stören** in the subordinate clause which is placed before the finite verb **will** at the end of the clause.

(b) **Als** der Mann durch den Park **ging, sah** er seinen Freund.
    *When the man walked through the park he saw his friend.*
    The subordinate clause begins with **als** and ends with **ging**. This sentence illustrates another very common pattern of German word order '**verb comma verb**' which always occurs when the subordinate clause is followed by the main statement.

(c) Er kam früh in der Schule an**, weil** sein Wecker ihn um halb sieben **aufgeweckt hatte**.

*He arrived early at school because his alarm clock had woken him up at half past six.*

The subordinate clause begins with **weil** and ends with **hatte**. In this example we have the pluperfect tense of a separable verb with the past participle **aufgeweckt** being placed before the finite verb **hatte** at the end of the clause.

**(d)** Er konnte seine Frau nicht sehen, **weil** sie **ausgehen mußte.**

*He couldn't see his wife because she had to go out.*

The subordinate clause begins with **weil** and ends with **mußte**. In this example we have an infinitive of a separable verb **ausgehen** placed before the finite verb **mußte**, a modal verb at the end of the clause.

Points to note:

- Clauses must be separated from each other by commas in German.
- The finite verb is placed at the end of a subordinate clause.
- If there are other parts of verbs, such as infinitives or past participles in a subordinate clause they will immediately precede the finite verb at the end of the clause. The infinitives or past participles of separable verbs will be written as one word as **aufgeweckt** and **ausgehen** in examples **(c)** and **(d)**.

## Word order within the clause

### (a) Direct and Indirect Objects – accusative and dative

Basically there are three patterns to remember:

**(1)** If both objects are nouns, then the dative precedes the accusative.
(Nouns – Dative Accusative NDA)
Er gab **dem Jungen das Buch**. *He gave the boy the book.* (indirect object followed by direct object)

**(2)** If both objects are pronouns, then the accusative precedes the dative.
(Pronouns – Accusative Dative PAD)
Er gab **es ihm**.           *He gave it to him.* (direct object followed by indirect object)

**(3)** If one object is a pronoun and the other a noun, the pronoun always comes first, the case is irrelevant
Er gab **es** dem Jungen.           *He gave it to the boy.*
Er gab **ihm** das Buch.           *He gave him the book.*

### (b) Time, manner, place – adverbial phrases (TMP)

The order of adverbial phrase in main or subordinate clauses is usually: Time ❶, Manner ❷, Place ❸.

Er kam um neun Uhr mit dem Zug in Berlin an.           *He arrived in Berlin by train at nine o'clock.*
        ❶                  ❷                  ❸

We usually mention the place first and the time last in English. Frequently in German the time phrase begins the sentence which means that *inverted word order* is required. This is often done for emphasis or to give the sentence balance:

Um neun Uhr **kam er** mit dem Zug in Berlin an.
        ❶                  ❷                  ❸

### (c) Position of reflexive and personal pronoun objects within a clause

**(i)** Main clauses:
- The reflexive or personal pronoun object immediately follows the finite verb in a main statement:
  Er hat **sich** gewaschen.           *He has washed himself.*
  Ich habe **sie** gesehen.           *I have seen her.*
- When there is *inverted word order* the reflexive or personal pronoun object will follow the subject if it is a pronoun:
  Gestern wusch er **sich** nicht.           *He did not wash himself yesterday.*
  Letzte Woche gab er **ihm** ein Buch.           *He gave him a book last week.*
- When there is *inverted word order* the reflexive or personal pronoun object will precede the subject if it is a noun:
  Gestern wusch **sich** der kleine Junge nicht.           *The little boy did not wash himself yesterday.*
  Letzte Woche gab **ihm** der Lehrer ein Buch.           *The teacher gave him a book last week.*

**(ii)** Subordinate clauses:
- In a subordinate clause it is better German to place the reflexive or personal pronoun object before a noun subject:

Da **sich** meine Schwester erkältet hat, ... *As my sister has caught a cold...*
Da **ihn** mein Mann in der Stadt gesehen hat, ... *As my husband has seen him in the town...*

- If the subject is a pronoun the reflexive or personal pronoun object will immediately follow it:
Weil er **mir** das Buch gezeigt hatte, ... *Because he had shown me the book...*
Während er **sich** die Hände wusch, ... *While he was washing his hands...*

## (d) Position of 'nicht'

Look at these examples carefully:

(i) In main clauses:

| | |
|---|---|
| Wir haben ihn lange **nicht** gesehen. | *We have not seen him for a long time.* |
| Heute abend kannst du **nicht** ausgehen. | *You cannot go out this evening.* |
| Stehen Sie bitte **nicht** auf! | *Please don't get up!* |
| Gestern war es **nicht** kalt. | *It was not cold yesterday.* |
| Sie ist **nicht** meine Frau. | *She is not my wife.* |
| Gestern ist sie **nicht** in die Schule gegangen. | *She didn't go to school yesterday.* |
| Er mag mich **nicht** sehr. | *He does not like me very much.* |

In the first three examples *nicht* is placed as near to the end of the sentence as possible. In the other examples it is placed next to the word it is qualifying.

In simpler sentences *nicht* is placed last:

| | |
|---|---|
| Wir sehen ihn **nicht.** | *We do not see him.* |
| Vergiß mich **nicht!** | *Don't forget me!* |

(ii) In subordinate clauses:

| | |
|---|---|
| Wenn er es **nicht** sieht, ... | *If he does not see it...* |
| Da es **nicht** so kalt ist, ... | *As it is not so cold...* |
| Weil sie **nicht** meine Tochter ist, ... | *Because she is not my daughter...* |
| Obwohl er **nicht** schnell läuft, ... | *Although he does not run quickly...* |
| Obwohl er **nicht** in die Schule geht, ... | *Although he is not going to school...* |
| Obwohl er **nicht** in die Schule gegangen ist, ... | *Although he has not gone to school...* |

These examples are very like the ones above, but the rules about the **finite verb** and its parts in a subordinate clause mean that the negative cannot go right to the end.

To a large extent placing a negative within a clause is common sense, as long as you remember the other rules of word order which override everything else.

### Revision tip

Make a revision card about the rules of word order.

# 1.14 Numerals and expressions of time

(a) The cardinal and ordinal numerals are listed on page 79 in Chapter 4
- Note that **eins** is used when counting but if a noun is used or implied you must use **ein** with the appropriate case ending:
Wie viele Koffer hat sie? Sie hat nur **einen**.
*How many cases has she got? She has only one.*
- **Hundert** and **Tausend** can be used as neuter nouns:
Da waren **Hunderte/Tausende** von Kindern.
*Hundreds/Thousands of children were there.*
- To form the ordinal numerals 1st, 2nd, etc, simply add -**e** to the cardinal number as far as 19th and -**st** from 20th plus the appropriate adjective ending from pattern 1 on page 33. Be careful about 1st, 3rd and 8th which are slightly irregular: **der erste** –1st, **der dritte** – 3rd, **der achte** – 8th, for the others see Chapter 4, page 79.
- To write an ordinal number in a date in German use the figure with a fullstop as in this example: am **1.** Januar 1998 is *on the first of January*.
- At the head of a letter the date is in the accusative case: **den 2. Oktober** for example.
- **mal** is used in German with the ordinal for 'time':
**das erstemal** *the first time*, **zum drittenmal** *for the third time*

Note also: **einmal** *once*, **erstens** *firstly*; **zweimal** *twice*, **zweitens** *secondly*; **dreimal** *three times*, **drittens** *thirdly*; **viermal** *four times* (and so on).

**(b)** Time by the clock is listed in Chapter 4 on page 80.

- Some other useful phrases include:
  **heute morgen** *this morning*, **heute nachmittag** *this afternoon*, **heute abend** *this evening*, **heute nacht** *tonight (i.e. during the coming night)*, **heute vor acht Tagen** *a week ago*, **heute in acht Tagen** *today week*, **drei Wochen lang** *for three weeks*, **Er fährt auf vier Wochen nach Köln**. *He is going to Cologne for four weeks.*
- Definite time is expressed by the accusative case:
  **jeden Abend** *every evening*, **nächsten Montag** *next Monday*, **den ganzen Tag** *all day long*, **Guten Morgen** *Good morning*, **Guten Tag** *Good day*, **Guten Abend** *Good evening*, **Gute Nacht** *good night* are also in the accusative.
- Indefinite time is expressed by the genitive case:
  **Eines Tages** wird er sich erholen. *One day he will get better.*

**(c)** 'When' in German

- **Wann** asks a question:
  **Wann** fährt der Zug ab? *When does the train leave?*
- **Als** refers to a single occasion in the past:
  **Als** er nach Hause kam, spielte er Fußball.
  *When he came home he played football.*
- **Wenn** is used for *when* in sentences referring to present or future time or repeated occasions in the past. In this instance **wenn** means *whenever*.
  **Wenn** er krank ist, muß er zu Hause bleiben. *When he is ill he has to stay at home.*
  **Wenn** sie nach Frankreich fuhren, pflegten sie immer mit der Fähre zu reisen. *When(ever) they went to France, they used to travel by ferry.*

# 1.15 The use of ß

The rule about the use of this letter/symbol is that the **ß** is used after a long vowel sound, before a **t** and at the end of a word: **er muß, der Fluß, draußen, ihr müßt.** A **-ss-** is used between two vowels when the first one is short: **wir müssen, die Flüsse** etc. There are lots of other examples in this section and in the vocabulary section of this book.

# 1.16 Strong verb list

This list gives the third person singular form (**er/sie/es** form) of the strong and irregular verbs you need to know for GCSE in the present, imperfect and perfect tenses plus the meaning of the infinitive. It also tells you which verb to use in the perfect and pluperfect tenses. Use this list when revising and remember that compounds of verbs have the same vowel changes, so **aufstehen** is like **stehen**. **Sein** and **werden** have been left off this list as they are given in full on page 51.

| Infinitive | Meaning | Present | Imperfect | Perfect |
|---|---|---|---|---|
| backen | *to bake* | bäckt | backte | hat gebacken |
| befehlen | *to command* | befiehlt | befahl | hat befohlen |
| beginnen | *to begin* | beginnt | begann | hat begonnen |
| beißen | *to bite* | beißt | biß | hat gebissen |
| bekommen | *to get, obtain* | bekommt | bekam | hat bekommen |
| bersten | *to burst* | birst | barst | ist geborsten |
| bewegen | *to induce* | bewegt | bewog | hat bewogen |
| biegen | *to bend* | biegt | bog | hat gebogen |
| bieten | *to offer* | bietet | bot | hat geboten |
| binden | *to bind, tie* | bindet | band | hat gebunden |

| Infinitive | Meaning | Present | Imperfect | Perfect |
|---|---|---|---|---|
| bitten | *to ask, beg* | bittet | bat | hat gebeten |
| blasen | *to blow* | bläst | blies | hat geblasen |
| bleiben | *to remain* | bleibt | blieb | ist geblieben |
| brechen | *to break* | bricht | brach | hat gebrochen |
| brennen | *to burn* | brennt | brannte | hat gebrannt |
| bringen | *to bring* | bringt | brachte | hat gebracht |
| denken | *to think* | denkt | dachte | hat gedacht |
| dringen | *to pierce, penetrate* | dringt | drang | ist gedrungen |
| einladen | *to invite* | lädt ein | lud ein | hat eingeladen |
| empfehlen | *to recommend* | empfiehlt | empfahl | hat empfohlen |
| erlöschen | *to die down, go out (of fire, light)* | erlischt | erlosch | ist erloschen |
| erschrecken | *to be frightened* | erschrickt | erschrak | ist erschrocken |
| essen | *to eat* | ißt | aß | hat gegessen |
| fahren | *to drive, ride* | fährt | fuhr | ist gefahren |
| fallen | *to fall* | fällt | fiel | ist gefallen |
| fangen | *to catch* | fängt | fing | hat gefangen |
| finden | *to find* | findet | fand | hat gefunden |
| fliegen | *to fly* | fliegt | flog | ist geflogen |
| fliehen | *to flee* | flieht | floh | ist geflohen |
| fließen | *to flow* | fließt | floß | ist geflossen |
| fressen | *to eat (of animals)* | frißt | fraß | hat gefressen |
| frieren | *to freeze* | friert | fror | hat gefroren |
| geben | *to give* | gibt | gab | hat gegeben |
| gehen | *to go* | geht | ging | ist gegangen |
| gelingen | *to succeed* | gelingt | gelang | ist gelungen |
| genießen | *to enjoy* | genießt | genoß | hat genossen |
| geschehen | *to happen* | geschieht | geschah | ist geschehen |
| gewinnen | *to gain, win* | gewinnt | gewann | hat gewonnen |
| gießen | *to pour* | gießt | goß | hat gegossen |
| gleichen | *to resemble* | gleicht | glich | hat geglichen |
| gleiten | *to glide* | gleitet | glitt | ist geglitten |
| graben | *to dig* | gräbt | grub | hat gegraben |
| greifen | *to seize* | greift | griff | hat gegriffen |
| halten | *to hold, stop* | hält | hielt | hat gehalten |
| hängen | *to hang, be suspended* | hängt | hing | hat gehangen |
| heben | *to lift* | hebt | hob | hat gehoben |
| heißen | *to be called* | heißt | hieß | hat geheißen |
| helfen | *to help* | hilft | half | hat geholfen |
| kennen | *to know* | kennt | kannte | hat gekannt |
| klingen | *to sound* | klingt | klang | hat geklungen |
| kommen | *to come* | kommt | kam | ist gekommen |
| kriechen | *to creep* | kriecht | kroch | ist gekrochen |
| laden | *to load* | lädt | lud | hat geladen |
| lassen | *to let* | läßt | ließ | hat gelassen |
| laufen | *to run* | läuft | lief | ist gelaufen |
| leiden | *to suffer* | leidet | litt | hat gelitten |
| leihen | *to lend* | leiht | lieh | hat geliehen |
| lesen | *to read* | liest | las | hat gelesen |
| liegen | *to lie* | liegt | lag | hat gelegen |
| lügen | *to tell lies* | lügt | log | hat gelogen |
| meiden | *to avoid* | meidet | mied | hat gemieden |
| messen | *to measure* | mißt | maß | hat gemessen |
| nehmen | *to take* | nimmt | nahm | hat genommen |
| nennen | *to name* | nennt | nannte | hat genannt |
| pfeifen | *to whistle* | pfeift | pfiff | hat gepfiffen |
| preisen | *to praise* | preist | pries | hat gepriesen |
| rennen | *to run* | rennt | rannte | ist gerannt |
| raten | *to advise, guess* | rät | riet | hat geraten |
| reiben | *to rub* | reibt | rieb | hat gerieben |

| Infinitive | Meaning | Present | Imperfect | Perfect |
|---|---|---|---|---|
| reißen | *to tear* | reißt | riß | hat gerissen |
| reiten | *to ride* | reitet | ritt | hat geritten |
| riechen | *to smell* | riecht | roch | hat gerochen |
| rufen | *to call* | ruft | rief | hat gerufen |
| scheiden | *to part* | scheidet | schied | ist geschieden |
| scheinen | *to appear, shine* | scheint | schien | hat geschienen |
| schieben | *to shove, push* | schiebt | schob | hat geschoben |
| schießen | *to shoot* | schießt | schoß | hat geschossen |
| schlafen | *to sleep* | schläft | schlief | hat geschlafen |
| schlagen | *to strike, hit* | schlägt | schlug | hat geschlagen |
| schleichen | *to creep* | schleicht | schlich | ist geschlichen |
| schließen | *to shut* | schließt | schloß | hat geschlossen |
| schmelzen | *to melt* | schmilzt | schmolz | ist geschmolzen |
| schneiden | *to cut* | schneidet | schnitt | hat geschnitten |
| schreiben | *to write* | schreibt | schrieb | hat geschrieben |
| schreien | *to cry out, shout* | schreit | schrie | hat geschrien |
| schreiten | *to stride* | schreitet | schritt | ist geschritten |
| schweigen | *to be silent* | schweigt | schwieg | hat geschwiegen |
| schwellen | *to swell* | schwillt | schwoll | ist geschwollen |
| schwimmen | *to swim* | schwimmt | schwamm | ist geschwommen |
| schwingen | *to swing* | schwingt | schwang | hat geschwungen |
| schwören | *to swear* | schwört | schwor | hat geschworen |
| sehen | *to see* | sieht | sah | hat gesehen |
| senden | *to send* | sendet | sandte | hat gesandt |
| singen | *to sing* | singt | sang | hat gesungen |
| sinken | *to sink* | sinkt | sank | ist gesunken |
| sitzen | *to sit* | sitzt | saß | hat/ist gesessen |
| spinnen | *to spin* | spinnt | spann | hat gesponnen |
| sprechen | *to speak* | spricht | sprach | hat gesprochen |
| springen | *to spring, jump* | springt | sprang | ist gesprungen |
| stechen | *to prick, sting* | sticht | stach | hat gestochen |
| stehen | *to stand* | steht | stand | hat gestanden |
| stehlen | *to steal* | stiehlt | stahl | hat gestohlen |
| steigen | *to ascend* | steigt | stieg | ist gestiegen |
| sterben | *to die* | stirbt | starb | ist gestorben |
| stoßen | *to push, knock, bump* | stößt | stieß | hat gestoßen |
| streichen | *to paint, spread* | streicht | strich | hat gestrichen |
| streiten | *to argue, fight* | streitet | stritt | hat gestritten |
| tragen | *to carry, wear* | trägt | trug | hat getragen |
| treffen | *to hit, meet* | trifft | traf | hat getroffen |
| treiben | *to drive* | treibt | trieb | hat getrieben |
| treten | *to step, kick (football)* | tritt | trat | hat getreten |
| trinken | *to drink* | trinkt | trank | hat getrunken |
| tun | *to do* | tut | tat | hat getan |
| verbieten | *to forbid* | verbietet | verbot | hat verboten |
| verderben | *to spoil* | verdirbt | verdarb | hat verdorben |
| vergessen | *to forget* | vergißt | vergaß | hat vergessen |
| verlieren | *to lose* | verliert | verlor | hat verloren |
| verschwinden | *to disappear* | verschwindet | verschwand | ist verschwunden |
| verzeihen | *to pardon* | verzeiht | verzieh | hat verziehen |
| wachsen | *to grow* | wächst | wuchs | ist gewachsen |
| waschen | *to wash* | wäscht | wusch | hat gewaschen |
| weisen | *to show* | weist | wies | hat gewiesen |
| wenden | *to turn* | wendet | wandte | hat gewandt |
| werfen | *to throw* | wirft | warf | hat geworfen |
| wiegen | *to weigh* | wiegt | wog | hat gewogen |
| winden | *to wind* | windet | wand | hat gewunden |
| wissen | *to know* | weiß | wußte | hat gewußt |
| ziehen | *to draw, pull* | zieht | zog | hat gezogen |
| zwingen | *to force* | zwingt | zwang | hat gezwungen |

# Chapter 2
# *Test yourself on grammar*

## 2.1 Introduction

The answers to these tests are given in Chapter 3. When you have done each test, check your answers. If you are not satisfied with your performance, check the relevant Grammar section (shown in brackets) and then test yourself again. Always test yourself in writing!

## 2.2 Test 1 – nouns (Unit 1.2)

Give the gender, plural and meaning of the following nouns:

| | | | |
|---|---|---|---|
| **(a)** | Nacht | **(k)** | Wald |
| **(b)** | Zeitung | **(l)** | Glas |
| **(c)** | Kellner | **(m)** | Gemälde |
| **(d)** | Schüssel | **(n)** | Stundenplan |
| **(e)** | Schnellimbiß | **(o)** | Vetter |
| **(f)** | Tochter | **(p)** | Briefkasten |
| **(g)** | Vogel | **(q)** | Verband |
| **(h)** | Auge | **(r)** | Kamm |
| **(i)** | Küche | **(s)** | Schülerin |
| **(j)** | Schuh | **(t)** | Kino |

## 2.3 Test 2 – case endings with adjectives and prepositions (Units 1.5 and 1.8)

Fill in the gaps in the following sentences using the appropriate case endings:
- **(a)** Um d... neu... Parkhaus zu erreichen, biegen wir an d... erst... Kreuzung links ab.
- **(b)** Mein... klein... Schwester hat ein... dick... Katze mit klein... Ohren.
- **(c)** In Münster besichtigen wir d... alt... Rathaus und d... schön... Kaufhäuser in d... Stadtmitte.
- **(d)** Wir haben kein... Tisch in unser... Wohnzimmer.
- **(e)** Er gab sein... klein... Tochter ein... groß... Handtasche.
- **(f)** D... Onkel mein... Freund... wohnt in ein... klein... Dorf auf d... Lande.
- **(g)** Gut... Wein kostet sechs Mark d... Flasche in England.
- **(h)** Leute ohne klein... Kinder können d... halb... Preis bezahlen.
- **(i)** Weiter... Informationen über d... Hotel finden Sie in unser... neu... Broschüre.
- **(j)** Gestern habe ich ein sehr nett... englisch... Mädchen kennengelernt, sie hatte lang..., blond... Haare und blau... Augen.

## 2.4 Test 3 – pronouns (Unit 1.7)

Replace the nouns underlined in these sentences with pronouns in the right case:
- **(a)** <u>Der Hund</u> läuft durch <u>den Garten</u>, um <u>seinen Besitzer</u> zu lecken.
- **(b)** <u>Die Leute</u> standen auf <u>dem Martplatz</u> und sahen <u>die kleinen Vögel</u> an.
- **(c)** <u>Der Junge</u> schrieb <u>einen Brief</u> an <u>seine Brieffreundin</u> in München.
- **(d)** <u>Die Familie</u> fuhr mit <u>ihren Freunden</u> nach Österreich.
- **(e)** <u>Der Vater</u> gab <u>seinem Sohn</u> <u>ein Buch</u>.

In the following sentences replace the pronoun in English with the equivalent pronoun in German in the right case:
- **(f)** Er hat (*me*) nicht gesehen. (*What*) machte ich da?
- **(g)** Mein Vater gab (*her*) ein Geschenk. (*Who*) war sie?
- **(h)** Meine Mutter sprach mit (*them*). (*They*) waren sehr glücklich.
- **(i)** (*Someone*) gab (*us*) ein neues Fahrrad.
- **(j)** Liesel und Lotte, steht (*you*) heute früh auf?

## 2.5 Test 4 – prepositions (Unit 1.8)

Complete the following sentences by using two of the prepositions listed after each sentence. You will also need to know the correct case endings. Sometimes you need to use one of the contracted forms e.g. **im** or **ins**.
- **(a)** Sie saßen … d… Tisch, als er … d… Tür klopfte. (**in, an, um**)
- **(b)** Er fuhr d… Straße … , um … d… Stadtmitte einkaufen zu gehen. (**an, entlang, in**)
- **(c)** Es gibt Popkonzerte … d… Stadthalle. Sie liegt d… Rathaus… (**gegenüber, für, in**)
- **(d)** Das größte Problem … d… Umwelt sind Autos, deswegen sieht man nicht so viele Schmetterlinge … d… Lande. (**für, unter, auf**)
- **(e)** … d… Sommerferien fuhren wir … d… Küste. (**zu, während, an**)
- **(f)** Als er … d… Zug ankam, sah er … Fenster hinaus. (**zu, mit, aus**)
- **(g)** … viel… Jahren konnte man nicht … d… Grenze gehen. (**über, durch, vor**)
- **(h)** Ein Tankwagen ist … ein… Personenwagen gefahren, und viele Liter Öl sind… d… Tankwagen ausgelaufen. (**aus, mit, in**)
- **(i)** Morgens gehen wir … d… Wald und nachmittags gehen wir … d… Stadt spazieren. (**in, durch, auf**)
- **(j)** Der Bus kam … neun Uhr … d… Marktplatz an. (**in, auf, um**)

## 2.6 Test 5 – verb forms and tenses (Unit 1.9)

Give the 'du' form of the following verbs in the present tense and the meaning of the infinitive:
- **(a)** geben
- **(b)** begegnen
- **(c)** halten
- **(d)** aufstehen
- **(e)** sein
- **(f)** finden
- **(g)** sich bewerben
- **(h)** vergessen
- **(i)** können
- **(j)** bringen

Give the 'wir' form and the meaning of the perfect tense of the following verbs:
- **(a)** reisen
- **(b)** teilnehmen
- **(c)** haben
- **(d)** schwimmen
- **(e)** begleiten
- **(f)** pfeifen
- **(g)** denken
- **(h)** telefonieren
- **(i)** essen
- **(j)** schließen

Give the '**er**' form and the meaning of the imperfect tense of the following verbs:

(a)  gehen

(b)  sich unterhalten

(c)  empfehlen

(d)  versuchen

(e)  anrufen

(f)  vorbereiten

(g)  müssen

(h)  werden

(i)  schlafen

(j)  ziehen

Give the '**du**' form, the second person singular familiar form of the command form or imperative of the following verbs and say what it means:

(a)  geben

(b)  antworten

(c)  ausfüllen

(d)  schreiben

(e)  erklären

(f)  lesen

(g)  ergänzen

(h)  kopieren

(i)  wählen

(j)  aufstehen

## 2.7  Test 6 – word order with conjunctions (Unit 1.13)

Rewrite these sentences joining them together with the conjunction specified. Pay particular attention to the word order rules in German:

(a)  Begin with **bevor** and make these two sentences into one:

Er ging zu Bett. Er trank ein Glas Milch.

(b)  Begin with **weil** and make these two sentences into one:

Er war so krank. Er konnte nicht ausgehen.

(c)  Join these two sentences with **denn** in the middle:

Sie konnte nicht viel sehen. Sie hatte ihre Brille zu Hause gelassen.

(d)  Begin with **wenn** and make these two sentences into one:

Er schläft nicht ein. Wir werden mit ihm spielen können.

(e)  Begin with **da** and make these two sentences into one:

Es war so kalt gewesen. Wir mußten den ganzen Nachmittag zu Hause bleiben.

(f)  Begin with **obwohl** and make these two sentences into one:

Ich war nicht krank. Ich wollte im Bett bleiben

(g)  Begin with **nachdem** and make these two sentences into one:

Er hatte viele Einkäufe gemacht. Er fuhr sofort nach Hause.

(h)  Join these two sentences making them one with **sondern** in the middle:

Wir sind nicht ins Theater gegangen. Wir haben im Garten gearbeitet.

(i)  Join these two sentences together using **so daß** in the middle:

Das Wetter war schlecht. Wir konnten nicht viel wandern.

(j)  Begin with **als** and make these two sentences into one:

Der Wecker weckte ihn früh auf. Er ging sofort ins Badezimmer.

## 2.8  Test 7 – other examples of German word order (Unit 1.13)

(a)  Replace the nouns in **bold** with pronouns and change the word order if necessary:

Der kleine Junge zeigte **seinem neuen Freund sein neues Fahrrad.**

(b)  Insert the word **nicht** into this sentence to make it negative:

Gestern ist sie ins Theater gegangen.

(c)  Use the verb in brackets in the perfect tense to complete this sentence:

Er (**ankommen**) erst gegen 6 Uhr abends wieder zu Hause.

**(d)** Use the verb in brackets in the future tense to complete this sentence:
   Die Eltern (**sich freuen)** auf die Sommerferien.

**(e)** Place the phrases in brackets in the right order to form a complete sentence:
   (fuhren wir) (letzte Woche) (in die Schweiz) (mit dem Zug).

## 2.9  Test 8 – relative pronouns (Unit 1.7)

This test is for those of you entered for the Higher Tier examinations only.

Supply the correct form of the relative pronoun in German in these sentences, the English word in brackets translates the word that is missing:

**(a)** Der Mann, … ich gestern sah, ist mein Onkel.                  (*whom*)

**(b)** Die Frau, … Haus ich miete, wohnt nicht mehr da.              (*whose*)

**(c)** Die Eltern, mit … der Lehrer spricht, sind zornig.            (*whom*)

**(d)** Der Tisch, … die Bücher liegen, ist sehr alt.                 (*on which*)

**(e)** Das Heft, … in meiner Schultasche ist, gehört mir nicht.      (*that*)

**(f)** In vielen Städte hat man eine Nummer, … man wählen kann.      (*which*)

**(g)** Der Freund, bei … Bruder ich wohne, arbeitet in Frankfurt    (*whose*)

**(h)** Wer ist der Mann, … in diesem Häuschen wohnt?                 (*who*)

**(i)** Ich hatte eine Freundin, mit … ich oft den Abend verbrachte. (*whom*)

**(j)** Leute, … Vegetarier sind, essen kein Fleisch.                (*who*)

# Chapter 3
## *Test yourself*
## *suggested answers*

### 3.1 Test 1

**(a)** die Nacht, die Nächte, *night*
**(b)** die Zeitung, die Zeitungen, *newspaper*
**(c)** der Kellner, die Kellner, *waiter*
**(d)** die Schüssel, die Schüsseln, *bowl, basin*
**(e)** der Schnellimbiß, die Schnellimbisse, *snack*
**(f)** die Tochter, die Töchter, *daughter*
**(g)** der Vogel, die Vögel, *bird*
**(h)** das Auge, die Augen, *eye*
**(i)** die Küche, die Küchen, *kitchen*
**(j)** der Schuh, die Schuhe, *shoe*
**(k)** der Wald, die Wälder, *wood*
**(l)** das Glas, die Gläser, *glass*
**(m)** das Gemälde, die Gemälde, *painting*
**(n)** der Stundenplan, die Stundenpläne, *timetable*
**(o)** der Vetter, die Vettern, *cousin*
**(p)** der Briefkasten, die Briefkästen, *post-box*
**(q)** der Verband, die Verbände, *club*
**(r)** der Kamm, die Kämme, *comb*
**(s)** die Schülerin, die Schülerinnen, *schoolgirl*
**(t)** das Kino, die Kinos, *cinema*

### 3.2 Test 2

**(a)** Um das neue Parkhaus zu erreichen, biegen wir an der ersten Kreuzung links ab.
**(b)** Meine kleine Schwester hat eine dicke Katze mit kleinen Ohren.
**(c)** In Münster besichtigen wir das alte Rathaus und die schönen Kaufhäuser in der Stadtmitte.
**(d)** Wir haben keinen Tisch in unserem Wohnzimmer.
**(e)** Er gab seiner kleinen Tochter eine große Handtasche.
**(f)** Der Onkel meines Freundes wohnt in einem kleinen Dorf auf dem Lande.
**(g)** Guter Wein kostet sechs Mark die Flasche in England.
**(h)** Leute ohne kleine Kinder können den halben Preis bezahlen.
**(i)** Weitere Informationen über das Hotel finden Sie in unserer neuen Broschüre.
**(j)** Gestern habe ich ein sehr nettes englisches Mädchen kennengelernt, sie hatte lange, blonde Haare und blaue Augen.

## 3.3 Test 3

(a) Er läuft dadurch, um ihn zu lecken.
(b) Sie standen darauf und sahen sie an.
(c) Er schrieb ihn an sie in München.
(d) Sie fuhr mit ihnen nach Österreich.
(e) Er gab es ihm.
(f) Er hat mich nicht gesehen. Was machte ich da?
(g) Mein Vater gab ihr ein Geschenk. Wer war sie?
(h) Meine Mutter sprach mit ihnen. Sie waren sehr glücklich.
(i) Jemand gab uns ein neues Fahrrad.
(j) Liesel und Lotte, steht ihr heute früh auf?

## 3.4 Test 4

(a) Sie saßen um den Tisch, als er an der Tür klopfte.
(b) Er fuhr die Straße entlang, um in der Stadtmitte einkaufen zu gehen.
(c) Es gibt Popkonzerte in der Stadthalle. Sie liegt dem Rathaus gegenüber.
(d) Das größte Problem für die Umwelt sind Autos, deswegen sieht man nicht so viele Schmetterlinge auf dem Lande.
(e) Während der Sommerferien fuhren wir an die Küste.
(f) Als er mit dem Zug ankam, sah er zum Fenster hinaus.
(g) Vor vielen Jahren konnte man nicht über die Grenze gehen.
(h) Ein Tankwagen ist in einen Personenwagen gefahren, und viele Liter Öl sind aus dem Tankwagen ausgelaufen.
(i) Morgens gehen wir durch den Wald und nachmittags gehen wir in der Stadt spazieren.
(j) Der Bus kam um neun Uhr auf dem Marktplatz an.

## 3.5 Test 5

### 'Du' form – present

(a) du gibst, *to give*
(b) du begegnest, *to meet*
(c) du hältst, *to hold*
(d) du stehst auf, *to get up*
(e) du bist, *to be*
(f) du findest, *to find*
(g) du bewirbst dich, *to apply*
(h) du vergißt, *to forget*
(i) du kannst, *to be able to*
(j) du bringst, *to bring*

### 'Wir' form – perfect

(a) wir sind gereist, *we have travelled*
(b) wir haben teilgenommen, *we have taken part*
(c) wir haben gehabt, *we have had*
(d) wir sind geschwommen, *we have swum*
(e) wir haben begleitet, *we have accompanied*
(f) wir haben gepfiffen, *we have whistled*

**(g)** wir haben gedacht, *we have thought*
**(h)** wir haben telefoniert, *we have telephoned*
**(i)** wir haben gegessen, *we have eaten*
**(j)** wir haben geschlossen, *we have shut*

## 'Er' form – imperfect

**(a)** er ging, *he went*
**(b)** er unterhielt sich, *he conversed*
**(c)** er empfahl, *he recommended*
**(d)** er versuchte, *he tried*
**(e)** er rief an, *he rang up*
**(f)** er bereitete vor, *he prepared*
**(g)** er mußte, *he had to*
**(h)** er wurde, *he became*
**(i)** er schlief, *he slept*
**(j)** er zog, *he pulled*

## Second person singular – imperative

**(a)** gib! *give*
**(b)** antworte! *answer*
**(c)** füll aus! *fill in*
**(d)** schreib! *write*
**(e)** erklär! *explain*
**(f)** lies! *read*
**(g)** ergänze! *complete*
**(h)** kopiere! *copy*
**(i)** wähl! *choose*
**(j)** steh auf! *get up*

# 3.6  Test 6

**(a)** Bevor er zu Bett ging, trank er ein Glas Milch.
**(b)** Weil er so krank war, konnte er nicht ausgehen.
**(c)** Sie konnte nicht viel sehen, denn sie hatte ihre Brille zu Hause gelassen.
**(d)** Wenn er nicht einschläft, werden wir mit ihm spielen können.
**(e)** Da es so kalt gewesen war, mußten wir den ganzen Nachmittag zu Hause bleiben.
**(f)** Obwohl ich nicht krank war, wollte ich im Bett bleiben.
**(g)** Nachdem er viele Einkäufe gemacht hatte, fuhr er sofort nach Hause.
**(h)** Wir sind nicht ins Theater gegangen, sondern wir haben im Garten gearbeitet.
**(i)** Das Wetter war schlecht, so daß wir nicht viel wandern konnten.
**(j)** Als der Wecker ihn früh aufweckte, ging er sofort ins Badezimmer.

# 3.7  Test 7

**(a)** Der kleine Junge zeigte es ihm.
**(b)** Gestern ist sie nicht ins Theater gegangen.
**(c)** Er ist erst gegen 6 Uhr abends wieder zu Hause angekommen.
**(d)** Die Eltern werden sich auf die Sommerferien freuen.
**(e)** Letzte Woche fuhren wir mit dem Zug in die Schweiz.

## 3.8 Test 8

**(a)** Der Mann, den ich gestern sah, ist mein Onkel.
**(b)** Die Frau, deren Haus ich miete, wohnt nicht mehr da.
**(c)** Die Eltern, mit denen der Lehrer spricht, sind zornig.
**(d)** Der Tisch, worauf die Bücher liegen, ist sehr alt.
**(e)** Das Heft, das in meiner Schultasche ist, gehört mir nicht.
**(f)** In vielen Städte hat man eine Nummer, die man wahlen kann.
**(g)** Der Freund, bei dessen Bruder ich wohne, arbeitet in Frankfurt.
**(h)** Wer ist der Mann, der in diesem Häuschen wohnt?
**(i)** Ich hatte eine Freundin, mit der ich oft den Abend verbrachte.
**(j)** Leute, die Vegetarier sind, essen kein Fleisch.

# Chapter 4
# *Vocabulary*

## 4.1 Introduction

- This vocabulary chapter contains the basic words you need to know for GCSE.
- In their GCSE syllabuses all the Exam Boards have a list of about 1500 words: this list is called the Minimum Core Vocabulary. The exams are based on these lists.
- There are lots of differences between the lists of different Boards.
- The first section of words, Numbers, Days, etc, is a section common to all Boards.
- The words in this chapter have been categorised into the Areas of Experience which are the topic categories that all Boards use.
- There is also a section on IT vocabulary. These words are not on the Exam Boards' lists.

All the examining boards will use words outside these lists for the more difficult questions – so the minimum you need to know is what is listed here.

It is very important to learn as much vocabulary as you can, not just so that you recognise a word and its meaning when you hear it or read it, but so that you can use it correctly in context in your own speaking or writing in German.

Vocabulary cannot be learned haphazardly. You need to be systematic. There is no short cut to success, you just have to keep working at it and devise your own system for ensuring that you learn as much as you can in the time available. Here are some tips about how to increase your vocabulary in German:

- You should keep your own vocabulary note-book, writing in it any new words you come across in your work and listing them under the Areas of Experience.
- Set yourself a target of so many words to be learned each week. Remember to learn the gender and plural of each noun and the principal parts of each strong or irregular verb. Other details about verbs are important, like whether they take **haben** or **sein** in the perfect tenses, are they separable or inseparable, are they strong or weak. These details should be logged and learned. Remember the secret is to establish a routine and stick to it.
- Be systematic, work through the lists in this chapter and add to them as you are doing work on the Area of Experience in question.
- Do not try to learn too many words at one go and always ensure that you test yourself in writing.
- It is a good idea to work with a friend and test one another when you think you have both learned the list properly.
- Listen to German radio programmes, especially daily news bulletins which often have similar items to ours. Note down any words you do not recognise and look them up in a dictionary, then learn them.
- Read German short stories, newspapers and magazines and do the same thing.
- Take part in a German exchange if you can, staying in a German family for a short period and immersing yourself in the German-speaking atmosphere. This is one of the best ways of improving your vocabulary quickly.
- Set up a correspondence with a German-speaking friend and write letters to one another, half in German, half in English. You could do the same by exchanging recorded cassettes on a regular basis. This way both you and your German friend will improve your knowledge of one another's language.
- Finally the watchword is 'little and often', once you have learned a new word or phrase, try to use it!

# 4.2 Important words

## Words common to all Boards
### Numbers

**die Zahlen** numbers
**null** 0
**eins** 1
**zwei** 2
**drei** 3
**vier** 4
**fünf** 5
**sechs** 6
**sieben** 7
**acht** 8
**neun** 9
**zehn** 10
**elf** 11
**zwölf** 12
**dreizehn** 13
**vierzehn** 14
**fünfzehn** 15
**sechzehn** 16
**siebzehn** 17
**achtzehn** 18
**neunzehn** 19
**zwanzig** 20
**einundzwanzig** 21
**zweiundzwanzig** 22
**dreißig** 30
**vierzig** 40
**fünfzig** 50
**sechzig** 60
**siebzig** 70
**achtzig** 80
**neunzig** 90
**hundert** 100
**hunderteins** 101
**hundertzwei** 102
**zweihundert** 200
**tausend** 1000
**tausendeins** 1,001
**fünftausend** 5,000
**eine Million** 1,000,000
**die Ordinalzahlen** ordinal numbers
**erste** first
**zweite** second
**dritte** third
**vierte** fourth
**fünfte** fifth
**sechste** sixth
**sieb(en)te** seventh
**achte** eighth
**neunte** ninth
**zehnte** tenth
**elfte** eleventh
**zwölfte** twelfth
**dreizehnte** thirteenth

**vierzehnte** fourteenth
**fünfzehnte** fifteenth
**sechzehnte** sixteenth
**siebzehnte** seventeenth
**achtzehnte** eighteenth
**neunzehnte** nineteenth
**zwanzigste** twentieth
**einundzwanzigste** twenty-first
**fünfzigste** fiftieth
**hundertste** hundredth

### Days

**die Tage der Woche** the days of the week
**Montag** Monday
**Dienstag** Tuesday
**Mittwoch** Wednesday
**Donnerstag** Thursday
**Freitag** Friday
**Samstag/Sonnabend** Saturday
**Sonntag** Sunday
**heute** today
**gestern** yesterday
**morgen** tomorrow
**vorgestern** the day before yesterday
**übermorgen** the day after tomorrow
**am vorigen/vorhergehenden Tag** the day before
**am nächsten/folgenden Tag** the next day
**am Freitag** on Friday
**dienstags** on Tuesdays
**jeden Mittwoch** every Wednesday
**morgens** in the morning
**nachmittags** in the afternoon
**abends** in the evening
**nachts** at night

### Months

**die Monate** the months
**Januar** January
**Februar** February
**März** March
**April** April
**Mai** May
**Juni** June
**Juli** July
**August** August
**September** September
**Oktober** October
**November** November
**Dezember** December
**im Dezember** in December

### Date

**Den wievielten haben wir heute?/Der wievielte ist heute?** What's the date today?

**Wir haben den ersten Juni**   It's the first of June
**Es ist der zwanzigste**   It's the twentieth
**Es ist der sieb(en)te April neunzehnhundertsechsundneunzig**   It's the seventh of April 1996

## Seasons

**die Jahreszeiten**   the seasons
**der Frühling**   Spring
**der Sommer**   Summer
**der Herbst**   Autumn
**der Winter**   Winter
**im Frühling/Sommer**   in Spring/Summer
  **im Herbst/Winter**   in Autumn/Winter

## Time

**die Zeit**   the time
**Wieviel Uhr ist es?/**
  **Wie spät ist es?**   What's the time?
**Es ist acht Uhr**   It's eight o'clock
**Es ist fünf (Minuten) nach drei/drei Uhr fünf**   It's five minutes past three
**Es ist Viertel nach/vor neun**   It's a quarter past/to nine
**Es ist halb fünf/vier Uhr dreißig**   It's half past four
**Es ist zwanzig vor sechs/fünf Uhr vierzig**   It's twenty to six
**Es ist Mittag/zwölf Uhr mittags**   It's twelve noon
**Es ist Mitternacht**   It's midnight
**morgens**   a.m.
**nachmittags**   p.m.
**abends**   p.m. (after 5 p.m.)
**um fünf Uhr morgens**   at five in the morning

## Prepositions

### With Accusative

**bis**   until
**durch**   through
**entlang**   along
**für**   for
**gegen**   against
**ohne**   without
**um**   around, at (time)

### With Dative

**aus**   from, out of
**außer**   apart from
**bei**   with, at the house of
**gegenüber**   opposite
**mit**   with
**nach**   to, after
**seit**   since, for
**von**   from, by
**zu**   to

### With Accusative and Dative

**an**   at, to, in
**auf**   on, onto
**hinter**   behind
**in**   in, into
**neben**   next to
**über**   over, across, above
**unter**   under, among
**vor**   before, in front of
**zwischen**   between

### With Genitive

**statt**   instead of
**trotz**   in spite of
**während**   during
**wegen**   because of

## Conjunctions

### Co-ordinating Conjunctions

**aber**   but
**denn**   for
**oder**   or
**sondern**   but
**und**   and

### Subordinating Conjunctions

**als**   when
**bevor**   before
**bis**   until
**da**   since
**damit**   so that
**daß**   that
**nachdem**   after
**obwohl**   although
**seitdem**   since
**während**   whilst
**weil**   because
**wenn**   when, if
**wo**   where

# 4.3 Useful words

## Question words

**wann?**   when?
**warum?**   why?
**was für?**   what sort of?
**was?**   what?

**welche?**   which?
**wer?**   who?   **wie?**   how?
**wie lange?**   how long?
**wie weit?**   how far?
**wieviel(e)?**   how much? how many?
**wo?**   where?

**wo ... her?**  where from?
**woher?**  where from?
**wohin?**  where to?

## Quantities

**anderthalb**  one and a half
**die Anzahl**  number
**ein bißchen**  a little
**das Gramm**  gram
**halb**  half
**die Hälfte**  half
**der Haufen (-)**  pile, heap
**das Kilo (-s)**  kilo
**der Kilometer (-)**  kilometer
**der/das Liter (-)**  litre
**die Meile (-n)**  mile
**die meisten**  most
**der/das Meter (-)**  meter
**ein paar**  a few
**das Paar (-e)**  pair
**die Portion (-en)**  portion
**das Prozent (-e)**  percent
**die Tube (-n)**  tube (e.g. toothpaste)
**das Viertel (-)**  quarter
**der/das Zentimeter**  centimetre

## Negatives

**nicht**  not
**nicht mehr**  no longer
**nichts**  nothing
**nie**  never
**niemand**  nobody
**weder ... noch**  neither ... nor

## Other words

**aber**  but
**alles**  everything
**als**  when
**also**  so
**außerdem**  otherwise
**beide**  both

**d.h. (das heißt)**  i.e. (that is)
**damit**  so that
**denn**  for, because
**doch**  but, however
**ebenso**  just as
**einander**  one another
**einschließlich**  inclusive
**entweder ... oder**  either ... or
**etwas**  something
**hochachtungsvoll**  yours faithfully
**jedoch**  however
**jemand**  someone
**jener**  that
**los**  loose, off
**mal**  just
**man**  one
**nun**  now, well
**obgleich**  although
**obwohl**  although
**oder**  or
**pro**  per
**selbst**  oneself
**so**  well
**sogar**  even
**sondern**  but
**trotzdem**  nevertheless
**und**  and
**usw. (und so weiter)**  and so on
**vielleicht**  perhaps
**weil**  because
**z.B. (zum Beispiel)**  for example
**zwar**  in fact

## Modal verbs

**dürfen**  to be allowed to
**können**  to be able to
**mögen**  to like to
**müssen**  to have to
**sollen**  to be supposed to
**wollen**  to want to

# 4.4 Area of Experience A – Everyday activities

### Home life

### At home

**der Abfall (¨e)**  litter
**die Adresse (-n)**  address
**der Besitzer (-)**  owner
**das Bild (-er)**  picture
**der Boden (¨)**  floor
**die Bürste (-n)**  brush
**das Dach (¨er)**  roof
**die Decke (-n)**  ceiling
**die Diele (-n)**  floorboard
**das Fenster (-)**  window
**der Fußboden (¨)**  floor
**die Gardine (-n)**  curtain
**das Gemälde (-)**  painting

**der Haken (-)**  hook, peg
**das Haus (¨er)**  house
**die Hausarbeit (-en)**  housework
**der Haushalt (-e)**  household
**der Hausmeister (-)**  caretaker
**die Hausnummer (-n)**  house number
**die Heizung (-en)**  heating (radiator)
**der Käfig (-e)**  cage
**die Kerze (-n)**  candle
**der Knopf (¨e)**  button, knob
**der Komfort (-s)**  comfort, luxury
**der Korb (¨e)**  basket
**die Lampe (-n)**  lamp
**das Licht (-er)**  light
**die Möbel (pl)**  furniture
**das Möbelstück (-e)**  piece of furniture

der **Müll**   rubbish
der **Mülleimer** (-)   rubbish bin
der **Nagel** (-)   nail
die **Ordnung** (-en)   order, tidiness
das **Parterre** (-s)   ground floor
das **Pflaster** (-)   plaster, pavement
das **Porzellan**   porcelain
das **Regal** (-e)   shelf
die **Schachtel** (-n)   box
die **Schere** (-n)   scissors
das **Schloß** (-sser)   lock
der **Schrank** (-e)   cupboard
die **Steckdose** (-n)   electric socket
der **Strom**   electricity
die **Stufe** (-n)   step
das **Tor** (-e)   gate
die **Treppe** (-n)   stairs
das **Tuch** (-er)   cloth
die **Tür** (-en)   door
die **Uhr** (-en)   clock, watch, hour
der **Vorhang** (-e)   curtain
die **Wand** (-e)   wall
die **Wäsche**   washing
die **Zentralheizung**   central heating

## The rooms

das **Badezimmer** (-)   bathroom
der **Balkon** (-s)   balcony
der **Dachboden** (-)   attic
das **Eßzimmer** (-)   dining room
der **Flur** (-e)   corridor, hall
die **Garage** (-n)   garage
der **Keller** (-)   cellar
die **Küche** (-n)   kitchen
das **Schlafzimmer** (-)   bedroom
das **Untergeschoß** (-sse)   cellar, basement
die **Wäscherei** (-en)   laundry room
der **Weinkeller** (-)   wine cellar
das **Wohnzimmer** (-)   living room
das **Zimmer** (-)   room

## Materials

die **Baumwolle**   cotton
das **Eisen**   iron
das **Gold**   gold
aus **Holz**   made of wood
das **Holz** (-er)   wood
der **Karton** (-s)   cardboard
das **Leder**   leather
das **Metal** (-le)   metal
das **Perlon**   nylon
das **Plastik**   plastic
die **Seide**   silk
das **Silber**   silver
der **Stoff** (-e)   material
die **Wolle**   wool

## Adjectives

**bequem**   comfortable
**elektrisch**   electric
**elektro-**   electric…

**entfernt**   distant
**fern**   distant
**gemütlich**   comfortable/cosy
**möbliert**   furnished
**modern**   modern
**modisch**   fashionable
**neu**   new
**ordentlich**   tidy
**praktisch**   practical, convenient
**schmutzig**   dirty
**schön**   beautiful
**unordentlich**   untidy

## Verbs

**abheben** (sep)   to lift (e.g. lid, hat)
**ablegen** (sep)   to put down
**abschließen** (sep)   to lock up
**anmachen** (sep)   to turn on (e.g. light)
**anschnallen** (sep)   to snap on, to fasten
**anstreichen** (sep)   to paint
**anzünden** (sep)   to light
**aufpassen** (sep) **(auf)**   to take care of
**aufschließen** (sep)   to unlock
**ausmachen** (sep)   to turn off (e.g. light)
**ausschalten** (sep)   to switch off
**drücken**   to press, to push
**einschalten** (sep)   to switch on
**hängen**   to hang
**heizen**   to heat
**kaufen**   to buy
**klingeln**   to ring
**lassen**   to let, to allow
**mähen**   to mow
**malen**   to paint
**nehmen**   to take
**pflücken**   to pick , to pluck
**sitzen**   to sit
**sitzenbleiben** (sep)   to remain seated
**stecken**   to put
**stellen**   to place, to put
**streichen**   to stroke, to paint, to cross out
**umziehen** (sep)   to move house

## The living room

der **Aschenbecher** (-)   ashtray
das **Bücherregal** (-e)   bookshelf
das **Büfett** (-e)   sideboard
die **Computeranlage** (-n)   computer equipment
der **Fernseher** (-)   TV set
das **Kissen** (-)   cushion
der **Lehnstuhl** (-e)   armchair
das **Radio** (-s)   radio
der **Schreibtisch** (-e)   desk
der **Sessel** (-)   armchair
das **Sofa** (-s)   sofa
die **Stehlampe** (-n)   standard lamp
die **Stereoanlage** (-n)   stereo
die **Tapete** (-n)   wallpaper
der **Teppich** (-e)   carpet
das **Videogerät** (-e)   video recorder

## The bedroom

das **Bett** (-en)  bed
das **Bettuch** (¨er)  sheet
die **Bettwäsche**  bed linen
das **Bettzeug**  bedding
die **Decke** (-n)  blanket
das **Federbett** (-en)  quilt, duvet
die **Garderobe** (-n)  wardrobe
die **Haarbürste** (-n)  hairbrush
der **Kleiderschrank** (¨e)  wardrobe
das **Kopfkissen** (-)  pillow
in **Ordnung**  in order
das **Plakat** (-e)  poster
der **Wecker** (-)  alarm clock

## The bathroom

das **Bad** (¨er)  bath
das **Badetuch** (¨er)  bath towel
die **Badewanne** (-n)  bath(tub)
die **Dusche** (-n)  shower
das **Handtuch** (¨er)  handtowel
der **Kamm** (¨e)  comb
das **Kölnisch Wasser**  eau de Cologne
das **Parfüm** (-s)  perfume
der **Rasierapparat** (-e)  electric razor
der **Schwamm** (¨e)  sponge
die **Seife** (-n)  soap
der **Spiegel** (-)  mirror
die **Toilette** (-n)  toilet
das **Toilettenpapier**  toilet paper
das **Waschbecken** (-)  wash basin
die **Zahnbürste** (-n)  toothbrush
die **Zahncreme** (-n)  toothpaste
die **Zahnpasta** (-ten)  toothpaste

## Routine verbs

**abnehmen** (sep)  to take off, to remove
**anhaben** (sep)  to wear (dresses, trousers etc)
sich **anziehen** (sep)  to get dressed
**aufhaben** (sep)  to have on, to wear (hats, caps etc)
**aufstehen** (sep)  to get up
**aufwachen** (sep)  to wake up
sich **ausschlafen** (sep)  to have a good sleep
sich **ausziehen** (sep)  to get undressed
sich **bürsten**  to brush
sich die **Zähne putzen**  to clean one's teeth
**duschen**  to shower
**einschlafen** (sep)  to fall asleep
**frühstücken**  to have breakfast
sich **kämmen**  to comb one's hair
sich **rasieren**  to shave
**schlafen**  to sleep
sich **schminken**  to put on make-up
**schneiden**  to cut
**tragen**  to carry, to wear
sich **umziehen** (sep)  to change clothes
**verschlafen**  to oversleep
**wecken**  to wake

## The kitchen

der **Becher** (-)  mug
der **Dosenöffner** (-)  tin-opener
das **Gas** (-e)  gas
das **Geschirr**  crockery
der **Geschirrspülautomat**
  (-en)  dishwasher
der **Herd** (-e)  cooker, oven
der **Kalender** (-)  calendar
der **Kühlschrank** (¨e)  fridge
der **Lappen** (-)  cloth, rag
das **Mehl**  flour
der **Mikroherd** (-e)  microwave oven
die **Mikrowelle** (-n)  microwave(s)
der **Ofen** (¨)  oven
die **Pfanne** (-n)  pan
das **Rezept** (-e)  recipe
die **Schüssel** (-n)  dish
die **Spülmaschine** (-n)  dishwasher
der **Stuhl** (¨e)  chair
die **Tiefkühltruhe** (-n)  deep-freeze
der **Tisch** (-e)  table
der **Topf** (¨e)  pot, saucepan
der **Wandschrank** (¨e)  wall cupboard
die **Waschmaschine** (-n)  washing machine
der **Wischlappen** (-)  cloth, floorcloth

## The garden

der **Baum** (¨e)  tree
die **Blume** (-n)  flower
der **Garten** (¨)  garden
das **Gras** (¨er)  grass
die **Hütte** (-n)  hut
das **Loch** (¨er)  hole
die **Nelke** (-n)  carnation
die **Pflanze** (-n)  plant
der **Rasen** (-)  lawn
der **Rasenmäher** (-)  lawnmower
die **Rose** (-n)  rose
der **Stein** (-e)  stone
die **Tulpe** (-n)  tulip
das **Unkraut**  weed
der **Zaun** (¨e)  fence

## Pets

der **Goldfisch** (-e)  goldfish
das **Haustier** (-e)  pet
der **Hund** (-e)  dog
der **Kanarienvogel** (¨)  canary
das **Kaninchen** (-)  rabbit
die **Katze** (-n)  cat
das **Meerschweinchen** (-)  guinea pig
die **Schildkröte** (-n)  tortoise
der **Wellensittich** (-e)  budgerigar

## The housework

das **Bügeleisen** (-)  iron
der **Staubsauger** (-)  vacuum cleaner
das **Waschpulver** (-)  washing powder

## Verbs

**abräumen** (sep)   to tidy up
**abspülen** (sep)   to wash up
**abstauben** (sep)   to dust
**abtrocken** (sep)   to dry up
**abwaschen** (sep)   to wash up
**aufräumen** (sep)   to tidy up
**backen**   to bake
**braten**   to fry, to roast
**bügeln**   to iron
**decken**   to cover, to lay (the table)
**kochen**   to cook
**nähen**   to sew
**putzen**   to clean
**reinigen**   to clean
**reparieren**   to repair
**schälen**   to peel
**spülen**   to rinse
**trocknen**   to dry
**waschen**   to wash

## Houses

**das Appartement (-s)**   appartment
**der Block (¨e)**   block (e.g. of flats)
**der Bungalow (-s)**   bungalow
**das Doppelhaus (¨er)**   semi-detached house
**das Einfamilienhaus (¨er)**   detached house
**das Fachwerk**   half-timbering
**das Hochhaus (¨er)**   high-rise building
**das Reihenhaus (¨er)**   terraced house
**der Wohnblock (¨e)**   block of flats
**die Wohnung (-en)**   flat

## School

## In class

**das Abitur**   A-level exam
**die Abschlußprüfung (-en)**   school-leaving exam
**die Ahnung (-en)**   idea, presentiment
**der Anfang (¨e)**   beginning
**die Antwort (-en)**   answer
**die Aufgabe (-n)**   exercise
**der Aufsatz (¨e)**   essay
**der Ausdruck (¨e)**   expression
**der Ausgang (¨e)**   exit
**der Austausch (-e)**   school exchange
**das Beispiel (-e)**   example
**die Beschreibung (-en)**   description
**das Ende**   end
**zu Ende**   at an end
**der Erfolg (-e)**   success
**die Erlaubnis (-isse)**   permission, permit
**das Examen (-)**   exam
**das Fach (¨er)**   subject
**der Fehler (-)**   mistake
**die Ferien** (pl)   holidays
**die Frage (-n)**   question
**die Ganztagsschule (-n)**   all-day schooling
**das Geräusch (-e)**   noise
**die Hausaufgabe (-n)**   homework

**die Idee (-n)**   idea
**die Klasse (-n)**   class
**die Klassenarbeit (-en)**   class test
**die Klassenfahrt (-en)**   class trip
**der Klassenkamarad (-en)**   class friend
**der Krach (¨e)**   din, racket
**die Kreide (-n)**   chalk
**der Kreis (-e)**   circle
**der Lärm**   noise
**die Leistung (-en)**   achievement, performance
**die Leitung (-en)**   guidance
**die Linie (-n)**   line
**die Mittagspause (-n)**   lunch time
**die Mittlere Reife**   GCSE (German equivalent)
**die Mühe (-n)**   trouble
**die Note (-n)**   mark
**die Oberprima**   upper sixth
**die Oberstufe (-n)**   sixth-form
**die Pause (-n)**   break
**das Pflichtfach (¨er)**   compulsory subject
**die Prüfung (-en)**   test, exam
**der Punkt (-e)**   point, mark (in exam)
**die Regel (-n)**   rule
**die Rolle (-n)**   role
**der Schluß (¨sse)**   end
**die Schulaufgaben** (pl)   homework
**die Seite (-n)**   side, page
**das Semester (-)**   term
**die Strafarbeit (-en)**   extra work at school
**der Studienplatz (¨e)**   place to study
**die Stunde (-n)**   lesson
**der Stundenplan (¨e)**   timetable
**die Tafel (-n)**   board, blackboard
**die Taste (-n)**   key, button
**das Teil (-e)**   part
**der Titel (-)**   title
**die Übung (-en)**   exercise
**die Unterprima**   lower sixth
**der Unterricht**   lessons
**die Verbesserung (-en)**   improvement
**die Verpflegung (-en)**   catering
**die Vokabel (-n)**   word
**die Weiterbildung**   Further Education
**das Wort (-e)** or **(¨er)**   word
**die Zahl (-en)**   number
**das Zeugnis (-se)**   report (e.g. school report)

## Subjects

**die Biologie**   biology
**die Chemie**   chemistry
**die Erdkunde**   geography
**die Fremdsprache (-n)**   foreign language
**die Geographie**   geography
**die Geschichte**   history
**die Handarbeit**   needlework
**die Hauswirtschaft**   home economics
**die Informatik**   IT
**das Kochen**   cookery
**die Kunst**   art

das **Latein**   Latin
das **Maschinenschreiben**   typing
**Mathe**   maths
die **Mathematik**   maths
das **Nähen**   needlework
die **Naturwissenschaft (-en)**   science
die **Physik**   physics
die **Religionslehre**   religious education
die **Religion**   religion
die **Sozialkunde**   social studies
die **Sozialwissenschaft (-en)**   social sciences
die **Sprache (-n)**   language
die **Stenographie**   shorthand
die **Technik**   technology
das **Turnen**   gymnastics
das **Wahlfach (¨er)**   optional subject
das **Werken**   handicraft
die **Wirtschaftslehre**   economics
die **Wirtschaftswissenschaft**   economics

## Adjectives

**hitzefrei**   time off school because of heat
**mündlich**   oral
**richtig**   correct
**schulfrei**   school holiday
**schwierig**   difficult
**schwer**   difficult, heavy
**streng**   severe, strict

## The places

die **Aula (-s)**   assembly hall
die **Berufschule (-n)**   technical college
die **Fachhochschule (-n)**   college
der **Gang (¨e)**   corridor
die **Gesamtschule (-n)**   comprehensive school
die **Grundschule (-n)**   primary school
das **Gymnasium (-ien)**   grammar school
die **Hauptschule (-n)**   secondary modern
  school
die **Hochschule (-n)**   technical college,
  university
der **Hof (¨e)**   playground
das **Internat (-e)**   boarding school
die **Kantine (-n)**   canteen
der **Kindergarten (¨)**   nursery school
das **Klassenzimmer (-)**   classroom
das **Labor (-s)**   lab, laboratory
das **Lehrerzimmer (-)**   staffroom
die **Realschule (-n)**   secondary school
der **Saal (Säle)**   hall
die **Schule (-n)**   school
der **Schulhof (¨e)**   playground
der **Speisesaal (-äle)**   dining hall/room
der **Sportplatz (¨e)**   sportsfield
das **Sprachlabor (-s)**   language lab
die **Stube (-n)**   study
die **Turnhalle (-n)**   gymnasium
die **Universität (-en)**   university
die **Volkshochschule (-n)**   adult education
  centre

## The equipment

das **Blatt (¨er)**   sheet of paper, page
der **Bleistift (-e)**   pencil
der **Farbstift (-e)**   colour pencil
der **Filzstift (-e)**   felt tip pencil
der **Füller (-)**   fountain pen
das **Heft (-e)**   exercise book
der **Kugelschreiber (-)**   biro
der **Kuli (-s)**   biro
das **Lineal (-e)**   ruler
das **Papier (-e)**   paper
der **Radiergummi (-s)**   rubber
das **Schulbuch (¨er)**   schoolbook
die **Schulmappe (-n)**   school bag
der **Stift (-e)**   pencil
der **Tageslichtprojektor (-en)**   overhead
  projector
der **Taschenrechner (-)**   pocket calculator
die **Tinte (-n)**   ink
das **Wörterbuch (¨er)**   dictionary

## The people

der **Direktor (-en)**   headmaster
der **Klassensprecher (-)**   class representative
der **Lehrer (-)**   teacher
der/die **Rektor/in (-nen)**   headteacher
der **Schuldirektor (-en)**   headmaster
der **Schüler (-)**   schoolboy
der **Student (-en)**   student

## Verbs

**abschreiben** (sep)   to copy (in an exam)
**anfangen** (sep)   to begin
**ankreuzen** (sep)   to mark with a cross
**antworten**   to answer
**aufhören** (sep)   to stop, to give up
**aufmachen** (sep)   to open
**aufschreiben** (sep)   to write down
**auskommen mit** (sep)   to manage
**beachten**   to heed, to observe
**beantworten**   to answer
**beginnen**   to begin
**benutzen**   to use
**buchstabieren**   to spell
**dransein** (sep)   to take one's turn
**durchfallen** (sep)   to fail (e.g. an exam)
**enden**   to end
**erlauben**   to allow
**erreichen**   to achieve, to reach
**finden**   to find
**hören**   to hear
**kapieren**   to understand
**kopieren**   to copy
**korrigieren**   to correct
**sich langweilen**   to be bored
**lernen**   to learn
**nachsitzen** (sep)   to be kept in
**rechnen**   to calculate
**reichen**   to reach, to be sufficient

**schaffen**  to pass (exam), to manage
**schließen**  to close, to finish
**Schluß machen**  to finish
**schreiben**  to write
**schwänzen**  to play truant
**sitzenbleiben** (sep)  to repeat a year
**starten**  to start
**stehen**  to stand
**stimmen**  to be correct
**studieren**  to study
**teilen**  to share
**teilnehmen** (sep) **an**  to take part in
**tun**  to do
**übersetzen**  to translate
**umdrehen** (sep)  to turn over
**sich umdrehen** (sep)  to turn round
**verbessern**  to improve
**verbieten**  to forbid
**verbinden**  to connect
**verbringen**  to spend (time)
**verfügen**  to have at one's disposal
**vergessen**  to forget
**verlassen**  to leave
**vernachlässigen**  to neglect
**verstehen**  to understand
**versuchen**  to try
**vorbereiten**  to prepare
**weiterstudieren** (sep)  to continue studying
**wiederholen**  to repeat
**zeigen**  to show
**zugreifen** (sep)  to help oneself
**zuhören** (sep)  to listen

### Food and drink
### Meals

**das Abendbrot (-e)**  supper
**das Abendessen (-)**  evening meal
**das Frühstück (-e)**  breakfast
**die Mahlzeit (-en)**  meal, mealtime
**das Mittagessen (-)**  lunch
**das Picknick (-s)**  picnic
**der Schnellimbiß (-sse)**  snack
**die Vorspeise (-n)**  starter

### Vegetables

**der Blumenkohl**  cauliflower
**die Bohne (-n)**  green bean
**die Bratkartoffel (-n)**  fried potato
**der Champignon (-s)**  mushroom
**die Erbse (-n)**  pea
**das Gemüse**  vegetables
**die Karotte (-n)**  carrot
**die Kartoffel (-n)**  potato
**der Kohl(-e)**  cabbage
**der Kopfsalat (-e)**  lettuce
**der Pilz (-e)**  mushroom
**Pommes frites (-)**  chips
**der Reis**  rice
**der Rosenkohl**  Brussel sprout
**der Rotkohl**  red cabbage

**die Salzkartoffel (-n)**  boiled potato
**das Sauerkraut**  pickled cabbage
**die Zwiebel (-n)**  onion

### Fruit

**die Ananas (-)**  pineapple
**der Apfel (¨)**  apple
**die Apfelsine -(n)**  orange
**die Aprikose (-n)**  apricot
**die Banane (-n)**  banana
**die Birne (-n)**  pear
**die Erdbeere (-n)**  strawberry
**die Himbeere (-n)**  raspberry
**die Kirsche (-n)**  cherry
**das Obst**  fruit
**die Orange (-n)**  orange
**die Pampelmuse (-n)**  grapefruit
**der Pfirsich (-e)**  peach
**die Pflaume (-n)**  plum
**die rote Johannisbeere (-n)**  redcurrant
**die schwarze Johannisbeere (-n)**
  blackcurrant
**die Stachelbeere (-n)**  gooseberry
**die Tomate (-n)**  tomato
**die Traube (-n)**  grape
**die Weintraube (-n)**  grape
**die Zitrone (-n)**  lemon

### Meat

**der Braten (-)**  roast (i.e. a roast dish)
**das Brathähnchen (-)**  roast chicken
**das Fleisch**  meat
**das Geflügel**  poultry
**das Hähnchen (-)**  chicken
**das Kalbfleisch**  veal
**das Kotelett (-e)**  chop
**das Lammfleisch**  lamb
**die Leber (-n)**  liver
**das Rindfleisch**  beef
**der Schinken (-)**  ham
**der Schnitzel (-)**  cutlet
**das Schweinefleisch**  pork
**der Speck (-e)**  bacon

### On the table

**das Besteck (-e)**  cutlery
**der Essig**  vinegar
**die Flasche (-n)**  bottle
**die Gabel (-n)**  fork
**das Gewürz (-e)**  spice
**das Glas (¨er)**  glass
**die Kaffeekanne (-n)**  coffeee pot
**das Kännchen (-)**  little pot (for tea or coffee)
**das/der Ketchup**  ketchup
**der Krug (¨e)**  jug, pitcher
**der Löffel (-)**  spoon
**das Messer (-)**  knife
**der Pfeffer**  pepper
**das Salz**  salt
**der Senf (-e)**  mustard

die Soße (-n)  sauce
die Tasse (-n)  cup
die Teekanne (-n)  teapot
der Teller (-)  plate
die Untertasse (-n)  saucer
der Zucker  sugar

## At the snack bar

der Aufschnitt  cold meat
ein belegtes Brot (-e)  open sandwich
die Bockwurst (-̈e)  sausage
das Bonbon (-s)  sweet
die Bratwurst (-̈e)  sausage
das Brot (-e)  bread
das Brötchen (-)  bread roll
die Butter  butter
das Butterbrot (-e)  sandwich
die Chips  crisps
die Currywurst (-̈e)  curried sausage
das Ei (-er)  egg
der Eintopf (-̈e)  stew
das Eis (-e)  ice cream
die Erfrischung (-en)  refreshment
der Erfrischungsstand (-̈e)  refreshment stall
die Frikadelle (-n)  rissole
das Gebäck (-e)  biscuits
das Graubrot (-e)  bread made from more than one type of flour
der Hamburger (-)  hamburger
der Honig  honey
der Imbiß (-sse)  snack
die Imbißstube (-n)  snackbar
der Käse (-)  cheese
der Kaugummi (-s)  chewing gum
das/der Keks (-e)  biscuit
das Kompott (-e)  stewed fruit
der Kuchen (-)  cake
die Leberwurst (-̈e)  liver sausage
die Margarine  margarine
die Marmelade (-n)  jam
die Nudel (-n)  noodle
die Nuß (-̈sse)  nut
das Omelett (-s)  omelette
die Praline (-n) (-s)  chocolate
das Rührei (-er)  scrambled egg
der Salat (-e)  salad
die Schokolade (-n)  chocolate
das Schwarzbrot (-e)  black bread
die Semmel (-n)  roll
das Spiegelei (-er)  fried egg
die Süßigkeiten (pl)  sweets
die Trinkhalle (-n)  refreshment kiosk
die Wurst (-̈e)  sausage
das Würstchen (-)  small sausage

## Desserts

die Creme (-s)  cream
der Eisbecher (-)  ice-cream sundae
die Frucht (-̈e)  fruit
der/das Joghurt (-s)  yoghurt
der Nachtisch (-e)  dessert

der Pudding (-s)  pudding, dessert
die Sahne  cream
die Schlagsahne  whipped cream
das Speiseeis  ice cream
die Torte (-n)  flan, gateau
die Vanille  vanilla

## Drinks

der Alkohol (-e)  alcohol
der Apfelsaft (-̈e)  apple juice
das Bier (-e)  beer
die Cola (-s)  Coca-Cola
das Getränk (-e)  drink
der Kaffee (-s)  coffee
der Kakao (-s)  cocoa
die Limonade (-n)  lemonade
die Milch  milk
das Milch-Mixgetränk (-e)  milkshake
das Mineralwasser (-)  mineral water
der Orangensaft (-̈e)  orange juice
das Pils (-)  beer
der Rotwein (-e)  red wine
der Saft (-e)  juice
der Schnaps (-̈e)  schnapps, spirits
der Sekt (-e)  champagne
die Spirituosen (pl)  spirits
der Sprudel (-)  mineral water, lemonade
der Strohhalm (-e)  drinking straw
der Tee (-s)  tea
der Wein (-e)  wine
der Weißwein (-e)  white wine

## The restaurant

die Bedienung (-en)  service
das Café (-s)  café
der Durst  thirst
das Essen (-)  food, meal
der Fisch (-e)  fish
die Forelle (-n)  trout
das Gericht (-e)  course (of a meal)
der Geschmack (-̈er)  taste
die Getränkekarte (-n)  list of drinks, wine list
das Hauptgericht (-e)  main course
Herr Ober!  waiter!
der Hunger  hunger
inbegriffen/inbgr.  included
die kalte Platte (-n)  cold dish
der Kellner (-)  waiter
die Kellnerin (-nen)  waitress
der Koch (-̈e)  cook
das Menü (-s)  menu
die Nachspeise (-n)  dessert, sweet
die Preistafel (-n)  price list
der Raucher (-)  smoker
die Rechnung (-en)  bill
das Restaurant (-s)  restaurant
die Sardine (-n)  sardine
sonst noch etwas?  anything else?
die Speisekarte (-n)  menu
die Spezialität (-en)  speciality
die Suppe (-n)  soup

die **Terrasse** (-n)   terrace
die **Toilette** (-n)   toilet
das **Trinkgeld** (-er)   tip
die **Wahl** (-en)   choice
die **Weinkarte** (-n)   wine list
die **Weinliste** (-n)   wine list
**zum Mitnehmen**   take-away (food)

## Restaurant verbs

**anbieten** (sep)   to offer
**bedienen**   to serve
**bestehen aus**   to consist of
**bestellen**   to order
**empfehlen**   to recommend
**essen**   to eat
**riechen**   to smell
**schmecken**   to taste (good)
**trinken**   to drink

## Health and fitness

### Sports

das **Angeln**   angling
die **Athletik**   athletics
das **Badminton**   badminton
der **Federball** (¨e)   badminton
der **Fußball** (¨e)   football
die **Gymnastik**   gymnastics
der **Handball** (¨e)   handball
das **Jagen**   hunting
das **Reiten**   riding
das **Tennis**   tennis
das **Tischtennis**   table tennis
das **Windsurfen**   windsurfing

### Sport words

der **Anmeldeschein** (-e)   registration form
das **Endspiel** (-e)   final (of competition)
das **Ergebnis** (-se)   result
das **Fitneßzentrum** (-ren)   sports centre
der **Fußballplatz** (¨e)   football pitch/ground
der **Lauf** (Läufe)   race
der **Lautsprecher** (-)   loudspeaker
die **Liga** (-en)   league
die **Meisterschaft** (-en)   championship
die **Niederlage** (-n)   defeat
der **Pokal** (-e)   cup
die **Reitschule** (-n)   riding school
die **Runde** (-n)   lap
der **Sieg** (-e)   victory
der **Ski** (-s)   ski
das **Spiel** (-e)   game, match
der **Sport**   sport
die **Sportart** (-en)   type of sport
der **Sportplatz** (¨e)   sports field
das **Sportverein** (-e)   sports club
das **Sportzentrum** (-ren)   sports centre
das **Stadion** (-ien)   stadium
der **Stehplatz** (¨e)   standing room
das **Tor** (-e)   goal

die **Turnhalle** (-n)   gymnasium
das **Turnier** (-e)   competition
**unentschieden**   drawn (game)
die **Veranstaltung** (-en)   event
der **Verein** (-e)   club
der **Wettkampf** (¨e)   competition
**wie steht das Spiel?**   what's the score?

## Sports gear

die **Angelrute** (-n)   fishing-rod
der **Ball** (¨e)   ball
der **Jogginganzug** (¨e)   jogging suit
das **Netz** (-e)   net
der **Schläger** (-)   racquet, bat
der **Schlittschuh** (-e)   ice skate
der **Sessellift** (-e)   chairlift
der **Skilift** (-e)   ski-lift
der **Trainingsanzug** (¨e)   track suit

## The people

der **Fan** (-s)   fan
der **Fußballspieler** (-)   footballer
der **Läufer** (-)   runner
die **Mannschaft** (-en)   team
das **Mitglied** (-er)   member
das **Publikum**   audience, crowd
der **Radfahrer** (-)   cyclist
der **Sportler** (-)   sportsman
der **Zuschauer** (-)   spectator

## Verbs

**anschauen** (sep)   to look at
**ansehen** (sep)   to watch, to look at
**atmen**   to breathe
**aufgeben** (sep)   to give up
**ausfallen** (sep)   to be cancelled
**fangen**   to catch
**gewinnen**   to win
**halten**   to hold, keep, stop
**joggen**   to jog
**klettern**   to climb
**laufen**   to run
**nachschauen** (sep)   to watch, to have a look
**nachsehen** (sep)   to check
**pfeifen**   to whistle
**radfahren** (sep)   to cycle
**rennen**   to run
**rudern**   to row
**schauen**   to look, to see
**schwimmen**   to swim
**schwitzen**   to sweat
**segeln**   to sail
**sehen**   to see
**siegen**   to win
**Ski fahren**   to ski
**Ski laufen**   to ski
**spielen**   to play
**Sport treiben**   to practise sport
**springen**   to jump
**stattfinden** (sep)   to take place

**steigen** to climb
**trainieren** to train
**treiben** to do (e.g. sports, studies)
**turnen** to do gymnastics
**werfen** to throw

## The body

**der Arm (-e)** arm
**das Auge (-n)** eye
**der Bart (¨e)** beard
**der Bauch (¨e)** belly
**das Bein (-e)** leg
**das Blut** blood
**die Brust (¨e)** breast, chest
**der Daumen (-)** thumb
**der Finger (-)** finger
**der Fuß (-üsse)** foot
**das Gesicht (-er)** face
**die Glatze (-n)** bald head
**das Haar (-e)** hair
**der Hals (¨e)** neck, throat
**die Hand (¨e)** hand
**die Haut (Häute)** skin
**das Herz (-en)** heart
**das Knie (-)** knee
**der Kopf (¨e)** head
**der Körper (-)** body
**die Lippe (-n)** lip
**der Magen (¨)** stomach
**der Mund (¨er)** mouth
**die Nase (-n)** nose
**das Ohr (-en)** ear
**der Rücken (-)** back
**der Schnurrbart (¨e)** moustache
**die Schulter (-n)** shoulder
**die Stimme (-n)** voice
**der Zahn (¨e)** tooth
**die Zehe (-n)** toe
**die Zunge (-n)** tongue

## Health and illness

**AIDS** AIDS
**die Allergie (-n)** allergy
**der Appetit** appetite
**die Bauchschmerzen (pl)** stomach ache
**das Bauchweh** stomach ache
**die Behandlung (-en)** treatment
**die Besserung (-en)** improvement, recovery
**die Besuchszeit (-en)** visiting time
**der Blutdruck** blood pressure
**die Diät (-en)** diet
**der Durchfall** diarrhoea
**die Entzündung (-en)** inflammation
**die Erkältung (-en)** cold
**das Fieber** temperature
**die Gesundheit** health
**der Gips (-e)** plaster cast
**die Grippe** flu
**die Halsschmerzen (pl)** sore throat
**das Hansaplast** Elastoplast

**der Heuschnupfen** hay fever
**die Infektion (-en)** infection
**die Klinik (-en)** clinic
**die Kopfschmerzen (pl)** headache
**das Krankenhaus (¨er)** hospital
**die Krankenkasse (-n)** health insurance company
**der Krankenschein (-e)** medical insurance card
**der Krankenwagen (-)** ambulance
**die Krankheit (-en)** illness
**der Kurort (-e)** spa
**die Magenschmerzen (pl)** stomach ache
**das Medikament (-e)** medicine
**die Medizin** medicine
**die Ohnmacht** faint
**die Operation (-en)** operation
**die Pille (-n)** pill
**das Rezept (-e)** prescription
**die Salbe (-n)** ointment
**der Schmerz (-en)** pain
**der Schnupfen** cold
**der Sonnenbrand (¨e)** sunburn
**das Sonnenöl (-e)** sun cream
**die Sprechstunde (-n)** consulting hours, surgery
**die Tablette (-n)** tablet, pill
**der Termin (-e)** appointment
**das Thermometer (-)** thermometer
**die Verletzung (-en)** injury
**die Verstopfung (-en)** constipation
**das Weh** ache
**die Wunde (-n)** wound
**die Zahnschmerzen (pl)** toothache
**die Zigarette (-n)** cigarette

## The people

**der Arzt (¨e)** doctor
**der Doktor (-en)** doctor
**der Facharzt (¨e)** specialist doctor
**der/die Kranke (-n)** sick person
**der Krankenpfleger (-)** male nurse
**die Krankenschwester (-n)** female nurse
**der/die Patient/in (-nen)** patient
**der Zahnarzt (¨e)** dentist

## Verbs

**bluten** to bleed
**einreiben (sep)** to rub in
**sich erholen** to recover, to get better
**sich erkälten** to catch a cold
**sich fühlen** to feel
**Heimweh haben** to be homesick
**husten** to cough
**niesen** to sneeze
**pflegen** to nurse, to look after
**röntgen** to X-ray
**stechen** to sting
**untersuchen** to examine
**sich verbrennen** to burn oneself

**verletzen**   to injure
**verschreiben**   to prescribe
**wehtun** (sep)   to hurt
**weinen**   to cry
**zittern**   to shiver

## Adjectives

**erkältet**   having a cold
**krank**   ill
**schlaflos**   sleepless
**seekrank**   seasick
**übel**   ill
**verletzt**   injured
**verstopft**   constipated

# 4.5  Area of Experience B – Personal and social life

## Self, family and personal relationships

### Family

**das Alter**   age
**die Ehe (-n)**   marriage
**der Familienname (-n)**   surname
**der Familienstand**   married status
**die Geburt (-en)**   birth
**der Nachname (-n)**   surname
**das Taschengeld**   pocket money
**der Vorname (-n)**   first name
**der Wohnort (-e)**   place of residence

### The people in the family

**das Baby (-s)**   baby
**der Bruder (¨)**   brother
**der Cousin (-s)**   cousin
**die Ehefrau (-en)**   wife
**die Eheleute** (pl)   married couple
**der Ehemann (¨er)**   husband
**das Ehepaar (-e)**   couple
**das Einzelkind (-er)**   only child
**die Eltern** (pl)   parents
**der Enkel (-)**   grandchild
**die Enkelin (-nen)**   granddaughter
**die Enkelkinder** (pl)   grandchildren
**die Familie (-n)**   family
**die Geschwister** (pl)   brothers and sisters
**die Großeltern** (pl)   grandparents
**die Großmutter (¨)**   grandmother
**der Großvater (¨)**   grandfather
**der Junge (-n)**   boy
**das Kind (-er)**   child
**die Kusine (-n)**   cousin (female)
**der Mann (¨er)**   man, husband
**die Mutter (¨)**   mother
**Mutti**   Mum
**der Neffe (-n)**   nephew
**die Nichte (-n)**   niece
**die Oma (-s)**   granny
**der Onkel (-)**   uncle
**der Opa (-s)**   grandad
**die Schwester (-n)**   sister
**die Schwiegereltern** (pl)   parents-in-law
**die Schwiegermutter (¨)**   mother-in-law

**der Schwiegersohn (¨)**   son-in-law
**der Schwiegervater (¨)**   father-in-law
**der Sohn (¨e)**   son
**die Tante (-n)**   aunt
**die Tochter (¨)**   daughter
**der Vater (¨)**   father
**Vati**   dad
**der/die Verlobte (-n)**   fiancé/fiancée
**der Verwandte (-n)**   relative
**der Vetter (-n)**   cousin (male)
**die Witwe (-n)**   widow
**der Witwer (-)**   widower
**der Zwilling (-e)**   twin

## Adjectives

**arm**   poor
**atemlos**   breathless
**betrunken**   drunk
**bewußtlos**   unconscious
**blaß**   pale
**blond**   blond, fair
**dick**   fat
**dünn**   thin
**fit**   fit
**geschieden**   divorced, separated
**gestorben**   dead
**gesund**   healthy
**häßlich**   ugly
**hübsch**   pretty
**jung**   young
**ledig**   single (not married)
**lockig**   curly
**mager**   thin
**männlich**   masculine
**reich**   rich
**schlank**   slim
**schwanger**   pregnant
**stark**   strong
**tot**   dead
**unfit**   unfit
**verheiratet**   married
**verlobt**   engaged
**vollschlank**   plump
**weiblich**   female, feminine

## Friends

der Besuch (-e)   visit
die Bitte (-n)   request
die Brieffreundschaft (-en)   correspondence
   with a penfriend
der Briefwechsel (-)   correspondence
der Einführungsbrief (-e)   introductory
   letter
die Einladung (-en)   invitation
die Entschuldigung (-en)   apology
das Fest (-e)   party
die Gastfreundschaft   hospitality
das Geschenk (-e)   present
das Gespräch (-e)   conversation
die Herkunft (¨e)   origin
der Kuß (¨sse)   kiss
die Laune (-n)   mood
die Liebe (-n)   love
der Mädchenname (-n)   maiden name
die Partnerstadt (¨e)   twin town
die Party (-s)   party
die Stimmung (-en)   mood
die Unterhaltung (-en)   conversation
die Verabredung (-en)   arrangement
die Vorstellung (-en)   introduction
der Zettel (-)   note

## The people

der/die Bekannte ( n)   acquaintance
der Brieffreund (-e)   penfriend
die Dame (-n)   lady
der Erwachsene (-n)   adult
der Freund (-e)   friend
die Gruppe (-n)   group
die Jugend   young people
der Jugendliche (-n)   young person
der Kamerad (-en)   comrade
das Mädchen (-)   girl
der Mensch (-en)   person, man
der Nachbar (-n)   neighbour
der Partner (-)   partner
die Person (-en)   person
der Typ (-en)   bloke, type, guy

## Adjectives

aktiv   active
angenehm   pleasant
behilflich   helpful
bekannt   well-known
beliebt   popular
blöd   mad, stupid
brav   good, well-behaved
doof   stupid
dumm   stupid
ehrlich   honest
ernst   serious
faul   lazy
fleißig   hard-working
frech   cheeky

freundlich   friendly
geduldig   patient
gut gelaunt   in a good mood
herzlich   warm, warm-hearted
humorvoll   humorous
intelligent   intelligent
interessant   interesting
klug   clever
langweilig   boring
lustig   amusing
neugierig   curious
ruhig   quiet
scheu   shy
schlau   clever, cunning
schüchtern   shy
sportlich   sporty
sympathisch   nice, kind
unfreundlich   unfriendly
verrückt   crazy
verwöhnt   spoilt
vorsichtig   careful
zärtlich   affectionate

## Verbs

abholen (sep)   to collect, to meet
ablehnen (sep)   to decline, to reject
sich ärgern   to get annoyed
ausführen (sep)   to take someone out
   (e.g. to cinema)
ausgehen (sep)   to go out
aussehen (sep)   to look, to appear
befreundet sein   to be friends
begegnen   to meet
begleiten   to accompany
begrüßen   to greet
beißen   to bite
bekommen   to receive
bellen   to bark
besuchen   to visit
bieten   to offer
bringen   to bring
einladen (sep)   to invite
empfangen   to greet, to welcome
erkennen   to recognise
erstaunen   to surprise
erwarten   to expect
feiern   to celebrate
Feuer haben   to have a light
sich freuen   to be pleased
geben   to give
hassen   to hate
heiraten   to marry
heißen   to be called
helfen   to help
kennen   to know (people, places)
kennenlernen (sep)   to get to know
küssen   to kiss
lächeln   to smile
lachen   to laugh
leben   to live

**lieben**   to love
**mitbringen** (sep)   to bring with you
**mitfahren** (sep)   to travel with
**mitkommen** (sep)   to come with you
**mitmachen** (sep)   to join in
**mitnehmen** (sep)   to take with you
**nennen**   to name, to call
**schenken**   to give as a present
**schütteln**   to shake
**sorgen für**   to care for
**treffen**   to meet
**überraschen**   to surprise
**sich verabschieden**   to say goodbye
**vermissen**   to miss (e.g. a person)
**sich verstehen**   to get on well
**sich vorstellen** (sep)   to introduce oneself
**wachsen**   to grow
**willkommen**   to welcome
**winken**   to wave
**wohnen**   to live
**wünschen**   to wish
**zurückgeben** (sep)   to give back

## Clothes

**der Anzug** (¨e)   suit
**der Badeanzug** (¨e)   swimsuit
**die Badehose** (-n)   swimming trunks
**die Bluse** (-n)   blouse
**der Gürtel** (-)   belt
**der Handschuh** (-e)   glove
**die Haube** (-n)   bonnet, cap
**das Hemd** (-en)   shirt
**die Hose** (-n)   trousers
**der Hut** (¨e)   hat
**die Jacke** (-n)   jacket
**die Jeans** (-)   jeans
**das Kleid** (-er)   dress
**die Kleider** (pl)   clothes
**die Kleidung**   clothes
**das Kostüm** (-e)   costume, suit
**die Krawatte** (-n)   tie
**der Mantel** (¨)   coat
**die Mütze** (-n)   cap
**der Pulli** (-s)   pullover
**der Pullover** (-s)   pullover
**der Rock** (¨e)   skirt
**die Sandale** (-n)   sandal
**der Schal** (-e)   shawl, scarf
**der Schlafanzug** (¨e)   pyjamas
**der Schlips** (-e)   tie
**der Schuh** (-e)   shoe
**die Socke** (-n)   sock
**der Stiefel** (-)   boot
**der Strumpf** (¨e)   sock
**die Strumpfhose** (-n)   tights
**das T-Shirt** (-s)   tee-shirt
**das Taschentuch** (¨er)   handkerchief
**die Unterhose** (-n)   underpants
**die Unterwäsche**   underclothes

## Extras

**das Armband** (¨er)   bracelet
**die Armbanduhr** (-en)   wristwatch
**die Brieftasche** (-n)   wallet
**die Brille** (-n)   glasses
**der Geldbeutel** (-)   purse
**die Geldbörse** (-n)   purse
**die Halskette** (-n)   necklace
**die Handtasche** (-n)   handbag
**die Kette** (-n)   necklace, bracelet
**der Lippenstift** (-e)   lipstick
**die Mappe** (-n)   briefcase
**der Ohrring** (-e)   earring
**das Portemonnaie** (-s)   purse
**der Regenschirm** (-e)   umbrella
**der Ring** (-e)   ring
**der Schmuck**   jewellery
**die Tasche** (-n)   pocket

## Free time and social activities

## Free time

**das Album** (Alben)   album
**der Aufkleber** (-)   sticker
**der Bastler** (-)   person who likes DIY
**der Clown** (-s)   clown
**der Computer** (-)   computer
**das Dia** (-s)   slide
**die Einfahrt** (-en)   entrance
**der Eintritt** (-e)   entrance
**das Eintrittsgeld** (-er)   entrance fee
**der Fernseher** (-)   TV set
**das Feuerzeug** (-e)   cigarette lighter
**der Fotoapparat** (-e)   camera
**die Freizeit**   free time
**der Führer** (-)   leader
**der Humor**   humour
**das Interesse** (-n)   interest
**die Jagd** (-en)   hunt
**die Kamera** (-s)   camera
**die Küche** (-n)   cooking
**der Leiter** (-)   leader
**Lieblings-**   favourite...
**das Mitglied**   member
**die Pfeife** (-n)   pipe
**die Puppe** (-n)   doll
**das Rad** (¨er)   bicycle
**der Rollschuh** (-e)   rollerskate
**der Rucksack** (¨e)   rucksack
**der Rundfunk**   radio
**die Sammlung** (-en)   collection
**der Spaß**   fun
**die Spielwaren** (pl)   toys
**das Spielzeug** (-e)   toy
**der Tabak**   tobacco
**der Urlaub** (-e)   holiday
**der Verband** (¨e)   club
**der Wanderer** (-)   hiker
**die Wanderkarte** (-n)   walker's map
**die Wanderschuhe**   walking shoes

der Weg (-e)   way, track
der Wegweiser (-)   signpost

## Places

die Ausstellung (-en)   exhibition
die Bar (-s)   bar
die Diskothek (-en)   disco
das Freizeitzentrum
   (-zentren)   leisure centre
die Galerie (-n)   gallery
die Imbißhalle (-n)   snack bar
die Imbißstube (-n)   cafe/snack bar
der Jugendklub (-s)   youth club
das Jugendzentrum (-en)   youth club
die Kegelbahn (-en)   bowling alley
der Klub (-s)   club
die Kneipe (-n)   pub, restaurant
das Konzert (-e)   concert
das Lokal (-e)   pub
der Schalter (-)   counter, box office
das Schwimmbad (-̈er)   swimming pool
das Schwimmbecken (-)   swimming pool
der Tiergarten (-̈)   zoo
der Zirkus (-se)   circus
der Zoo (-s)   zoo

## Activities

die Freizeitsbeschäftigung (-en)   leisure
   activity
das Hobby (-s)   hobby
das Kegeln   bowling
das Schach   chess
der Spaziergang (-̈e)   walk
das Stricken   knitting
die Unterhaltung (-en)   entertainment
die Wanderung (-en)   walk, hike

## Adjectives

all-   every, all
allerlei   all sorts
allgemein   general
ander-   other
bestimmt   certain
derselbe   the same
doppelt   double
eigen   of one's own
einige   some
einzeln   individual, separate
einzig   only, sole
folgend   following
genug   enough
gewiß   certain, definite
gewöhnlich   usual
irgend   some, any
jeder   every
knapp   scarce
letzte   last
mehrere   several
nächste   next
sämtlich   all

solch   such
total   total
viel   a lot
vorig   last (previous)
zusätzlich   additional

## Movement

anhalten (sep)   to stop
sich beeilen   to hurry up
betreten   to enter, to step on
eilen   to hurry
es eilig haben   to be in a hurry
gehen   to go
hereinkommen (sep)   to come in
sich hinsetzen (sep)   to sit down
holen   to fetch
sich setzen   to sit down
stehenbleiben (sep)   to stop
überqueren   to cross
vorbeikommen (sep)   to go past
vorgehen (sep)   to go ahead
weggehen (sep)   to go away

## Reading

die Anzeige (-n)   advert (in paper)
der Autor (-en)   author
die Autorin (-nen)   author(ess)
das Buch (-̈er)   book
das Gedicht (-e)   poem
der Horrorroman (-e)   horror novel
die Illustrierte (-n)   magazine
der Kriminalroman (-e)   thriller novel
das Lesen   reading
der Liebesroman (-e)   novel about love
die Literatur   literature
das Magazin (-e)   magazine
die Presse   press
die Reklame (-n)   advertisement
der Roman (-e)   novel
der Schriftsteller (-)   author
die Schriftstellerin (-nen)   author(ess)
das Taschenbuch (-̈er)   paperback
die Werbung (-en)   advertisement
die Zeitschrift (-en)   magazine
die Zeitung (-en)   newspaper

## At the cinema/theatre

die Abendkasse (-n)   box office
die Aufführung (-en)   performance
die Bühne (-n)   stage (e.g. of theatre)
der Dokumentarfilm (-e)   documentary
der Eingang (-̈e)   entrance
die Eintrittskarte (-n)   entrance ticket
die Erfrischungen (pl)   refreshments
der Farbfilm (-e)   colour film
der Film (-e)   film
das Kino (-s)   cinema
der Krimi (-s)   thriller (book or film)
der Kriminalfilm (-e)   thriller
der Rang (-̈e)   tier

die **Reihe** (-n)  row
das **Schauspiel** (-e)  play
der **Spielfilm** (-e)  feature film
das **Stück** (-e)  piece, play (theatre)
der **Trickfilm** (-e)  cartoon
die **Vorstellung** (-en)  performance
der **Vorverkauf** (-̈e)  advance booking

## Music

der **Anfänger** (-)  beginner
die **Anlage** (-n)  system
der **Band** (-̈er)  tape
die **CD**  CD
der **Chor** (-̈e)  choir
der **Dirigent** (-en)  conductor
das **Instrument** (-e)  instrument
der **Jazz**  jazz
die **Kapelle** (-n)  band
die **Kassette** (-n)  cassette
der **Kassettenrecorder** (-)  cassette recorder
das **Konzert** (-e)  concert
die **Langspielplatte** (-n)  LP record
das **Lied** (-er)  song
die **Musik**  music
der **Musiker** (-)  musician
die **Oper** (-n)  opera
das **Orchester** (-)  orchestra
die **Platte** (-n)  record
der **Plattenspieler** (-)  record player
die **Popmusik**  pop music
der **Sänger** (-)  singer
die **Schallplatte** (-n)  record
der **Schlager** (-)  hit pop tune
die **Stereoanlage** (-n)  stereo
das **Ton** (-̈e)  sound
das **Tonband** (-̈er)  tape
das **Tonbandgerät** (-e)  tape recorder
der **Walkman** (-s)  walkman

## Instruments

die **Blockflöte** (-n)  recorder
die **Flöte** (-n)  flute
die **Geige** (-n)  violin
die **Gitarre** (-n)  guitar
das **Klavier** (-e)  piano
das **Schlagzeug**  drums
die **Trompete** (-n)  trumpet

## TV

der **Ansager** (-)  announcer
der **Dokumentarfilm** (-e)  documentary
die **Dokumentarsendung**(-en)
  documentary programme
der **Fernsehapparat** (-e)  TV set
die **Nachrichten** (pl)  news
das **Programm** (-e)  channel
der **Regisseur** (-e)  producer
die **Regisseurin** (-nen) (f)  producer
der **Schauspieler** (-)  actor
die **Sendung** (-en)  programme

die **Tagesschau** (-en)  TV News
das **Theater** (-)  theatre
das **Theaterstück** (-e)  play
die **Wetteraussichten**  weather prospects
die **Wettervorhersage** (-n)  weather forecast

## Verbs

sich **amüsieren**  to amuse oneself
**angeln**  to fish
**aufführen** (sep)  to stage, to put on
**aufnehmen** (sep)  to photograph, to record
**basteln**  to make models
**bauen**  to build
**behalten**  to keep
**bergsteigen** (sep)  to climb
**besitzen**  to possess
**biegen**  to bend
**binden**  to tie
**bummeln**  to wander, to stroll
**drehen**  to turn
**erhalten**  to receive, to get
**fernsehen** (sep)  to watch TV
**fischen**  to fish
**fotografieren**  to photograph
**gefallen**  to please
**gehören**  to belong to
**gernhaben** (sep)  to like
**graben**  to dig
**grillen**  to grill, to barbecue
**haben**  to have
sich **interessieren für**  to be interested in
**jäten**  to weed
**kegeln**  to bowl
**kleben**  to stick
**lesen**  to read
**lieber haben**  to prefer
**Lust haben**  to feel like
**machen**  to do, to make
**messen**  to measure
**plaudern**  to chat
**rauchen**  to smoke
**reiten**  to ride
**sammeln**  to collect
**schießen**  to shoot
**Schlittschuh laufen**  to go ice-skating
**schwärmen für**  to be crazy about
**singen**  to sing
**sinken**  to sink
**stricken**  to knit
**tanzen**  to dance
**üben**  to practise
**wandern**  to hike

## Holidays

## On holiday

der **Aufenthalt** (-e)  stay
der **Ausblick** (-e)  view, outlook
der **Ausflug** (-̈e)  excursion
die **Auskunft** (-̈e)  information
die **Aussicht** (-en)  view

der Blick (-e)   view, look
die Broschüre (-n)   brochure
die Fahrt (-en)   journey
die Fahrzeit (-en)   journey times
die Führung (-en)   guided tour
die Grenze (-n)   border
die Herbergseltern (pl)   wardens of youth hostel
die Heimfahrt (-en)   home journey
die Herbstferien (pl)   autumn holidays
im voraus   in advance
die Information (-en)   information
das Inland   inland
die Kontrolle (-n)   check (e.g. at customs)
die Kosten (pl)   the costs
die Miete (-n)   rent
die Osterferien (pl)   Easter Holidays
die Pauschalreise (-n)   package holiday
der Plan (¨e)   plan
die Reise (-n)   journey
der Reiseleiter (-)   guide
die Reiseleiterin (-nen) (f)   guide
der Reisenden (-)   traveller
die Reservierung (-en)   reservation
die Rundfahrt (-en)   tour
die Sonderfahrt (-en)   special excursion
der Sonnenschein   sunshine
die Staatsangehörigkeit (-en)   nationality
die Stadtführung (-en)   guided tour
die Stadtrundfahrt (-en)   tour of the city
der Steward (-e)   steward
die Stewardeß (-essen)   stewardess
der Tourist (-en)   tourist
die Tradition (-en)   tradition
die Weinprobe (-n)   wine-tasting
die Zollerklärung (-en)   customs declaration
die Zollkontrolle (-n)   customs control
der Zuschlag (¨e)   supplement

## Holiday gear

das Andenken (-)   souvenir
die Ansichtskarte (-n)   picture postcard
die Aufname (-n)   photo, recording
der E-111-Schein   E111 certificate
das Foto (-s)   photo
der Fotoapparat (-e)   camera
das Geschenk (-e)   present
die Karte (-n)   card, ticket, map
der Paß (-ässe)   passport
die Postkarte (-n)   postcard
der Prospekt (-e)   brochure
der Proviant   provisions
der Schirm (-e)   umbrella, shade
der Schlafsack (¨e)   sleeping bag
die Sonnenbrille (-n)   sunglasses
die Sonnencreme (-n)   suncream
die Sonnenmilch   suntan lotion
das Sonnenöl (-e)   suntan oil
das Souvenir (-s)   souvenir
der Stadtplan (¨e)   town plan

das Ticket (-s)   (air) ticket
das Visum (Visa or Visen)   visa
der Wohnwagen (-)   caravan

## Places

das Amt (¨er)   office
der Badeort (-e)   seaside resort
das Freibad (¨er)   open-air pool
das Hallenbad (¨er)   indoor pool
das Informationsburo (-s)   information office
der Kurort (-e)   spa
die Unterkunft (¨e)   accommodation
das Verkehrsamt (¨er)   tourist office
die Wechselstube (-n)   bureau de change
die Weinstube (-n)   wine bar
der Zoll (¨e)   customs

## Camping

die Batterie (-n)   battery
das Campinggas   calor gas for camping
der Campingkocher (-)   camping stove
der Campingplatz (¨e)   campsite
die Elektrizität   electricity
das Klo (-s)   toilet
das Streichholz (¨er)   match
das Trinkwasser   drinking water
der Waschraum (¨e)   washroom
das Wasser   water
der Wasserhahn (¨e)   tap
das Zelt (-e)   tent
der Zeltplatz (¨e)   campsite

## In the hotel/youth hostel

der Aufzug (¨e)   lift
DJH   German Youth Hostel Assoc.
das Doppelbett (-en)   double bed
das Doppelzimmer (-)   double room
das Einzelbett (-en)   single bed
das Einzelzimmer (-)   single room
der Fahrstuhl (¨e)   lift
das Fremdenzimmer (-)   room (in guest house)
der Gast (¨e)   guest
der Gastgeber (-)   host
das Gasthaus (häuser)   guest house
der Gasthof (¨e)   hotel
die Gaststätte (-n)   hotel
der Herbergsvater (¨)   youth hostel warden
die Herbergsmutter (¨)   youth hostel warden
das Hotel (-s)   hotel
inklusiv/inkl.   including
die Jugendherberge (-n)   youth hostel
der Lift (-e)   lift
der Luxus   luxury
der Name (-n)   name
die Pension (-en)   guest house
der Schlafraum (¨e)   dormitory
der Schlüssel (-)   key
die Toilette (-n)   toilet

die Übernachtung (-en)   overnight stay
das WC (-s)   WC

## At hotel reception

das Anmeldeformular (-e)   registration form
der Anmeldezettel (-)   booking-in form
die Anmeldung (-en)   booking, registration
der Ausweis (-e)   ID card
der Empfang   reception
die Empfangsdame (-n)   receptionist
das Formular (-e)   form (to be completed)
das Geburtsdatum (-en)   date of birth
der Geburtsort (-e)   place of birth
das Geschlecht (-er)   sex (i.e. male or female)
die Halbpension   half board
die Heimatstadt (-̈e)   home town
das Hotelverzeichnis (-se)   hotel register
der Personalausweis (-e)   personal ID card
die Staatsangehörikeit (-en)   nationality
die Unterschrift (-en)   signature
die Vollpension   full board
der Wohnort (-e)   place of residence
der Wohnsitz (-e)   domicile

## Holiday verbs

abgeben (sep)   to hand in (i.e. lost property)
sich anmelden (sep)   to book in, to report
aufschlagen (sep)   to pitch ( a tent)
aufstellen (sep)   to pitch (a tent)
ausfüllen (sep)   to complete (a form)
sich auskennen (sep)   to know one's way
  around
auspacken (sep)   to unpack
sich ausruhen (sep)   to relax, to rest
baden   to bathe
bemerken   to notice
beobachten   to observe, to watch
besichtigen   to see (the sights)
bleiben   to stay
blicken auf   to look at
buchen   to book
einpacken (sep)   to pack, to wrap
sich entspannen   to relax
sich erkundigen   to enquire
es gibt   there is, there are
faulenzen   to laze about
fließen   to flow
fressen   to eat (animals)
sich freuen auf   to look forward to
führen   to lead
füttern   to feed (animals)
gucken   to look
kauen   to chew
läuten   to sound, to ring
legen   to lay
liegen   to lie
mieten   to hire, to rent
organisieren   to organise
packen   to pack
planen   to plan

reservieren   to reserve
sich sonnen   to sun oneself
spazierengehen (sep)   to go for a walk
suchen   to look for
übernachten   to stay overnight
sich verirren   to get lost
vermieten   to rent out
verzollen   to declare (i.e. at customs)
vorhaben (sep)   to plan
zelten   to camp

## Abstractions

die Angst (-̈e)   fear
die Aushilfe (-n)   help
der Blödsinn   madness, stupidity
die Enttäuschung (-en)   disappointment
die Furcht   fear
das Glück   luck, fortune
die Hoffnung (-en)   hope
die Kraft (-̈e)   strength
das Mitleid   sympathy
die Persönlichkeit (-en)   personality
die Qualität (-en)   quality
die Ruhe   peace, quietness
die Schuld   debt, blame
der Schutz   protection
die Sicherheit   safety
die Sorge (-n)   care, worry
der Stil (-e)   style, way, manner
die Überraschung (-en)   surprise
das Vergnügen (-)   pleasure
die Verzeihung   pardon
die Vorsicht   caution
die Wut   rage, fury
der Zorn   anger

## Expressions

abgemacht!   agreed
Achtung!   careful!
alles Gute!   all the best!
auf Wiedersehen!   goodbye
bitte   please
bzw. (beziehungsweise)   that is to say
der Dank   thanks
danke   thank you
danke schön   thank you very much
das geht   I'm fine
das stimmt   that's right
der wievielte?   what date?
einverstanden   agreed
Entschuldigung!   excuse me!
es hat geklappt   it worked
es kommt darauf an   it depends
es macht nichts   it doesn't matter
es tut mir leid   I'm sorry
gleichfalls   same to you
der Glückwunsch (-̈e)   congratulation
der Gruß (-̈e)   greeting
Grüß Gott!   hello
gute Besserung!   get well soon!

gute Nacht   goodnight
gute Reise!   good trip!
guten Abend!   good evening
guten Appetit!   enjoy your meal!
guten Morgen!   good morning
guten Tag!   good day!
hallo!   hello
herein!   come in!
herzlichen Glückwunsch   congratulations
herzliches Beileid   with deepest sympathy
Hilfe!   help!
ja   yes
jawohl   yes indeed
keine Ahnung!   no idea!
Mahlzeit!   enjoy your meal!
na?   well?
natürlich   of course
nein   no
nichts zu danken   don't mention it
prima!   great!
Prost!   cheers!
Quatsch!   rubbish!
raus!   get out!
Schade!   what a pity!
selbstverständlich   of course
Servus   hello, goodbye
stimmt das?   is that right?
Tschüs!   cheerio
viel Glück   good luck
viel Spaß   have good fun
vielen Dank   many thanks
wie bitte?   I beg your pardon?
wie geht's?   how are you?
wieso?   how do you mean?
wohl   well, I suppose
zum Wohl!   cheers!

## General verbs

sich bedanken   to thank
bedauern   to regret
bedeuten   to mean
beschreiben   to describe
sich beschweren   to complain
bestätigen   to confirm
bitten (um)   to ask for
danken   to thank
sich entschuldigen   to apologise
erklären   to explain
erzählen   to tell, to relate
fragen   to ask
gratulieren   to congratulate
leid tun   to be sorry
loben   to praise
mitteilen (sep)   to communicate, to tell
nicken   to nod
quatschen   to chatter
raten   to advise
sagen   to say
schreien   to shout, to shriek
sprechen   to speak

streiten   to quarrel
sich unterhalten   to chat
versprechen   to promise
vorschlagen (sep)   to suggest

## Adjectives

ärgerlich   annoyed
böse   angry
dankbar   thankful
durstig   thirsty
enttäuscht   disappointed
erschöpft   exhausted
erstaunt   surprised
froh   happy
fröhlich   happy
gespannt   excited
glücklich   happy, fortunate
heiter   cheerful
hoffnungsvoll   hopeful
hungrig   hungry
lieb   dear
müde   tired
nervös   nervous
optimistisch   optimistic
satt   full up, satisfied
schlecht gelaunt   in a bad mood
schwind(e)lig   dizzy
stolz   proud
traurig   sad
überrascht   surprised
unglücklich   unfortunate, unhappy
unzufrieden   unsatisfied
verbunden   thankful, obliged
wütend   furious
zornig   angry
zufrieden   satisfied

## Special occasions

## Occasions

der Adventskranz (¨e)   Advent wreath
die Bescherung (-en)   giving out of
   Christmas presents
der erste Weihnachtstag (-e)   Christmas Day
evangelisch   Protestant
der Fasching (-e)   carnival
der Feiertag (-e)   public holiday
das Fest (-e)   party
die Festspiele (pl)   festival
der Festtag (-e)   special day, holiday
fröhliche Weihnachten   Happy Christmas
der Geburtstag (-e)   birthday
das Geschenk (-e)   present
der Gott (¨er)   God
der Gottesdienst (-e)   church service
der Heilige Abend (-e)   Christmas Eve
das Hoch   toast
die Hochzeit (-en)   wedding
die Kapelle (-n)   chapel
der Karfreitag (-e)   Good Friday
der Karneval (-s)   carnival

**der Katholik (-en)** Catholic man
**die Katholikin (-nen)** Catholic woman
**katholisch** Catholic
**die Kirmes (-sen)** fair
**die Messe (-n)** mass, trade fair
**mit besten, freundlichen Grüßen** with best wishes
**das Neujahr (-e)** New Year
**das Oktoberfest (-e)** Munich Beer Festival
**die Olympischen Spiele** (pl) Olympic Games
**der Osterhase (-n)** Easter Bunny
**der Ostermontag (-e)** Easter Monday
**Ostern** Easter
**der Ostersonntag** Easter Sunday
**Pfingsten** Whit
**der Protestant (-en)** Protestant man
**die Protestantin (-nen)** Protestant woman
**Sankt Nikolaus** Santa Claus
**Silvester** New Year's Eve
**Weihnachten** Christmas
**der Wunsch (¨e)** wish
**der zweite Weihnachtstag** Boxing Day

## Incidents

**das Abenteuer (-)** adventure
**der Brand (¨e)** fire
**der Diebstahl (¨e)** theft
**das Ding (-e)** thing
**das Drama (-en)** drama
**die Drogenszene (-n)** drug scene
**der Fall (¨e)** event, case
**das Feuer (-)** fire
**der Feuerlöscher (-)** fire extinguisher
**der Feuerwehrwagen (-)** fire engine
**die Flamme (-n)** flame
**die Form (-en)** shape
**die Gefahr (-en)** danger
**das Gericht (-e)** court of law
**die Geschichte (-n)** story, tale
**die Hilfe** help
**die Lebensgefahr** danger to life
**die Maske (-n)** mask
**der Mord (-e)** murder
**der Notausgang (¨e)** emergency exit
**der Notfall (¨e)** emergency

**die Papiere** (pl) identity papers
**der Schaden (¨)** damage
**tödlich verunglückt** killed in an accident
**der Unfall (¨e)** accident
**das Unglück (-e)** accident, misfortune
**die Warnung (-en)** warning

## The people

**der Dieb (-e)** thief
**der Einbrecher (-)** burglar
**die Feuerwehr** fire brigade
**die Menge** crowd
**der Notdienst (-e)** emergency service
**die Polizei** police
**der Taschendieb (-e)** pickpocket
**der Verbrecher (-)** criminal

## Verbs

**aufbrechen** (sep) to force open
**brechen** to break
**brennen** to burn
**einbrechen** (sep) to break in
**einfallen** (sep) to collapse
**fallen** to fall
**fallen lassen** to drop
**fassen** to grab, to take hold of
**fehlen** to be missing
**festhalten** (sep) to hold onto
**fliehen** to run away
**gelingen** to succeed
**geschehen** to happen
**hinfallen** (sep) to fall (down)
**klappen** to work out well
**klopfen** to knock, beat, hit
**kontrollieren** to check
**passieren** to happen
**Pech haben** to have bad luck
**schlagen** to hit, to strike
**stehlen** to steal
**sterben** to die
**verlieren** to lose
**vermeiden** to avoid
**verschwinden** to disappear
**vorkommen** (sep) to happen
**zusammenstoßen** (sep) to collide

# 4.6 Area of Experience C – The world around us

## Home town and local area

### The town

**die Allee (-n)** avenue
**die Ampel (-n)** traffic lights
**die Anlage (-n)** park
**das Blumenbeet (-e)** flower bed

**die Brücke (-n)** bridge
**der Brunnen (-)** well, fountain
**der Bürgersteig (-e)** pavement
**die Bushaltestelle (-n)** bus stop
**das Denkmal (¨er)** monument
**die Ecke (-n)** corner
**der Flohmarkt (¨e)** flea market

frisch gestrichen  fresh paint
der Fußgänger (-)  pedestrian
die Fußgängerzone (-n)  pedestrian zone
die Gasse (-n)  lane
der Gehsteig (-e)  pavement
die Glocke (-n)  bell
der Hafen (÷)  port
die Haltestelle (-n)  bus/tram stop
die Hauptstadt (÷e)  capital city
die Innenstadt (÷e)  city centre
der Markt (÷e)  market
der Marktplatz (÷e)  marketplace
die Nähe  vicinity
der Park (-s)  park
die Parkanlage (-n)  park
der Parkplatz (÷e)  car park
der Platz (÷e)  place, square
der Rand (÷er)  edge
die Sackgasse (-n)  cul-de-sac
die Sehenswürdigkeit (-en)  attractions
der Spielplatz (÷e)  playground
die Stadtmitte (-n)  town centre
die Stadt (÷e)  town
das Stadtteil (-e)  part of a town, quarter
das Stadtwappen (-)  municipal coat of arms
das Stadtzentrum  town centre
die Stockung (-en)  traffic jam
die Straße (-n)  street
die Umgebung (-en)  surroundings
die Unterführung (-en)  subway, underpass
der Verkehr  traffic
der Vorort (-e)  suburb
die Vorstadt (÷e)  suburb
der Zeitungsstand (÷e)  newspaper stand
das Zentrum (Zentren)  centre

## The buildings

die Altstadt (÷e)  old town
die Bibliothek (-en)  library
die Burg (-en)  castle
der Dom (-e)  cathedral
das Fundamt (÷er)  lost-property office
das Gebäude (-)  building
die Kirche (-n)  church
das Münster (-)  cathedral
das Museum (-een)  museum
die Polizeiwache (-n)  police station
das Rathaus (÷er)  town hall
das Revier (-e)  police station
das Schloß (÷sser)  castle
der Turm (÷e)  tower
das Wirtshaus (häuser)  pub, tavern

## The shops

die Apotheke (-n)  chemist's
die Bäckerei (-en)  bakery
die Bücherei (-en)  bookshop
die Buchhandlung (-en)  bookshop
die Drogerie (-n)  drugstore
die Konditorei (-en)  cake shop

der Laden (÷)  shop
das Lebensmittelgeschäft (-e)  grocer's
die Metzgerei (-en)  butcher's
die Reinigung (-en)  cleaner's
das Reisebüro (-s)  travel agent
das Schreibwarengeschäft (-e)  stationer's
die Schreibwarenhandlung (-en)  stationer's
das Sportgeschäft (-e)  sports shop
der Supermarkt (÷e)  supermarket
die Wechselstube (-n)  bureau de change

## Shopping

das Angebot (-e)  offer
der Artikel (-)  article
der Ausverkauf (÷e)  sale
die Auswahl (-en)  selection, choice
der Automat (-en)  vending machine
der Beutel (-)  bag
die Büchse (-n)  tin, can
die Dose (-n)  tin
die Einkaufsliste (-n)  shopping list
der Einkaufswagen (-)  shopping trolley
einschließlich  inclusive, included
die Ermäßigung (-en)  reduction (in cost)
die Garantie (-n)  guarantee
die Gebrauchsanweisung (-en)  instructions for use
die Gebühr (-en)  fee, charge
das Geld (-er)  money
die Geldrückgabe (-n)  money back
das Gerät (-e)  appliance
die Geschäftszeiten (pl)  business hours
die Größe (-n)  size
haltbar bis  use by (the sell-by date)
die Kanne (-n)  can
die Kasse (-n)  check-out
der Kiosk (-e)  kiosk
die Konfektion (-en)  clothing (ready to wear)
kostenlos  free of charge
der Kunde (-n)  client, customer
die Kundin (-nen) (f)  client, customer
die Lebensmittel (pl)  food
die Liste (-n)  list
das macht ...  that makes ...
die Marke (-n)  brand, make
die Mehrwertsteuer/MwSt  VAT
die Mode (-n)  fashion
die Öffnungszeiten (pl)  opening times
das Pfand (÷er)  deposit on bottle
der Preis (-e)  price
die Quittung (-en)  receipt
die Rolltreppe (-n)  escalator
die Scheibe (-n)  slice
die Schlange (-n)  queue, tail
der Schlußverkauf (÷e)  closing-down sale
die Selbstbedienung  self-service
der Sommerschlußverkauf (÷e)  end-of-summer sale
das Sonderangebot (-e)  special offer

**der Sonderpreis (–e)** special price
**die Tasche (–n)** bag
**die Theke (–n)** counter
**die Tüte (–n)** bag
**umsonst** free
**die Ware (–n)** product, goods

## Adjectives

**alkoholfrei** non-alcoholic
**altmodisch** out of date
**ausverkauft** sold out
**billig** cheap
**bitter** bitter
**erhältlich** obtainable
**fett** fatty
**frei** free
**frisch** fresh
**gebacken** baked
**gebraten** roast, baked, fried
**gebührenpflichtig** fee payable
**gemischt** mixed
**geöffnet** open
**geschlossen** closed
**gestreift** striped
**getrennt** separate (paying bill)
**gratis** free of charge
**kariert** checked
**klassisch** classical
**kostbar** expensive
**köstlich** costly
**offen** open
**preiswert** cheap, good value
**schick** elegant, chic
**silbern** silver
**süß** sweet
**teuer** expensive
**wert** worth
**wertvoll** valuable
**zollfrei** duty-free

## Places

**die Abteilung (–en)** department (e.g. in shop)
**die Bude (–n)** stall (market)
**das Einkaufszentrum (–en)** shopping centre
**das Erdgeschoß (–sse)** ground floor
**die Etage (–n)** storey, floor
**die Fußgängerzone (–n)** pedestrian precinct
**das Kaufhaus (¨er)** department store
**das Obergeschoß (–sse)** upper floor
**das Schaufenster (–)** shop window
**der Stock** floor, storey
**das Stockwerk (–e)** floor, storey
**die Umkleidekabine (–n)** fitting room
**das Warenhaus (häuser)** department store

## Shopping verbs

**anprobieren** (sep) to try on
**sich bedienen** to serve yourself
**einführen** (sep) to insert

**einkassieren** (sep) to collect (e.g. money)
**Einkäufe machen** to go shopping
**einkaufen** to shop
**kassieren** to collect (e.g. money)
**kosten** to cost
**kriegen** to get
**öffnen** to open
**passen** to suit
**probieren** to try out
**in Raten zahlen** to pay by instalments
**schieben** to push
**Schlange stehen** to stand in a queue
**speichern** to store
**sich umsehen** (sep) to look round
**verkaufen** to sell
**zahlen** to pay
**ziehen** to pull
**zuhaben** (sep) to be closed
**zumachen** (sep) to close

## At the Post Office

**der Absender (–)** sender (e.g. of letter)
**die Anschrift (–en)** address (on letter)
**der Brief (–e)** letter
**der Briefkasten (¨)** letter-box
**die Briefmarke (–n)** stamp
**der Briefumschlag (¨e)** envelope
**der Eilbrief (–e)** express letter
**der Einwurf (¨e)** slot for letters/coins
**der Empfänger (–)** recipient, addressee
**die Leerung (–en)** collection of mail
**die Luftpost** airmail
**das Päckchen (–)** packet
**die Packung (–en)** packet
**das Paket (–e)** parcel
**die Post** post office
**das Postamt (¨er)** post office
**die Postanweisung (–en)** postal order
**das Postleitzahl (–en)** post code
**das Postwertzeichen (–)** stamp
**das Schließfach (¨er)** PO box
**der Stempel (–)** rubber stamp
**das Telegramm (–e)** telegram
**der Umschlag (¨e)** envelope

## At the bank

**die Anweisung (–en)** payment
**die Bank (–en)** bank
**die Banknote (–n)** banknote
**DM** German Mark
**der Euroscheck (–s)** Eurocheque
**der Franken** Swiss franc
**das Geld (–er)** money
**der Geldwechsel (–)** currency exchange
**der Groschen (–)** 10 Pfennig coin
**das Konto (–s)** account
**die Kreditkarte (–n)** credit card
**der Kurs (¨e)** rate of exchange
**die Mark** German Mark
**das Markstück (–e)** Mark coin

die Münze (-n)   coin
der Pfennig (-e)   Pfennig
das Pfund (-e)   pound
der Rappen (-)   Swiss centime
der Reisescheck (-s)   travellers cheque
der Scheck (-s)   cheque
die Scheckkarte (-n)   cheque card
der Schein (-e)   bank-note
der Schilling (-e)   shilling
die Sparkasse (-n)   savings bank

## Bank verbs

ausgeben (sep)   to spend (money)
einlösen (sep)   to cash (cheque)
einzahlen (sep)   to pay in (into an account)
leihen   to lend
lösen   to cash, to buy (tickets)
sparen   to save
unterschreiben   to sign
verdienen   to earn
wechseln   to change

## The natural and made environment

## Environment

der Bach (¨e)   stream, brook
der Bauernhof (¨e)   farm
der Berg (-e)   mountain
das Blatt (¨er)   leaf (of tree)
das Dorf (¨er)   village
der Dschungel (-)   jungle
die Erde   earth
das Feld (-er)   field
der Fluß (Flüsse)   river
das Flußufer (-)   river bank
der Föhn (-e)   foehn (wind)
das Gebirge (-)   mountain range
die Gegend (-en)   area
das Gift (-e)   poison
der Gipfel (-)   summit, peak
die Großstadt (¨e)   large city
der Grund (¨e)   ground
das Heu   hay
der Himmel   sky, heaven
das Hochgebirge   high mountains
der Hügel (-)   hill
das Industriegebiet (-e)   industrial area
die Industriestadt (¨e)   industrial town
die Insel (-n)   island
die Jahreszeit (-en)   season of year
die Kohle (-n)   coal
das Korn (¨er)   seed, grain
das Land (¨er)   country
die Landschaft (-en)   countryside
die Luft   air
das Mittelgebirge   low mountain range
der Mond (-e)   moon
die Natur   nature
der Ort (-e)   place
die Ortschaft (-en)   village, town

der Pfad (-e)   path
die Quelle (-n)   source
der Rauch   smoke
der See (-n)   lake
die See (-n)   sea
der Sonnenaufgang (¨e)   sunrise
der Sonnenuntergang (¨e)   sunset
die Spitze (-n)   summit
der Steig (-e)   steep track
der Stern (-e)   star
der Strom (¨e)   large river
das Tal (¨er)   valley
der Tannenbaum (bäume)   fir tree
die Tiefebene (-n)   lowland plain
der Tropfen (-)   drop (e.g. water)
das Ufer (-)   river bank
die Umwelt   environment
der Wald (¨er)   forest
die Welt (-en)   world
die Wiese (-n)   meadow

## Animals

der Affe ( n)   monkey, ape
der Bär (-en)   bear
die Biene (-n)   bee
der Elefant (-en)   elephant
die Ente (-n)   duck
die Gans (¨e)   goose
das Huhn (¨er)   hen
das Insekt (-en)   insect
das Krokodil (-e)   crocodile
die Kuh (¨e)   cow
der Löwe (-n)   lion
die Maus (¨e)   mouse
die Mücke (-n)   mosquito
das Nilpferd (-e)   hippo
das Pferd (-e)   horse
der Pinguin (-e)   penguin
die Ratte (-n)   rat
das Schaf (-e)   sheep
der Schmetterling (-e)   butterfly
das Schwein (-e)   pig
die Spinne (-n)   spider
das Tier (-e)   animal
der Tiger (-)   tiger
das Vieh   livestock
der Vogel (¨)   bird
die Wespe (-n)   wasp

## At the seaside

die Ebbe (-n)   low tide
der Eimer (-)   bucket
die Flut (-en)   high tide
der Kai (-s)   quay
die Küste (-n)   coast
die Luftmatratze (-n)   airbed
das Meer (-e)   sea
der Sand   sand
der Strand (¨e)   beach
das Strandbad (¨er)   seawater swimming pool

**die Tide (-n)** tide
**die Welle (-n)** wave

## The colours

**blau** blue
**braun** brown
**die Farbe (-n)** colour
**gelb** yellow
**grau** grey
**grün** green
**hell** bright
**lila** lilac, mauve
**orange** orange
**rosa** pink
**rot** red
**schwarz** black
**türkis** turquoise
**weiß** white

## Adjectives

**flach** flat
**gefährlich** dangerous
**gerade** straight
**glitschig** slippy, slippery
**hoch** high, tall
**höher** higher
**steil** steep
**still** quiet
**tief** deep
**umweltfeindlich** ecologically harmful
**umweltfreundlich** eco-friendly
**weit** far

## Situations

**auf dem Lande** in the country
**an Bord** on board
**da** there
**daher** from there
**dahin** there
**dort** there
**dort drüben** over there
**dorthin** there
**draußen** outside
**drinnen** inside
**drüben** over there
**fort** away
**geradeaus** straight on
**heim** home
**her** towards the speaker
**hier** here
**hin** away from the speaker
**hinein** in
**hinten** behind
**irgendwo** somewhere or other
**links** left
**die Mitte (-n)** middle
**mitten** in the middle
**nach Hause** (to) home
**in der Nähe von** in the vicinity of
**nirgendwo** nowhere

**oben** above, upstairs
**quer** at right angles
**rechts** right
**rückwärts** backwards
**der Schatten (-)** shadow
**überall** everywhere
**unten** below, downstairs
**unterwegs** on the way
**vorne** at the front
**vorwärts** forwards
**weg** away
**weiter** further
**zu Fuß** on foot
**zu Hause** at home
**zurück** back

## Compass locations

**der Norden** north
**der Osten** east
**der Süden** south
**der Westen** west

## How much?

**etwa** approximately, about
**fast** almost
**ganz** quite, very
**gar nicht** not at all
**insgesamt** altogether, all in all
**kaum** scarcely
**mehr** more
**mindestens** at least
**minus** minus
**nur** only
**soviel** as much, so much
**überhaupt** on the whole
**ungefähr** about, approximately
**völlig** completely
**wenig** little
**wenigstens** at least
**wieder** again
**ziemlich** quite

## How?

**allein** alone
**am besten** best
**am liebsten** best of all, most of all
**auch** also
**außer Betrieb** out of order
**besonders** especially
**genau** exactly
**genauso** just
**gern** willingly
**glücklicherweise** fortunately
**hoffentlich** hopefully
**langsam** slowly
**leider** unfortunately
**leise** softly, gently
**schnell** quickly
**sehr** very
**total** totally

**unbedingt** absolutely
**ungern** reluctantly
**vor allem** above all
**wahrscheinlich** probably
**wirklich** really
**zufällig** by chance
**zusammen** together

## When?

**anschließend** afterwards
**auf einmal** all at once, at the same time
**bald** soon
**der Beginn (-e)** beginning
**damals** then, at that time
**danach** afterwards
**dann** then
**das Datum (-en)** date
**diesmal** this time
**eines Tages** one day
**einmal** once
**endlich** at last
**erst** first, firstly
**erst** not until, only
**früh** early
**gestern** yesterday
**gleich** immediately
**heute** today
**heutzutage** nowadays
**immer** always
**immer noch** still
**inzwischen** meanwhile
**irgendwann** sometime or other
**jetzt** now
**jeweils** each time
**lange** for a long time
**das Mal (-e)** time
**meistens** mostly
**der Mittag (-e)** midday
**Mitternacht (-e)** midnight
**morgen** tomorrow
**nachdem** after
**nachher** afterwards
**neulich** recently
**noch** still, yet
**nochmal** again
**noch nicht** not yet
**nochmals** again
**plötzlich** suddenly
**pünktlich** punctual
**schließlich** finally
**schon** already
**sofort** immediately
**sogleich** straight away
**spät** late
**später** later
**übermorgen** day after tomorrow
**vor kurzem** a short time ago
**vorgestern** day before yesterday
**die Weile (-n)** while
**wenn** when

**die Zeit (-en)** time
**zuerst** at first
**zunächst** at first
**zur Zeit** at the time

## How long?

**der Abend (-e)** evening
**der Alltag (-e)** weekday
**der Augenblick (-e)** moment
**das Jahr (-e)** year
**das Jahrhundert (-e)** century
**die Minute (-n)** minute
**der Moment (-e)** moment
**der Monat (-e)** month
**der Morgen (-)** morning
**der Nachmittag (-e)** afternoon
**die Nacht (-e)** night
**die Sekunde (-n)** second
**die Stunde (-n)** hour
**der Tag (-e)** day
**die Viertelstunde (-n)** quarter of an hour
**der Vormittag (-e)** morning
**die Woche (-n)** week
**das Wochenende (-n)** weekend

## How often?

**abends** in the evening
**gewöhnlich** usually
**jährlich** yearly
**manchmal** sometimes
**mittags** at lunchtimes, at midday
**monatlich** monthly
**morgens** in the mornings
**nachmittags** in the afternoons
**nachts** at night
**normalerweise** normally
**oft** often
**regelmäßig** regular
**selten** rarely
**stündlich** hourly
**täglich** daily
**vormittags** in the mornings
**werktags** on working days
**wochentags** on weekdays
**wöchentlich** weekly

## Adjectives

**häufig** frequent
**monatelang** lasting for months
**rechtzeitig** punctual
**stundenlang** lasting several hours

## The weather

**der Blitz (-e)** lightning
**Celsius** Celsius, centigrade
**der Donner (-)** thunder
**das Eis** ice
**es donnert** there is lightning
**es regnet** it's raining
**es schneit** it's snowing

der Frost (¨e)   frost
das Gewitter (-)   thunderstorm
der Grad (-e)   degree
der Hagel   hail
die Hitze (-n)   heat
die Höchsttemperatur (-en)   highest
   temperature
die Kälte   cold
das Klima (-s)   climate
die Nässe   damp, wet
der Nebel (-)   fog
der Niederschlag (¨e)   precipitation
der Regen   rain
der Schauer (-)   shower
der Schnee   snow
die Sonne (-n)   sun
der Sturm (¨e)   storm
die Temperatur (-en)   temperature
das Tief (-s)   depression
die Tiefsttemperatur (-en)   lowest
   temperature
das Wetter   weather
der Wetterbericht (-e)   weather report
die Wettervorhersage (-n)   weather forecast
der Wind (-e)   wind
die Wolke (-n)   cloud

## Weather adjectives

bedeckt   cloudy, overcast
bewölkt   cloudy
dunkel   dark
feucht   damp
heiß   hot
kalt   cold
kühl   cool
mild   mild
naß   wet
neblig   foggy
niedrig   low
nördlich   northerly
östlich   easterly
regnerisch   rainy
schwül   sultry
sonnig   sunny
stürmisch   stormy
südlich   southerly
trocken   dry
warm   warm
wechselhaft   changeable
westlich   westerly
windig   windy
wolkenlos   cloudless
wolkig   cloudy

## Weather verbs

blitzen   to flash (lightning)
donnern   to thunder
frieren   to be cold, to freeze
regnen   to rain
scheinen   to shine

schneien   to snow

## Shapes and sizes

breit   wide
eng   narrow
enorm   enormous
klein   small
kurz   short
lang   long
mittelgroß   of average height
rund   round
schmal   narrow

## People
## Positive adjectives

am liebsten   favourite
ausgezeichnet   excellent
befriedigend   satisfactory
berühmt   famous
besser   better
beste (r,s)   best (superlative of good)
echt   genuine, real
erfolgreich   successful
fabelhaft   splendid
fein   fine
günstig   favourable
gut   good
herrlich   wonderful
klasse   terrific
lecker   delicious
merkwürdig   remarkable
nett   nice
phantastisch   fantastic
rein   clean
sauber   clean
sehenswert   worth seeing
selbständig   independent
sicher   certain, safe
toll   super
wahr   true
wunderbar   wonderful
wunderschön   wonderful

## Negative adjectives

beschädigt   damaged
dreckig   dirty
drogenabhängig   addicted
falsch   false, incorrect
furchtbar   terrible
fürchterlich   terrible
giftig   poisonous
kaputt   broken
kompliziert   complicated
mangelhaft   defective, weak
mies   rotten, lousy
sauer   sour
scheußlich   dreadful
schlecht   bad
schlimm   bad

schrecklich   awful
schwach   weak
verdammt   damned
vergebens   of no avail

## Physical adjectives

ähnlich   similar
alt   old
anders (als)   different (from)
anstrengend   strenuous
bereit   ready
bunt   bright
deutlich   clear
dringend   urgent
eben   just, flat
egal   equal, same
fertig   ready
fließend   fluent
fremd   strange, foreign
geboren (geb.)   born

genau   exact
glatt   smooth
golden   golden
groß   big
hart   hard
historisch   historical
kinderleicht   childishly simple
klar   obvious
komisch   amusing, strange
laut   loud
leer   empty
leicht   light, easy
normal   normal
scharf   sharp
seltsam   strange
spannend   exciting
typisch   typical
unglaublich   unbelievable
voll   full
wach   awake

# 4.7  Area of Experience D – The world of work

## Job applications
### Work

die Aktentasche (-n)   briefcase
die Arbeit (-en)   work
das Arbeitspraktikum (-praktika)   work experience
die Ausbildung (-en)   training
der Beruf (-e)   profession
der Berufswunsch (-e)   choice of job
die Bewerbung (-en)   job application
das Berwerbungsformular (-e)   application form
die Bezahlung (-en)   pay, payment
die Bildung   education
die Chance (-n)   chance, opportunity
der Computer (-)   computer
das Diplom (-e)   diploma
der Eindruck (-e)   impression
der Feierabend (-e)   end of work, evening
das Geld (-er)   money
die Gelegenheit (-en)   opportunity
die Genehmigung (-en)   approval, permit
halbtags   half-day/part-time
der Handel   trade
der Job (-s)   job
der Kurs (-e)   course
der Lebenslauf (-e)   curriculum vitae
die Lehre (-n)   apprenticeship
die Litfaßsäule (-n)   advertising column
die Möglichkeit (-en)   possibility
die Qualifikation (-en)   qualification
der Ruhetag (-e)   day off
die Schreibmaschine (-n)   typewriter
die Stelle (-n)   place, job

die Stellenanzeige (-n)   job advertisement
der Streik (-s)   strike
der Tarif (-e)   price, rate
der Tourismus   tourism
der Umtausch (-e)   exchange
der Werktag (-e)   working day
der Wochentag (-e)   week day

### The people

der Arbeitgeber (-)   employer
der Arbeitnehmer (-)   employee
der Chef (-s)   boss
Sehr geehrte Damen und Herren   Dear sir/madam
Sehr geehrter Herr Kurz!   Dear Mr. Kurz
der Kollege (-n)   colleague
die Kollegin (-nen) (f)   colleague
der Lehrling (-e)   apprentice

### Places

der Betrieb (-e)   factory, firm
das Büro (-s)   office
die Fabrik (-en)   factory
die Firma (-en)   firm
das Geschäft (-e)   shop, business
die Handlung (-en)   business, trade
die Industrie (-n)   industry
die Werkstatt (-en)   workshop

### Verbs relating to work

abschicken (sep)   to send off
annehmen (sep)   to accept
arbeiten   to work
ausrichten (sep)   to organise, to deliver
austragen (sep)   to deliver (i.e. letters)

**behandeln**  to deal with
**beilegen** (sep)  to enclose
**sich bewerben**  to apply (for a job)
**bezahlen**  to pay
**einschreiben** (sep)  to send recorded delivery
**einwerfen** (sep)  to post, to put in slot
**funktionieren**  to work (i.e. to function)
**gebrauchen**  to use
**kündigen**  to hand in one's notice
**lehren**  to teach
**operieren**  to operate
**programmieren**  to programme
**schicken**  to send
**sein**  to be
**senden**  to send
**streiken**  to strike
**tippen**  to type
**unterrichten**  to teach
**werden**  to become
**zählen**  to count
**zeichnen**  to draw

## Jobs

**der/die Angestellte (-n)**  employee
**der Apotheker (-)**  chemist
**der Arbeiter (-)**  worker
**der Assistent (-en)**  assistant
**der Babysitter (-s)**  babysitter
**der Bäcker (-)**  baker
**der Bauer (-n)**  farmer
**die Bäuerin (-nen)**  farmer's wife
**der Beamte (-n)**  official, civil servant
**der Briefträger (-)**  postman
**der Detektiv (-e)**  detective
**der Dolmetscher (-)**  interpreter
**der Drogist (-en)**  chemist
**der Elektriker (-)**  electrician
**der Fabrikarbeiter (-)**  factory worker
**der Fahrer (-)**  driver
**der Feuerwehrmann (¨er)**  fireman
**der Fleischer (-)**  butcher
**der Fotograf (-en)**  photographer
**der Friseur (-e)**  hairdresser
**der Geschäftsmann (¨er)**  business man
**der Handarbeiter (-)**  manual worker
**der Händler (-)**  tradesman, dealer
**der Handwerker (-)**  skilled manual worker
**die Hausfrau (-en)**  housewife
**der Ingenieur (-e)**  engineer
**der Journalist (-en)**  journalist
**der Juwelier (-e)**  jeweller
**der Kassierer (-)**  cashier
**die Kassiererin (-nen)** (f)  cashier
**die Kauffrau (-en)**  businesswoman
**der Kaufmann (¨er)**  businessman
**der Kinderpfleger (-)**  children's nurse
**der Konditor (-en)**  pastry cook
**die Krankenschwester (-n)**  female nurse
**der Künstler (-)**  artist
**der Landarbeiter (-)**  agricultural worker
**der Lehrer (-)**  teacher

**der Maler (-)**  painter
**die Malerin (-nen)** (f)  painter
**der Mechaniker (-)**  mechanic
**der Metzger (-)**  butcher
**der Pilot (-en)**  pilot
**der Rentner (-)**  pensioner
**der Schauspieler (-)**  actor
**der Schneider (-)**  tailor
**der Sekretär (-e)**  secretary
**die Sekretärin (-nen)** (f)  secretary
**der Soldat (-en)**  soldier
**der Taxifahrer (-)**  taxi driver
**der Verkäufer (-)**  salesman
**der Vertreter (-)**  representative
**der Zahnarzt (¨e)**  dentist
**das Zimmermädchen (-)**  maid

## Adjectives

**aktuell**  current
**angestellt**  on the staff
**arbeitslos**  unemployed
**beruflich**  professional
**berufstätig**  employed
**beschäftigt**  busy
**bürgerlich**  civil
**möglich**  possible
**nötig**  necessary
**notwendig**  necessary
**städtisch**  municipal
**technisch**  technical
**unmöglich**  impossible
**wichtig**  important

## Communication

### The telephone

**der Anruf (-e)**  phone call
**der Anrufbeantworter (-)**  answerphone
**am Apparat**  speaking!
**der Apparat (-e)**  phone
**auf Wiederhören**  good bye
**besetzt**  occupied, engaged
**bleiben Sie am Apparat!**  hold the line!
**das Ferngespräch (-e)**  long-distance call
**der Fernsprecher (-)**  public phone
**der Hörer (-)**  receiver
**die Kabine (-n)**  booth
**das Kleingeld**  small change
**der Notruf (-e)**  emergency call
**die Nummer (-n)**  number
**das Ortsgespräch (-e)**  local call
**das Telefon (-e)**  telephone
**das Telefonbuch (¨er)**  phone book
**die Telefonkabine (-n)**  phone kiosk
**die Telefonnummer (-n)**  phone number
**die Telefonzelle (-n)**  phone box
**die Vorwahl (-en)**  dialling code
**die Vorwahlnummer (-n)**  code

### Telephone verbs

**anrufen** (sep)  to phone

aufheben (sep)   to pick up (receiver)
auflegen (sep)   to replace (receiver)
sich melden   to answer the phone
rufen   to call
telefonieren   to phone
wählen   to dial

## Useful IT vocabulary

Abenteuerspiel (n)   adventure game
Sicherheitskopie (f)/Backup (n)   back-up
fett   bold (print style)
booten/starten   boot
blättern/Datei durchgehen   browsing
Pufferspeicher (m)   buffer memory
Fehler (m)/Bug (m)   bug
Computer-unterstütztes Lernen   Computer
    Assisted Learning
Verbrauchsmaterial (n)   consumable (paper
    etc.)
Positionsanzeiger (m)/Schreibmarke (f)
    cursor
Ausschneiden und Einfügen   cut and paste
Datum (n)/Datensatz (m)   datum
Datenbank (f)   database
debuggen/Fehler beseitigen/Fehler suchen
    debug
löschen   delete
digital   digital
digitalisieren   digitise
(Inhalts)verzeichnis (n)   directory
Diskettensystem/Betriebssystem (n)   Disc
    Operating System (DOS)
(Disketten)laufwerk (n)   disc drive
(an)zeigen/darstellen   display
ausgeben (in Rohform)/dumpen   dump (to
    print out a screen)
editieren/aufbereiten (zum Ausdruck)   edit
Aufbereitung (f)/Gestaltung (f) (des Textes)
    editing
Lernprogramm (n)   educational software
elektronische Post (f)   electronic mail
fernkopieren (sep)/faxen   fax
Feld (n)/Datensatz (m)   field (on database)
Datei (f)   file
Diskette (f)   floppy disc
formatieren   format
Spielprogramm (n)/Spielsoftware (f)
    games software
Hardcopy (f)/(Bildschirm)ausdruck (m)
    hard copy
Festplatte (f)   hard disc
Hardware (f)   hardware
hervorheben (sep)/inverse Darstellung (f)
    highlighting
Informatik (f)/Info'technologie (f)
    information technology
Eingabe (f)   input
interaktiv   interactive
Interface (n)/Schnittstelle (f)   interface
Joystick (n)   joystick
Taste (f)   key
Tastatur (f)   keyboard

Stichwort (n)/Schlüsselbegriff (m)   keyword
(auf)listen (sep)   list
laden   load (a computer program)
Menü (n)/Benutzerführung (f)   menu
mischen/(Daten)verknüpfen/
    zusammenführen (sep)   merge
Mikrochip (m)/IC (m)   microchip
Mikrocomputer/Computer (m)
    microcomputer
Modem (n)   modem
Bildschirm (m)/Monitor (m)   monitor
Maus (f)   mouse
fast korrespondenzfähige
    Druckqualität (f)   Near Letter Quality
    (NLQ)
Korrespondenzfähigkeit (f) Netz (n)/
    Netzwerk (n)   network
off-line   off-line
Bürotechnik (f)   office technology
on-line   on-line
Ausgabe (f)   output
Paket (n)   package
Passwort (n)   password
Peripheriegerät (n)   peripheral (printer etc.)
Tortendiagramm (n)/Kuchendiagramm (n)
    pie chart
Drucker (m)   printer
Druckertreiber (m)   printer driver
Programm (n)   program
Prompt (n)/Eingabeaufforderung (f)/
    Systemanfrage (f)   prompt
Schreiblesespeicher (m)/Speicher (m) mit
    wahlfreiem Zugriff/Arbeitsspeicher (m)
    Random Access Memory (RAM)
Festwertspeicher (ROM) (m)/
    Nur-Lesespeicher (m)   Read Only
    Memory (ROM)
Record (n)/Datensatz (m)   record (database)
speichern/sichern   save
Bildschirm (m)   screen
Bildschirmanzeige (f)   screen display
scröllen (Bild hochschieben)/rollen
    scrolling
Programm (n)/Software (f)   software
Tabellenkalkulation(sprogramm (n)) (f)
    spreadsheet
Stapel (m), Einschub (m)   stack (Apple
    Hypercard)
Zeichenfolge (f)   string
Telekommunikation (f)   telecommunications
Bildschirmtext (m)/BTX (m)   viewdata
    system
Textfenster (n)/Grafikfenster (n)
    text/graphics window
Traktor (m) (für Papiervorschieb)/
    Traktoreinzug (m)   tractor feed
Hilfsprogramm (n)/Utility (n)   utility
Bildschirmtextterminal (m) or (n)   viewdata
    terminal
Sprachsynthesizer/elektronische Stimme
    voice synthesiser
Textverarbeitung (f)   word processing

# 4.8 Area of Experience E – The international world

## Tourism at home and abroad

### Transport

**die Abfahrt (en)** departure
**der Abflug (-̈e)** departure of flights
**die Abreise (-n)** departure
**die Ankunft (-̈e)** arrival
**der Ausstieg (-e)** exit (i.e. on a bus)
**die Dauer** duration
**der Einstieg (-e)** entrance (i.e. onto a bus)
**die Entfernung (-en)** distance
**der Fahrausweis (-e)** ticket
**das Fahrgeld (-er)** fare
**die Fahrkarte (-n)** ticket
**der Fahrplan (-̈e)** timetable
**der Fahrpreis (-e)** fare
**der Fahrschein (-e)** ticket
**der Flug (-̈e)** flight
**der Flughafen (-̈)** airport
**der Flugplatz (-̈e)** airfield, airport
**die Hafenstadt (-̈e)** port
**die Haltestelle (-n)** bus/tram stop
**die Hauptstraße (-n)** main road
**die Hauptverkehrszeit (-en)** rush hour
**der Kanal (-̈e)** canal
**der Koffer (-)** suitcase
**das Kreuz (-e)** cross, intersection
**öffentliche Verkehrsmittel** public transport
**die Richtung (-en)** direction
**die Rückgabe** return of luggage
**der Taxistand (-̈e)** taxi rank
**die Uhrzeit (-en)** clock time
**die Verspätung (-en)** delay
**zugestiegen** to have got on a bus, train, etc

### The people

**der Busfahrer (-)** bus passenger
**der Fluggast (-̈e)** airline passenger
**der Nichtraucher (-)** non-smoker
**der Passagier (-e)** passenger
**der Radfahrer (-)** cyclist

### Vehicles

**das Boot (-e)** boat
**der Bus (-sse)** bus
**der Dampfer (-)** steamer
**die Fähre (-n)** ferry
**das Fahrrad (-̈er)** bicycle
**das Fahrzeug (-e)** vehicle
**das Flugzeug (-e)** aeroplane
**der Lastwagen (-)** lorry
**der LKW (-s)** lorry
**die Maschine (-n)** machine, plane
**das Mofa (-s)** moped
**das Motorrad (-̈er)** motorbike
**der Reisebus (-se)** coach
**das Schiff (-e)** ship
**die Straßenbahn (-en)** tram
**das Taxi (-s)** taxi

### Travel verbs

**abbiegen** (sep) to turn, to turn off (a road)
**abfahren** (sep) to depart
**abfliegen** (sep) to fly, to take off
**abreisen** (sep) to leave
**per Anhalter fahren** to hitch-hike
**ankommen** (sep) to arrive
**aussteigen** (sep) to get off/out
**per Autostop fahren** to hitch-hike
**dauern** to last
**einsteigen** (sep) to get on/in
**entwerten** to cancel ( a ticket)
**fahren** to go, to travel
**kommen** to come
**landen** to land
**losfahren** (sep) to set off
**reisen** to travel
**trampen** to hitch-hike
**umsteigen** (sep) to change (e.g. train)
**umtauschen** (sep) to exchange
**verpassen** to miss (e.g. a bus)
**verreisen** to go away
**warten** to wait
**sich zurechtfinden** (sep) to find one's way
**zurückfahren** (sep) to return, to drive back
**zurückkehren** (sep) to return
**zurückkommen** (sep) to come back

### Cars

**ADAC** German equivalent of AA
**das Auto (-s)** car
**die Autowäsche (-n)** carwash
**die Baustelle (-n)** building site, roadworks
**das Benzin** petrol
**der Diesel** diesel
**der Fahrgast (-̈e)** passenger
**der Führerschein (-e)** driving licence
**die Geldstrafe (-n)** spot fine
**das Glatteis** ice (on roads)
**die Landkarte (-n)** map
**der Luftdruck** air pressure
**das Normalbenzin** regular petrol
**das Öl** oil
**die Panne (-n)** breakdown
**das Parkhaus (-̈er)** multi-storey car park
**der Parkschein (-e)** parking ticket
**die Parkuhr (-en)** parking meter
**das Parkverbot** no parking
**der PKW (-s)** car
**der Rasthof (-̈e)** service station
**die Raststätte (-n)** service station
**der Reifendruck** tyre pressure

**die Reifenpanne (-n)** puncture
**die Reparatur (-en)** repair
**die Reparaturwerkstatt (¨en)** car repairers
**SB** self-service
**das Schild (-er)** sign
**selbsttanken** self-service for fuel
**die Sperre (-n)** barrier
**der Stau (-s)** traffic jam
**die Strafe (-n)** fine, punishment
**das Strafgeld (-er)** fine
**Super verbleit** 4-star petrol (leaded)
**das Superbenzin** 4-star petrol
**die Tankstelle (-n)** petrol station
**der Tankwart (-e)** petrol attendant
**unverbleit** unleaded
**der Verkehr** traffic
**die Versicherung (-en)** insurance
**der Wagen (-)** car

## Roads

**Anlieger frei** residents only
**die Ausfahrt (-en)** exit (e.g. on motorway)
**die Autobahn (-en)** motorway
**die Durchfahrt (-en)** way through
**der Durchgang (¨e)** thoroughfare
**die Einbahnstraße (-n)** one-way street
**die Hauptstraße (-n)** main road
**die Kreuzung (-en)** crossing
**die Kurve (-n)** curve, bend
**die Landstraße (-n)** country road
**die Überfahrt (-en)** crossing
**der Übergang (¨e)** crossing
**die Umleitung (-en)** diversion
**die Vorfahrt (-en)** right of way
**die Zufahrt (-en)** approach road

## Car parts

**die Bremse (-n)** brakes
**der Katalysator (-en)** catalytic converter
**der Kofferraum (¨e)** boot (of car)
**der Motor (-en)** engine
**das Rad (¨er)** wheel
**der Reifen (-)** tyre
**der (Sicherheits)gurt (-e)** seat belt
**das Steuerrad (¨er)** steering wheel

## Car verbs

**abschleppen** (sep) to tow away
**bestrafen** to punish
**bremsen** to brake
**einordnen** (sep) to get into lane
**freihalten** (sep) to keep clear
**Gang einschalten** to change gear
**hupen** to sound the horn
**parken** to park
**prüfen** to test, to check
**tanken** to fill up with petrol
**überholen** to overtake
**volltanken** (sep) to fill up (petrol)
**weiterfahren** (sep) to drive on

## Adjectives

**bleifrei** leadfree
**direkt** direct, non-stop
**einfach** simple, single (ticket)
**fahrplanmäßig** scheduled
**gesperrt** closed to traffic
**gestattet** allowed, permitted
**gültig** valid
**kurvenreich** winding
**öffentlich** public
**planmäßig** according to plan
**verbleit** leaded
**verboten** forbidden
**versichert** insured

## By train

**das Abteil (-e)** compartment (of train)
**der Anschluß (¨sse)** connection
**die Bahn (-en)** railway
**der Bahnhof (¨e)** station
**die Bahnhofshalle (-n)** station concourse
**der Bahnsteig (-e)** platform
**die Deutsche Bundesbahn /DB** German
 Railways
**die Eisenbahn (-en)** railway
**die Endstation (-en)** terminus
**der Entwerter (-)** ticket cancelling machine
**der Fahrkartenschalter (-)** ticket office
**das Fundbüro (-s)** lost property office
**das Gepäck** luggage
**die Gepäckaufbewahrung** left-luggage office
**das Gepäcknetz (-e)** luggage rack
**der Gepäckträger (-)** porter
**das Gleis (-e)** platform
**der Hauptbahnhof (¨e)** main station
**hin und zurück** return
**die Notbremse (-n)** communication cord
**der Portier (-s)** porter
**die Rückfahrkarte (-n)** return ticket
**der Schaffner (-)** ticket collector
**das Schließfach (¨er)** left-luggage locker
**die Station (-en)** station
**die Tageskarte (-n)** day ticket
**die U-Bahn (-en)** underground
**die U-Bahnstation (-en)** tube station
**der Warteraum (¨e)** waiting room
**der Wartesaal (-säle)** waiting room
**das Wartezimmer (-)** waiting room

## Trains

**der D-Zug (¨e)** fast train
**der Eilzug (¨e)** fast train
**der Intercity-Zug (¨e)** Intercity train
**der Liegewagen (-)** sleeping car (couchette)
**der Nahverkehrszug (¨e)** local train
**der Personenzug (¨e)** passenger train
**die S-Bahn (-en)** urban railway
**der Schlafwagen (-)** sleeping car
**der Schnellzug (¨e)** express train
**die Schwebebahn (-en)** cable railway

**der Speisewagen (-)**  restaurant car
**der TEE-Zug (¨e)**  trans-european express
**der Zug (¨e)**  train

## Countries

**Afrika**  Africa
**Amerika**  America
**das Ausland**  abroad
**Belgien**  Belgium
**das Bundesland**  Federal Republic of
  Germany
**die Bundesrepublik/BRD**  German
  Federal Republic
**Dänemark**  Denmark
**Deutschland**  Germany
**die ehemalige DDR**  former DDR
**England**  England
**Europa**  Europe
**Frankreich**  France
**Griechenland**  Greece
**Großbritannien**  Great Britain
**Holland**  Holland
**Irland**  Ireland
**Italien**  Italy
**Jugoslawien**  Yugoslavia
**Luxemburg**  Luxemburg
**die Niederlande**  Netherlands
**Nordamerika**  North America
**Nordirland**  Northern Ireland
**Norwegen**  Norway
**Österreich**  Austria
**Polen**  Poland
**Portugal**  Portugal
**die Republik Irland**  Irish Republic
**Rumänien**  Romania
**Rußland**  Russia
**Schottland**  Scotland
**Schweden**  Sweden
**die Schweiz**  Switzerland
**die Slowakei**  Slovakia
**Spanien**  Spain
**Südamerika**  South America
**Tschechische Republik**  Czech Republic
**die Tschechoslowakei**  Czechoslovakia
**die Türkei**  Turkey
**Ungarn**  Hungary
**die USA** (pl)  USA
**die Vereinigten Staaten** (pl)  USA
**Wales**  Wales

## Nationalities

**der Amerikaner (-)**  American (person)
**der Ausländer (-)**  foreigner
**der Brite (-n)**  Briton
**der/die Deutsche (-n)**  German (person)
**der Einwohner (-)**  inhabitant
**der Engländer (-)**  Englishman
**der Franzose (-n)**  Frenchman
**der Holländer (-)**  Dutchman
**der Ire (-n)**  Irishman
**die Irin (-nen)**  Irishwoman

**der Italiener (-)**  Italian
**der Jude (-n)**  Jewish man
**die Jüdin (-nen)**  Jewish woman
**der Nordire (-n)**  Northern Ireland man
**die Nordirin (-nen)**  Northern Ireland woman
**der Österreicher (-)**  Austrian
**der Schweizer (-)**  Swiss (man)
**der Spanier (-)**  Spaniard
**der Waliser (-)**  Welshman

## Adjectives

**amerikanisch**  American
**deutsch**  German
**englisch**  English
**französisch**  French
**irisch**  Irish
**jüdisch**  Jewish
**nordirisch**  Northern Irish
**österreichisch**  Austrian
**portugiesisch**  Portuguese
**schottisch**  Scottish
**schweizerisch**  Swiss
**spanisch**  Spanish
**tschechisch**  Czech
**walisisch**  Welsh

## Life in other countries and communities

### Rivers

**die Donau**  Danube
**die Mosel**  Mosel
**der Rhein**  Rhine
**die Themse**  Thames

### Regions

**Bayern**  Bavaria

### Mountains

**Alpen** (pl)  Alps

### Seas

**der Atlantik**  Atlantic
**der Bodensee**  Lake Constance
**der Ärmelkanal**  English Channel
**das Mittelmeer**  Mediterranean Sea
**die Nordsee**  North Sea
**die Ostsee**  Baltic Sea

### Cities

**Köln**  Cologne
**München**  Munich
**Rom**  Rome
**Wien**  Vienna

## World events and issues

### Problems

**die Abgase**  exhaust fumes
**die Absicht (-en)**  intention, purpose
**das Altpapier**  waste paper

die **Arbeitslosigkeit**   unemployment
der **Ausweis** (-e)   identity card
das **Bedürfnis** (-se)   need, necessity
die **Beziehung** (-en)   relation
die **Diskussion** (-en)   discussion
**EG**   European Community
der **Gastarbeiter** (-)   foreign worker
das **Gegenteil** (-e)   opposite
die **Gemeinde** (-n)   community
die **Gesellschaft** (-en)   society
der **Grund** (-̈e)   reason
die **Heimat** (-en)   home country
die **Idee** (-n)   idea
der **Krieg** (-e)   war
die **Lage** (-n)   situation
das **Land** (-̈er)   state (of Germany)
das **Leben**   life
die **Leute** (pl)   people
die **Mauer** (-n)   wall
die **Meinung** (-en)   opinion, meaning
das **Mißverständnis** (-se)   misunderstanding
das **Mittel** (-)   means
der **Ordner** (-)   steward, marshall
der **Politiker** (-)   politician
das **Problem** (-e)   problem
der **Raum** (-̈e)   room, space
die **Sache** (-n)   thing, affair
die **Serie** (-n)   series
die **Sorte** (-n)   sort, type
der **Spielraum**   room to move
der **Staat** (-en)   state
die **Steuer** (-n)   tax
die **Umfrage** (-n)   survey, poll
**umsonst**   in vain

der **Umweltschutz**   conservation
der **Unsinn**   nonsense
die **Ursache** (-n)   cause
die **Verbindung** (-en)   connection
die **Verschmutzung**   pollution
die **Wende** (-n)   change, re-unification
das **Wunder** (-)   miracle
das **Ziel** (-e)   aim, destination, target
die **Zukunft**   future

## Verbs

**beschließen**   to decide on, to end
**bestehen**   to exist
**brauchen**   to need
**denken**   to think
**sich erinnern**   to remember
**folgen**   to follow
**glauben**   to believe
**hoffen**   to hope
**leiden**   to suffer
**liegenlassen** (sep)   to leave behind
**sich lohnen**   to be worth while
**meinen**   to mean, to think
**nachdenken** (sep)   to think, to reflect
**recht haben**   to be right
**recyceln**   to re-cycle
**scheinen**   to seem
**schützen**   to protect
**träumen**   to dream
**unrecht haben**   to be wrong
**wissen**   to know
**zunehmen** (sep)   to increase

# Chapter 5
# *Listening*

## 5.1 Introduction

- Listening Tests are included at both Foundation and Higher Tiers for all the examining groups. The material for all tests will be pre-recorded using native speakers. Only material which is appropriate to the spoken language will be used in the tests.
- You must be entered for either the Foundation Tier or the Higher Tier of the Listening Test. You cannot opt out. You should decide with your teacher which tier you will take in the January of your final year. If you are entered for the Higher Tier, you cannot do the Foundation Tier.
- The material for the listening test will be taken from the five Areas of Experience, so make sure you have learned the vocabulary in this book thoroughly.
- Remember you are not expected to understand every single word in this kind of test, only the ones you need to understand to answer the questions.

## 5.2 Preparing for the Listening Test

The best kind of preparation for these kinds of test is to listen to as much spoken German as you can.
- You can watch German TV and films on some satellite channels if you have the necessary access.
- You can listen to German radio programmes. Details of which stations can easily be picked up in this country are available from: Deutsche Welle, 50588 Köln, Germany and Deutschlandradio Marketing GmbH, Raderbergürtel 40, 50968 Köln, Germany.
- If you have a German penfriend why not ask him or her to record some German radio programmes for you and send them to you. You could exchange cassettes instead of letters with your penfriend speaking German to you and you recording your reply in English, that way you both get some listening practice.
- If travelling by car listen to a German cassette on the way. If on a coach, take your walkman with you and listen to German.
- Get a friend to read out the transcript and then do the same for him or her.
- It is a good idea to practise some of the past listening papers from your examining group, especially near the examination period. These are available usually in school or direct from your examining group. The addresses of all the groups are on pages 9–19.
- This book is accompanied by a CD of GCSE-type questions. Write down the words you do not recognise and then look at the transcript which will help you to understand what you are hearing when you get stuck. Look up any words you do not know in a dictionary and note them in your own vocabulary book under the relevant area of experience. Learn them thoroughly!

## 5.3 During the examination

- Fill in the front of your booklet quickly so that you can spend as much time as possible reading through the questions. Make sure you know your candidate and centre number.

- Spend as much time as possible reading through the questions.
- Listen carefully to the instructions and make sure that you have learnt all the possible rubrics in German so that you will understand the instructions on the tape.
- Make sure you have read and understood the instructions on the answer paper.
- Remember that the mark allocation for each question will give you a clue as to what information is required and how much detail you need to supply in your answer.
- Always attempt every question, even if you have to guess.
- The rubrics to the questions will almost always be in German: make sure that you can understand the rubric. The German rubrics are listed on pages 4–6.
- Remember that you do not have to write in full sentences. Many of the questions will be box-ticking types but if you do have to write in German, then a short or one word answer will score full marks.
- There is often a clue to the answer in the rubric on the question paper or in the instructions on the recording, so make sure you read the rubrics and listen to the instructions very carefully.
- If you are allowed to make notes during the listening examination, it is best to make your notes in German, not English. Try to listen for the relevant details and write down the important words in German as you hear them.

# 5.4 Foundation Tier examination questions

This is what you need to know about the Listening Test at Foundation Tier.
- Most of the questions will be in German. You must answer in German or tick a box or give a visual answer (e.g. draw a symbol in the box). However, there will be a small percentage of questions in English and you will see that if the rubric is in English then you should answer in English.
- At Foundation Tier you will be asked to understand specific detail.
- You are not expected to understand every word.
- The following questions are on the CD which accompanies this book. In the examination each extract will be repeated after a pause. On the accompanying CD the recordings are not repeated, so when you have listened to a recording once, go back and listen again.
- The following are examples of the sort of questions you can expect in your examination in the Foundation Tier at GCSE. They are short items or dialogues where you have to tick a box. There is a transcript of all the recorded material used in these questions on pages 121–125.

## Recording 1

You want to travel to Koblenz. You are told what time the next train leaves. What time does the train leave? Tick the box which has the appropriate time on the clock next to it.

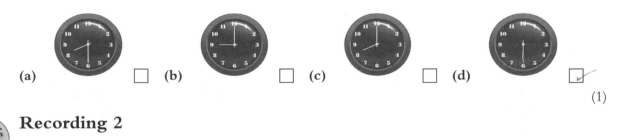

(a) ☐　(b) ☐　(c) ☐　(d) ☑

(1)

## Recording 2

You want to get to the airport. You are told to catch a bus. Which number should you take?

(a) 5 ☐　(b) 15 ☐　(c) 35 ☑　(d) 25 ☐

(1)

> ### **E**xaminer's tip
>
>
> Recordings 1 and 2 are asking you to listen for numbers or times. Remember timetables are usually on a 24-hour basis in Germany. Numbers and expressions of time are in Chapter 4.

## Recording 3

Ihre Brieffreundin ist im Supermarkt. Was kauft sie? Kreuzen Sie ein Kästchen an!

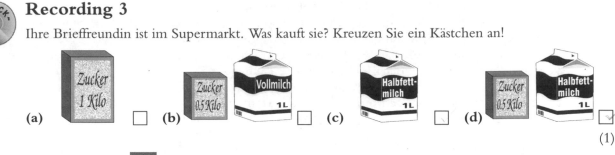

(a) ☐    (b) ☐    (c) ☐    (d) ☑

(1)

> **E**xaminer's tip
>
> This question requires you to be able to recognise weights and measures of goods you can buy in a supermarket.

## Recording 4

Sie sind im Informationsbüro und suchen das Hotel Leve, das in der Nähe ist. Man sagt Ihnen, wo es sich befindet. Wo ist es? Kreuzen Sie das Kästchen an, wo das Hotel auf der Karte ist!

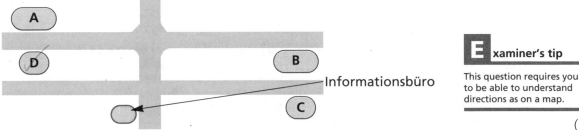

Informationsbüro

> **E**xaminer's tip
>
> This question requires you to be able to understand directions as on a map.

(1)

## Recording 5

In der Konditorei, wer bestellt was? Kreuzen Sie das richtige Kästchen an!

|        | Eis | Kaffee | Tee | Torte | Strudel |
|--------|-----|--------|-----|-------|---------|
| Karl   |     | ✓      |     |       |         |
| Jürgen |     |        |     | ✓     |         |
| Uschi  |     |        | ✓   |       | ✓       |
| Lotte  | ✓   |        |     |       |         |

> **E**xaminer's tip
>
> This question requires you to identify who is ordering what, so you need to listen for the names and what they each order.

(5)

## Recording 6

Am Telefon auf dem Campingplatz, was will der Fahrer? Markiere, ob der Satz **richtig** (R) oder **falsch** (F) ist!

(a) Der Kunde heißt Kinder.    `F`
(b) Er will zwei Nächte bleiben.    `F`
(c) Es gibt vier Personen in der Familie.    `R`
(d) Es gibt keine Duschen in den Waschräumen.    `F`
(e) Der Kunde will mit einem Scheck zahlen.    `R`

> **E**xaminer's tip
>
> This is a true/false choice based on what you hear. You need to understand the statements in the suggested answers to check if they match what you hear. Read the questions very carefully.

(5)

## Recording 7

You have just arrived at your German penfriend Paul's house. Paul's mother is showing you round for the first time. Complete the details below about what she tells you. You should write your notes in English.

(a) From the window of your room you can see ....the...sea...buildings...... *and sailing boats* (*3 things*)    (3)

(b) The bathroom is ....very............ near Paul's room.    (1)

(c) The bathroom is equipped with ...shower...+...toilet...... (*2 things*)    (2)

(d) Breakfast is at ......8...o'clock.......... (*time*) ✓ *8:30*    (1)

(e) Breakfast will be served in ...the...kitchen............ (*place*)    (1)

> **E**xaminer's tip
>
> Remember your answers have to be in English and you are looking for precise details.

# 5.5 Foundation and Higher Tier examination questions

These longer items in more than one section could occur in either a Foundation Tier paper or a Higher Tier paper. (Higher Tier students should read the last two bullet points in the introduction to Unit 5.6 on page 116.)

## Recording 8

Zwei Deutsche sprechen über Münster, eine Stadt in Nordrhein-Westfalen. Markiere, ob der Satz **richtig** (R) oder **falsch** (F) ist!

**(a)** Münster ist eine schöne, große Stadt in Süddeutschland.  `F`

**(b)** Münster hat ein gutes Einkaufsviertel.  `R`

**(c)** Man kann in Münster studieren.  `R`

**(d)** Man kann auf dem Aasee segeln.  `R`

**(e)** Man kann am Montag vor dem Dom parken.  `R`

**(f)** In der Zeit von 9 Uhr morgens bis Mitternacht kann man gut in Münster essen und trinken.  `R`    (6)

> **E**xaminer's tip
>
> This kind of question is asking you to understand and draw conclusions from what you hear. You must use all the time given to read the statements and understand them because they do not necessarily contain the same words as the recorded material.

## Recording 9

Monika and her friend Brigitte are talking on the phone about Monika's trip to the sales with Helga. The conversation is in two parts. For each question tick the correct box or boxes.

### Part 1

**(a)** What time did Monika and Helga leave home?
- **(i)** 8. 30 am  ☐
- **(ii)** 7. 30 am  ☑
- **(iii)** 8. 00 am  ☐    (1)

**(b)** How did they arrive in the town centre?
- **(i)** on foot  ☐
- **(ii)** by train  ☐
- **(iii)** by tram  ☑    (1)

**(c)** Why did they go to town?
- **(i)** to ride in the train  ☐
- **(ii)** to look at the fashions  ☐
- **(iii)** to buy things at reduced prices  ☑    (1)

### Part 2

**(d)** Who bought what?

|          | black dress | green dress | long dress |
|----------|-------------|-------------|------------|
| **Monika** | ☑ | ☐ | ☑ |
| **Helga**  | ☐ | ☑ | ☐ |

(3)

**(e)** Where did Helga buy her bathing costume?
- **(i)** in the sports department  ☑
- **(ii)** from France  ☐
- **(iii)** on the North Sea coast  ☐    (1)

**(f)** What did Monika buy for her husband?
- **(i)** a suit  ☐
- **(ii)** shoes  ☐
- **(iii)** socks  ☑    (1)

> **E**xaminer's tip
>
> In the examination you will be given time to read the questions in each section before hearing the recorded material. Get used to doing this as a matter of course and concentrate on the questions in each section separately.

## Recording 10

In der Apotheke hören Sie ein Gespräch zwischen einem Kunden und dem Apotheker. Beantworten Sie die Fragen auf deutsch!

**Abschnitt 1**

**(a)** Warum war der Kunde in der Apotheke?

Er hat ...*Kopfweh*... und ...*Fiebe*... (2)

**(b)** Wie viele Tabletten sollte der Kunde einnehmen, und wie oft?

Er sollte ...*zwei*... Tabletten ...*dreimal*... am Tag einnehmen. (2)

**(c)** Wie lange sollte der Kunde im Bett bleiben?

Er sollte ...*zwei / drei Tage*... im Bett bleiben. (2)

**(d)** Was sollte der Kunde trinken?

Er sollte ...*warme Getränke*... trinken. (1)

**Abschnitt 2**

**(e)** Wie viele Tabletten kosten 8 DM?

...*Zwanzig*... Tabletten kosten 8 DM. (1)

**(f)** Warum empfiehlt der Apotheker einen Hustensaft?

Weil der Kunde ...*Husten*... hat. (1)

**(g)** Was kostet die Flasche Hustensaft?

Sie kostet ...*6 M die Flasche*... (1)

> **E**xaminer's tip
>
> Read the questions to each section carefully and separately, one section at a time. You are required to give answers in German and specific details are expected, so look at the allocation of marks to each question to see how much detail is expected.

# 5.6 Higher Tier examination questions

- The recordings for Higher Tier will be faster and longer than at Foundation Tier and the vocabulary will be beyond the minimum core vocabulary list issued by your examination board.
- There may be background noise and recordings may be split into sections.
- One main difference between Foundation and Higher Tier questions is that at Higher Tier you will be expected to draw conclusions and detect emotions.
- The following are examples of the sort of questions you can expect in your examination in the Higher Tier at GCSE.

## Recording 11

Zwei Deutsche sprechen über sich, was sie gern haben und machen. Haken Sie die drei richtigen Aussagen für beide ab!

**Abschnitt 1**
**Georg**

**(a)** **(i)** bleibt gern zu Hause ☐
    **(ii)** haßt Ausländer ☑
    **(iii)** fährt gern ins Ausland ☐
    **(iv)** geht gern aus ☐ (1)

**(b)** **(i)** treibt Sport ganz gern ☑
    **(ii)** haßt allerlei Sportarten ☐
    **(iii)** treibt am liebsten Sport ☐
    **(iv)** treibt Sport nicht gern ☐ (1)

**(c)** **(i)** sammelt alles mögliche ☑
    **(ii)** tanzt gern ☐

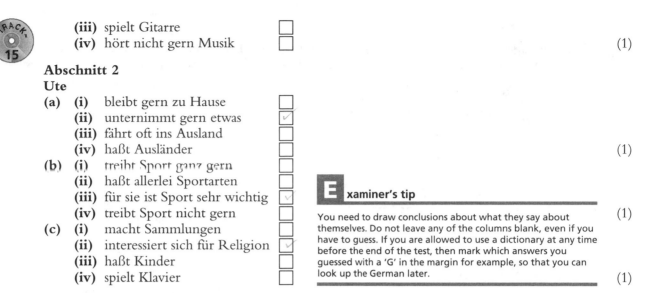

**TRACK 15**

(iii) spielt Gitarre ☐
(iv) hört nicht gern Musik ☐ (1)

**Abschnitt 2**
**Ute**

(a) (i) bleibt gern zu Hause ☐
(ii) unternimmt gern etwas ☑
(iii) fährt oft ins Ausland ☐
(iv) haßt Ausländer ☐ (1)

(b) (i) treibt Sport ganz gern ☐
(ii) haßt allerlei Sportarten ☐
(iii) für sie ist Sport sehr wichtig ☑
(iv) treibt Sport nicht gern ☐ (1)

(c) (i) macht Sammlungen ☐
(ii) interessiert sich für Religion ☑
(iii) haßt Kinder ☐
(iv) spielt Klavier ☐ (1)

> **E**xaminer's tip
>
> You need to draw conclusions about what they say about themselves. Do not leave any of the columns blank, even if you have to guess. If you are allowed to use a dictionary at any time before the end of the test, then mark which answers you guessed with a 'G' in the margin for example, so that you can look up the German later.

## Recording 12

Ein Deutscher und seine Frau besprechen eine Reise nach London. Kreuzen Sie das Kästchen unter der Person an, die folgendes sagt:

**TRACK 16**

**Abschnitt 1**

|  |  | der Mann | die Frau |
|---|---|---|---|
| (a) | Diese Person will mit dem Flugzeug fliegen. | ☑ | ☐ |
| (b) | Diese Person ist nie seekrank. | ☐ | ☑ |
| (c) | Diese Person ißt nicht gern im Restaurant an Bord. | ☑ | ☐ |
| (d) | Diese Person sieht gern die Landschaft an. | ☐ | ☑ |
| (e) | Diese Person will mit der Fähre fahren. | ☐ | ☑ |

**TRACK 17**

**Abschnitt 2**

|  |  | der Mann | die Frau |
|---|---|---|---|
| (f) | Diese Person zieht kurzere Reisen vor. | ☑ | ☐ |
| (g) | Diese Person will direkt in der Innenstadt ankommen. | ☐ | ☑ |
| (h) | Diese Person schlägt vor, durch den Tunnel zu fahren. | ☑ | ☐ |
| (i) | Diese Person sagt, daß die Züge nicht immer pünktlich ankommen. | ☑ | ☐ |
| (j) | Diese Person sagt, daß sie mit dem Zug ganz in der Nähe ihres Hotels ankommen werden. | ☐ | ☑ |

(10)

> **E**xaminer's tip
>
> This is a typical Higher Tier question where you have to work out people's opinions. Each question needs careful analysis.

## Recording 13

**TRACK 18**

Sie hören dem Wetterbericht im Radio zu. Beantworten Sie die Fragen auf deutsch!

(a) Was ist die allgemeine Wetterlage am 8. April in Deutschland?

.............................................................................. (1)

(b) In welchem Teil Deutschlands wird das beste Wetter sein?

.............................................................................. (1)

(c) Was wird der nächtliche Tiefstwert im Norden sein?

.............................................................................. (1)

(d) In welchem Teil Deutschlands wird es nieseln?

.............................................................................. (1)

(e) In welchem Teil Deutschlands wird die kälteste Tageshöchsttemperatur sein?

.............................................................................. (1)

> **E**xaminer's tip
>
> Specific detail needs to be extracted from the recorded material. It would be a good idea to look at the tapescript for this question to familiarise yourself with the specialist vocabulary. Complete sentences are not required in this sort of question.

## Recording 14

Sie erwarten einen Telefonanruf von der Mutter Ihrer Brieffreundin Inge Braun. Inge wird in ein paar Wochen ankommen, um einige Tage bei Ihnen zu verbringen. Füllen Sie die Lücken aus!

**Inges Ankunft**

Wie abgemacht wird Inge ....*zwei Wochen*... in York ankommen. Sie wird ...*Nahstzug*... von London nehmen und wird um ...*14 Uhr*..... auf dem Hauptbahnhof ankommen. Falls du sie nicht vom ...*Fahtzug*... erkennst, trägt sie einen ...*blaue Mütze*....., einen blauen Anorak und ...*eine gelbe Hose*..... Sie wird auch eine Zeitschrift unter ...*dem linken Arm*.. tragen. (7)

> **E**xaminer's tip
>
> Times and specific details are important in this question. Be careful with the adjective case endings you will need to use correctly in your answers. See page 33 in Chapter 1.

## Recording 15

You are acting as an interpreter for a group of American tourists who are visiting Bremen. You are listening to a German guide. You have to tell your American friends what your German guide is saying. Fill in the blanks in English.

**Part 1**

The tour lasts ......................... (a). It begins at the ............................. (b) and ends in the Schnoorviertel where there are ................... (c) and ..................... (d) to be found. There are good places to eat and drink ............................. (e). The meeting place for tourists and inhabitants alike is the ......................... (f) which has been there since ...................... (g). The market place is ............................. (h) and trams are the only vehicles allowed to cross it.

**Part 2**

On the left side of the market place is the townhall which was built in ......................... (a). Guided tours of the townhall take place at ................ , ................. (b) and .............. (c) on weekdays from March to ......................... (d). Under the townhall is the famous Ratskeller which was built in ........... (e). In the Schnoorviertel, which is one of the ......................... (f) of the town of Bremen, many of the tiny houses date from the ...................... (g) and ...................... (h) centuries and are now fully restored. There are ............................................... (i) and ................. (j) – all people, who work there. You can buy ................... (k) there. They are inexpensive. (25)

> **E**xaminer's tip
>
> You need to listen carefully to the recorded material for this question and look at the transcript to find the words you do not know. 25 pieces of information are needed.

## Recording 16

Ein Freund beschreibt das Hotel, wo er und seine Frau letztes Jahr auf Urlaub waren. Haken Sie die fünf Sätze ab, die richtig sind!

**(a)** Es gab keine Probleme im Hotel. ☐
**(b)** Sie waren nicht im dritten Stock. ☐
**(c)** Sie mußten oft im Restaurant warten. ☐
**(d)** Das Essen im Hotel war ausgezeichnet. ☐
**(e)** Man hatte eine gute Auswahl an Weinen. ☐
**(f)** Die Kellner waren immer hilfreich. ☐
**(g)** Das Wetter war wirklich schön, besonders während der zweiten Woche. ☐
**(h)** Zu jeder Zeit konnten sie Freunde und Familie anrufen. ☐

**(i)** Das Hotel hatte ein modernes Hallenbad. ☐

**(j)** Sie wollten nur Mineralwasser im Hotel trinken. ☐ (5)

## Recording 17

Drei junge Deutsche sprechen über ihre Berufswahl. Beantworten Sie die Fragen!

**(a) Helke**

    **(i)** Wohin wird sie nach dem Abitur gehen?

    Sie wird ..................................................gehen. (1)

    **(ii)** Was wird sie studieren?

    Sie wird ............................... studieren. (1)

    **(iii)** Was wird sie vielleicht werden?

    Sie wird ................................................... werden. (2)

**(b) Jürgen**

    **(i)** Was will er machen?

    Er will ..................................................arbeiten. (2)

    **(ii)** Seit wann will er den Älteren helfen?

    ..................................................... (1)

**(c) Gisela**

    **(i)** Was will sie werden?

    ..................................................... (1)

    **(ii)** Warum kann sie nicht mit alten Menschen arbeiten?

    Weil sie........................................................ (2)

    **(iii)** Was muß sie tun, um alles über das Frisieren zu lernen?

    Sie muß........................................................ (2)

## Recording 18

Ein Gespräch mit Klaus über die Arbeitswelt. Beantworten Sie die Fragen auf deutsch!

**(a)** Wo arbeitet Klaus?

.................................................................................... (2)

**(b)** Seit wann arbeitet er dort?

.................................................................................... (1)

**(c)** Warum gefällt ihm die Arbeit?

.................................................................................... (2)

**(d)** Wohin können die Kunden reisen? (*2 Länder*)

.................................................................................... (2)

**(e)** Was wird er tun, um mehr zu verdienen?

.................................................................................... (2)

## Recording 19

Karl beantwortet Fragen über Drogen und Rauchen. Markieren Sie die folgenden Sätze **richtig** (R) oder **falsch** (F)!

### Abschnitt 1

(a) Karl hat nie Drogen genommen. ☐

(b) Karl glaubt, man kann von Drogen abhängig werden. ☐

(c) Karl hat keine Zigaretten geraucht. ☐

(d) Karl ist der Meinung, daß das Rauchen gefährlich ist. ☐

(e) Karl war vierzehn Jahre alt, als er zu rauchen begann. ☐

### Abschnitt 2

(f) Junge Leute nehmen Drogen, weil sie an Streß in der Schule leiden. ☐

(g) Man fühlt sich erwachsen, wenn man sich langweilt. ☐

(h) Die Mädchen fühlen sich attraktiv, wenn sie rauchen. ☐

(i) Karl würde sich viel fitter fühlen, wenn er nicht mehr rauchte. ☐

(j) Die drogenabhängigen Leute sollten "nein" sagen können. ☐　　(10)

> **E**xaminer's tip
>
> Not every word in the statements above occurs in the recorded material. Listen to the recording very carefully. Look at the transcript and look up any words you do not recognise.

## Recording 20

Nachrichten im Radio: ein Eisenbahnunglück. Beantworten Sie die Fragen auf deutsch!

### Abschnitt 1

(a) Wo fand das Unglück statt?

............................................................................ (1)

(b) Wie schnell fuhr der Zug, der in den anderen hineinfuhr?

............................................................................ (1)

(c) Warum stand der zweite Zug still?

............................................................................ (1)

(d) Wie viele Leute sind tot?

............................................................................ (1)

### Abschnitt 2

(e) Was hat Herr Lemmer gehört und gesehen?

............................................................................ (2)

(f) Warum eilte er hin?

............................................................................ (1)

(g) Worauf warteten so viele Leute?

............................................................................ (1)

(h) Wissen wir genau, wie viele Verletzte es waren?

...,............................................................................ (1)

(i) Was wird im Krankenhaus gemacht?

............................................................................ (1)

(j) Was müssen die Ärzte in den Krankenhäusern dringend haben?

............................................................................ (1)

## Recording 21

Nachrichten im Radio: ein Verkehrsunfall. Beantworten Sie die Fragen auf deutsch!

(a) Wo findet der Verkehrsunfall statt?

............................................................................ (1)

**(b)** Wie viele sind tot?

.................................................................................... (1)

**(c)** Wie alt war der Unglücksfahrer?

.................................................................................... (1)

**(d)** Wie alt war der jüngste Mensch bei diesem Unfall?

.................................................................................... (1)

**(e)** Was mußte die Polizei tun?

.................................................................................... (2)

# 5.7 Transcripts for examination questions

## Recording 1

**Frau**       Der nächste Zug nach Koblenz fährt um achtzehn Uhr dreißig von Gleis 9 ab.

## Recording 2

**Mann**       Sie fahren am besten mit dem Autobus Linie fünfunddreißig zum Flughafen.

## Recording 3

**Frau**       Also, was kaufe ich? Ich brauche ein halbes Kilo Zucker und einen Liter Halbfettmilch.

## Recording 4

**Mann**       Das Hotel Leve ist nicht weit entfernt. Gehen Sie links aus dem Gebäude und dann geradeaus. Nehmen Sie die zweite Straße links. Das Hotel ist am Ende auf der linken Seite.

## Recording 5

| | |
|---|---|
| **Lotte** | Karl, was möchtest du? |
| **Karl** | Also, ich nehme eine Tasse Kaffee mit Milch, bitte. |
| **Lotte** | Und du, Jürgen? |
| **Jürgen** | Ja, für mich ein Stück Schwarzwälder Kirschtorte, bitte. |
| **Lotte** | Und Uschi, was möchtest du? |
| **Uschi** | Eine Tasse Tee mit Zitrone und ein Stück Apfelstrudel, bitte. Und zuletzt, Lotte, was möchtest du? |
| **Lotte** | Ich möchte ein Himbeereis, bitte. |

## Recording 6

| | |
|---|---|
| **Kunde** | Haben Sie Platz für eine Nacht? |
| **Empfangsdame** | Für heute abend? |
| **Kunde** | Nein, für den elften August. |
| **Empfangsdame** | Für ein Zelt? |
| **Kunde** | Nein, für einen Wohnwagen. |
| **Empfangsdame** | Ja, wir haben einen Platz am elften August, wie viele Personen? |
| **Kunde** | Vier, meine Frau, zwei Kinder und ich. |
| **Empfangsdame** | Gut, wie heißen Sie? |
| **Kunde** | Schmidt. |
| **Empfangsdame** | Also, S–C–H–M–I–D–T. |
| **Kunde** | Ja, gibt es Duschen in den Waschräumen? |
| **Empfangsdame** | Ja, natürlich. |
| **Kunde** | Was kostet die eine Nacht? |
| **Empfangsdame** | Dreißig Mark fünfzig pro Nacht. |
| **Kunde** | Darf ich mit einem Scheck zahlen? |
| **Empfangsdame** | Ja, das ist in Ordnung. |
| **Kunde** | Gut, danke, auf Wiederhören! |
| **Empfangsdame** | Auf Wiederhören! |

## Recording 7

**Die Mutter**

Hier ist dein Zimmer. Leider ist es nicht sehr groß, aber es hat eine schöne Aussicht über den See. Komm! Es gibt schöne Bäume dort drüben, und du kannst die Segelboote sehen. Das Badezimmer ist hier rechts neben Pauls Zimmer. Im Badezimmer sind eine Dusche und die Toilette. Wir stehen um acht Uhr auf und frühstücken eine halbe Stunde später in der Küche. Wir essen nicht oft im Eßzimmer.

## Recording 8

| | |
|---|---|
| **Frau** | Wie würdest du Münster beschreiben? |
| **Mann** | Münster ist eine schöne, große Stadt in Nordrhein-Westfalen. Es hat viele große Kaufhäuser, ein modernes Theater, eine Universität, mehrere Kinos, ein sehr altes historisches Rathaus, viele Wohnhäuser und einen alten Dom. |
| **Frau** | Was tust du in deiner Freizeit in Münster? |
| **Mann** | Ich gehe oft ins Theater, um Theaterstücke oder Opern zu sehen, oder ich segle auf dem Aasee, wo man auch Paddelboote mieten kann. |
| **Frau** | Gibt es einen Markt? |
| **Mann** | Ja sicher, am Mittwoch und am Samstag kann man nicht auf dem Platz vor dem Dom parken, weil der Markt auf dem Parkplatz stattfindet. |
| **Frau** | Wohnst du gern in Münster? |
| **Mann** | Ja, es gibt so viele Sehenswürdigkeiten, und die Konditoreien, Gasthäuser und Restaurants sind den ganzen Tag offen. Es macht viel Spaß, in Münster zu leben. |

## Recording 9

**Part 1**

**Monika**

Hallo, Brigitte, hier spricht Monika, schön, daß du zu Hause bist. Ich wollte dir nur etwas vom Sommerschlußverkauf erzählen, der heute morgen angefangen hat. Schon um halb acht ging ich mit Helga aus dem Haus, denn wir wollten so viele passende Sachen wie möglich zu herabgesetzten Preisen kaufen. Wir fuhren zuerst mit dem Zug und dann mit der Straßenbahn in die Innenstadt. Da viele Leute vor den Türen der Kaufhäuser standen, eilten wir zum ersten Kaufhaus, in das wir gehen wollten. Pünktlich um halb neun öffneten sich die Türen, und wir drängten uns durch die Menge zur Damenabteilung.

**Part 2**

| | |
|---|---|
| **Brigitte** | Hast du etwas gekauft? |
| **Monika** | Ja sicher. Ich kaufte mir ein kurzes, schwarzes Kleid und ein langes, blaues Kleid, während Helga sich ein grünes Kleid aussuchte. Das blaue Kleid war besonders billig, denn es war von neunundfünfzig Mark auf dreißig Mark herabgesetzt. Letztes Jahr, als wir an der Nordseeküste waren, war Helgas Badeanzug zu klein, deshalb gingen wir heute in die Sportabteilung, wo Helga einen neuen, gelben Badeanzug aus Frankreich kaufte. Er war sehr billig und hübsch. |
| **Brigitte** | Hast du sonst noch etwas gefunden? |
| **Monika** | Ja, natürlich suchte ich auch etwas für meinen Mann. Wir kauften ihm Unterhemden und Socken. Als wir das Kaufhaus verließen, rief ich meinen Mann an, um ihm zu sagen, er würde Schuhe und Anzüge zu günstigen Preisen finden. Vielleicht hat er heute Zeit hinzugehen. Du solltest auch hingehen. |
| **Brigitte** | Ja, ich gehe gleich nach dem Mittagessen, tschüs! |
| **Monika** | Viel Glück! Wiederhören! |

## Recording 10

**Abschnitt 1**

| | |
|---|---|
| **Kunde** | Guten Morgen, ich habe Kopfweh und ein bißchen Fieber. Ich fühle mich gar nicht wohl. Können Sie mir etwas empfehlen? |
| **Apotheker** | Ja, natürlich. Ich würde diese Tabletten empfehlen. Sie sollten zwei davon dreimal am Tag mit Wasser einnehmen. Ich würde auch raten, daß Sie ins Bett gehen und zwei oder drei Tage im Bett bleiben. Sie sollten nicht viel essen, sondern viele warme Getränke trinken. Sie haben wahrscheinlich eine kleine Grippe. |

**Abschnitt 2**

| | |
|---|---|
| **Kunde** | Was kosten die Tabletten? |
| **Apotheker** | Eine Packung zu zwanzig kostet acht Mark. |
| **Kunde** | Leider habe ich auch Husten, haben Sie etwas dagegen? |
| **Apotheker** | Ja sicher, ich empfehle diesen Hustensaft mit Honig darin. Sie sollten ihn auch dreimal am Tag einnehmen. Er kostet sechs Mark die Flasche, und hoffentlich wird der Husten schnell viel besser werden. |

# Recording 11

**Abschnitt 1**

| | |
|---|---|
| **Ute** | Georg, was für einen Brieffreund suchst du? |
| **Georg** | Jemanden wie ich, der gern verreist. Er muß auch gern moderne Sprachen lernen. |
| **Ute** | Und muß er auch Sport treiben? |
| **Georg** | Ich selbst treibe Sport ganz gern, aber ich lese lieber und höre gern klassische Musik. Ich spiele gern Klavier, zum Beispiel. |
| **Ute** | Und interessierst du dich für andere Hobbys? |
| **Georg** | Ja, zu Hause habe ich eine große Briefmarkensammlung, viele Photos, und ich sammle Ansichtskarten. |

**Abschnitt 2**

| | |
|---|---|
| **Georg** | Und du, Ute, was für eine Brieffreundin suchst du? |
| **Ute** | Ich suche eine Brieffreundin, die sich für viel begeistern kann und aktiv ist. Wie ich, soll sie Sport treiben. Ich interessiere mich sehr für Sport. Ohne Sport würde ich mich nicht wohlfühlen. |
| **Georg** | Und interessierst du dich für andere Sachen? |
| **Ute** | Ja, ich gehe oft in die Kirche, ich arbeite gern mit jungen Kindern und ich spiele Gitarre sehr gern. |

# Recording 12

**Abschnitt 1**

| | |
|---|---|
| **Frau** | Ich möchte lieber mit dem Zug nach Ostende und dann mit der Fähre nach Harwich fahren. Von Zeit zu Zeit bin ich doch etwas seekrank, aber normalerweise ist die See ganz ruhig und ich fühle mich wohl. Vor allem esse ich gern im Restaurant an Bord. |
| **Mann** | Ach nein, die Seefahrt dauert so lange. Wenn wir mit dem Flugzeug fliegen, ist die Reise viel kürzer. Du weißt, du bist fast immer seekrank. Ich leide gar nicht daran, und meiner Meinung nach schmeckt das Essen an Bord aber schrecklich. |
| **Frau** | Ja, aber man sieht nichts als Himmel und Wolken, wenn man fliegt. Mit dem Zug kann man die Landschaft von Holland sehen, und die Überfahrt ist oft herrlich, besonders bei gutem Wetter. Man sieht auch etwas von England, wenn man mit dem Zug von Harwich nach London fährt. |

**Abschnitt 2**

| | |
|---|---|
| **Mann** | Meine Liebe, das Flugzeug ist viel schneller, und wir können deswegen eine längere Zeit in London verbringen. |
| **Frau** | Ja, aber der Flughafen liegt so weit von der Innenstadt entfernt. Sicher dauert der Flug nach Gatwick ungefähr zwei Stunden, aber es dauert noch zwei Stunden, bis man im Hotel in der Innenstadt ankommt. |
| **Mann** | Na gut, ich habe eine Idee, wir können mit dem Zug durch den Kanaltunnel fahren. Es gibt Pannen dann und wann, aber du würdest sicher nicht seekrank werden. |
| **Frau** | Ja, du hast Recht, und der Zug durch den Tunnel kommt mitten im Stadtzentrum an. Gut, das machen wir! |

# Recording 13

**Mann**

Hier ist der Wetterbericht für heute, den achten April. Allgemeine Wetterlage: eine Hochdruckzone über Mitteleuropa bestimmt das Wetter in Deutschland. Im Norden meist sonnig, aber kalt. Tageshöchsttemperaturen um acht Grad. Nächtliche Tiefstwerte um zwei Grad. Im Süden stark bewölkt oder neblig mit Sprühregen. Tageshöchsttemperatur um sechs Grad. In Mitteldeutschland herrscht Nebel. Tageshöchsttemperatur fünf Grad. Wind von Nordwesten. Aussicht: keine durchgreifende Änderung.

## Recording 14

### Frau Braun

Hallo. Hier spricht Frau Braun, die Mutter von deiner Brieffreundin Inge. Willst du deiner Mutter bitte folgendes sagen? Also, Inge kommt, wie abgemacht, in zwei Wochen in York an. Sie wird um vierzehn Uhr auf dem Hauptbahnhof ankommen. Sie wird den D-Zug von London nehmen. Falls du sie nicht sofort vom Farbfoto erkennst, trägt sie eine blaue Mütze, einen blauen Anorak und eine gelbe Hose. Sie wird auch eine Zeitschrift unter dem linken Arm tragen. Alles klar? Auf Wiederhören!

## Recording 15

### Abschnitt 1
### Lotte

Guten Tag, meine Damen und Herren, ich heiße Lotte und bin Ihre Stadtführerin. Die ganze Tour wird etwa anderthalb Stunden dauern. Wir fangen hier am Hauptbahnhof an, und am Ende werden wir die Atmosphäre des Schnoorviertels genießen, wo man die alten kleinen Häuser in den engen Straßen der Altstadt finden kann.

Zuerst gehen wir in die Innenstadt zum Marktplatz. Die Bremer nennen ihren Markplatz *die gute Stube*, denn hier in den Gebäuden um den Markplatz herum kann man besonders gut essen und trinken. Seit dem Jahre 1404 ist das Denkmal Roland der Treffpunkt für Tausende von Touristen und Einwohnern. Der Marktplatz ist in der Fußgängerzone, nur die Straßenbahn fährt hier durch.

### Abschnitt 2
### Lotte

Auf der linken Seite sehen wir das Rathaus, das in den Jahren 1405 bis 1409 errichtet wurde. Führungen finden wochentags um 10, 11 und 12 Uhr, von März bis Ende Oktober statt. Unter dem Rathaus ist der berühmte Ratskeller, der einer der ältesten Stadtweinkeller ist. Der Ratskeller wurde im Jahre 1408 gebaut.

Jetzt gehen wir durch das Schnoorviertel, das eines der ältesten Stadtviertel Bremens ist. Die vielen, zum Teil winzigen Häuser aus dem siebzehnten und achzehnten Jahrhundert sind jetzt völlig restauriert. In diesen kleinen Straßen sind Sie nämlich nicht in einem Museum, sondern in einem Viertel, wo Leute – Architekten, Schriftsteller, Töpfer und Glasbläser – arbeiten. Hier können Sie bummeln und schöne, preiswerte Souvenirs kaufen. Diese Tour endet hier. Auf Wiedersehen und alles Gute für Ihre Reise durch Deutschland.

## Recording 16

### Mann

Wir übernachteten in einem großen, modernen Hotel, das dicht am Bodensee lag. Das Hotel war gut eingerichtet. Es gab ein Freibad, ein Restaurant und eine kleine Tanzhalle. Meine Frau und ich hatten ein Doppelzimmer mit Dusche im zweiten Stock. Nach dem zweiten Tag wurde die Dusche leider kaputt. Danach konnten wir uns nur in der Badewanne waschen. Außer der Dusche war alles im Zimmer in bester Ordnung. Wir hatten Telefon, Fernseher und Videorekorder. Wir konnten auch Kaffee oder Tee im Zimmer kochen.

Die Kellner im Restaurant waren sehr höflich. Wir brauchten nie auf das Essen zu warten. Es gab eine gute Weinkarte, und die Speisekarte war auch reichhaltig, das heißt, wir hatten eine sehr große Auswahl, und das Essen schmeckte wirklich lecker.

Leider war das Wetter nicht so schön, besonders während der zweiten Woche.

## Recording 17

| | | |
|---|---|---|
| (a) **Jürgen** | Was machst du denn Heike, wenn du die Schule verläßt? |
| **Heike** | Ach, im Moment habe ich keine klare Ahnung. Ich weiß nicht genau, was ich machen will. Wahrscheinlich werde ich nach dem Abitur auf die Universität gehen, um Medizin zu studieren. Vielleicht werde ich Ärztin in einem Krankenhaus werden. Was willst du machen, Jürgen? |
| (b) **Jürgen** | Ich weiß schon, was ich machen will. Ich möchte gerne mit alten Menschen in einem Altersheim arbeiten. Schon seit drei Jahren will ich den Älteren helfen. Was hältst du davon Gisela? |
| (c) **Gisela** | Ich könnte so was nicht machen, ich bin zu ungeduldig. Ich will Friseurin werden, wenn ich die Schule verlasse. Ich weiß, daß ich bei einer Friseurin in die Lehre gehen muß, um alles über das Frisieren zu lernen. Hoffentlich werde ich ein bißchen Geld verdienen können, während ich meine Lehre mache. |

## Recording 18

**Beamtin**    Was für einen Job hast du, Klaus?

**Klaus**    Ich habe einen neuen Job in einem Reisebüro in der Weidenstraße in der Stadtmitte. Ich arbeite schon seit drei Wochen dort.

**Beamtin**    Gefällt dir die Arbeit?

**Klaus**    Die Arbeit macht mir viel Spaß. Ich komme mit vielen Leuten zusammen, die überallhin – nach Amerika, England, Spanien, Italien – fahren wollen. Heutzutage ist die Auswahl so groß.

**Beamtin**    Verdienst du gut?

**Klaus**    Nicht sehr viel, aber genug. Ich werde ein paar Monate hier arbeiten, bis ich eine bessere Stelle bekommen kann.

## Recording 19

**Abschnitt 1**

**Freundin**    Hast du je Drogen probiert, Karl?

**Karl**    Nein, meiner Meinung nach ist es sehr gefährlich, Drogen zu probieren, weil man davon abhängig werden kann.

**Freundin**    Aber du rauchst Zigaretten, nicht wahr?

**Klaus**    Ja, ich war zehn Jahre alt, als ich meine erste Zigarette rauchte. Ich weiß jetzt, daß Rauchen ganz dumm ist. Es kann auch sehr gefährlich sein.

**Abschnitt 2**

**Frau**    Kennst du andere junge Leute, die Drogen nehmen oder Zigaretten rauchen?

**Klaus**    Ja, manche aus meiner Klasse rauchen oder nehmen Drogen.

**Frau**    Warum nehmen sie Drogen?

**Klaus**    Weil sie sich langweilen, weil es Spaß macht, oder weil es so viel Streß in der Schule gibt.

**Frau**    Und das Rauchen?

**Klaus**    Sie rauchen, weil sie sich erwachsen und attraktiv fühlen wollen, besonders die Mädchen.

**Frau**    Und du?

**Klaus**    Ich glaube, ich sollte nicht mehr rauchen. Ich würde viel fitter sein, ich würde auch nicht mehr husten und ich könnte joggen gehen. Die jungen Leute, die Drogen nehmen, sind einfach schwach und sollten lernen, "nein" zu sagen.

## Recording 20

**Abschnitt 1**

**Frau**

Heute morgen fand ein Zugunglück auf der Strecke zwischen Köln und Düsseldorf statt. Ein Zug fuhr mit einer Geschwindigkeit von 45 km pro Stunde in einen anderen Zug hinein, der bei Rotlicht stillstand. Nach Angaben der Polizei sind 22 Leute tödlich verunglückt, darunter 5 Kinder.

**Abschnitt 2**

**Frau**    Unser Reporter hat vor kurzem mit einem Augenzeugen gesprochen.

**Reporter**    Herr Lemmer, was haben Sie gesehen?

**Herr Lemmer**    Es war furchtbar. Ich hörte eine schreckliche Explosion, wie eine Bombe, und sah viel Rauch. Ich eilte hin, um den Leuten beim Rausklettern zu helfen. Viele mußten auf den Rettungswagen warten… Es war furchtbar… Es war zum Weinen.

**Reporter**    Die Verletzten werden in die Krankenhäuser gebracht – es steht noch nicht fest wie viele. Die Lage ist sehr schlimm, einige werden schon operiert. Es wird dringend Blut gebraucht.

## Recording 21

**Frau**

Heute nachmittag sind bei einem schweren Verkehrsunfall auf einer Landstraße in der Nähe von Münster vier Menschen ums Leben gekommen. Ein Zwanzigjähriger ist mit seinem Auto frontal mit dem Wagen einer Familie zusammengestoßen. Die beiden Eltern, ihre siebenjährige Tochter und der Unglücksfahrer waren sofort tot. Die Polizei mußte die Landstraße für vier Stunden sperren.

# 5.8 Suggested answers for examination questions

## Recording 1

(d)

## Recording 2

(c)

## Recording 3

(d)

## Recording 4

(d)

## Recording 5

|        | Eis | Kaffee | Tee | Torte | Strudel |
|--------|-----|--------|-----|-------|---------|
| **Karl**   |     | ✗      |     |       |         |
| **Jürgen** |     |        |     | ✗     |         |
| **Uschi**  |     |        | ✗   |       | ✗       |
| **Lotte**  | ✗   |        |     |       |         |

## Recording 6

**(a)**  F
**(b)**  F
**(c)**  R
**(d)**  F
**(e)**  R

## Recording 7

**(a)**  the lake (**den See**), trees (**Bäume**) and sailing boats (**Segelboote**)
**(b)**  on the right (**rechts**)
**(c)**  a shower (**eine Dusche**) and the toilet (**die Toilette**)
**(d)**  half past eight (i.e. *half an hour after we get up at 8 o'clock*)
**(e)**  in the kitchen (**in der Küche**)

## Recording 8

**(a)**  F (It is in **Nordrhein–Westfalen**, not Süddeutschland.)
**(b)**  R (good – **viele große Kaufhäuser**)
**(c)**  R (university – **eine Universität**)
**(d)**  R (The **Aasee** is a lake where you can sail – **ich segle auf dem Aasee**)
**(e)**  R (Mondays you can park; on market days **am Mittwoch und am Samstag** you cannot)
**(f)**  R (Cafes, restaurants and cakeshops are open all day – **den ganzen Tag offen**)

## Recording 9

Part 1  **(a)**  **(ii)**
        **(b)**  **(iii)**
        **(c)**  **(iii)**
Part 2  **(d)**  Monika: a black and a long blue dress; Helga: a green dress
        **(e)**  **(i)**
        **(f)**  **(iii)**

## Recording 10

**Abschnitt 1  (a)**   Er hat **Kopfweh** und **Fieber**.

       **(b)** Er sollte **zwei** Tabletten **dreimal** am Tag einnehmen.

       **(c)** Er sollte **zwei oder drei Tage** im Bett bleiben.

       **(d)** Er sollte **viele warme Getränke** trinken.

**Abschnitt 2 (e)** **Zwanzig** Tabletten kosten 8 DM.

       **(f)** Weil der Kunde **Husten** hat.

       **(g)** Sie kostet **sechs Mark**.

## Recording 11

**Abschnitt 1**

**(a)** (iii)

**(b)** (i)

**(c)** (i)

**Abschnitt 2**

**(a)** (ii)

**(b)** (iii)

**(c)** (ii)

## Recording 12

**Abschnitt 1**

**(a)** der Mann

**(b)** der Mann

**(c)** der Mann

**(d)** die Frau

**(e)** die Frau

**Abschnitt 2**

**(f)** der Mann

**(g)** die Frau

**(h)** der Mann

**(i)** der Mann

**(j)** die Frau

## Recording 13

**(a)** eine Hochdruckzone

**(b)** im Norden

**(c)** um zwei Grad

**(d)** im Süden

**(e)** in Mitteldeutschland

## Recording 14

in zwei Wochen; den D-Zug; vierzehn Uhr; Farbfoto; blauen Hut; eine gelbe Hose; dem linken Arm

## Recording 15

**Part 1**

**(a)** about one and a half hours

**(b)** main railway station

**(c)** little old houses

**(d)** narrow streets

**(e)** in the buildings around the market place

**(f)** the Roland monument

**(g)** 1404

**(h)** in the pedestrianised zone

**Part 2**

**(a)** 1405 to 1409

**(b)** 10, 11

**(c)** 12

**(d)** the end of October

**(e)** 1408

**(f)** oldest parts

**(g)** seventeenth

**(h)** eighteenth

**(i)** architects, writers, potters

**(j)** glass blowers

**(k)** souvenirs

## Recording 16

**Correct statements**

**(b)** (They were not on the third floor – **im zweiten Stock**.)

**(d)** (The food in the restaurant was excellent – **die Speiskarte war reichhaltig**.)

**(e)** (There was a good choice of wine – **es gab eine gute Weinkarte**.)

**(f)** (The waiters were helpful – **die Kellner waren sehr höflich, wir brauchten nie auf das Essen zu warten**.)

**(h)** (They had a telephone in their room – **wir hatten Telefon usw**.)

**Incorrect statements**

**(a)** (They had problems with the shower.)

**(c)** (They never had to wait in the restaurant.)

**(g)** (The weather was not so hot in the second week.)

**(i)** (The hotel did not have an indoor pool.)

**(j)** (They did not want to drink just mineral water.)

## Recording 17

(a) (i)   auf die Universität
      (ii)  Medizin
      (iii) Ärztin in einem Krankenhaus
(b) (i)   mit alten Menschen in einem Altersheim
      (ii)  Seit drei Jahren
(c) (i)   Sie will Friseurin werden
      (ii)  zu ungeduldig ist
      (iii) bei einer Friseurin in die Lehre gehen

## Recording 18

(a) **Er arbeitet in einem Reisebüro in der Stadtmitte** (or **auf der Weidenstraße**). – You need to give two pieces of information out of the three available: 1 mark for the travel agency and 1 mark for either in the **Weidenstraße** or in the town centre.

(b) **Seit drei Wochen** – there is no need to write a complete sentence.

(c) **Die Arbeit macht ihm viel Spaß.** (1 mark) **Er kommt mit vielen Leuten zusammen.** (1 mark)

(d) Any two of: **nach Amerika, England, Spanien, Italien**. (1 mark each)

(e) **Nach ein paar Monaten wird er sich eine bessere Stelle suchen.** (1 mark for any idea of staying in the present job for a few months and 1 mark for getting a better job)

## Recording 19

Abschnitt 1 (a)   R   (He has never tried drugs.)
                (b)   R   (You can become dependent on drugs.)
                (c)   F   (He has smoked since he was 10.)
                (d)   R   (He thinks smoking is stupid and dangerous.)
                (e)   F   (No, he was 10.)
Abschnitt 2 (f)   R   (Yes, stress in school is one of the reasons for taking drugs.)
                (g)   F   (You do not feel grown up if you are bored.)
                (h)   R   (They smoke because they want to feel attractive.)
                (i)   R   (Yes, he would feel fitter.)
                (j)   R   (Yes, drug dependent people should try to say 'no'.)

## Recording 20

Abschnitt 1 (a)   auf der Strecke zwischen Köln und Düsseldorf
                (b)   mit einer Geschwindigkeit von 45 Kilometern pro Stunde
                (c)   Er hatte Rotlicht.
                (d)   22 Leute
Abschnitt 2 (e)   Er hat eine Explosion gehört und viel Rauch gesehen.
                (f)   um den Leuten (beim Rausklettern) zu helfen
                (g)   Sie warteten auf den Rettungswagen.
                (h)   Nein, es steht noch nicht fest wie viele.
                (i)   Es wird operiert.
                (j)   Sie müssen Blut haben.

## Recording 21

(a)   auf einer Landstraße in der Nähe von Münster
(b)   Vier Menschen sind ums Leben gekommen.
(c)   Er war zwanzig Jahre alt.
(d)   Sie war sieben Jahre alt.
(e)   Die Polizei mußte die Landstraße für vier Stunden sperren. *Two pieces of information required here: closing the road (1 mark) and for four hours (1 mark).*

# Chapter 6
# *Speaking*

## 6.1 Introduction

This is what you need to know about the Speaking Test:
- You must be entered either for the Foundation or the Higher Tier of the Speaking Test. You cannot opt out.
- You cannot be entered for both Tiers: you must choose one or the other: your teacher will discuss the correct tier of entry with you.
- There will be a variety of tasks to complete: there will always be two or three role-play situations.
- You may have to give a short presentation in German.
- Most of the role-play tasks will be in pictorial form and you must try to practise looking at the symbols so you know what to expect. Some of the role-plays may be written in German and you will have to be able to interpret what you are expected to do from the sentences.
- You do not have to translate word for word the task specified on the card. However it is very important to ensure that you get the right message across to the examiner.
- It is also important that you take time to practise and improve your pronunciation as there will be marks available for this in the examination.
- It would be a good idea to make recordings of yourself in German so that you can identify the mistakes that you make.

## 6.2 Grade criteria

The GCSE Speaking Test (AT2) will test your ability to do a variety of tasks, depending on which examination group you have been entered for. It is important to check the syllabus details carefully with your teacher and in the syllabus analysis section at the beginning of this book.

### Grade C

Candidates undertake transactions and develop conversations which include past, present and future events. They express personal opinions and show an ability to deal with some unpredictable elements. Although there are some errors, they convey a clear message and their pronunciation and intonation are generally accurate.
- All students are expected to take part in a role-play. This may be based on a rubric in the target language and/or visual stimulus.
- In addition students take part in a role-play which includes an unpredictable element.
- Students take part in a conversation which may be preceded by a short presentation.

### Grade A

Candidates initiate and carry through transactions, take part in conversation and narrate events. They express and justify ideas and points of view and produce longer sequences of speech using a variety of vocabulary, structures and time references. They speak confidently with good pronunciation and intonation. The message is clear, although there may still be errors, especially when candidates use more complex structures.

- Candidates take part in a role-play which includes an unpredictable element.
- Candidates take part in a conversation which may be preceded by a presentation and which must include a narrative.
- Candidates are expected to express and justify points of view.

# 6.3  Preparing for the examination

- It is important to learn new words: start learning vocabulary as soon as possible. Try to learn 10–15 new words every day.
- Marks will be lost if you use English words or if you use the wrong word entirely.
- You may find it helpful to record the words on to a cassette: that way you will be able to work on improving your pronunciation as well as increasing your knowledge of the German language.
- Revise your grammatical rules thoroughly: spend time learning your tenses thoroughly.
- Take notes on small postcards.
- Be able to ask questions as well as being able to recognise question words.
- Get as much practice as possible speaking German.
- Try speaking German to your friends: it will seem strange initially, but in time aim to spend 10 minutes each day using German.
- Use German in your lessons at school as much as possible.
- Make recordings of yourself in German and ask your teacher or the German assistant to mark your recordings for you.
- Record yourself doing the role-plays on the CD and then listen to yourself and note down the mispronunciations, the hesitancy and the grammatical errors; then do the tasks again until you feel confident.

# 6.4  Introduction to conversation

This is what you need to know about the conversation part of your examination:
- First read through the analysis of the examination groups to find out what to expect in the conversation part of your examination.
- If you are doing MEG or Edexcel (London) you will start with a presentation. If you are doing any of the other examination groups, you do not need to read the following section.

## Presentation

- MEG says that you may make use of illustrative materials: e.g. postcards, photographs, etc. If you want to talk about your hobby, you can bring things to the examination to help you to explain things in more detail as well as assisting your teacher in asking you appropriate questions.
- NEAB says that you must not use support materials.
- MEG gives you a separate mark for your presentation.
- NEAB gives you one mark for the presentation and conversation.
- MEG says that you may take notes into the examination room to remind you of what you want to say. You are not allowed to read from written notes. You should make short headings to help you during your presentation.

**E**xaminer's tip

If you are talking about your holiday to Spain last summer your notes could look like this:
1  nach Spanien geflogen: lange Reise; geschlafen und gegessen
2  in einer Villa am Strand: geschwommen; mich gesonnt
3  nach Benidorm gefahren: Souvenirs gekauft; es gab viele Leute
4  Am Abend: ins Restaurant; in der Disko; Leute kennengelernt
5  diesen Sommer: nach London?

Your teacher will be looking out for the following things:
- Use of past, present and future tenses. It may not always be possible to use all three tenses, but in

your preparation for this part of the examination, it is important to try to find ways in which to include as much variety as possible.

- Unusual vocabulary and structures: try to offer an opinion, even in a simple form: **Die Ferien waren gut, weil das Wetter so heiß war. Ich möchte wieder nach Amerika fahren, weil es dort so viel zu sehen gibt.**
- The ability to give a good presentation; however, you should also be able to respond to questions from your teacher.

Avoid choosing 'Myself' as a topic for your presentation: it may seem an easy choice, but there is the possibility of overlapping with other topics and this is to be avoided.

Here are some suggestions for your presentation:

- my holidays
- my family
- my house
- my favourite past-time/hobby
- my visit to Germany
- my part-time job
- my favourite music
- my plans for next year
- my school.

## An example of a presentation

So, hier ist unsere Schule: Die Schule ist eine gemischte Gesamtschule mit ungefähr achthundert Schulkindern. Die Schule wurde 1960 gebaut, und sie ist ziemlich altmodisch. Wir haben sechs Gebäude: alte und neue. Hier ist ein Foto von unserer Bibliothek: Sie ist sehr modern, und darin gibt viele Computers und CD-Romen. Ich mache gern die Hausaufgaben dort.

Hier sind unser Sportplatz und die Turnhalle: Man kann fast alle Sportarten darin treiben. Leider gibt es kein Schwimmbad, aber im Sommer dürfen wir zum Schwimmbad gehen, das in der Stadtmitte liegt. Wir haben auch viele Sportklubs, und es gibt auch Sportturniers. Ich spiele in der Hockeymannschaft und ich muß zweimal in der Woche trainieren.

Hier ist das älteste Gebäude: Darin sind die meisten Klassenzimmer. Es gibt Tische und Stühle für die Kinder, und oft findet man auch einen Tageslichtprojektor, einen Kassettenrekorder und einen Computer. Die Klassenzimmer hier sind relativ klein, aber im Winter sind die Zimmer sehr warm, in dem modernen Gebäude ist es nicht so warm im Winter.

In der Pause am Morgen und in der Mittagspause kann man in der Kantine essen. Das Mittagessen kostet viel, und es schmeckt nicht so gut. Es gibt keine große Auswahl; hier ist eine der Speisekarten und einige Fotos. Die meisten Kinder bringen Butterbrote mit. Wir dürfen in der Kantine und in den Klassenzimmern essen.

Hier ist unsere Schuluniform. Ich finde sie ganz praktisch, aber ich würde lieber andere Klammotten tragen. Im Sommer ist es nicht so gut, besonders wenn das Wetter schön ist, dann würde ich lieber etwas anderes tragen.

Wie ist deine Schule in Deutschland? Ist sie modern, und so groß wie unsere?

# 6.5 Foundation Tier conversation

> **E**xaminer's tip
>
> Write out short paragraphs about your hobbies, your interests in TV viewing; your favourite books etc. Memorise them carefully and record them on a cassette. Use these as speaking and listening practice for the GCSE. You will also be able to use these in the written examination when you have to write letters.

- You will be assessed under the categories of pronunciation, content (range of language), independence and accuracy.
- You should practise your pronunciation as much as possible as marks are frequently lost in this category. Practise with the CD.
- You will have to be able to use a range of tenses: past, present and future.

- You should be able to offer opinions in as many topics as possible. You should make a list of words which express positive and negative opinions and you should then practise these expressions so that your pronunciation and intonation are correct. Here are some examples:

| Positive | Negative |
|---|---|
| es ist toll | es ist nicht so gut |
| das ist echt gut | ich finde das schlimm |
| ich finde das interessant | das gefällt mir nicht |
| es gibt immer viel zu tun | es ist ziemlich langweilig |

- If you are being entered for Foundation Tier, you should be able to answer the following questions:

## Holidays

| | |
|---|---|
| Wohin fährst du gern? Warum? | Ich fahre gern nach…, weil… |
| Mit wem fährst du? | Ich fahre mit meiner Familie/meinen Freunden. |
| Wie fährst du dorthin? | Ich fahre mit… |
| Wo wohnst du am liebsten in den Ferien? | Auf einem Campingplatz, usw. |
| Warst du schon in Deutschland? | Ja, ich war in Berlin/nein, leider noch nicht. |
| Was hast du letzten Sommer gemacht? | Ich bin… gefahren/ich war in… |
| Wenn du viel Geld hättest, wohin würdest du lieber fahren? | Nach Portugal. |

## You and your family

| | |
|---|---|
| Wie heißt du? | Ich heiße… |
| Wie alt bist du? | Ich bin… Jahre alt. |
| Wann hast du Geburtstag? | Mein Geburtstag ist am…? |
| Wann bist du geboren? | Ich bin neunzehnhunderteinundachtzig geboren. |
| Wie viele Personen sind in deiner Familie? | Wir sind vier: mein Vater, meine Mutter, meine Schwester und ich. |
| Was ist dein Vater von Beruf? | Er ist Polizist. |
| Was macht deine Mutter? | Sie arbeitet in einem Laden in der Stadtmitte. |
| Wie groß bist du? | Ich bin einen Meter fünfundfünfzig groß. |
| Hast du Haustiere? | Ich habe eine Maus/keine Haustiere/einen Hund. |

## School

| | |
|---|---|
| Was für eine Schule besuchst du? | Ich besuche eine Gesamtschule/ein Gymnasium. |
| Wie ist die Schule? | Die Schule ist relativ groß/modern/alt. |
| Was lernst du? | Ich lerne Deutsch, Englisch, Mathematik, Physik. |
| Was magst du gern? | Ich mag gern Kunst, weil es interessant ist. |
| Und nicht gern? | Ich lerne nicht gern Mathe, weil ich sie so schwer finde. |
| Wann beginnt der Unterricht? | Der Unterricht beginnt um fünf vor neun. |
| Wann endet der Unterricht? | Um Viertel vor vier. |
| Wie ist die Uniform? | Die Uniform ist dunkelblau: Für Mädchen gibt es einen grauen Rock und einen dunkelblauen Pullover; für Jungen gibt es graue oder schwarze Hosen und eine dunkelblaue Jacke. |
| Was machst du zu Mittag? | Ich esse in der Schule/ich gehe nach Hause. |
| Wie schmeckt das Schulessen? | Es ist gut/lecker/nicht so gut. |
| Gibt es Klubs? | Wir haben Sportklubs und Musikklubs. |

## Future plans

| | |
|---|---|
| Was sind deine Pläne für nächstes Jahr? | Ich werde auf der Schule bleiben. |
| | Ich werde in die Oberstufe gehen. |
| | Ich werde eine Lehre machen. |

## House and home

| | |
|---|---|
| Wo wohnst du? | Ich wohne in Durham. |
| Wohnst du in einem Haus oder in einer Wohnung? | Ich wohne in einem Doppelhaus. |
| Wie viele Zimmer hat dein Haus? | Es gibt sechs Zimmer: vier Schlafzimmer, ein Wohnzimmer und eine Küche. |

Gibt es einen Garten bei dir zu Hause?

Wie ist dein Schlafzimmer?

Wir haben einen Vorgarten mit Blumen.

Mein Zimmer ist rosa, und ich habe ein Bett, einen Tisch, einen Fernseher und einen Hifi-Turm.

Mußt du zu Hause helfen?

Bekommst du Taschengeld?

Was machst du damit?

Ich muß mein Bett machen/abwaschen.

Ja, zehn Pfund pro Woche.

Ich kaufe Kleider/ich spare für die Ferien.

## Daily routine

Wann stehst du auf?

Was machst du zunächst?

Wann gehst du ins Bett?

Was ißt du zum Frühstück?

Ich stehe um acht Uhr auf.

Ich wasche mich und ziehe mich an.

Gegen elf Uhr.

Ich esse Toast und Marmelade und trinke Tee dazu.

Wann verläßt du das Haus, um in die Schule zu gehen?

Wie kommst du zur Schule?

Was machst du abends zu Hause?

Und danach?

Um halb neun.

Mit dem Bus.

Ich mache die Hausaufgaben.

Ich sehe fern oder ich gehe mit Freunden aus.

# 6.6 Higher Tier conversation

Here is what you need to know about the examination:

- You will be assessed on your communication skills and also on the quality of your language.
- You will be asked to show your knowledge of tenses by being asked questions about what you did in the past, what you normally do and what you will do in the future. Your final grade depends on how well you produce the different tenses.
- Your answers need to be longer than at Foundation Tier. You will be asked more open-ended questions to allow you to answer at length (e.g. **Können Sie mir etwas über Ihre Ferien erzählen?**) and you must show that you can talk at length using a wide variety of vocabulary and structures.
- You will not be allowed to give a pre-learnt speech. Your teacher will interrupt you when s/he realises that this is what you are doing.
- Your teacher will have a list of the topics to be covered in the Higher Tier conversation and s/he may give you this list as well as some questions to learn. You should concentrate on the topics which your teacher gives you.
- The topics which you are most likely to encounter at this Tier are: family, house and home, your home town and area, your holidays, your school, your future plans, your friends, shopping, food and meals, daily routine, special occasions, the world of work, pocket money and weekend/part-time jobs.
- In the examination give long answers, try to use a variety of structures and vocabulary, try to put expression and meaning into what you are saying and prepare some questions to ask your teacher: remember this is a conversation and not a boring monologue.
- Although your answers must not be pre-learnt, it is nevertheless important that you are able to speak for about a minute on these topics.
- Record your presentation on a cassette and listen to it as often as you like. Ask a friend to practise the conversation with you. Ask them to interrupt you and ask an unexpected question.

## Family

### Kannst du mir etwas über dich und deine Familie sagen?

Ich heiße Lisa und ich bin sechzehn Jahre alt. Ich wohne in Durham in Nordostengland. Ich bin ziemlich klein und schlank. Ich habe braune Haare und grüne Augen wie meine Mutter. Mein Vater ist vor drei Jahren gestorben.

### Hast du Geschwister?

Ich habe einen Bruder, der Peter heißt. Er ist jünger als ich, und ich helfe ihm oft bei seiner Schularbeit. Meine ältere Schwester wohnt jetzt in London. Sie ist Studentin an der Uni.

**Fährst du oft nach London, um sie zu besuchen?**

Das hängt von meinem Taschengeld ab: Es kostet viel, mit dem Zug dorthin zu fahren. Ich hoffe im September nach London zu fahren.

**Hast du ein gutes Verhältnis zu deiner Schwester?**

Ja, wir können fast alles besprechen und wir haben dieselben Hobbys. Wir gehen gern ins Kino und wir treiben Sport.

**Und zu deinem Bruder?**

Das ist umgekehrt: Er geht mir auf die Nerven. Er kommt immer in mein Schlafzimmer, er ist frech und auch ein bißchen faul.

## House and home

**Kannst du mir etwas über dein Haus sagen?**

Ich wohne mit meiner Familie in einer Wohnung am Stadtrand. Die Wohnung ist in einem modernen Wohnblock. Ich wohne im dritten Stock. Die Wohnung ist ganz modern: Es gibt ein Wohnzimmer mit einer Eßecke, drei Schlafzimmer, ein Badezimmer mit Dusche und auch eine große Küche. Wir essen oft in der Küche, weil sie so groß ist.

**Wohnst du gern dort?**

Obwohl dieWohnung klein ist, ist es sehr gemütlich, und mein Zimmer ist sehr bequem.

**Was gibt es in deinem Schlafzimmer?**

Ein Bett (natürlich), ein Sofa, einen Fernseher und ein Videogerät. Mein Zimmer ist weiß und rosa tapeziert, ich habe die Farben gewählt. Wenn meine Freunde zu mir kommen, sitzen wir herum und plaudern.

**In was für einem Haus würdest du wohnen, wenn du reich wärst?**

Ich hätte gern ein Einfamilienhaus mit einem Garten vor und hinter dem Haus. Ich arbeite gern mit Pflanzen, und weil wir im dritten Stock wohnen, haben wir keinen Garten.

## Your home town

**Beschreibe deine Heimatstadt**

Ich wohne seit zehn Jahren in Colchester. Colchester liegt in Südostengland nicht weit von London: ungefähr eine Stunde mit dem Zug. Colchester ist die älteste Stadt in England, und viele Touristen kommen in meine Stadt.

**Was gibt es denn für Touristen zu sehen?**

Es gibt die alte Burg; viele Museen und ein gutes Einkaufszentrum. Außerhalb der Stadt gibt es einen modernen Zoo mit allerlei Tieren. Die Parkgebühren sind teuer, und es gibt am Wochenende viele Staus. Man kann auch Ausflüge nach Cambridge und an die Küste machen.

**Was kann man abends machen?**

Es gibt viele Kneipen und auch eine Disko. Wenn man Sport treiben will, gibt es ein neues Sportzentrum und auch eine moderne Kegelbahn. Leider kostet es viel Geld, ins Sportzentrum zu gehen. Nicht weit von Colchester gibt es Mersea: eine kleine Stadt am Meer, wo man Wasserski laufen kann und wo man auch schwimmen kann. Das Wasser ist aber ziemlich kalt, auch im Sommer. Das Wetter hier ist wirklich sonnig. Meiner Meinung nach gibt es nicht genug für junge Leute in Colchester. Wir finden die Stadt langweilig und wir brauchen mehr Klubs und Aktivitäten.

## Hobbys

**Was machst du in deiner Freizeit?**

Ich bin sehr sportlich, ich treibe sehr gern Sport. Samstags spiele ich Fußball für die Schulmannschaft, und am Samstagnachmittag gehe ich zu einem Fußballspiel. Während der Woche spiele ich auch Basketball, und ich gehe schwimmen.

**Bist du Mitglied eines Klubs?**

Ja, ich spiele in einem Tennisklub und auch in einem Squashklub.

**Bist du schon mal nach Wembley gefahren, um ein Fußballspiel oder ein Basketballspiel zu sehen?**

Vor zwei Jahren waren die Harlem Globetrotters hier in England, und ich bin mit einer Schulgruppe nach Wembley gefahren, um das Spiel zu sehen. Es hat viel Spaß gemacht. Die Harlem Globetrotters haben sehr gut gespielt. Ich hoffe, diesen Sommer Basketball in Amerika zu spielen.

**Wieso?**

Unsere Schule macht einen Austausch mit einer Schule in Washington, und ich nehme daran teil. Es kostet viel, und im Moment arbeite ich abends, um extra Geld zu verdienen und für die Ferien zu sparen.

## Future plans

**Nach den GCSE's, was für Pläne hast du?**

Wenn ich gute Noten bekomme, werde ich auf die Oberstufe gehen um weiterzustudieren. Es gibt keine Oberstufe hier an meiner Schule, aber es gibt ein gutes College in der Stadtmitte. Für mich ist es wichtig die Schule zu verlassen. Ich kann neue Leute kennenlernen und auch die Lehrer dort kennen mich nicht. Ich brauche keine Uniform zu tragen.

**Was wirst du denn studieren?**

Ich werde Deutsch und Physik und Chemie studieren. Dann, nach dem Abitur, werde ich auf die Uni gehen, vielleicht in London, ich bin nicht sicher. Ich möchte eine Stelle in einer großen Firma finden. Ich könnte auch in Deutschland arbeiten.

**Und wenn die Resultaten nicht so gut sind?**

Dann werde ich eine Lehre bei einer Firma hier in der Stadt machen: ich werde Geld und Qualifikationen kriegen.

**Gibt es Probleme hier mit der Arbeitslosigkeit?**

Ein bißchen, aber es wird jetzt besser.

## Holidays

**Was für Pläne hast du für diesen Sommer?**

Ich habe schon einen Ferienjob in einem Geschäft gefunden. Ich werde vier Wochen arbeiten, dann fahre ich los! Ich fahre mit einer Gruppe nach Spanien. Meine Freundin hat eine Villa am Meer in Südspanien, und wir fahren mit ihren Eltern nach Malaga, und wir werden zwei Wochen dort bleiben. Wir werden uns sonnen und Souvenirs kaufen.

**Ist das dein erster Besuch im Ausland?**

Nein, vor zwei Jahren bin ich mit meiner Familie nach Frankreich gefahren. Wir haben einen Wohnwagen in den Alpen gemietet. Das Wetter war echt gut, und wir haben viele Ausflüge gemacht. Wir haben einen Tag in der Schweiz verbracht. Die Landschaft war so schön, und es war so sauber. Es war nicht so teuer in Frankreich, aber in der Schweiz waren die Preise viel höher.

# 6.7 Role-plays

## Foundation Tier

You will need to perform role-plays involving transactional language e.g. in a shop, in a restaurant, shopping for souvenirs, asking the way.

## Higher Tier

You will be asked to carry out more complex role-plays with some unexpected questions or where the situation is less structured and thus more open-ended. With some examination groups the role-play will be accompanied by pictures – check with your teacher.

## Examination technique

In the role-play it is most important to get the message over. When the response is being marked, the examiner will be judging you on your ability to get the message over to a native speaker. Although grammatical errors will be tolerated, pronunciation is vital if you are to get the message over. Use the CD to help you to improve your accent and intonation.

## Role-play situations

The role-play situations will be based on the Areas of Experience used by all of the examination boards. However there are certain situations which lend themselves to role-play and you should be aware of this. These situations are:

- in a cafe/in a snackbar/in a restaurant
- asking the way
- using public transport: buses, trams, trains
- at the camp-site/at the youth hostel/at the hotel
- staying with a family

- at the doctor's
- shopping for food/drink/clothes/souvenirs
- at the bank/at the post office
- talking to a friend and making arrangements to go out.

The teacher's role and suggested answers for the following role-plays are on the CD which accompanies this book. Look at the task first, prepare your answers with a dictionary, then listen to your CD. There is a tone which tells you to stop your machine and give the appropriate response.

## Examples of role-play type 1: Foundation Tier

### Role-play 1

You are in a snackbar in Germany. Your teacher will play the part of the waiter/waitress.

(a)     (b)     (c)     (d)     (e)

(10)

### Role-play 2

You are in Hamburg Hauptbahnhof and you want to buy a second class return to Bonn. You must find out what platform the train leaves from, how much the ticket costs, the time of departure and whether you have to change.

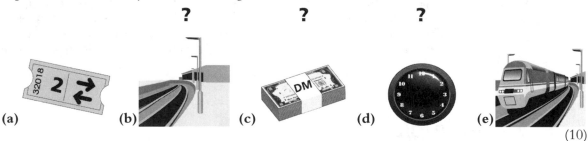

(a)     (b)     (c)     (d)     (e)

(10)

### Role-play 3

You are visiting your pen-pal for the first time. You have to telephone your pen-pal's parents to inform them that you have now arrived in Germany. You have to tell them where you are waiting, what you are wearing and something else about yourself.

(a)     (b)     (c)     (d)     (e)

(10)

### Role-play 4

You are in the bus station in Lübeck. You want to book a seat on the coach to Travemünde on Saturday morning. You have a student card. You want to check the times of the coach.

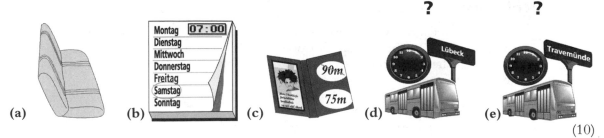

(a)     (b)     (c)     (d)     (e)

(10)

**Role-play 5**
You are at a campsite in Switzerland. Your teacher will play the part of the warden.
**(a)** Begrüßen Sie den Besitzer/die Besitzerin.

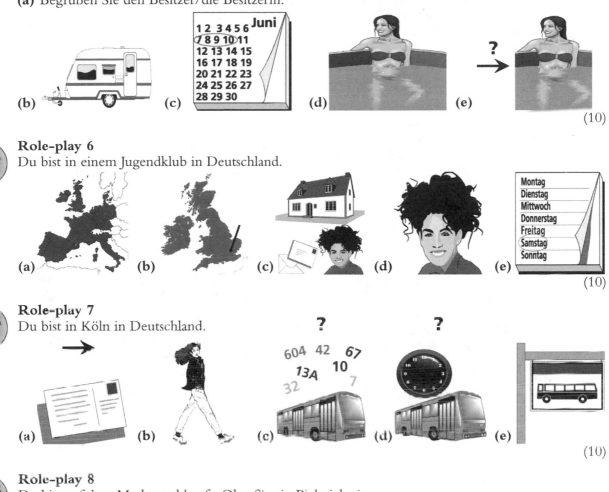

(b)          (c)          (d)          (e)

(10)

**Role-play 6**
Du bist in einem Jugendklub in Deutschland.

(a)          (b)          (c)          (d)          (e)

(10)

**Role-play 7**
Du bist in Köln in Deutschland.

(a)          (b)          (c)          (d)          (e)

(10)

**Role-play 8**
Du bist auf dem Markt und kaufst Obst für ein Picknick ein.

Du mußt  kaufen. Bevor du  kaufst, mußt du nach den Preisen fragen.

(5)

# Examples of role-play type 2: Foundation and Higher Tier

- You will have to do this type of role-play at both Higher and Foundation Tier. This is the overlap role-play.
- The tasks will be more open-ended: this means that instead of having to communicate one simple idea, you may have to make a choice or explain a more complicated idea.
- The examiner is looking for a higher level of German from you, but minor errors will be tolerated.
- There will be one question where you will have to respond to an unprepared question from the examiner.
- In the role-plays at Higher Tier there are usually some unexpected questions. When you are preparing the role-play, try to think logically about what the examiner could ask you if you were really in a real-life situation.

**E** xaminer's tip

Du or Sie?
When you are preparing the role-play it is important to note to whom you are talking.
If it is someone that you know as a friend, then you will be expected to use **du**. If,
however the teacher is playing the part of a receptionist in a hotel or another adult
that you do not know so well, then you will have to use **Sie**. At Higher Tier marks are
deducted for the incorrect choice of 'register'.

**Role-play 9**

Sie sind in Deutschland und Sie suchen eine Stelle für sechs Monate.

**(a)** Geben Sie Ihren Namen und sagen Sie, warum Sie da sind.

**(b)** Sagen Sie, was für Arbeit Sie schon gemacht haben.

**(c)** Beantworten Sie die Frage.

**(d)** Beantworten Sie die Frage.

**(e)** Fragen Sie etwas über die Stelle. (10)

**Role-play 10**

You are discussing your holiday plans with a friend.

**(a)** Say that you are going to Germany this year.

**(b)** Answer the question.

**(c)** Answer the question.

**(d)** Say that you have booked your ticket.

**(e)** Say that you will send him/her a postcard. (10)

**Role-play 11**

Sie sprechen mit einem Freund. Sie gehen heute abend aus, aber Sie müssen spätestens um 10 Uhr zurück sein.

**(a)**   **(b)**   **(c)**   **(d)**   **(e)** (10)

**Role-play 12**

You are staying with a friend in Köln during a school exchange. S/he wants to go out with you one evening so you show him/her your programme. Negotiate with your friend the best time to go out and also decide where you are going. S/he will start the conversation.

```
Montag:       9.00:   Willkommen in der Schule
             14.00:   Tischtennisspiel in der Sporthalle
Dienstag:             mit den Gastfamilien
Mittwoch:     9.00:   Besuch in der Stadt
             13.00:   Ausflug in die Berge
Donnerstag:   9.00:   Schule bis 1200 Uhr
             14.00:   Einkaufen
Freitag:              Rückfahrt nach England
```

**(a)** Was?

**(b)** Welchen Tag?

**(c)** Wann?

**(d)** Wie? (10)

**Role-play 13**

Sie sind auf Urlaub und Ihr Freund ist seit gestern morgen krank.

**(a)** Sagen Sie, was mit Ihrem Freund los ist.

**(b)** Geben Sie andere Symptome an.

**(c)** Beantworten Sie die Frage.

**(d)** Fragen Sie nach weiterem Rat. (10)

**Role-play 14**

Du bist in einem Fundbüro in einem Bahnhof.

(10)

## Examples of role-play type 3: Higher Tier

This is what you need to know about this type of role-play:

● This role-play will contain a greater degree of unpredictability.

● These role-plays take the form of a series of pictures depicting a day out, a holiday, an accident or other event. You can usually decide if the subject of the story was you or someone else. You must tell the story in the past tense, so revise carefully from Chapter 1.

● The type of role-play will be dependent on your examination group. For MEG there will be a series of pictures and words for you to use to tell a story in the past tense. For NEAB you may have to come to an agreement with someone about where to go, what to do and what time to go. For WJEC/London you will have a role-play similar to type 2 but with two unpredictable elements instead of one.

**E**xaminer's tip

Learn the following imperfect and perfect forms of past tenses:

| es gab | there was/there were | ich habe gegessen | I ate |
|--------|----------------------|-------------------|-------|
| ich bin gefahren | I went | ich habe gekauft | I bought |
| ich bin gegangen | I went | ich bin angekommen | I arrived |
| ich habe gesehen | I saw | ich bin ausgegangen | I went out |

**Role-play 15**

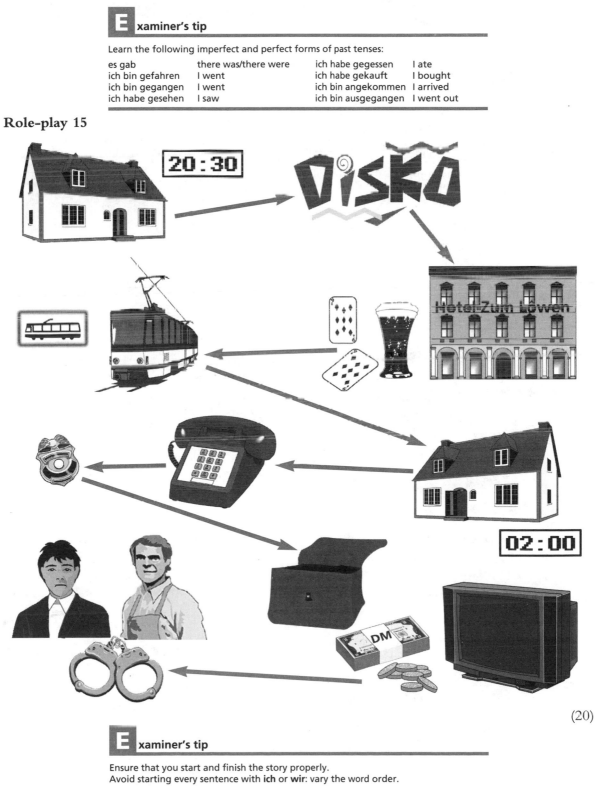

(20)

**E**xaminer's tip

Ensure that you start and finish the story properly.
Avoid starting every sentence with **ich** or **wir**: vary the word order.

**Role-play 16**

## Spanien
### Costa Brava

Luxushotel
3 Minuten vom Meer
alle Zimmer mit Dusche und WC: Sonderpreise im Sommer
modern eingerichtet
Restaurant; Bar; Freizeitraum; Fernsehraum; Freibad
Babysitters
Disko: dienstags, donnerstags, samstags
schöner Strand mit Booten zum Mieten
Windsurfen; Wasserski; Wasserball
Parkplatz und Garagen
Bus vom Flughafen zum Hotel

**E** xaminer's tip

There are key words used in the picture stories and you should know how to use them:

| | |
|---|---|
| Besuch in der Stadt | wir haben die Stadt besucht |
| Stadtbesichtigung | ich habe die Stadt besichtigt |
| Abfahrt | wir sind abgefahren |
| Ankunft | wir sind angekommen |
| Beschreibung | er war relativ groß/klein usw. |
| Rückfahrt | wir sind nach Hause gefahren |

(20)

**Role-play 17**

**S O N D E R A U S F L U G**
*am 4. August*
Bonn – Wiesbaden (Dampfer)
10 Stunden
Abfahrt: 6.00 Uhr
etwa 170 Kilometer
Jugendliche DM 48
modernes Schiff mit Bar und Restaurant
Stadtbesichtigung Koblenz
Unterkunft in Wiesbaden
Reisebustour: DM 20
Rückfahrt mit dem Zug nach Bonn am 5. August
Reservieren Sie sofort

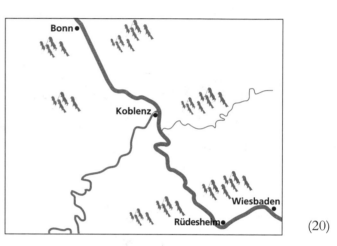

(20)

**Role-play 18**

Your Austrian penpal is in England and is surprised that students have to wear school uniform. S/he thinks it is a silly outdated idea. You are convinced that it is a good idea.

**(a)** Beschreiben Sie Ihre Uniform
**(b)** Erklären Sie, daß es eine gute Idee ist.
**(c)** Geben Sie Gründe dafür.

Remember that your teacher has to argue with you and you have to convince him/her of your point of view. (10)

**Role-play 19**

You are on holiday in Switzerland and you have just read this advertisment. You telephone your Swiss friend to arrange a day out there. The examiner will begin the conversation.

### *Sportzentrum*
*Luzern*
*Rollschuhbahn*
*Rodelbahn*
*Schnellimbiß*
*Spiel und Spaß*
*Täglich: 9.00 bis 20.00*

- Aktivitäten
- Was mitbringen
- Treffpunkt

Du rufst einen Freund/eine Freundin an. Ich bin dein Freund/deine Freundin.

Dein(e) Lehrer(in) beginnt.

(10)

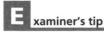 **E** xaminer's tip

Some other useful expressions:

nachdem wir die Burg besucht haben, sind wir ins Museum gegangen
bevor wir abgefahren sind, gab es einen Unfall

| | |
|---|---|
| kurz darauf | shortly afterwards |
| plötzlich | suddenly |
| zwei Stunden später | two hours later |

# 6.8 Teacher's role and suggested answers

## Role-play 1

| | |
|---|---|
| **Teacher** | Guten Tag, wie kann ich Ihnen helfen? |
| **You** | Guten Tag, ich möchte eine Bratwurst. |
| **Teacher** | Mit oder ohne Senf? |
| **You** | Mit Senf, bitte. |
| **Teacher** | Und zu trinken? |
| **You** | Ein Glas Limonade, bitte. |
| **Teacher** | Kommt sofort. |
| **You** | Wieviel macht das zusammen? |
| **Teacher** | Das macht 10 Mark 90. |
| **You** | Kann ich von hier telefonieren? |
| **Teacher** | Das Telefon ist im Untergeschoß. |

## Role-play 2

| | |
|---|---|
| **Teacher** | Wie kann ich Ihnen helfen? |
| **You** | Einmal nach Bonn hin und zurück zweiter Klasse. |
| **Teacher** | In Ordnung. |
| **You** | Von welchem Gleis fährt der Zug? |
| **Teacher** | Gleis 6. |
| **You** | Was kostet das? |
| **Teacher** | 70 Mark. |
| **You** | Wann fährt der Zug ab? |
| **Teacher** | Um halb zehn. |
| **You** | Muß ich umsteigen? |
| **Teacher** | Nein, der Zug fährt durch. |

## Role-play 3

| | |
|---|---|
| **Teacher** | Hallo Lenzer! Wer ist am Apparat. |
| **You** | Guten Tag Herr Lenzer. Hier spricht … |
| **Teacher** | Da bist du endlich. Wie war die Reise? |
| **You** | Ziemlich lang. |
| **Teacher** | So, wo bist du jetzt? |
| **You** | Auf dem Bahnhof. Ich warte vor dem Schalter. |
| **Teacher** | Ich hole dich mit dem Auto ab. Wie siehst du aus? |
| **You** | Ich bin mittelgroß und habe kurze Haare. |
| **Teacher** | Und was trägst du heute? |
| **You** | Ich habe Jeans und einen Pullover an. |

## Role-play 4

| | |
|---|---|
| **You** | Ich möchte einen Platz nach Travemünde reservieren. |
| **Teacher** | Wann wollen Sie fahren? |
| **You** | Am Samstagmorgen. |
| **Teacher** | Wir haben noch Platz. |
| **You** | Gibt es eine Ermäßigung für Studenten? |
| **Teacher** | Ja. Ihren Ausweis, bitte. |
| **You** | Wann fährt der Bus von Lübeck ab? |
| **Teacher** | Der erste Bus fährt um 6 Uhr. |
| **You** | Wann kommt der Bus in Travemünde an? |
| **Teacher** | Sehen wir mal … um elf Uhr. |

## Role-play 5

| | |
|---|---|
| **You** | Guten Tag/Guten Abend. Haben Sie noch Platz frei? |
| **Teacher** | Für ein Zelt? |
| **You** | Nein, für einen Wohnwagen. |
| **Teacher** | Für wie lange? |

| You | Für drei Nächte. |
| Teacher | Wir haben noch Platz. |
| You | Kann man hier in der Nähe schwimmen gehen? |
| Teacher | Es gibt ein Schwimmbad im Dorf. |
| You | Wie kommt man am besten zum Schwimmbad? |

## Role-play 6

| Teacher | Guten Abend. |
| You | Woher kommst du? |
| Teacher | Ich komme aus Deutschland. |
| You | Ich bin Engländer(in). |
| Teacher | Was machst du hier in Deutschland? |
| You | Ich besuche meinen Brieffreund. |
| Teacher | Wie findest du deinen Besuch? |
| You | Der Besuch gefällt mir. |
| Teacher | Und wann fährst du nach Hause? |
| You | Nächste Woche. |

## Role-play 7

| You | Wie komme ich am besten zur Post? |
| Teacher | Sie gehen hier geradeaus, dann nehmen Sie die zweite Straße rechts. |
| You | Kann ich zu Fuß gehen? |
| Teacher | Leider müssen Sie mit dem Bus fahren. |
| You | Welche Linie? |
| Teacher | Linie 6A. |
| You | Wann fährt der nächste Bus ab? |
| Teacher | Um 15 Uhr. |
| You | Und wo ist die Bushaltestelle? |
| Teacher | Gleich vor der Sparkasse. |

## Role-play 8

| Teacher | Wie kann ich Ihnen helfen? |
| You | Ich möchte ein Kilo Äpfel. |
| Teacher | Sonst noch etwas? |
| You | Wieviel kosten die Pfirsiche? |
| Teacher | 1 Mark 40 das Stück. |
| You | 6 Pfirsiche. |
| Teacher | Ist das alles? |
| You | Haben Sie Erdbeeren? |
| Teacher | Sie kosten 5 Mark das Kilo. |
| You | Ein Kilo, bitte/nein danke, das ist mir zu teuer. |

## Role-play 9

| Teacher | Guten Tag, wie kann ich Ihnen helfen? |
| You | Ich suche einen Ferienjob bei Ihrer Firma. Ich heiße … |
| Teacher | Haben Sie eine Stelle in England? |
| You | (e.g. Ja, ich arbeite samstags, und ich habe letzten Sommer in einem Café gearbeitet.) |
| Teacher | Seit wann lernen Sie Deutsch? |
| You | (e.g. Seit 5 Jahren.) |
| Teacher | Wie lange können Sie bei uns arbeiten? |
| You | (e.g. Sechs Monate.) |
| Teacher | Also, Sie haben einen Job. |
| You | (e.g. Wie viele Stunden muß ich jeden Tag arbeiten? Muß ich eine Uniform tragen?) |

## Role-play 10

| Teacher | Was sind deine Pläne für die Ferien? |
| You | Ich fahre nach Deutschland. |
| Teacher | Wie fährst du dorthin? |
| You | (e.g. Mit dem Bus/mit dem Zug.) |

| | |
|---|---|
| **Teacher** | Wie lange dauert die Reise mit dem Bus/Zug? |
| **You** | (e.g. Ungefähr zwei Tage.) |
| **Teacher** | Das ist aber lange! |
| **You** | Ich habe schon meinen Platz reserviert. |
| **Teacher** | Prima! |
| **You** | Ich werde dir eine Postkarte schicken. |

## Role-play 11

| | |
|---|---|
| **Teacher** | Wir gehen heute abend in den Klub. Kommst du mit? |
| **You** | Ja gerne! Wann und wo treffen wir uns? |
| **Teacher** | Um 8 Uhr vor dem Kino. |
| **You** | Was ziehst du an? |
| **Teacher** | Jeans und ein T-Shirt. |
| **You** | Wann ist die Disko aus? |
| **Teacher** | Um 11 Uhr. |
| **You** | Leider kann ich nicht mitkommen, ich muß schon um 10 Uhr zu Hause sein. Wenn ich mitkomme, muß ich die Disko früh verlassen. |

## Role-play 12

| | |
|---|---|
| **Teacher** | Möchtest du lieber auf eine Party kommen oder in die Disko gehen? |
| **You** | (e.g. In die Disko.) |
| **Teacher** | Wann kannst du gehen? |
| **You** | (e.g. Entweder Dienstag oder Mittwochabend.) |
| **Teacher** | Leider ist es für mich an diesen zwei Tagen nicht möglich. Wie wäre es mit Montag? |
| **You** | Ja, das geht auch. |
| **Teacher** | Wann endet das Tischtennisspiel? |
| **You** | Gegen vier Uhr. |
| **Teacher** | Das paßt ja prima! |
| **You** | Wie fahren wir dorthin? |
| **Teacher** | Ich hole dich mit dem Auto ab. |
| **You** | Wann und wo? |
| **Teacher** | Um 19 Uhr bei der Gastfamilie. |

## Role-play 13

| | |
|---|---|
| **Teacher** | Was ist mit dir los? |
| **You** | (Mein Freund hat Magenschmerzen.) |
| **Teacher** | Hat er andere Symptome? |
| **You** | (Ja. Er hat auch Fieber.) |
| **Teacher** | Wann fahrt ihr nach England? |
| **You** | (In zwei Tagen/in einer Woche/morgen.) |
| **Teacher** | Am besten bleibt er im Bett. |
| **You** | (Was soll er machen? Darf er trinken? Darf er essen?) |

## Role-play 14

| | |
|---|---|
| **Teacher** | Kann ich dir helfen? |
| **You** | Ich habe meine Tasche mit meinem Badeanzug verloren. |
| **Teacher** | Wo hast du sie gelassen? |
| **You** | Im Zug. |
| **Teacher** | Und wann war das? |
| **You** | Gestern morgen um 10 Uhr. |
| **Teacher** | Wann fährst du nach England? |
| **You** | (e.g. Nächste Woche/morgen.) |
| **Teacher** | Leider haben wir keine Tasche wie deine hier im Moment. |
| **You** | Können Sie mich anrufen oder mir einen Brief senden? |
| **Teacher** | Freilich, wenn wir sie finden. |

## Role-play 15

| | |
|---|---|
| **Teacher** | So, du warst neulich in Deutschland bei einer Gastfamilie. Eines Abends bist du ausgegangen. Kannst du mir etwas darüber erzählen? |

| | |
|---|---|
| **You** | Ja, letzten Sommer, als ich auf Urlaub in Deutschland war, bin ich eines Abends mit meiner Freundin ausgegangen. Wir sind in eine Disko gegangen. Wir haben das Haus um halb neun verlassen, und in der Disko haben wir getanzt, und wir haben viel Spaß gehabt. |
| **Teacher** | Was hast du dann gemacht? |
| **You** | Nachdem wir die Disko verlassen haben, sind wir in ein Hotel gegangen. Dort haben wir einige Bier getrunken und Karten gespielt. Eine Stunde später sind wir zur Straßenbahnhaltestelle gegangen, um nach Hause zu fahren. |
| **Teacher** | Wann hast du das Haus erreicht? |
| **You** | Wir sind endlich um 2 Uhr morgens nach Hause gekommen und wir haben bemerkt, daß die Haustür offen war. Wir waren schockiert, und sobald wir das Haus betreten hatten, war alles klar. Einbrecher hatten eingebrochen und viel gestohlen. Wir haben die Polizei angerufen. |
| **Teacher** | So ein Pech! |
| **You** | Ja. Die Polizisten haben uns gefragt, was gestohlen wurde. Wir haben alles erklärt: Sie haben den Fernseher aus dem Wohnzimmer genommen und auch eine Handtasche und Geld. Wir haben alles beschrieben, und ein Polizist hat es aufgeschrieben. |
| **Teacher** | Was ist dann passiert? |
| **You** | Die Polizei ist wieder zur Polizeiwache gefahren, und wir sind ins Bett gegangen. Zwei Wochen später, als ich wieder in England war, habe ich gehört, daß sie die zwei Einbrecher verhaftet hatten. Ende gut, alles gut! |

## Role-play 16

| | |
|---|---|
| **Teacher** | Du warst neulich auf Urlaub in Spanien. Kannst du mir etwas darüber sagen? |
| **You** | Letzten Sommer habe ich meine Ferien in Spanien verbracht. Wir sind von Gatwick nach Malaga geflogen. Die Reise war nicht zu lang. Als wir in Spanien ankamen, sind wir in den Hotelbus eingestiegen, weil das Hotel an der Küste lag. Es dauerte nur eine halbe Stunde, bis wir das Hotel erreichten. |
| **Teacher** | Wie war das Hotel? |
| **You** | Das Hotel war ganz modern und lag direkt am Strand. Es gab 40 Zimmer, einige mit Balkon, und sie hatten alle Dusche und WC. Mein Zimmer war im ersten Stock mit schöner Aussicht aufs Meer. Und im Hotel gab es ein Restaurant, wo wir oft am Abend gegessen haben. Es gab auch ein schönes geheiztes Freibad, wo man zweimal pro Woche Wasserball spielen konnte. Das Hotel hatte auch eine Disko für Kinder und Erwachsene – das war echt gut. |
| **Teacher** | Wieso? |
| **You** | Ich habe ein nettes Mädchen kennengelernt, und wir haben den Rest der Ferien zusammen verbracht. Am Strand haben wir uns gesonnt, und ich habe auch Windsurfen gemacht. Für mich war das schwierig - ich bin oft ins Wasser gefallen. Wir sind auch Wasserski gelaufen: Es hat viel gekostet, und es war sehr ermüdend. Die Ferien sind zu schnell vorbeigegangen, und ich mußte nach England zurückfahren. |
| **Teacher** | Hoffst du, das Mädchen wiederzusehen? |
| **You** | Sie hat mir ihre Adresse und ihre Telefonnummer gegeben. Wir haben einige Briefe geschrieben und wir hoffen, nächstes Jahr zusammen Urlaub zu machen. |

## Role-play 17

| | |
|---|---|
| **You** | Letzten Sommer, als ich in Deutschland war, habe ich eine Bootsfahrt auf dem Rhein gemacht. Wir sind von Bonn nach Wiesbaden gefahren. Wir sind am Montagmorgen um 7 Uhr mit dem Bus abgefahren. Eine halbe Stunde später waren wir auf dem Schiff. |
| **Teacher** | Wie war das Wetter? |
| **You** | Am Morgen war es kühl, aber es gab auch Sonne. Unterwegs habe ich viel geknipst. Wir haben eine Stunde in Koblenz verbracht. Ich habe einige Souvenirs gekauft, und dann sind wir in eine Konditorei gegangen, um Kaffee und Kuchen zu kaufen. Es war echt gut, aber es war ein bißchen teuer. |
| **Teacher** | Wohin sind Sie dann gefahren? |
| **You** | Von Koblenz sind wir weitergefahren. Wir haben die Lorelei gesehen, und es war ganz still auf dem Wasser. Danach haben wir zu Abend im Restaurant auf dem Boot gegessen. Das Essen hat mir gut geschmeckt, und wir haben auch viel Wein probiert! |

| | |
|---|---|
| **Teacher** | War das Rheinwein? |
| **You** | Natürlich! |
| **Teacher** | Nach dem Abendessen, waren sie da alle müde? |
| **You** | Ein bißchen, aber wir hatten Karten für die Bustour in Wiesbaden reserviert. Die Stadt sah ganz schön am Abend aus. Wir haben unser Hotel gegen elf Uhr wieder erreicht, und ich war todmüde. Ich bin sofort eingeschlafen. |
| **Teacher** | Was haben Sie am Dienstagmorgen gemacht? |
| **You** | Am folgenden Morgen sind wir mit dem Zug wieder nach Bonn gefahren. Die Reise mit dem Zug war ein bißchen langweilig, aber unterwegs habe ich geschlafen. |
| **Teacher** | Hoffen Sie, wieder nach Deutschland zu fahren? |
| **You** | Vielleicht: Das hängt vom Geld ab. |

## Role-play 18

| | |
|---|---|
| **Teacher** | Ich finde es ganz schlimm, daß die Schulkinder hier immer noch eine Uniform tragen müssen. Für mich ist es altmodisch. |
| **You** | Das finde ich nicht. Ich finde die Uniform ganz praktisch. |
| **Teacher** | Wieso? Eine Jacke und einen Schlips zu tragen? Das ist aber doof. |
| **You** | Nein, hier in der Schule sehen alle Kinder gleich aus. Es gibt keine Probleme, wenn man nicht soviel Geld für Klamotten hat. Man muß dieselben Kleider tragen. Die Schule ist keine Modenschau. |
| **Teacher** | Aber es ist unbequem. Im Sommer, wenn es heiß ist... |
| **You** | Wir haben auch eine Sommeruniform: keinen Schlips und keine Jacke. Im Winter ist die Jacke schön, weil es hier in der Schule immer so kalt ist. |
| **Teacher** | Vielleicht, aber wenn man Jeans und Pullis trägt, ist es einem auch warm. |
| **You** | Aber wie sehen die Kinder aus? |
| **Teacher** | Es ist natürlich sehr bunt! |
| **You** | Hier in England tragen wir gern eine Uniform: Es ist bequem, man weiß schon am Abend vorher, was man am nächsten Tag tragen wird; es gibt wenige Probleme in den Schulen, in denen Uniform getragen wird. Wir haben unsere Klamotten für das Wochenende. Wenn man älter ist und in einem Büro arbeitet, dann sollte man auch eine Uniform tragen. Polizisten, Krankenschwestern: Es gibt viele Berufe, wo man eine Uniform tragen muß. In der Schule ist es auch eine gute Idee. |
| **Teacher** | Vielleicht hast du recht. |

## Role-play 19

| | |
|---|---|
| **Teacher** | Schulz. |
| **You** | Hallo, hier spricht... Wie geht's? |
| **Teacher** | Es geht. Was machen wir am Freitag? |
| **You** | Es gibt ein neues Freizeitzentrum in Luzern. Möchtest du hingehen? |
| **Teacher** | Ja, gute Idee. Was kann man dort machen? |
| **You** | Wir können entweder rollschuhlaufen oder rodeln. |
| **Teacher** | Hast du Rodeln schon probiert? |
| **You** | Ja, letztes Jahr auf Urlaub in den Alpen. Es war toll und sehr spannend. |
| **Teacher** | OK. Kann man da alles entleihen, und ist es teuer? |
| **You** | Freilich; nein es ist nicht so teuer. |
| **Teacher** | Was machen wir denn zu Mittag? Soll ich Butterbrote mitbringen? |
| **You** | Es gibt dort eine gute Imbißstube. Das Essen schmeckt gut und ist preiswert. |
| **Teacher** | Sehr schön. Wann und wo treffen wir uns? |
| **You** | Um halb zehn vor der Kirche auf dem Marktplatz. |
| **Teacher** | Wieviel Geld brauche ich? |
| **You** | Ich nehme dreißig Franken mit. Tschüs. |
| **Teacher** | Tschüs. |

# 6.9 Coursework

- One of the main changes with the new examination is the opportunity for students to complete coursework.
- Decisions will rest with Teachers and pupils themselves as to whether they choose the writing or oral coursework.
- Remember that you may not use the following example as your coursework for the new examination.
- Ask your Teacher for as much assistance as possible and make good use of the sections on using the dictionary to improve your writing as well as checking your work in the grammar sections.
- There is an example of a test type below.

## Looking for a holiday job in a German-speaking country: sample questions and answers

**E**xaminer's tip

Try to think of the type of questions that you would be asked for a part-time job in the United Kingdom. If you have a Saturday job, try to remember what you were asked. The most important part of this type of examination is to answer the questions properly. You will *not* always need a full sentence. How often do you use a full sentence in English?

1   **Wie heißen Sie?**
    Ich heiße Samantha Jones. Ich heiße Sam mit Vornamen und Jones mit Nachnamen.
2   **Woher kommen Sie?**
    Aus England. Ich wohne in Basildon, nicht weit von London.
3   **Seit wann lernen Sie Deutsch?**
    Seit vier Jahren.
4   **Wo haben Sie Ihr Deutsch gelernt?**
    Auf einer Schule in Basildon./Auf einem Ferienkurs in Deutschland.
5   **Wie lange möchten Sie hier arbeiten?**
    Vier oder sechs Wochen.
6   **Wann können Sie anfangen?**
    Anfang Juli oder vielleicht früher.
7   **Haben Sie schon in einem Hotel gearbeitet?**
    Letzten Sommer habe ich in einem Hotel in Southend gearbeitet. Es hat Spaß gemacht.
8   **Haben Sie einen Nebenjob?**
    Ich arbeite am Wochenende in einem Supermarkt und ich gehe babysitten.
9   **Haben Sie Fragen für mich?**
    Ja, wie viele Stunden muß ich täglich arbeiten?/Muß ich eine Uniform tragen?/Muß ich am Wochenende auch arbeiten?/Wieviel Geld kriege ich pro Woche?/Gibt es auch Schichtarbeit?

# Chapter 7
# *Reading*

## 7.1 Introduction

This is what you need to know about the test at Foundation Tier.
- You must be entered for either Foundation Tier or the Higher Tier of the Reading Test. You cannot opt out.
- You cannot be entered for both Tiers: you must choose one or the other. Your teacher will ask you in January which tier you wish to take.
- You will have to read a variety of materials in German and there will be a variety of question types to answer.
- The reading materials will be taken from the five Areas of Experience listed in the introduction to this book.
- Most of the questions will be in German. You must answer in German or tick a box or give a visual answer (e.g. draw a symbol in a box). You must not answer in English. However, a small percentage of the questions will be in English and if the questions are set in English, then answer in English.
- At Foundation Tier the visual or reading material will usually be relatively short.
- You will have to be able to read German handwriting: get as much practice as possible.
- At Foundation Tier you will be asked to understand specific detail (at Higher Tier you will have to draw conclusions).
- You are not expected to understand every word and there will be little time to spend attempting to translate the passage that you have to read.
- You will be able to use a dictionary: however use the dictionary carefully (see Introduction) and do not waste time looking up every word.

## 7.2 How to prepare for the examination

You will need to ask for or borrow magazines and leaflets from school.
You will need a dictionary so that you can look up words when you get stuck.
You must try to read as must German as possible.
There are certain items of vocabulary that are always going to be tested:
- family members
- numbers
- times
- days of the week
- physical descriptions
- items of clothing
- places in a town
- weather
- shops
- landmarks in the country
- directions and distances
- time expressions
- school subjects.

## 7.3 During the examination

- Fill in the front of your examination booklet as soon as possible. (Be sure that you know your candidate and centre number beforehand.)
- The instructions to the questions will nearly always be in German. Start to read the instructions as soon as possible.
- Use the instructions properly: there is often a clue to the answer, so read the instructions carefully.
- Before attempting to answer any of the questions: write down in German or English what you would reasonably expect the answer to be.
- Remember that you do not have to answer in full sentences.
- Ensure that you have answered the question that has been asked. Many of the questions will be box-ticking types but if you do have to write in German, then short or one-word answers will often score full marks.
- Remember that you will be able to use a dictionary. However, do not waste time looking up every single word. The idea of this paper is to test your comprehension of a passage of German: it is not designed as a translation exercise.

## 7.4 Foundation Tier examination questions

In the new examination you will be asked some questions in German. It is important to remember to check that you have answered the question asked. Do you know your question words? (See 4.3 page 80.)

In the examination you will encounter many different question types. Here are some of the types and a brief explanation of each one:
- Grids for completion: in this type of exercise you could be presented with a series of adverts for hotels and there would be a grid to complete on the availability and cost of facilities.
- Multiple choice: in this type of exercise you are offered a selection of answers and you have to use the question and passage to guide you to the correct answer.
- True/false questions: in this type of exercise you are offered a selection of statements and you have to use your skill and knowledge of the language to decide if each is correct or wrong.
- Matching: there could be a series of pictures or photographs which have to be matched to the correct headlines.
- Forms to complete: as the title suggests this will involve the recognition of key words used on forms in German-speaking countries.
- Completing charts/timetables
- Guided note-taking: this is another new skill area and one which you will need to practise.
- Guided summary: this is another new task and in time you will be able to confidently select the words and phrases needed to enable you to complete the exercise. You will have to be able to write good accurate sentences. (See 1.13 page 63.)
- Interpreting: this will involve you looking at a variety of source materials to interpret what is happening and to explain to a non-native speaker of German.
- Re-ordering texts: this will involve the choice of sentences to ensure that the article makes sense.

Now do the following questions: the answers can be found in 7.7.

1  Wo wird man dieses Schild sehen?
   **(a)** in einem Supermarkt ☐
   **(b)** in einem Bahnhof ☐
   **(c)** an einer Autobahn ☐
   **(d)** in einem Restaurant ☐

(1)

2 Was kann man im dritten Stock machen?
   **(a)** essen ☐
   **(b)** telefonieren ☐
   **(c)** duschen ☐
   **(d)** bezahlen ☐

| SCHNELLRESTAURANT |
| IM DRITTEN STOCK |
| durchgehend geöffnet! |

(1)

3 Wo wird man das Schild sehen?
   **(a)** in einem Krankenhaus ☐
   **(b)** in einer Stadt ☐
   **(c)** in einer Bank ☐
   **(d)** in einem Bahnhof ☐

| ES IST VERBOTEN, |
| DEN FAHRER WÄHREND |
| DER FAHRT ZU SPRECHEN |

(1)

4 Sie sind im Hotel. Wo können Sie frühstücken?
   **(a)** im Restaurant ☐
   **(b)** in der Küche ☐
   **(c)** am Ausschank ☐
   **(d)** in der Gaststube ☐

(1)

5 Sie suchen eine Hose für Ihren Bruder. Welche Abteilung ist das?
   **(a)** Möbel ☐
   **(b)** Herrenmode ☐
   **(c)** Schreibwaren ☐
   **(d)** Werkzeuge ☐

(1)

6 Sie haben Zahnschmerzen. Wohin müssen Sie gehen?
   **(a)** zum Augenarzt ☐
   **(b)** zum Zahnarzt ☐
   **(c)** zum Rechtsanwalt ☐
   **(d)** zum Frauenarzt ☐

(1)

7 Was für Sportmöglichkeiten gibt es in Maria Alm? Gib vier Antworten.

**MARIA ALM mit Hintermoos und Hinterthal**
800–2.900 m / Salzburger Land

Urlaubsfreuden in sonniger Bergwelt: Erholung – Sport – Geselligkeit – familienfreundlich. Großartiger Naturpark, 80 km Wanderwege, geführte Bergwanderungen, Tennis – Reiten – Minigolf. Urlaub für Fischer – eigenes Fischwasser. Sessellift; schöner Moorbadesee, nur 5 km entfernt. Informieren Sie sich über unser reichhaltiges, preiswertes Urlaubsangebot.

Auskünfte u. Prospekte: Verkehrsverein A-5761 Maria Alm 65, Telefon 00 43 / 65 84 / 316

   **(a)** ..................................................................
   **(b)** ..................................................................
   **(c)** ..................................................................
   **(d)** ..................................................................

(4)

8 You come across the following when looking for a new pen-friend to write to:

Ich suche Brieffreunde
Hobbys: Squash, Langlauf
Schwimmen, Lesen, Musik
Meine Lieblingssänger sind Reinhard Mey, Udo Jürgens und Peter Hofmann. Da mein Englisch schwach ist, korrespondiere ich nur in Deutsch. Meine Brieffreunde sollten im Alter von 15 Jahren aufwärts sein.

   **(a)** What hobbies does the writer have? (Name three) .....................

   **(b)** Why must she write in German? .....................

   **(c)** What age would she like her penfriend to be? .....................

(5)

9   This letter is taken from a magazine's problem page.

### Älterer Bruder

LESERIN: Ich habe ein Problem. Mein Bruder ärgert mich oft. Er nimmt oft mein Glas, wenn ich trinken will. Auch glaubt er, mir befehlen zu können, nur weil er älter ist. Weil er das macht, werde ich immer nervös, wenn er in der Nähe ist. Aber trotzdem mag ich ihn. Ich würde ihn gern bessern, aber ich weiß nicht wie. Vielleicht mache ich auch etwas falsch. Wissen Sie Rat?

**(a)**   Who is annoying the reader?

.............................................................................

**(b)**   Name one annoying thing he does .............................

.............................................................................

**(c)**   Why doesn't the reader do anything about it? ..............

.............................................................................

(3)

10   You are staying with Tanja, who shows you this letter.

Katwijk, den 14 August

*Liebe Tanja*

*ich sende Dir herzliche Grüße von unserer Ferien-Fahrradtour nach Holland. Es ist ganz toll hier! Wir sind gestern an der Küste angekommen. Wir haben einen schönen Zeltplatz gefunden, direkt am Strand. Leider ist das Wasser sehr schmutzig, so daß ich nicht gerne darin schwimme.*

*Auf der Fahrt hierher ist uns etwas Aufregendes passiert. Meine Freunde und ich haben in einem kleinen Dorf auf einer Wiese übernachtet. Als wir am Morgen aus dem Zelt kamen, waren unsere Fahrräder verschwunden. Wir haben vielleicht einen Schreck bekommen! Wir haben überall gesucht, aber wir konnten sie nicht finden. Als wir uns gerade entschlossen hatten, zur Polizei zu gehen, kam eine Frau aus dem Bauernhaus und winkte uns zu. "Ich habe Eure Räder in den Schuppen gestellt, damit niemand sie fortnehmen kann", sagte sie. "Und jetzt kommt erst mal rein, frühstücken!" Wir waren natürlich sehr froh und ließen uns die frische Milch und die warmen Brötchen schmecken. Dann setzten wir unsere Reise fort.*

*Bis bald!*
*Viele Grüße*
*Dein Markus*

**(a)**   Wie fährt Markus durch Holland? ..................................

**(b)**   Warum mag er im Meer nicht schwimmen? ...................

**(c)**   Wo hat die Gruppe die erste Nacht verbracht? .............

**(d)**   Wer hat die Fahrräder genommen? ...............................

**(e)**   Was haben die Jungen zum Frühstück gegessen und getrunken? .......

(5)

**11** Ihre Freunde/Freundinnnen suchen Brieffreunde. Können Sie einige finden?

Vorname: **Anke**
Nachname: **Mosebach**
Alter: **17**
Straße: **Ostring 15**
Stadt: **D-3501 Fuldabrück**
Hobbys/Interessen: **Lesen, Volleyball, Basketball, Musik, Theater, Stricken**
besonders erwünscht: **Nationalität egal**
Persönliche Bemerkung: **Briefe auf Deutsch oder Englisch**

V: **Stefanie**
N: **Schäfer** A: **12**
Str: **Pestalozzistraße 14**
S: **D-3503 Lohfelden**
H/I: **Turnen, Tanzen, Leichtathletik, Schwimmen, Reiten**
bes.erw.: **England (London, Oxford, Liverpool)**
Bem.: **Mädchen erwünscht**

V: **Nicole**
N: **Offenhammer** A: **11**
Str: **Am Rain 14**
S: **D-3503 Lohfelden**
H/I: **Handball, Skifahren, Ballett**
bes.erw.: **England (London, Oxford oder andere Städte)**

V: **Joy**
N: **Harries** A: **13**
Str: **Schlade 42**
S: **D-2803 Weyhe-Leeste**
H/I: **Schwimmen, Lesen, Badminton**
bes.erw.: **USA, England**
Bem.: **In Deutsch oder Englisch schreiben, bitte mit Foto!**

V: **Silke**
N: **Rothensee** A: **13**
Str: **Fliederstraße 26**
S: **D-2803 Weyhe**
H/I: **Reiten, Basketball, Lesen, Briefe schreiben, Skifahren**
bes.erw.: **Island, Philippinen, Brasilien**
Bem.: **In Deutsch oder Englisch schreiben**

V: **Ulrike**
N: **Czybulka** A: **13**
Str: **Schloßgarten 23**
S: **D-2803 Weyhe-Leeste**
H/I: **Lesen, Handarbeiten, (Stricken, Sticken), Gitarre spielen, Hockey**
bes.erw.: **England, USA, Australien**
Bem.: **In Deutsch oder Englisch schreiben, bitte mit Foto!**

V: **Britta**
N: **Tödtmann** A: **16**
Str: **Kalberkamp 23**
S: **D-2803 Weyhe**
H/I: **Musik, Sport, Reisen, Tanzen, Tiere, Pflanzen, Sprachen**
bes.erw.: **USA, Finnland, England, China**

V: **Petra**
N: **Falke** A: **11**
Str: **Mückenbergstraße 42**
S: **D-3501 Söhrewald 3**
H/I: **Tanzen, Reiten, Malen, Musik hören**
bes.erw.: **Kanada, England**
bem.: **Kennwort: Marty**

V: **Caroline**
N: **Jäger** A: **12**
Str: **Friedhofsweg 37**
S: **D-3503 Lohfelden 2**
H/I: **Schwimmen, Reiten, Lesen, Fahrradfahren, Tennis**

**(a)** Louise is 13 and likes outdoor sports, especially riding.

................................................. (1)

**(b)** Anne is 16; she enjoys knitting and going to the theatre. She can write fluently in German.

................................................. (1)

**(c)** Vickki is 12 and lives in Oxford and enjoys a lot of sport.

................................................. (1)

**(d)** Anja, your own penpal from Finland, who is interested in nature wants to write to a German girl. ................................................. (1)

**12** Richtig oder falsch? Lesen Sie den Artikel durch. Schreiben Sie R oder F.

Hallo, ich heiße Bernhard und bin siebzehn. Ich komme aus Seefeld, das ist eine Stadt in Österreich. Hier kann man im Winter super Sport machen. Meine Hobbys sind Skifahren, Schlittschuhlaufen und Snowboarding. Mit dem Snowboard kann man fahren und springen! Das macht total Spaß!

Hallo! Ich bin vierzehn Jahre alt und heiße Katja. Ich wohne auch in Seefeld. Mein Hobby ist Skifahren. Ich mache Langlauf und Abfahrtslauf. Langlauf ist gut für die Kondition. Und Abfahrtslauf ist superschnell. Das ist total gut. Im Winter kommen viele Touristen hier nach Seefeld. Da ist viel los, und jeden Samstag gehe ich mit meinen Freundinnen in die Disco. Da treffen wir viele Leute aus der ganzen Welt!

Hallo, ich heiße Johann. Ich bin dreizehn und wohne in einem kleinen Dorf in der Nähe von Seefeld. Mein Hobby ist Snowboarding. Das machen jetzt viele Leute hier. Snowboarding ist besser als Skifahren! Skifahren finde ich langweilig. Snowboarding macht viel mehr Spaß.

**(a)** Katja findet Snowboarding toll. ☐
**(b)** Johann findet Skifahren langweilig. ☐
**(c)** Mit dem Snowboard kann man springen. ☐
**(d)** Langlauf ist gut für die Kondition. ☐
**(e)** Abfahrtslauf ist ein bißchen zu langsam. ☐

(5)

**13**

# Deutschland

Hier sind beliebte Moderatoren und Sendungen:

## Heike Makatsch

Ihr seht Heike auf der Titelseite. Sie ist 24 Jahre alt und wohnt mit ihren zwei Katzen in Düsseldorf (Nordrhein-Westfalen). Sie macht die Sendung *Interaktiv* auf dem deutschen Musiksender VIVA. Die Zuschauer finden Heike und ihre Sendung toll. Sie können Heike Briefe schreiben, ein Fax schicken oder sogar live mit Heike telefonieren. Natürlich gibt es auch viele Musik-Videos in dieser Sendung.

## Gerhard Leinauer

„Leini" (Gerhard Leinauer) ist 32 Jahre alt und kommt aus Augsburg (Bayern). Er ist ein fanatischer Sportler. Er ist Snowboardfahrer, Surfer und Mountainbiker. Im Deutschen Sportfernsehen (DSF) moderiert er die Sendung *Magic Sports*. Dort berichtet er über Beachvolleyball, Surfen, Mountainbiking und viele andere tolle Sportarten.

*Gute Zeiten, schlechte Zeiten*
*Gute Zeiten, schlechte Zeiten* ist eine Familienserie im Programm des Senders RTL. Diese Serie hat viele Fans in Deutschland. Drei Stars der Serie sind Jan Sosniok, Andreas Elsholz und Frank-Thomas Mende.

Können Sie die zwei Hälften finden?

| | |
|---|---|
| eine Musiksendung | gute Zeiten, schlechte Zeiten |
| eine Sportsendung | Interaktiv |
| eine Familienserie | Magic Sports |

(3)

---

## 7.5 Foundation and Higher Tier examination questions

---

**14** Lesen Sie alles, dann schreiben Sie den Artikel auf.

**Der Name der Rose**
**Produktion:** Neue Constantin Film, München
**Regie:** Jean-Jacques Annaud
**Nach dem Roman von Umberto Eco**

*Der Name der Rose* ist ein deutscher Film – mit internationalen Stars! Die Neue Constantin Film produzierte ihn im Jahr 1987. Der spannende "Krimi" aus dem 14. Jahrhundert war ein großer internationaler Erfolg.

**Die Geschichte:**
Der englische Mönch Bruder William von Baskerville (Sean Connery) kommt im Jahr 1327 in ein reiches Kloster in Norditalien. Der italienische Kaiser hat ihn dorthin geschickt: Bruder William soll ein politisches Treffen zwischen zwei Gruppen der Kirche organisieren. Er und sein Helfer Adson (Christian Slater) finden im Kloster drei tote Mönche. Bruder William will den Mörder finden. Er entdeckt geheime Schriften und Manuskripte, und er findet ein gefährliches Labyrinth. Schließlich haben William und Adson die Lösung des Rätsels: Sie wissen, wer der Mörder ist…

Können Sie die Sätze einordnen.

**(a)** um ein politisches Treffen zu organisieren.

**(b)** Er findet ein gefährliches Labyrinth im Kloster.

**(c)** Der englische Mönch Bruder William kommt in ein reiches Kloster in Norditalien an.

**(d)** Sein Helfer Adson findet im Kloster drei tote Männer.

**(e)** Schließlich haben die beiden die Lösung des Rätsels.

**(f)** Der Kaiser hat William dorthin geschickt,

**(g)** William will den Mörder finden.

**(h)** Im Kloster entdeckt William geheime Schriften und Manuskripte.

**(i)** Sie wissen wer der Mörder ist.

(9)

Fangen Sie mit **(c)** an.

**15**

## „Toll, drei Wochen keine Schule!"

Peter freut sich schon auf paradiesische Zeiten. Das wird sich erst zeigen, denke ich für mich. Ich bin der Klassenlehrer dieser 9 R 2, die in den nächsten Wochen ihr Betriebspraktikum machen soll. Alle Schüler der vorletzten Klassen (die 8.Klasse in der Hauptschule und die 9. in der Realschule) haben diese Möglichkeit. Sie sollen Erfahrungen in der Arbeitswelt sammeln: Berufe und Produktionsabläufe kennenlernen und den Umgang mit Menschen in der Arbeitswelt. Einige Wochen lang haben wir uns vorbereitet. Wir haben Lebensläufe und Bewerbungen geschrieben und die Jugend-Arbeits-Gesetze durchgenommen. (Verboten sind zum Beispiel Akkord-Arbeit und körperliche Strafen.) Wir haben über Versicherungen gesprochen und mit einem Computer nach den besonderen Neigungen und Fähigkeiten jedes Schülers gesucht. Einige Schüler fanden dann selbst eine Stelle für ihr Praktikum, andere bekamen Hilfe von der Schulleitung. An diesem Freitag freuen sich alle. Es ist der letzte Schultag vor dem Praktikum. Jeder hat eine Stelle gefunden. Auf meinem Tisch liegt die Liste von Firmen: eine Autowerkstatt, ein Hotel, ein Reisebüro, eine Bank, eine Bäckerei, eine Versicherung, eine Krankenkasse, die Stadtverwaltung, ein Supermarkt, ein Fotolabor, ein Postamt, ein Krankenhaus, ein Zahnarzt... Es ist fast alles dabei. Aufgeregt stellen die Schüler noch letzte Fragen (natürlich sind alle schon besprochen): „Wie lange müssen wir höchstens arbeiten?" (sechs Stunden täglich) „Wieviel Mittagspause steht uns zu?" (30 Minuten) „Müssen wir jeden Tag hin?" (sonntags nicht und ein Werktag ist frei) „Bekommen wir Geld dafür?" (Nein. Aber ihr sollt auch nicht als billige Arbeitskraft eingesetzt werden, sondern lernen und probieren!) „Was ist bei Krankheit?" (Schule anrufen und den Betrieb). „Tschüs, ... und viel Spaß!" wünsche ich allen. Denn am Montag geht's los.

**(a)** What are students hoping to gain by doing work experience?

.......................................................................... (1)

**(b)** In what two ways has the school prepared the pupils for work experience?

.......................................................................... (2)

**(c)** Why did they use the computers?

.......................................................................... (1)

**(d)** How many hours per day may the students work?

.......................................................................... (1)

**(e)** What are students supposed to do if they fall ill durng the work experience?

.......................................................................... (1)

**16** Lesen Sie den Artikel und schreiben Sie die Antworten auf.

## „Ich bin behindert – na und?"

**Regine Sattler (17) geht in die 10. Klasse des Drebber-Gymnasiums in Bremen. Regine mag Popmusik (ihre Lieblingsgruppe ist Take That), sie liest viel und sie sieht gern fern. Regine hat viele Freundinnen und Freunde, die sie oft zu Hause besuchen. Sie geht gern zur Schule – ihr Lieblingsfach ist Englisch. Regine ist ein normaler Teenager. Aber: Regine ist behindert – sie ist gelähmt.**

„Hallo, da seid ihr ja!" Regine öffnet die Tür. Sie fährt mit ihrem Rollstuhl ins Wohnzimmer. „Kommt herein, ich habe Kaffee gekocht!" Dann lacht sie: „Oder glaubt ihr, ich kann so etwas nicht – weil ich im Rollstuhl sitze?"
Regine ist seit ihrer Geburt gelähmt. Sie kann nicht gehen. Sie kann nicht allein aufstehen. Sie kann sich nicht allein waschen. Sie kann sich nicht allein anziehen, und sie kann nicht allein zur Toilette gehen. „Meine Mutter muß mir bei all dem helfen. Aber alles andere mache ich selber, meine Arme sind ja in Ordnung!" Seit drei Jahren geht Regine auf eine „normale" Schule – das Drebber-Gymnasium. „Vorher war ich in einer Behinderten-Schule. Ich bin nur am Wochenende nach Hause gekommen. Das war langweilig! Meine Geschwister gehen alle auf das Drebber-Gymnasium. Ich habe mir gesagt: Warum kann ich nicht auch dorthin gehen? Meine Noten waren gut genug!" Das Drebber-Gymnasium fand die Idee super. Seitdem holt der Schulbus Regine jeden Morgen ab. Ihre Freundin Annika wartet vor der Schule auf Regine und fährt ihren Rollstuhl in das Klassenzimmer. „Meine Klassenräume sind im Erdgeschoß", sagt Regine. „Das ist kein Problem. Und es gibt auch einen Lift – da paßt mein Rollstuhl prima rein!"

Wie reagierten die Schüler und Schülerinnen auf Regine? „Meine Klassenkameraden waren alle super. Einige von ihnen waren am Anfang etwas unsicher – aber ich habe ihnen genau erklärt, was ich kann und was ich nicht kann. Ich brauche Hilfe – na klar. Das ist doch nicht schlimm! Und außerdem: Ich helfe ihnen ja auch – im Unterricht oder bei den Hausaufgaben zum Beispiel."

Regine ist eine beliebte Schülerin. Ihre Klassenkameraden mögen sie sehr. Sie hat viele Freundinnen und Freunde in der Klasse. „Wir treffen uns oft nachmittags zum Musikhören und Reden. Manchmal fahren wir auch in die Stadt. Wir gehen ins Kino, oder wir essen ein Eis."

Das ist jedoch manchmal ein Problem: In viele Geschäfte kann Regine mit ihrem Rollstuhl nicht hinein. „Das macht mich wirklich wütend. Wir Behinderte sind doch keine „Menschen 2. Klasse"! Aber so fühlen wir uns manchmal!" sie ärgert sich auch über die Reaktionen von anderen Leuten: „Viele Menschen glauben, ich bin total dumm – nur weil ich im Rollstuhl sitze. Sie sagen dann zu meinen Freunden: „Das arme Mädchen, was hat sie denn?" Und mich ignorieren sie. Das nervt mich wirklich sehr!"

Regine hat einen Wunsch: „Die Leute sollen mich so akzeptieren, wie ich bin. Ich bin behindert – na und? Für mich und meine Freunde ist das kein Problem. Ich wünsche mir, daß jeder so denkt!"

(a) Was für Hobbys hat Regine? .................................................................................... (1)

(b) Seit wann ist sie behindert? ..................................................................................... (1)

(c) Wer hilft ihr im täglichen Leben? ............................................................................. (1)

(d) Was für Probleme gibt es für Regine, wenn sie durch die Schule rollt? Warum?

.................................................................................................................................... (2)

(e) Wie helfen ihre Kameraden ihr? ............................................................................... (1)

(f) Und was macht Regine für sie? ................................................................................. (1)

**17** Lesen Sie den Artikel und schreiben Sie dann die Antworten auf.

# ZOFF!
# Die neue Jugendsendung

Kennt ihr das? Ihr habt Ärger mit eurem Vater. Streit mit eurer besten Freundin, und niemand hilft euch. Für deutsche Jugendliche gibt es jetzt eine neue Fernsehsendung, die bei diesem Problem hilft. In *Zoff* sagen streitende Jugendliche ihre Meinung – kontrovers engagiert und ehrlich. Das jugendliche Publikum entscheidet, wer recht hat und wie der Streit beendet werden kann. Der *Zoff* Moderator Jürgen Blaschke sagt: „*Zoff* ist eine Jugendsendung, von der auch Erwachsene viel lernen können."

(a) Wovon handelt die neue Sendung?

.....................................................................................................................

(b) Was dürfen die Zuschauer während der Sendung machen?

.....................................................................................................................

(c) Was für Rat kann man bekommen?

.....................................................................................................................

(d) Warum sollen Erwachsene der Sendung auch zuschauen?

.....................................................................................................................

(4)

**18** You are interested in environmental issues. Read the article and answer the questions.

„Ich bade nicht in der Badewanne, sondern dusche. Dabei verbrauche ich weniger Wasser. Papier und Glas schmeiße ich nur in Spezialcontainer, die stehen in jedem Stadtteil. Dafür laufe ich gern ein paar Meter. Meine Mutter denkt auch an die Umwelt. Im Supermarkt macht sie zum Beispiel die Verpackungen ab und läßt sie einfach liegen. Meine Schwester und mein Vater interessieren sich wenig für den Umweltschutz. Sie sind zu bequem." **Ines, 18**

„Meine Eltern fahren auf der Autobahn langsamer. Sie sparen Benzin. Ich bin umweltbewußt erzogen worden. Wenn ich aus dem Zimmer gehe, mache ich immer das Licht aus. Im Winter drehe ich die Heizung ab, sobald ich das Haus verlasse. Beim Einkaufen achte ich auf die Verpackung. Joghurt zum Beispiel kaufe ich im Glas, nicht in Pappbechern." **Christoph, 15**

„Beim Einkaufen denke ich selten an die Umwelt. Außerdem gibt es viele Produkte nur in Dosen. Und mit dem Auto oder Motorrad bin ich schneller als mit dem Bus oder der Straßenbahn. Meiner Meinung nach darf man den Umweltschutz nicht dem einzelnen überlassen. Man muß ihn erzwingen. In Hamburg zum Beispiel durfte man vor Weihnachten nicht mehr in die Innenstadt fahren. Nur so kann man die Probleme lösen." **Stephan, 16**

**(a)** Name any way in which Ines is trying to save energy.

................................................................................................................ (1)

**(b)** What does she say about her sister?

................................................................................................................ (1)

**(c)** In what ways are Christopher's parents trying to save energy?

................................................................................................................ (1)

**(d)** What does Christoph do in winter to save energy at home?

................................................................................................................ (1)

**(e)** Why does Stephan travel by car?

................................................................................................................ (1)

**(f)** What arrangements were made in Hamburg last Christmas to ease congestion?

................................................................................................................ (1)

**19** Match the definitions to the words by putting the letters in the boxes.
**(a)** Sie liegt 50 Kilometer hoch über der Erde. Sie schützt vor zu viel ultravioletten Licht von der Sonne. Wegen eines Lochs wird die Erde wärmer; das Eis an Nordpol und Südpol schmilzt.
**(b)** Immer mehr Pflanzen und Tiere sterben aus, weil der Mensch ihre Umwelt kaputtmacht. Wir brauchen diese Pflanzenarten und Tierarten, um von ihnen zu lernen. Die Tiere und die Pflanzen machen unsere Welt schön.
**(c)** Giftiger Staub fällt auf die Blätter der Bäume, und wenn es regnet vermischt sich der Staub mit Wasser: Das ist saurer Regen, und er macht die Bäume kaputt. Man soll die Bäume schützen.
**(d)** Man soll etwas Gutes für die Umwelt tun: man geht zu Fuß; man läßt das Auto zu Hause; man kauft recyceltes Papier, Getränke in Flaschen usw.

umweltfreundlich ☐   Artenschutz ☐
Waldsterben ☐   Ozonschicht ☐

**20** Lesen Sie die Artikel.

**Phillippe,**
Der blonde Junge aus Belgien spricht französisch, holländisch und deutsch. In seinem Land spricht man alle diese Sprachen. Außerdem lernt er noch Englisch. Phillippe hatte in der Schule Schwierigkeiten mit Deutsch. Darum kam er in eine Sprachschule nach Köln und wohnte bei einer deutschen Familie. „Sprachen sind wichtig, denn dann kann man mit anderen besser Geschäfte machen", sagt der junge Belgier. In seiner Freizeit geht Phillippe Tennis spielen, oder er fährt Motocross. Musik hört er am liebsten von den Pixies und Primus, „die sind nicht so kommerziell."

**Astrid,**
Das Au-pair-Mädchen aus Dänemark ist ein halbes Jahr in Deutschland. Sie arbeitet in einer Familie mit kleinen Kindern. Morgens bringt sie den 5jährigen Sohn mit dem Fahrrad in den Kindergarten. Anschließend hilft sie im Haushalt und spielt mit der 2jährigen Tochter. Zu ihren Aufgaben gehören bügeln, aufräumen und manchmal kochen. Nachmittags geht sie in eine Sprachenschule. Dort trifft sie viele junge Leute aus anderen Ländern. Ihre beste Freundin kommt aus Norwegen. Kontakt zu deutschen Jugendlichen hat sie kaum. Sie findet das schade. „Sie sind etwas zurückhaltend", meint Astrid. „Bei uns in Kopenhagen sind wir lockerer."

**Matthew,**

Der englische Internatsschüler aus Kent weiß genau, was er will. Mit sieben Jahren beschloß er, Rechtsanwalt zu werden. Später will er in Oxford studieren. Sein Ziel ist eine Anstellung in San Francisco. „Stell dir vor: ein Büro in einem Wolkenkratzer – und das letzte Licht, das ausgeht, das ist meins." Um sein Ziel zu erreichen, besucht er eine Eliteschule. „Dort habe ich die besten Möglichkeiten. Es gibt die besten Lehrer, tolle Sportmöglichkeiten, und Rauchen und Trinken sind verboten", erzählt Matthew. Nur die schwarze Schuluniform gefällt ihm nicht so sehr. In der Freizeit trainiert er für Schwimmwettkämpfe seiner Schule. Selbst bei seinem letzten Sprachurlaub in Deutschland ging er fast jeden Tag ins Schwimmbad, um zu trainieren.

Wen beschreiben wir?

**(a)** Arbeitet mit Kindern

..................................................................................... (1)

**(b)** Darf in der Schule weder trinken noch rauchen

..................................................................................... (1)

**(c)** Kann viele Sprachen

..................................................................................... (1)

**(d)** Hilft einer Familie bei der Hausarbeit

..................................................................................... (1)

**(e)** Ist sehr sportlich

..................................................................................... (1)

**(f)** Findet Sprachen sehr wichtig für die Zukunft

..................................................................................... (1)

**(g)** Hofft, im Ausland zu arbeiten

..................................................................................... (1)

**(h)** Findet die Deutschen ein bißchen schüchtern

..................................................................................... (1)

# 7.6 Higher Tier examination questions

This is what you need to know about the exam:

- If you are entered for the Higher Tier you cannot do the Foundation Tier.
- The passages will be longer than at Foundation Level and the vocabulary will be beyond the Minimum Core Vocabulary list issued by your Board.
- Some of the material will be hand-written.
- One major difference between Foundation and Higher Tier is that at Higher Tier you will be asked to draw conclusions and detect feelings.

**21** Read this article about school life.

## Ein neues System – die alten Lehrer
### SCHULE IN DER ALTEN DDR

„Wir können im Unterricht etwas freier reden. Eine totale Offenheit ist aber noch nicht da. Wir haben jetzt neue Schulbücher bekommen. Der Lehrer in Gesellschaftskunde konnte damit aber nichts anfangen. Er war der gleiche wie vor der Wende. Wir haben Mißtrauensanträge gegen einige Lehrer gestellt. Die haben dann nicht mehr unterrichtet. Im Moment fällt Gesellschaftskunde aus, bis ein neuer Lehrer da ist. Der soll aus dem Westen kommen." **Vivien, 18 Jahre**

„Viele Lehrer haben früher die Sozialistische Partei unterstützt. Sie sind aber ganz still und versuchen nicht, uns zu beeinflussen. Sie sind mir lieber als die Wendehälse. Die tun so, als ob sie immer schon gegen die Regierung wären. Eine Lehrerin an unserer Schule macht das. Sie war früher stellvertretende Schulleiterin und mußte dieses Amt aufgeben." **Sebastian, 17 Jahre**

„Ich finde, der Unterricht ist gleich geblieben. Wir waren schon immer recht kritisch. Unsere Lehrer haben die Partei nie großartig unterstützt und gelobt. Und in Fächern wie Mathematik oder Physik merkt man nicht, welche politische Meinung der Lehrer hat." **Martin, 18 Jahre**

„Unser Geschichtslehrer war SED-Parteisekretär. Jetzt tut er so, als ob er sich nicht mehr für Politik interessiert. Aber jeder weiß, welche Meinung er hat. Im Unterricht lernen wir nicht mehr die Geschichte der SED. Nach der Wende haben wir beim Altertum angefangen. Jetzt ist das Mittelalter dran. Auch Musik- und Sportunterricht haben sich verändert. Wir müssen nicht mehr die alten politischen Kampflieder singen; beim Sport ist alles viel lockerer." **Beatrix, 18 Jahre**

„Früher haben wir oft über Themen geredet, die nicht zum Unterricht gehörten. Viele Lehrer wollen das jetzt nicht mehr. Die neue Hausordnung kommt nicht mehr vom Direktor, sondern von uns. Später sollen die Lehrer sagen, ob sie damit zufrieden sind." **Birgit, 17 Jahre**

hat." **Christiane, 18 Jahre**

„Früher mußten die Schüler die Meinung der Partei lernen. Jetzt diskutieren wir über Themen wie das Wahlsystem, die soziale Entwicklung oder Rechte und Pflichten der Medien." **Jens, 17 Jahre**

„In unserem Geschichtsunterricht halten wir Schüler kurze Vorträge. Der Lehrer sagt kaum etwas dazu. Jeder weiß, wie er vorher gedacht

Match the opinion to the correct person.

(a) thinks that there has been little change ............................................. (1)

(b) there is a more relaxed atmosphere in some subjects ............... ............... (1)

(c) there are new resources ............... ............... ............... (1)

(d) students have a greater say in lesson content ............... ............... (1)

22

## Eine fährt Rad und die andere lacht so gerne

Ich habe noch zwei Omas und bin darüber auch sehr froh. Deshalb will ich nun auch beide Omas beschreiben. Die erste Oma wurde am 9. April 70 Jahre alt. Für so ein ziemlich hohes Alter ist sie noch sehr fit und sportlich. Sie fährt noch oft mit ihrem Fahrrad, und das finde ich sehr toll. Sie ist zwar technisch total unbegabt und weiß nicht, wo und wie man die Gänge einschaltet, dafür hat sie andere starke Seiten. Sie ist auch immer sehr flott angezogen und trägt nur sehr schöne Sachen. Die sind gar nicht so altmodisch.

Wenn wir Kinder zu Oma kommen, dürfen wir meistens Dunkelbier trinken, und das genießen wir. Sie ist im großen und ganzen eine sehr liebe Oma und nimmt sich viel Zeit für uns. Die zweite Oma hatte am 25. Februar Geburtstag und wurde 76 Jahre alt. 1983 hatten Oma und Opa „goldene Hochzeit". Sie sind also schon sehr lange verheiratet: Im letzten Jahr sind sie umgezogen denn die alte Wohnung machte ihnen zuviel Arbeit. Wenn einer von uns Enkeln Geburtstag hat, gibt sie der Mutter dann Geld dafür, denn sie hat sehr, sehr viele Enkel und auch schon einige Urenkel.

Oma kann sehr herzlich lachen, so daß man einfach mitlachen muß. Sie ist zwar nicht so sportlich, wie die andere Oma, aber dafür ist sie ja auch älter. Oma wird schnell ohnmächtig, wenn es ganz plötzlich laut wird, oder wenn es sehr stinkt! So z.B. bei Farbe. Wenn wir bei Oma sind, gibt sie uns meistens etwas zum Knabbern, was uns natürlich sehr gefällt. Auch sie ist eine sehr nette Oma.

Beantworten Sie die folgenden Fragen.

(a) Was für Kleider trägt die erste Oma?

.........................................................................

(b) Was erlaubt die erste Oma den Enkelkindern?

.........................................................................

(c) Warum ist die zweite Oma neulich umgezogen?

.........................................................................

(d) Was gibt sie den Enkeln und den Urenkeln zum Geburtstag?

.........................................................................

(e) Wer ist die älteste: die erste oder die zweite Oma?

.........................................................................

(f) Wann wird die zweite Oma bewußtlos?

.........................................................................

23 Lesen Sie den Text und beantworten Sie die Fragen.

## Mythos Schönheit:

# Dünn, dünner, am dünnsten?

50 Prozent aller deutschen Mädchen glauben, daß sie zu dick sind. Schon Acht- oder Neunjährige sagen heute: „Ich wiege zuviel!" und versuchen abzunehmen. Wer hat schuld an diesem gefährlichen Trend? „Die dünnen Fotomodelle", sagen viele Leute. „Sie sind die neuen Stars – und die jungen Mädchen denken: es ist normal, so dünn zu sein!"
Models und Fotomodelle sind zu dünn – das stimmt. Kate Moss (19) aus England ist 1 Meter 70 groß und wiegt 43 kg – normal (und gesund!) für diese Größe sind 52kg. Keine Frage: Models sehen nicht aus wie „normale" Frauen und Mädchen – sie sind viel zu mager. Aber trotzdem sind sie neue Idole: „Junge Mädchen sehen jeden Tag diese mageren Models – in Zeitschriften und im Fernsehen. Diese Modelle sind Superstars: Sie sind jung, schön und erfolgreich. Kein Wunder, daß viele Mädchen glauben: Nur wer dünn ist, ist schön und hat Erfolg!" sagt die Berliner Psychologin Cordula Tröger. Für einige Mädchen wird der Wunsch, dünn zu sein, sogar zur gefährlichen Obsession: Sie werden magersüchtig (Ärzte nennen diese Krankheit anorexia nervosa).
Paula Karaisgos von der Modellagentur Storm sagt jedoch: „Wer magersüchtig ist, hat meist in seiner Kindheit viele Probleme gehabt. Unsere dünnen Models haben nicht schuld daran – die Ursachen für anorexia nervosa liegen woanders."
Der Medienexperte Peter Tauber sagt dazu: „Die Medien haben diesen Trend gestartet – und nicht die dünnen Supermodels. Die Medien zeigen am liebsten junge, schöne und dünne Menschen. Sie zeigen damit: Dünnsein ist gesund und attraktiv. Fast alle Leute denken heute schon so!"
Was sagen die Models zu diesem Thema? Claudia Schiffer (24) erzählt: „Ich habe mit 17 Jahren zum ersten Mal als Fotomodell gearbeitet. Damals sagte jeder: „Du bist zu dick – du mußt 10 kg abnehmen!" Jetzt bin ich dünn – aber ich esse nur wenig. Fast alle Models machen Diät – das ist für uns normal!" Nadia Auermann (21) aus Ostberlin hält jedoch nicht viel von Diäten: „Diäten sind ungesund. Ich esse, was ich will. Aber ich habe Glück – ich bleibe schlank."

(a) Warum finden so viele junge Mädchen, daß sie zu dick sind?

............................................................................................... (1)

(b) Was erhoffen sich die Mädchen vom Dünn sein?

............................................................................................... (1)

(c) Was sind oft die Folgen ihrer Hoffnungen?

............................................................................................... (1)

(d) Was für Ursachen gibt man für anorexia nervosa?

............................................................................................... (1)

(e) Ihrer Meinung nach, wer ist daran schuld: die Supermodels oder die Medien? Geben Sie mindestens zwei Gründe an. ...........................................

............................................................................................... (2)

24 Read the information below.

**Nicole, 17:**
„In manchen Dingen behandeln mich meine Eltern wie eine Erwachsene. Zum Beispiel, wenn ich Aufgaben erfüllen muß: Saubermachen, Babysitten, Haushalt. Manchmal behandeln sie mich auch wie ein Kind: Wenn ich am Wochenende ausgehen möchte oder etwas alleine machen will. Sie geben mir keinen Freiraum."

**Verena, 17:**
„Für mich war es schwierig, im Kreis meiner Freunde eine eigene Meinung zu haben. Früher habe ich einfach die Ansichten der anderen übernommen – ohne selber darüber nachzudenken. Erwachsenwerden ist für mich die Chance, etwas allein zu machen. Sich von Freunden und Eltern zu lösen und einen eigenen Weg zu finden, nicht mehr abhängig zu sein."

**Manuel, 17:**
„Manchmal habe ich auch Angst, daß das Leben, der Beruf und die Partnerschaft langweilig werden."

**Marc, 16:**
„Gut am Erwachsenwerden finde ich, daß man Auto fahren darf oder spät abends in Discos gehen kann. Angst habe ich davor, daß später nichts aus mir wird, daß ich keinen Job finde und daß ich die Verantwortung für eine eigene Familie nicht tragen kann."

**Marco, 13:**
„Meine Eltern wollen nicht akzeptieren, daß ich größer werde. Ich will nicht immer mit ihnen spazierengehen, sondern selbst etwas unternehmen."

**Susanne, 17:**
„Mit 14 mußte ich mich noch bei meinen Eltern durchsetzen, als ich mal weggehen wollte. Heute verstehe ich mich mit ihnen sehr gut. Auch in der Schule läuft alles prima. Ich habe gute Erfahrungen mit dem Erwachsenwerden gemacht. Das liegt wahrscheinlich daran, daß ich mit meinen Eltern über alle Probleme sprechen konnte. Positives beim Erwachsenwerden: Man bekommt immer mehr Rechte. Mit 18 kann man den Führerschein machen und wählen gehen."

**Khamphad, 15:**
„Mit meinen Eltern habe ich immer Krach. Sie verstehen meine Probleme nicht. Zum Beispiel streiten wir uns, weil ich jetzt einen Freund habe und abends ausgehe. Früher habe ich mich anders gefühlt. Da war ich nicht so reif. Ich weiß jetzt mehr und bin erfahrener."

Match the opinion to the correct person.

**(a)** Wants the chance to think for self and be more independent

................................................................... (1)

**(b)** Parents can be stuffy and at times over-protective

................................................................... (1)

**(c)** Parents cannot accept that he/she has grown up

................................................................... (1)

**(d)** Has a very open relationship with parents and is able to discuss everything

................................................................... (1)

**(e)** Is afraid of being unemployed and life having no real purpose

................................................................... (1)

**(f)** Has very stressful relationship

................................................................... (1)

**(g)** Is afraid that everything will eventually have no purpose

................................................................... (1)

**25** Lesen Sie den Artikel. Bitte ordnen Sie die Sätze. Sie müssen mit 3 beginnen.

# Altglas ist kein Müll, sondern ein Rohstoff

Altglas ist kein Müll, sondern ein Rohstoff, den man heute wieder zu neuen Flaschen und Gläsern aufbereitet. Diese Aufbereitung nennt man „Recycling".

Umweltbewußte Bürger werfen ihre leeren Flaschen und Gläser nicht mehr in den Mülleimer, sondern in Glassammelbehälter. Auch in deinem Heimatort stehen Container für Altglas.

Regelmäßig werden diese Behälter von einer Firma entleert. Mit einem Spezial-Lastkraftwagen wird an einem Kran der Container hochgezogen. Eine Klappe öffnet sich, und mit Scherbengeklirr fällt das Altglas auf die Ladefläche.

Ist der beladene Lastwagen zur Sammelstelle der Firma zurückgekehrt, beginnt dort eine mühevolle Arbeit:

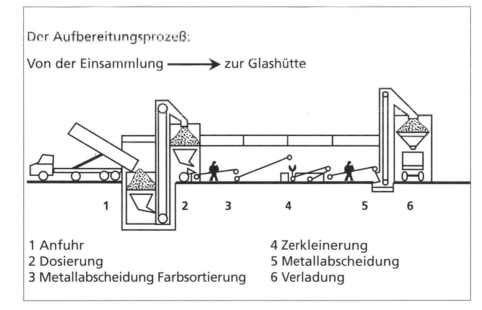

Der Aufbereitungsprozeß:

Von der Einsammlung ⟶ zur Glashütte

1 Anfuhr
2 Dosierung
3 Metallabscheidung Farbsortierung
4 Zerkleinerung
5 Metallabscheidung
6 Verladung

**1** Ein Aufzug befördert das gereinigte und sortierte Glas in einen großen Trichter. Von dort gelangt es mit einem Speziallastwagen zur Glashütte, wo es zu neuen Flaschen und Gläsern verarbeitet wird.

**2** Der Lastwagen fährt das Altglas an und kippt es in einen großen Behälter.

**3** Arbeiter beseitigen Fremdstoffe und sortieren die verschiedenen Glasarten nach Farben.

**4** Mit einem Aufzug wird das Glas in einen Dosierungsbehälter gefüllt. Von dort gelangt es auf ein Transportband.

**5** Das Glas wird in einer Mühle zerkleinert. Dann wird es gewaschen.

**6** Die Glassplitter werden auf Reinheit kontrolliert. Die letzten Fremdstoffe werden beseitigt.

## 7.7 Suggested answers to examination questions

1  (c)
2  (a)
3  (d)
4  (a)
5  (b)
6  (b)
7  **(a)**  Bergwandern
   **(b)**  Tennis
   **(c)**  Reiten
   **(d)**  Minigolf
8  **(a)**  any three from:
             squash
             cross-country skiing
             swimming
             reading
             listening to music
   **(b)**  Her English is weak.
   **(c)**  15 or over
9  **(a)**  Her elder brother
   **(b)**  He takes her glass when he wants a drink; he thinks he can boss her about because he is older.
   **(c)**  She doesn't know how.
10 **(a)**  mit dem Fahrrad
   **(b)**  das Wasser ist sehr schmutzig
   **(c)**  auf einer Wiese in einem kleinen Dorf
   **(d)**  eine Frau
   **(e)**  frische Milch und warme Brötchen
11 **(a)**  Louise: Silke Rothensee
   **(b)**  Anne: Anke Mosebach
   **(c)**  Vickki: Stefanie Schäfer
   **(d)**  Anja: Britta Tödmann
12 **(a)**  falsch
   **(b)**  richtig
   **(c)**  richtig
   **(d)**  richtig
   **(e)**  falsch
13 eine Musiksendung: Interaktiv
   eine Sportsendung:  Magic Sports
   eine Familienserie:   Gute Zeiten, schlechte Zeiten
14 (c) (f) (a) (h) (b) (d) (g) (e) (i)
15 **(a)**  to find out about the world of work/develop relationships with adults in the work place/get experience of the world of work
   **(b)**  written CV's and prepared job applications/insurance rules explained/employment law explained
   **(c)**  to find out about different types of jobs and to find out which jobs were best suited to their own skills and interests
   **(d)**  6 hours per day
   **(e)**  phone school and work place
16 **(a)**  Musik, Lesen, Fernsehen
   **(b)**  seit ihrer Geburt
   **(c)**  ihre Mutter
   **(d)**  keine Probleme; weil alle ihre Klassenzimmer im Erdgeschoß sind.
   **(e)**  Sie helfen ihr nur, wenn sie ihre Hilfe braucht.
   **(f)**  Sie hilft ihnen bei den Hausaufgaben und auch in den Unterrichtsstunden.
17 **(a)**  Von Problemen junger Leute
   **(b)**  Sie dürfen ehrlich ihre Meinung sagen

    **(c)**  ehrlich und hilfreich und kostenlos

    **(d)**  um etwas zu lernen

**18** **(a)**  always has a shower/recycles glass and paper

    **(b)**  not interested in/affected by environmental issues

    **(c)**  drive slower on the motorway to save petrol

    **(d)**  switches off heating when he goes out

    **(e)**  faster

    **(f)**  cars were banned from the town centre

**19** **(a)**  Ozonschicht

    **(b)**  Artenschutz

    **(c)**  Waldsterben

    **(d)**  umweltfreundlich

**20** **(a)**  Astrid

    **(b)**  Matthew

    **(c)**  Phillipe

    **(d)**  Astrid

    **(e)**  Matthew

    **(f)**  Phillipe

    **(g)**  Matthew

    **(h)**  Astrid

**21** **(a)**  Martin

    **(b)**  Beatrix

    **(c)**  Vivien

    **(d)**  Birgit

**22** **(a)**  sie trägt modische Kleider

    **(b)**  sie erlaubt ihnen, Bier zu trinken

    **(c)**  weil die andere Wohnung zuviel Arbeit machte

    **(d)**  Geld

    **(e)**  die zweite Oma

    **(f)**  wenn es zu laut wird, oder wenn es stinkt

**23** **(a)**  weil sie immer die dünnen Modelle sehen

    **(b)**  daß sie glücklicher und erfolgreich sein werden

    **(c)**  sie essen nicht genug und werden manchmal sogar magersüchtig

    **(d)**  anorexia nervosa beginnt in der Kindheit, wenn man Probleme mit den Eltern oder mit den Verhältnissen hat

    **(e)**  die Supermodelle, weil sie immer dünner werden und weil sie fast nie über Gesundheit und Diäten sprechen/die Medien, weil sie immer die Supermodelle zeigen und weil sie sagen, daß Dünnsein gesund und attraktiv ist

**24** **(a)**  Verena

    **(b)**  Nicole

    **(c)**  Marco

    **(d)**  Susanne

    **(e)**  Marc

    **(f)**  Khamphada

    **(g)**  Manuel

**25** 3, 4, 2, 5, 1, 6

# Chapter 8
# *Writing*

## 8.1 Introduction

Writing forms part of the GCSE examinations in both Foundation and Higher Tiers for all the examining groups in England, Wales and Northern Ireland. Make sure you know exactly what is expected of you by your particular examining group.

Here are some general tips about writing German and preparing for your writing tasks:

- Make sure you know exactly what you are being asked to do, how many words you have to write and how long you will have in the examination to write them.
- Remember virtually all the rubrics will be in German, so make sure you have studied the section on rubrics on pages 4–6 of this book and that you have learned them all carefully.
- You need to revise carefully all the vocabulary and grammar you have learned and ensure that you apply the rules consistently.
- You need to practise writing tasks regularly.
- Read the instructions on the question paper very carefully.
- If you have time, make a rough draft first.
- You will be allowed to use a dictionary in all your writing tasks.
- Some examining groups have a coursework alternative to the terminal writing examination. Check with your teacher and your syllabus before deciding which writing element of your GCSE examination to do. There is advice about coursework in 8.6.

## 8.2 Foundation Tier tasks

The following are the kinds of task you can expect at this level in your GCSE examinations:

- Messages of up to 30 words conveying information about a number of specific listed items.
- Lists
- Filling in some kind of proforma
- Writing a postcard giving listed or requested information
- Writing a letter.

The important things about these kinds of task are that the instructions will be in German and you will have to communicate the required message clearly. Number 1 is worked through for you.

### Messages, lists, proformas, postcards, letters

#### Messages

1  Du bist bei deiner Brieffreundin Ute in Hannover. Schreib ein paar Sätze an sie, um ihr zu erklären:
- du bist in die Stadt gefahren, um etwas für deinen Vater und deine Mutter zu kaufen
- was du für sie kaufen willst
- du wirst spät nach Hause kommen.
(Schreib ungefähr 30 Wörter!)

**E**xaminer's tip

Here you are asked to leave a note for your German penfriend Ute, saying that you have gone to town to buy something for your parents. You are also to say what you want to buy and that you will be late back. You can start by changing the person in the first part of the rubric: **Ich bin in die Stadt gefahren.**
Now what words do you know for presents? (**Ein Schlips oder ein Buch für Vati, eine Halskette oder Pralinen für Mutti** – your next sentence could be therefore, using the words in the rubric:
**Ich will ein Buch über Hannover für Vati und Pralinen für Mutti kaufen.**

*Ute,*

*ich bin in die Stadt gefahren. Ich will ein Buch über Hannover für Vati und Pralinen für Mutti kaufen. Es tut mir leid, aber ich werde spät nach Hause kommen. Kylie.*

The last part of the question asks you to explain that you will be late back. This is where you could include an idiom, **Es tut mir leid, aber ich werde spät nach Hause kommen**.

2 Du kommst nach Hause zurück. Du findest dieses Briefchen von deinem Brieffreund/deiner Brieffreundin auf dem Tisch in der Küche. Bevor du wieder ausgehst, schreibe eine Antwort und beantworte die Fragen! Du sollst ungefähr 30 Wörter schreiben.

*Mußte wieder ausgehen, Elke hat angerufen. Wir wollen morgen abend ins Kino. Kommst Du mit? Was willst Du heute nachmittag machen? Willst Du später Kaffee zu Hause trinken? Oder in einem Café?*

 **E** xaminer's tip

There are four questions which you need to answer, make sure you write something about them all. Do not try to use words you do not know.

## Lists

Writing or making a list is relatively easy at Foundation Tier. What you need to know is the relevant vocabulary, which you will of course find readily available in the core list issued by your examining group or under the appropriate Area of Experience. The most likely areas to be tested are:

- shopping
- clothes
- description of home or school
- hobbies and pastimes, description of a place.

3 Du fährst mit einem Freund bzw. einer Freundin auf Urlaub und du mußt ihm/ihr eine Liste senden.

Was soll er/sie mitbringen? Setze eine Liste auf!

........................................ ................ ......................

........................................ ................ ......................

........................................ ........................ ......

........................................ ......................

........................................ ......................

(10)

**E** xaminer's tip

You are asked here to list the items your friend should bring on holiday, ten things in all. What kinds of thing should you tell your friend to bring: clothes, camera, what else? Use only words you know.

4 Du gehst mit deinem deutschen Freund bzw. deiner deutschen Freundin zum Supermarkt, um alles für ein Picknick zu kaufen. Mach eine Einkaufsliste! Ihr kauft 12 Dinge.

(a) ................................................................

(b) ................................................................

(c) ................................................................

(d) ................................................................

(e) ................................................................

(f) ................................................................

(g) ................................................................

(h) ................................................................

(i) ................................................................

(j) ................................................................

(k) ................................................................

(l) ................................................................

(12)

**E** xaminer's tip

One word answers will do, but you could be a bit more adventurous and include some weights e.g. **ein Kilo Tomaten**. Look up and learn all the relevant vocabulary in Chapter 4.

**Proformas**

These are another kind of list requiring you to give very specific information. It could be details required on an application for a part-time job, an entry from your diary or calendar of events, personal details required when booking holiday accommodation or something similar.

5  Du suchst eine Stelle nach der Schule. Fülle das Formular aus!

| | | |
|---|---|---|
| Name | ................................................................................ | (1) |
| Vorname | ................................................................................ | (1) |
| Adresse | ................................................................................ | (1) |
| Geburtsdatum | ................................................................................ | (1) |
| Nationalität | ................................................................................ | (1) |
| Hobbys | ................................................................................ | (2) |
| Fächer studiert | ................................................................................ | (2) |
| Geschwister | ................................................................................ | (2) |

 **xaminer's tip**

The numbers in the brackets are the marks awarded for that section so you need to supply that number of pieces of information. You only need to use one-word answers in most instances.

6  Schreibe eine Seite in dein Tagebuch! Dein deutscher Freund/deine deutsche Freundin will wissen, was du in deiner Freizeit machst und wann.

| Tag | Was du in deiner Freizeit machst | Wann |
|---|---|---|
| Montag | ............................................................................... | |
| Dienstag | ............................................................................... | |
| Mittwoch | ............................................................................... | |
| Donnerstag | ............................................................................... | |
| Freitag | ............................................................................... | |
| Samstag | ............................................................................... | |
| Sonntag | ............................................................................... | |

(7)

 **xaminer's tip**

Again this is not a difficult task if you know the vocabulary for the things you do in your spare time. You probably need to write short sentences for what you do or use one-word answers e.g. **fischen** or better, **ich gehe fischen**. This is obviously vocabulary which you should know well.

**Postcards**

At this level you will not be expected to express opinions about your holiday for example, but to say simply what you did and where you went. These will be informal tasks and you will need to use **Du, Dein, Ihr, Euer,** which are all written with a capital letter on postcards or in messages and letters.

7  Du warst neulich mit der Schule in Deutschland. Du hast viel geknipst. Kannst du deinem Freund/deiner Freundin eine Postkarte senden und kannst du sagen, was du gemacht und gesehen hast. Sag etwas über das Wetter, die Stadt, das Essen und Trinken! Schreib ungefähr 40 Wörter!

**E** **xaminer's tip**

Check that you are using the correct tense as marks are frequently lost for writing in the present instead of the past tense.

8  Du hast das Wochenende bei einem Freund bzw. einer Freundin verbracht. Schreib eine Postkarte an ihn/sie, um ihm/ihr für das Wochenende zu danken. Sag, was du am liebsten hattest. (Schreib ungefähr 40 Wörter!)

**E** **xaminer's tip**

The important thing to remember in this example is that you must write in the past tense. You can use up some of the allocation of words with an appropriate beginning and ending.

**Letters**

Like postcards and messages, letters can either be on a particular topic suggested in the rubric or in answer to a letter printed on the question paper. Letters can be either informal or formal. At Foundation level you will not be expected to write more than about 70–100 words. It is worth knowing a few ways of beginning and ending both kinds of letter.

- An informal letter is usually written to a friend, a penfriend or a relative. You start such a letter as follows: **Lieber** (+ a boy's name) **Hans!** or **Liebe** (+ a girl's name) **Lotte!** It used to be normal to use the exclamation mark in German at the start of a letter but you can now use a comma if you wish, as we do in English. You must use the correct masculine and feminine forms.
- The start of the actual letter itself could then begin with a phrase like: **Herzliche Grüße aus...** or simply **Grüße aus...**
- In answer to a letter you have received, you could begin with: **Vielen Dank für Deinen letzten Brief, den ich gestern bekommen habe...**
- Other phrases you could use at the beginning of your letter: **Wie geht es Dir und Deiner Familie?/Im Moment geht es mir echt gut./Es tut mir leid, daß ich nicht früher geschrieben habe, aber wegen meiner Grippe habe ich keine Zeit gehabt...**
- There are many ways of ending an informal letter, here are some of the ones you can learn and adapt for your own purposes: **Mit vielen herzlichen Grüßen.../Mit den besten Grüßen .../Herzlichst.../Herzliche Grüße von uns allen...** These all mean much the same sort of thing: *With best wishes* or *Yours sincerely.* **Tschüs** *cheerio, bye for now,* is very informal and used between close friends. **Alles Gute** *all the best* is also informal. **Schreib bitte bald** (to one person) **Schreibt bitte bald** (to more than one person) means *write soon please* again writing informally.
- To start a formal letter you must use the correct form: **Sehr geehrter Herr** – *Dear Sir,* **Sehr geehrte Herren** – *Dear Sirs,* **Sehr geehrte Dame** – *Dear Madam,* **Sehr geehrter Herr Braun** – *Dear Mr Brown,* **Sehr geehrte Frau Schmidt** – Dear Mrs Smith, **Sehr geehrtes Fräulein Müller** – *Dear Miss Miller.*
- The most formal ending to letters is **Hochachtungsvoll** – *Yours faithfully* followed by your signature, but this is rarely used these days.
- You could precede this by a sentence like **Ich freue mich auf eine baldige Antwort** – *I look forward to a prompt/early reply.*

9 Du hast diesen Brief von deinem Freund/deiner Freundin in Österreich erhalten. Schreib eine Antwort (ungefähr 80 Wörter). Du sollst vier Fragen beantworten. Du mußt eine Frage vom zweiten Absatz beantworten.

(20)

*Graz, den 14. April*

*Hallo!*

*Ich möchte Euch allen für den wunderschönen Urlaub danken. Nun mußt Du mir sagen, wann Du uns besuchen kannst. Dieses Jahr noch vielleicht? Wie war die Rückfahrt vom Hafen? Du wolltest doch den Krimi im Fernsehen anschauen. Habt Ihr den Film gesehen, oder seid Ihr zu spät nach Hause gekommen? Ich kann meine Brieftasche nicht mehr finden. Vielleicht hab' ich sie bei Euch oder bei Deiner Tante liegengelassen. Hat sie Dir die Brieftasche gegeben?*

*Du gehst erst nächste Woche wieder in die Schule. Was machst Du bis dann?*

*Wie wirst Du Dein Geburtstagsgeld ausgeben? Hoffentlich war es ein guter Tag!*

*Laß bald von Dir hören!*

*Alles Gute!*

*S.*

 **xaminer's tip**

The first thing you have to do in this example is to choose which four questions to answer. Some of them are easier than others.

## 8.3 Foundation and Higher Tier tasks

The next few examples could be set at the more demanding level of the Foundation Tier and the lower, easier level of the Higher Tier papers. In general you are likely to have to write longer answers in the Higher Tier papers and you will be expected to give opinions about things rather than simply describe them.

10  Du schreibst einen Brief an eine deutsche Freundin/einen deutschen Freund über einen Besuch in deiner Stadt. Sie/Er wird eine Woche bei dir verbringen.

> Sag wo du wohnst und wie lange du Deutsch gelernt hast.
> Schreib Informationen über deine Familie – wie viele Geschwister, usw.
> Schreib Informationen über deine Hobbys (2) und deine Stadt. (3)
> Sag was du am Sonntag vorhast.
> Frag was sie/er am Samstag tun will.
> Endlich sollst du etwas über die Reise sagen. (20)

This is an informal letter which requires you to know the vocabulary about your family and yourself, the town where you live and the things you like doing. You should try to write accurate German using some simple idioms.

11  Du schreibst einen Brief an ein Hotel in Köln, um Zimmer zu reservieren. Vergiß nicht folgende Punkte!

Wann genau du nach Köln fährst; wie viele Tage du dort verbringst; wie viele Personen in deiner Familie sind; was für Unterkunft du willst. Du willst auch den Preis pro Nacht für die Unterkunft wissen, sowie den besten Weg vom Hauptbahnhof zum Hotel. Schreib ungefähr 80 Wörter. (20)

This is an open-ended question expecting you to decide the details to put into this formal letter to the hotel. Remember to use the formal beginning and ending to this letter and, where necessary, **Sie** and **Ihr**.

12  Für eine deutsche Schülerzeitung schreibst du einen Bericht über Schulen in England und in Deutschland. Schreib ungefähr 170 Wörter über die folgenden Aspekte:
- der Schultag
- der Schulunterricht
- die Schuluniform
- die Lehrer und Lehrerinnen
- ob du lieber in einer deutschen oder englischen Schule sein möchtest und warum. (20)

**E** xaminer's tip

You need to know the vocabulary about schools and to have learned how to express simple opinions in German.

## 8.4 Higher Tier tasks

The kinds of writing tasks set for the Higher Tier examinations will require you to be able to write clear accurate German, showing the ability to express ideas, facts and reactions to a narrative, report or description. To obtain the highest grades you should be able to develop your ideas, express opinions and write in a suitable style with a sense of grammatical structure, using a range of vocabulary and tenses. All the examining groups are looking for communication and accuracy. In most cases the split is 50% for communication and 50% for the accuracy and variety of the German you use. The length of the tasks is significantly increased up to 150 words for each piece of writing in the examination.

There are two types of writing task set at this level, letters and more creative writing in the form of articles or reports, plus the occasional narrative.

## Letters

These are either formal or informal as at Foundation Tier, but both sorts of letter at Higher level will be more demanding. You will also find that your work will be assessed for its accuracy plus the appropriateness, range and variety of the language you use.

### Informal letters

13 Du hast neulich einen Brief von deinem deutchen Brieffreund bzw. deiner deutschen Brieffreundin erhalten. Er/sie will dich nächste Woche besuchen. Leider ist das nicht möglich, weil du nach Schottland fahren mußt, um ein paar Tage bei deinem Onkel zu verbringen. Schreib an ihn/sie einen Brief und erkläre ihm/ihr diese Situation. (Schreib ungefähr 100 Wörter.)　(20)

> **E**xaminer's tip
>
> It is easy to include in your reply some good idiomatic phrases and different tenses. Do not forget to use capital letters for **Du** and **Dein** in your answer.

14 Du fährst bald nach Deutschland, um zwei Wochen bei einer Familie zu verbringen. Schreib einen Brief an die Familie (ungefähr 130 Wörter).

　　Sag　wie du fahren wirst
　　　　wann du ankommen wirst
　　　　wo du warten wirst
　　　　was du tragen wirst
　　　　was du machen möchtest
　　Frag etwas über das Wetter
　　　　was für Kleider du mitbringen mußt　(20)

> **E**xaminer's tip
>
> You need to know the vocabulary for going on a journey, clothes and what you like doing. You will need to use the future tense for a lot of this letter.

### Formal letters

These are likely to be job applications or letters seeking information or booking accommodation at a hotel, youth hostel, campsite or something similar. Learn these specific phrases thoroughly:

| | |
|---|---|
| eine Reservierung bestätigen | *to confirm a reservation/booking* |
| die Kosten angeben | *to indicate the costs* |
| ich wäre sehr dankbar, wenn Sie… könnten | *I should be very grateful if you could…* |
| ich möchte gerne wissen, ob… | *I should like to know whether…* |
| ich möchte Ihnen mitteilen, daß… | *I should like to inform you that…* |
| mit umgehender Post | *by return of post* |
| in Beantwortung auf Ihren Brief/Ihre Frage | *in reply to your letter/your question* |

15 Sie müssen drei Tage nächsten Monat in Köln verbringen. Sie werden im Büro der Express-Zeitung arbeiten. Sie möchten im Hotel Kolpinghaus übernachten. Schreiben Sie einen Brief an Herrn Weber, Hotel Kolpinghaus, Köln. (Schreiben Sie ungefähr 120 Wörter.)

　　Sagen Sie　wann Sie ankommen
　　　　　　wann Sie abfahren
　　　　　　wie Sie reisen
　　　　　　was für ein Zimmer Sie möchten
　　　　　　warum Sie dieses Hotel gewählt haben.
　　Fragen Sie　nach dem Abendessen
　　　　　　nach der Bestätigung
　　　　　　nach der Reservierung
　　　　　　nach den Kosten.　(20)

> **E**xaminer's tip
>
> This is a formal letter in which you need to use the formal/polite **Sie** and **Ihr** in German. Make sure that you have covered all the points mentioned in the rubric.

16 Letzte Woche warst du auf Urlaub in einer Jugendherberge. Du hast deine Kamera in der Jugendherberge gelassen. Schreib einen Brief an den Herbergsvater, Herrn Peters. (Schreib ungefähr 150 Wörter)

　　Sag ihm　　wann du da warst
　　　　　　wo du die Kamera liegengelassen hast
　　　　　　warum es für dich wichtig ist, sie zurückzuhaben
　　Beschreib　die Kamera
　　Frag　　　ob er die Kamera gefunden hat
　　Sag ihm　　dein Freund wird die Kamera von der Jugendherberge abholen, wenn er sie noch hat.
　　　　　　　　　　　　　　　　　　　　　　　　　(20)

> **E**xaminer's tip
>
> This is another example of a formal letter requiring you to give information and tell the warden of the youth hostel why you are concerned about your lost camera. There is opportunity for you to express the hope that it is still there and that you might get it back and say why it is important to you. Be careful about tenses and word order.

## Reports, articles and accounts

These are extended pieces of writing which will require you to use all your knowledge of grammar and vocabulary. It is a good idea before you write your actual answer to jot down the details you are expected to include in draft form. When you write your final version you can check them off and you will then know that you have not left out any important points.

They will be more creative than some of the other kinds of writing task. You will need to use your imagination to provide a plan of how you are going to tackle the question set. There are still likely to be some suggestions as to what you should include, but the task remains quite open ended and therefore demanding.

**17** Letztes Jahr hast du eine zweiwöchige Radtour mit vier Freunden in Deutschland gemacht. Schreib einen Bericht über diese Tour für die Schülerzeitung deines Brieffreundes in Deutschland. (Schreib ungefähr 150 Wörter.)

Vergiß nicht die folgenden Punkte:
- wann die Tour stattfand
- wo ihr übernachtet habt
- was ihr gesehen und gemacht habt
- das Wetter
- warum ihr so eine Tour gewählt habt
- die Reise dorthin und zurück. (20)

**E**xaminer's tip

You need to plan out about 20 words for each of the eight things mentioned as the points you should not forget. Be careful about the tense. Do not use pre-prepared material. Think what German you know that you can use in this context.

**18** Du hast vierzehn Tage Berufspraktikum in einem Büro gemacht. Schreib einen Artikel darüber. Erkläre, was du gemacht hast, wie du diese Arbeit gefunden hast, warum du diese Arbeit gewählt hast, was du davon gelernt hast, wie deine Kollegen waren. Schließlich: Wirst du so eine Stelle suchen, wenn du die Schule verläßt, und warum? (Schreib ungefähr 150 Wörter.)

(20)

**E**xaminer's tip

This question requires you to express opinions about a number of things to do with your work experience in an office. Do you know the German for what you might do in an office?

**19** Du hast eine Wanderung mit einigen Freunden auf das Land gemacht. Erzähle in einem Artikel, was geschehen ist. Die Bilder sollen dir helfen. (Schreib ungefähr 150 Wörter) (20)

 **xaminer's tip**

Not all the examining groups will set exactly this kind of task, but visuals to help you are quite frequent. You need to study them carefully. This account or article must be written in the past tense, in this case the imperfect tense. Before starting to write, jot down any relevant phrases and points of vocabulary. Make sure you are clear about the story line and which details you are going to include. If you know any expressions or idioms which fit into this account, then make use of them.

**20** Während eines Stadtbummels in Deutschland hast du einen Unfall gesehen. Schreib einen Bericht über den Unfall für die deutsche Versicherungsgesellschaft. Beschreib, was geschah.

Gib Informationen über die Fahrzeuge, die Zeit und das Wetter. Was geschah nachher? Wer hat geholfen, usw.? (Schreib ungefähr 150 Wörter.) (20)

**E** **xaminer's tip**

This report should be largely factual and written in the simple past tense. You need to know the vocabulary about traffic. Be sure to cover all the required details in your report.

# 8.5  Suggested answers to tasks

**2** Morgen abend gehe ich gern ins Kino. Welchen Film werden wir sehen? Heute nachmittag möchte ich schwimmen gehen. Danach können wir Kaffee und Kuchen in einem Café haben.

**3** Your list could include: eine Badehose/ein Badeanzug, Hemden, Blusen, Hosen, Röcke, eine Sonnenbrille, eine Kamera, ein Paß, Sandalen, Unterhosen, Unterwäsche, eine Landkarte, E–111–Schein

**4** Your list could include: Brötchen, Eier, Tomaten, Kopfsalat, Butter, Margarine, Käse, Chips, Schinken, Äpfel, Apfelsinen, eine Flasche Cola oder Limonade, Apfelsaft, Orangensaft, Bier, Milch, usw.

**5**

| | |
|---|---|
| Name | Miller |
| Vorname | Darren |
| Adresse | 25 Horsley Fields, Wolverhampton, West Midlands |
| Geburtsdatum | 12.05.1982 |
| Nationalität | Englisch |
| Hobbys: | Fischen, Fußball spielen, ich sammle Briefmarken |
| Fächer | Englisch, Deutsch, Mathematik, Naturwissenschaft, Erdkunde, Geschichte, usw. |
| Geschwister | ein Bruder, drei Schwestern |

**6** Activities: ich lese Bücher (z.B. Krimis), ich sehe fern, ich gehe fischen, ich spiele Fußball, ich treibe Sport, ich spiele Schach, ich spiele Tennis, ich höre Radio, ich höre Popmusik zu, ich spiele auf meinem Computer, ich gehe spazieren, ich knipse gern, ich gehe ins Kino, ich gehe ins Theater, ich spiele Gitarre, usw.

Times: am Morgen, am Nachmittag, am Abend, in der Nacht, während der Mittagspause, um 4 Uhr nachmittags, von acht bis zehn Uhr abends, während der Pause, um elf Uhr morgens, usw.

**7** Lieber Hans!

Grüße aus Münster. Das Wetter war prima! Wir haben den Dom besucht und in einem Paddelboot auf dem Aasee gepaddelt. Die Konditoreien waren wunderbar, aber ich hatte das Essen und Trinken meistens nicht gern. Tschüs Jack.

**8** Liebe Maria!/Lieber Kurt!

Ich bin schon wieder zu Hause. Ich schreibe, um Dich[1] für das wunderbare Wochenende bei Dir zu bedanken[2]. Es war schön, Dich wieder zu sehen[3], aber die Disko am Samstagabend[4] hatte ich am liebsten[5], es war wirklich toll! Bis zum nächsten Mal,

Deine Julie/Dein David

**Comment**: This is straightforward German. [1]It uses a capital letter for *Dich* and *Dir*. It has an *um… zu…* construction[2] with an infinitive at the end and [3]another infinitive construction separated from the rest of the sentence by a comma. [4]This is an expression of time and [5]uses the phrase in the rubric correctly.

**9** Liebe Susanne!/Lieber Stefan!

Vielen Dank für Deinen Brief, den ich gestern erhalten habe[1]. Hoffentlich werde ich Dich während der Sommerferien im August besuchen können[2]. Die Rückfahrt vom Hafen war ganz langweilig und langsam. Ich habe den Film im Fernsehen nicht gesehen, weil wir zu spät nach Hause kamen[3]. Leider habe ich Deine Brieftasche nicht gefunden.

An meinem Geburtstag waren viele Freunde und Freundinnen bei mir[4]. Wir hatten Spaß. Mit meinem Geburtstagsgeld habe ich eine CD von den 'Spice Girls' und einen neuen Tennisschläger gekauft[5].

Alles Gute! Deine Julie/Dein David

**Comments**: [1]A good standard opening. [2]Good use of future tense of a modal verb, note the word order of the infinitives. [3]Good use of tenses and a subordinate clause with *weil* with the verb at the end. [4]Prepositional phrase meaning 'at my house. [5]This is the answer to the question from the second paragraph about the birthday celebrations and the spending of the birthday money.

**10** Liebe Antje!/Lieber Kurt!

Nächste Woche wirst Du unsere Stadt besuchen[1]. Du wirst bei meiner Familie bleiben. Ich heiße Anne/John und ich habe eine jüngere Schwester, Karen und einen älteren Bruder, Robert[2]. Wir wohnen in Basildon, einer ziemlich großen Stadt[3] in Südostengland. Ich lerne Deutsch seit drei Jahren[4] und treibe gern Sport. Ich spiele Hockey/Fußball und schwimme sehr gern[5]. Basildon ist eine moderne Stadt mit einem Kino, einem neuen Theater und einem großen Einkaufszentrum. Es gibt auch ein Hallenbad, wo ich schwimmen gehe.[6]

Am Sonntagmorgen werden wir schwimmen gehen und am Nachmittag können wir einen Spaziergang machen.[7] Was möchtest Du am Samstag machen, wenn wir auch einen freien Tag haben werden?

Ich freue mich sehr auf Deinen Besuch[8] und wünsche Dir eine gute Reise nach England. Alles Gute,

Deine Anne/Dein John

**Comments**: [1]Good start with a correct use of the future tense. [2]Details about the family are given using comparative adjectives with the right endings. [3]This has to be in the same case as Basildon, i.e. the dative. [4]Correct use of the present tense with **seit** – learn this construction carefully.

[5]Hobbys are detailed. [6]Three things about the town. [7]What is planned for Sunday. [8]A good idiom with a preposition used correctly.

11  Sehr geehrte Damen und Herren,[1]

darf ich bitte zwei Doppelzimmer mit Dusche oder Bad für sieben Nächte ab dem elften August reservieren?[2] Es gibt vier Personen in unsrer Familie[3] und wir werden um achtzehn Uhr am elften August mit dem Zug in Köln ankommen.[4] Wie kommen wir vom Hauptbahnhof zum Hotel? Gibt es Taxis zum Beispiel?[5] Ich wäre sehr dankbar, wenn Sie mir die Kosten pro Nacht angeben könnten.[6] Ich freue mich auf Ihre baldige Antwort,

Hochachtungsvoll,[7] John Smith

**Comments**: [1]Formal opening to the manager of the hotel. [2]Request for the kind of accommodation, the number of nights and the date of arrival. [3]The number of people in the family. [4]The time of arrival and the date – note the correct use of the future tense. [5]One of the questions you were asked to ask in the rubric. [6]This is a sentence using formal structures which are explained on page 167. [7]Correct formal ending preceded by a standard request for a prompt answer.

12  Fast alle Schulen in England sind Ganztagsschulen, wo die Stunden um Viertel zehn nach einer Versammlung beginnen und nachmittags um halb vier enden. Wir haben nur fünf Tage in der Woche Unterricht, von Montag bis Freitag. In deutschen Schulen aber beginnen die Stunden früher, um 8 Uhr morgens, und enden um halb zwei nachmittags. Sie haben auch Unterricht am Samstagmorgen. In Deutschland gibt es keine Mittagspause wie in England, wo man in der Schule zu Mittag essen kann.

In den meisten englischen Schulen müssen wir alle, außer den Schulern in der Oberstufe, eine Schuluniform tragen. Deutsche Studenten haben Glück, sie brauchen keine Schuluniform zu tragen.

Der Unterricht in beiden Schulsystemen ist ähnlich, aber in Deutschland muß man mindestens fünf Fächer für das Abitur lernen, um es zu bestehen. Deutsche Studenten müssen auch regelmäßige Klassenarbeiten schreiben, so etwas Ähnliches gibt es nicht in England.

Die Lehrer in englischen Schulen sind nicht zu streng, sondern freundlich, in Deutschland sind sie etwas formeller. Meiner Meinung nach ist es besser in einer englischen Schule, weil wir keine Stunden am Samstag haben und Sport in der Schule unterrichtet wird.

**Comments**: This is a fairly simple piece of writing which contains some good relevant vocabulary – *Ganztagsschulen, Versammlung, Oberstufe, Mittagspause, bestehen, ähnlich, normalerweise, formell, mindestens.*

13  Lieber Rudi,/Liebe Uschi,

Vielen Dank für Deinen letzten Brief, den ich heute erhalten habe.

Es tut mir leid[1], daß Du nächste Woche nicht kommen kannst[2]. Leider muß ich meinen Onkel und meine Tante in Schottland besuchen.

Am Wochenende soll ich mit dem Auto nach Aberdeen fahren[3]. Ich werde vom nächsten Sonntag ab zwei Wochen bei meinen Verwandten verbringen[4]. Als mein Onkel letztes Jahr bei uns war, hat er mich eingeladen[5]. Also muß ich hin, sonst werden sie unzufrieden sein. Es ist wirklich schade, daß ich Dich diesmal nicht sehen kann. Hoffentlich wirst Du mich im nächsten Urlaub besuchen können.

Herzliche Grüße, Dein Robert/Deine Julie

**Comments**: [1] Good idiomatic phrase. [2]One of several modal verbs used correctly, this one in a subordinate clause - note the word order. [3]This sentence has an example of *time, manner, place* (TMP) in it. [4]Correct use of a future tense. [5]An example of *verb, comma, verb* (VCV) and correct use of the perfect and imperfect tenses. There is nothing in this letter which a candidate for the Higher Tier examination should find difficult.

**14** Liebe Anna,/Lieber Kurt,

Viele Grüße aus England, ich werde nächsten Monat nach Deutschland kommen, um bei Dir und Deiner Familie zwei Wochen zu verbringen. Ich werde mit der Fähre nach Ostende und dann mit dem Zug nach Münster fahren. Ich hoffe um 8 Uhr abends am 20sten Juli in Münster anzukommen, wenn der Zug pünktlich ist. Ich werde im Wartesaal warten. Ihr werdet mich sicher erkennen, weil ich eine braune Jacke mit einer gelben Rose im Knopfloch tragen werde.

Ich freue mich sehr auf diesen Besuch. Es wäre schön, wenn wir zu einer Kegelbahn gehen könnten, ich kegle sehr gern. Ich möchte auch Einkäufe machen. Ich frage mich, was für Kleider ich mitbringen sollte. Es hängt vom Wetter ab, nicht wahr? Wie ist das Wetter normalerweise im Sommer in Münster? Schreib bitte bald! Eure Julie/Euer David

**Comments**: Good use of the future tense here. A pleasing variety of sentence structure including *um... zu...* + infinitive, subordinate *wenn* and *weil* clauses with the verb at the end, correct use of the subjunctive in a conditional sentence. Some good vocabulary is used here – *sich freuen auf* (+acc), *Einkäufe machen, abhängen von* (+dat).

**15** Sehr geehrter Herr Weber,

nächsten Monat soll ich drei Tage in Köln verbringen, um im Büro der Express-Zeitung zu arbeiten. Ich habe dieses Hotel gewählt, weil ein Kollege, der in der Nähe von Köln wohnt, mir das Hotel Kolpinghaus empfohlen hat.

Darf ich bitte ein Einzelzimmer mit Dusche oder Bad für vier Nächte ab Montag dem 8. September reservieren? Ich werde am 8. September gegen 18 Uhr mit dem Zug in Köln ankommen, fahre dann am 12. um sieben Uhr dreißig vom Hauptbahnhof wieder ab.

Ich möchte gerne jeden Abend im Hotelrestaurant essen – ist das möglich? Ich wäre sehr dankbar, wenn Sie diese Reservierung bitte mit umgehender Post bestätigen und die Kosten angeben könnten. Ich freue mich auf Ihre baldige Antwort, Hochachtungsvoll

Peter Hunter

**Comments**: This formal letter has good variety of structure and vocabulary and more than covers the requirements of the rubric.

**16** Sehr geehrter Herr Peters!

Ich heiße John Smith/Julie Potter. Letzte Woche blieb ich bei Ihnen in der Jugendherberge. Als ich am Freitag zu Hause ankam, konnte ich zu meinem Erstaunen meine Kamera nicht finden. Ich suchte überall, aber die Kamera war nicht unter meinen Sachen, als ich meinen Rucksack auspackte.

Haben Sie vielleicht meine Kamera gefunden? Sie ist ziemlich neu, Marke Olympus II. Sie war in einer kleinen schwarzen Tasche mit einem roten Streifen darum. Ich habe sie wahrscheinlich im Zimmer Nummer 49 im Kleiderschrank liegengelassen. Es ist für mich wichtig, diese Kamera zurückzuhaben, weil sie ein Geburtstagsgeschenk von meiner alten Tante war. Wenn Sie die Kamera gefunden haben, könnten Sie sie meinem Freund, Kurt Müller geben. Er wohnt ganz in der Nähe von der Jugendherberge und er wird sie mir zurücksenden. Ich hoffe auf eine baldige Antwort.

Mit freundlichen Grüßen,

JohnSmith/Julie Potter

**Comments**: Good use of complex sentences with subordinate clauses and verbs in the right place. All the details in the rubric are covered. The ending is slightly less formal than *hochachtungsvoll* – yours faithfully, as this is to a youth hostel.

**17** Eine Radtour in Deutschland

Unsere Radtour fand letztes Jahr im Sommer statt. Wir waren vier – zwei Mädchen und zwei Jungen aus Colchester. Wir fuhren mit der Fähre von Harwich nach Ostende und dann mit dem Zug nach Köln. Zuerst übernachteten wir in Jugendherbergen, aber in der zweiten Woche fanden wir Campingplätze, wo wir bleiben konnten. Wir hatten Glück, das Wetter war herrlich. Es war so heiß und sonnig, daß wir viel Wasser trinken mußten.

In Köln haben wir den berühmten Dom besucht und danach sind wir durch viele hübsche Dörfer und kleine Städte nach Koblenz gefahren. Die Landschaft des Rheintals, die wir unterwegs gesehen haben, war atemberaubend.

Es war toll, zwei Wochen in dieser Gegend zu verbringen. Die Deutschen waren freundlich und hilfreich. Wir haben uns entschieden, diese Tour zu machen, weil es nicht zuviel kostete. Wir hatten auch die Gelegenheit, unser Deutsch zu verbessern. Die Rückreise mit dem Zug und der Fähre nach England war schnell, aber langweilig.

**Comments**: Note the requirement to express opinion is fulfilled with the reasons for going on the cycling tour.

**18** Neulich habe ich vierzehn Tage Berufspraktikum in einem Büro gemacht. Zuerst war es fremd, einen Anzug zu tragen und immer pünktlich ins Büro kommen zu müssen. Ich hatte auch keine Idee, was ich tun sollte. Meine Aufseherin erklärte mir, daß ich das Telefon abnehmen sollte, wenn es klingelte. Um das zu tun, mußte ich lernen, wie die Telefonanlage funktionierte. Glücklicherweise dauerte das nicht lange. Ich mußte auch den Kaffee kochen und viele Akten in den Aktenschrank ablegen. Ich fand das ziemlich langweilig, aber in der zweiten Woche erlaubte man mir, etwas Textverarbeitung am Computer zu machen. Das interessierte mich viel mehr.

Meine Kollegen waren sehr angenehm und halfen mir, alles im Büro zu verstehen. Ich wollte dieses Praktikum in einem Büro machen, denn ich interessiere mich sehr für Computer und werde so eine Stelle suchen, wenn ich die Schule verlasse. Ich habe viel über die Arbeit in einem Büro gelernt.

**19** An einem schönen Sommermorgen schlug ich eine Fußwanderung auf das Land vor. Meine Schwester Inge und die Nachbarskinder, Anna und Peter sollten mitkommen. Nachdem wir die Rucksäcke mit Proviant für den ganzen Tag vollgepackt hatten, sagten wir den Eltern, auf Wiedersehen und machten uns auf den Weg.

Drei Stunden lang schritten wir fröhlich durch die Wälder und an alten Bauernhöfen vorbei. Gegen halb eins machten wir unter den Bäumen halt, um das Mittagessen zu bereiten. Wir aßen Brot mit warmen Würstchen, die Anna über dem Feuer gebraten hatte, und tranken Limonade dazu.

Als wir wieder unterwegs waren, bemerkten wir am Himmel dunkle Wolken. Bald fing es an zu regnen. Leider hörte der starke Regen nicht auf, und wir waren schließlich völlig durchnäßt.

Sobald wir im nächsten Dorf ankamen, rief Inge unsren Vater an. Etwas ärgerlich holte er uns mit dem Auto von der Telefonzelle ab. Wir bedankten uns, und er fuhr so schnell wie möglich nach Hause zurück.

**Comments**: The above account is relevant to the pictures and accurately written in reasonably varied German. The variety is created by beginning sentences with adverbs or adverbial phrases like *bald, leider, an einem schönen Sommermorgen, drei Stunden lang*, each followed by the verb as the second idea. There are also a number of different subordinate clauses beginning with *als, nachdem, sobald* and a relative clause. Finally some relevant German expressions are used like: *sich auf den Weg machen, vorbeischreiten an* (+ dat), *unterwegs sein, sich bedanken.*

**20** Gestern nachmittag um dreiviertel vier ging ich in der Stadtmitte spazieren. Plötzlich begann es stark zu regnen, und die Fahrbahn wurde sofort naß und rutschig. Als ich die Hauptstraße entlangging, sah ich einen Unfall. Ein Junge auf einem Fahrrad kam zu schnell aus einer Nebenstraße und bog in die Hauptstraße ein. Ein Autofahrer, der einen grünen Volkswagen fuhr, konnte nicht anhalten. Er bremste und schleuderte, konnte aber den Radfahrer nicht vermeiden. Der Radfahrer ist überfahren worden. Ich bin der Meinung, daß der Autofahrer nicht schuld daran war. Glücklicherweise war der Junge nicht zu schwer verletzt. Während er auf der Straße lag, lief der Autofahrer los, um die Polizei und das Krankenhaus anzurufen. Ein paar Minuten später kamen ein Polizist und ein Krankenwagen an. Die Sanitäter hoben den Radfahrer vorsichtig in den Krankenwagen, um ihn ins Krankenhaus zu bringen. Der Polizist fragte, ob jemand den Unfall gesehen hätte. Ich erzählte ihm davon.

**Comments**: Covers the requirements of the rubric. Has good use of the simple past tense, clauses and infinitive phrases with *zu* and *um... zu...* Has some good phrases: *spazierengehen, bremsen, schleudern, bog in die Hauptstraße ein, ich bin der Meinung, daß..., schuld daran.*

# 8.6 Coursework

One of the main changes with the revised examination is the opportunity for students to complete coursework instead of taking a written examination at the end of their course.

The following examples and specimens are designed to assist you in the planning of your writing coursework.

- Remember that you may not use any of these examples as your coursework for your actual examination.
- Ask your teacher for as much assistance as possible and make good use of the sections on using a dictionary to improve your writing, as well as checking your work in the grammar section.

## Task type: Writing a letter in German to apply for a holiday job

Sie haben ein kleines Inserat gelesen:

> GESUCHT
> neues Hotel in Dortmund sucht Ferienpersonal.
> Können Sie Deutsch und Englisch?
> Wir brauchen Studenten/Studentinnen für allerlei Stellen.
> Schreiben Sie an unseren Personalleiter mit Ihren persönlichen Einzelheiten: Name, Alter,
> Sprachkenntnisse, Erfahrung, Lohn erwünscht, usw.

Sie möchten dort arbeiten. Schreiben Sie einen Brief. (100 Wörter)

**Suggested answer**

Sehr geehrte Damen und Herren,
ich habe neulich Ihr Inserat gelesen und ich suche eine Ferienstelle in Deutschland.

Mein Vorname ist Samantha und mein Familienname ist Smith. Ich bin siebzehn Jahre alt und ich komme aus England. Ich wohne in Basildon in Südostengland in der Nähe von London. Ich spreche Englisch als Muttersprache und ich lerne seit vier Jahren Deutsch. Ich habe Deutschland schon besucht und ich kann gut Deutsch sprechen.

Ich arbeite am Wochenende in einem großen Hotel: Ich mache die Betten und ich helfe den Gästen am Empfang.

Ich bin ab ersten Juli frei und ich könnte sechs Wochen arbeiten. Wieviel Geld werde ich verdienen? Muß ich eine Uniform tragen? Wie viele Stunden muß ich jeden Tag arbeiten? Kann ich im Hotel bleiben oder soll ich Unterkunft finden?

Ich freue mich auf Ihre baldige Antwort. Ich lege meinen Lebenslauf und einen internationalen Antwortschein bei.

Hochachtungsvoll,

**Examiner's tip**

Remember to check your sentence structure carefully. All accurate German is rewarded so that it is important to use capital letters for nouns, to check word order, and to check the verb constructions carefully.

## Task Type: Written report on a school holiday/visit to Germany

Du warst neulich mit einer Schulgruppe in Ulm auf einem Schüleraustausch. Du sollst jetzt etwas über die Reise, deine Erfahrungen schreiben. Du mußt auch über Vorteile und Nachteile eines Austausches schreiben.

**Examiner's tip**

If you have never been on a school exchange you will find this task difficult to complete. However, it is not difficult to imagine the type of activities that would be included in this visit. This would have to be in an essay format and you would have to use **man** verb forms; as well as being able to offer your opinion.

**Suggested answer**

Unsere Schule hat neulich einen Besuch nach Ulm gemacht. Es war ein Schüleraustausch und es gab ein gutes Programm. Man mußte täglich in die Schulstunden gehen: Das war ein bißchen schwierig, besonders wenn man auf deutsch redete. Die Englischstunden waren ziemlich interessant, und die deutschen Schulkinder durften nur Englisch reden, deswegen kennen sie viele Wörter und Sätze. In England in einer Deutschstunde dürfen wir entweder auf Deutsch oder auf Englisch reden.

Es gab auch eine Stadttour und man hat viel über die Stadt gelernt. Man konnte auch einkaufen gehen, und wir haben Souvenirs gekauft. Alles war ein bißchen teurer als in England, aber es hat uns trotzdem viel Spaß gemacht.

Man hat bei Familien gewohnt. Zuerst war es ein bißchen schwer: man konnte nicht fließend sprechen, und man dachte immer auf englisch, und dann versucht man auf deutsch zu übersetzen.

Die Familien waren sehr nett und freundlich, und man hat viele neue Leute kennengelernt. Wenn man älter ist, könnte man das Land wieder besuchen und bei den Freunden vorbeischauen. Man hat auch viel über ein neues Land gelernt: mehr als aus einem Schulbuch – etwas über die Sitten eines anderen Landes.

Man sollte auch deutsches Essen probieren. Natürlich war das Essen anders als zu Hause, aber es hat echt gut geschmeckt.

Meiner Meinung ist ein Austausch eine gute Idee: Man kann billig mit einer Gruppe reisen, neue Leute kennenlernen, die Sprachkenntnisse verbessern und seinen Horizont erweitern.

# *Complete GCSE paper*

## Introduction

In this chapter you have an example of a complete Foundation and Higher Tier GCSE paper. Probably the best time to attempt it is a week or two before your German exams start. The recordings for the listening tests are on the CD accompanying this book. Also, the transcripts of the recordings and the suggested answers are given later in the book.

- Try to do the papers under exam conditions.
- Try to adhere to the times allowed by your Examining Board for each paper.
- Ask your teacher to mark your work for the writing paper.
- In the following questions you will notice that both the *du* and *Sie* forms of the verb appear in different questions. Exam boards use either one or the other – check with your teacher which one will be used in your examination.

## The examination paper

LETTS SCHOOL EXAMINATIONS BOARD
General Certificate of Education Examination

GERMAN

Answer all four papers (Listening, Speaking, Reading, Writing).
Answer all the questions relating to your Tier (Foundation or Higher)

### Listening

**Instructions to candidates:**
Foundation Tier: attempt sections 1 and 2
Higher Tier: attempt sections 2 and 3
You must carry out the tasks specified.
You may use a dictionary in the preparation period before the exam.

### Section 1 (Foundation Tier)

### Recording 22

Auf dem Bahnhof. Beantworten Sie die Fragen auf Deutsch!

1 Woher kommt der Zug? Der Zug kommt .......................... (1)

2 Wie viele Minuten Verspätung hat der Zug? .......................... Minuten (1)

## Recording 23

Auf dem Bahnhof. Beantworten Sie die Fragen auf Deutsch!

1 Wann kommt der Zug auf diesem Bahnhof an? Der Zug kommt ......................... an. (1)

2 Wo sind die ersten Klasse Wagen? Sie sind ........................... (1)

3 Wohin fährt der Zug? Der Zug fährt nach .............................. (1)

4 Was muß man über den Zug wissen? Man muß ...........................................zahlen. (1)

## Recording 24

Sie sind auf Urlaub mit drei Freunden in Österreich. Sie kommen in einer Jugendherberge an. Beantworten Sie die Fragen auf deutsch oder haken Sie die richtige Antwort ab! Hören Sie gut zu!

1 Wie lange wollen Peter und seine Freunde in der Jugendherberge bleiben?

(a) zwei Wochen ☐     (c) eine Woche ☐

(b) einen Monat ☐     (d) einen Tag ☐     (1)

2 Um wieviel Uhr ist die Jugendherberge abends zu?

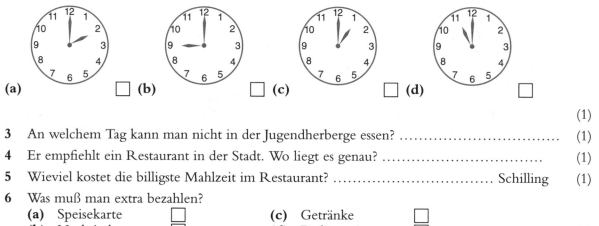

(a) ☐   (b) ☐   (c) ☐   (d) ☐

(1)

3 An welchem Tag kann man nicht in der Jugendherberge essen? .............................. (1)

4 Er empfiehlt ein Restaurant in der Stadt. Wo liegt es genau? ............................... (1)

5 Wieviel kostet die billigste Mahlzeit im Restaurant? ............................... Schilling (1)

6 Was muß man extra bezahlen?

(a) Speisekarte ☐     (c) Getränke ☐

(b) Nachtisch ☐     (d) Bedienung ☐     (1)

## Section 2 (Foundation and HigherTier)

## Recording 25

Sie planen einen Abend zu Hause. Was gibt es heute im Fernsehen?
Füllen Sie die Tabelle aus!

| | | |
|---|---|---|
| 20.00 | | (1) |
| | eine Serie | (1) |
| 21.45 | | (1) |
| 22.30 | | (1) |
| | Nachrichten und ...................... | (1) |
| | Sendeschluß | (1) |

## Section 3 (Higher Tier)

## Recording 26

Eine deutsche Familie ist auf Sommerurlaub. Beantworten Sie die Fragen auf deutsch! Hören Sie gut zu!

1 In welchem Land war die Familie? ................................................. (1)

2 Wie war das Wetter? .................................................. (1)

3 Wie oft gingen sie mit ihren Kanus paddeln? .................................................. (1)

4 Warum konnten sie so oft auf dem See paddeln? Weil .................................... (2)

5 Sie hatten einen Unfall. Wer war Schuld daran? .................................................. (1)

6 Auf was fuhr der Wohnwagen drauf? ................................................... (1)

## Recording 27

Uschi beschreibt ihren Ferienjob. Beantworten Sie die Fragen auf deutsch! Hören Sie gut zu!

1   Wo arbeitet Uschi?

.............................................................................................. (1)

2   Warum arbeitet sie?

........................................................................................ (2)

3   Was hofft sie, nächstes Jahr zu tun?

..................................................................... (1)

4   Was hat sie nicht gern?

...................................................................... (2)

5   Wieviel Geld verdient sie?

.................................................................... (1)

6   Was kann sie nachmittags tun, und warum?

......................................................................................................

...................................................................................................... (3)

## Recording 28

Zwei junge Deutsche unterhalten sich über Umweltverschmutzung.
Beantworten Sie die folgenden Fragen auf deutsch! Hören Sie gut zu!

**(1)**   Was beschreibt der Junge als enorm?

.................................... durch die .............................. (3)

**(2)**   Was verursacht die Verpestung der Luft in der Stadtmitte?

........................................ und ................................. (2)

**(3)**   Was könnten die jungen Leute tun, um die Umwelt zu schützen?
Zum Beispiel:

.................................................................... (2)

**(4)**   Was wäre gesünder für sie?

Es wäre gesünder .......................................................... (2)

**(5)**   Was sollte man recyceln? ............................................ (3)

**(6)**   Was wäre etwas Positives zu tun? ................................... (2)

## Speaking

**Instructions to candidates:**
Foundation Tier: attempt sections 1 and 2
Higher Tier: attempt sections 2 and 3
You must carry out the tasks specified.
You may use a dictionary in the preparation period before the exam.
You must assume that the Examiner speaks no English.

### Section 1 (Foundation Tier)

### Role-play 1

You are on holiday in Switzerland with your friend. You want a drink and something to eat.
Your teacher will play the part of the waiter or waitress.
Bereiten Sie die 5 Sätze vor.

(10)

### Role-play 2

Du bist in einem Hotel angekommen. Du möchtest hier übernachten. Bereite die 5 Sätze vor!

1    2    3    4    3    5

(10)

## Section 2 (Foundation and Higher Tier)

### Role-play 3

You have torn your friend's trousers. You go into the town to try to have them repaired.
Bereiten Sie die Sätze vor.

1    Sagen Sie, was passiert ist.
2    Fragen Sie, ob man sie reparieren kann.
3    Fragen Sie, wenn Sie sie wieder holen können.
4    Sagen Sie, wem sie gehört.
5    Beenden Sie das Gespräct.

(10)

### Role-play 4

Sie suchen einen Ferienjob in Deutschland. Sie können nur im August arbeiten.

1    Sagen Sie, wer am Apparat ist.                              (2)
2    Fragen Sie, ob es Stellen für Studenten gibt.               (2)
3    Sagen Sie, was Sie machen wollen.                           (2)
4    Beantworten Sie die Frage.                                  (2)
5    Beenden Sie das Gespräch.                                   (2)

## Section 3 (Higher Tier)

### Role-play 5

Sie waren neulich mit einer Gruppe in Deutschland. Sie haben das Programm nach England mitgenommen. Lesen Sie das Programm durch und erklären Sie dann, was während des Austausches passiert ist.

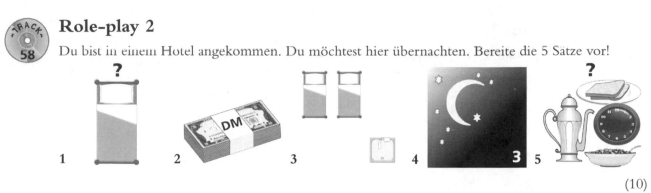

Partnerschafts – Club e.V
Castle Point (GB); Igny (F); Diepenbek (B); Köln Bez. 3 (d)
An der Ronne 10
5000 Köln 40
Tel:02234/76115

Jugendaustausch mit Castle Point vom 28. März bis 3. April

Liebe Jugend

freundlicherweise habt Ihr Euch bereit erklärt, in der o.a. Woche Gäste von Castle Point bei Euch aufzunehmen.
PROGRAMM:

| | |
|---|---|
| Dienstag 28.3.1997 | Albert-Schweizer-Schule |
| | ca. 18.30 Uhr Ankunft der Gäste |
| Mittwoch 29.3.1997 | Führung durch das Kölner Rathaus mit Empfang und |
| | anschließender Stadtrundfahrt, Stadtbummel |
| | Abfahrt: 9.00 Uhr |
| | Rückkehr gegen 17.00 Uhr an die Schule |
| Donnerstag 30.3.1997 | Tagesausflug nach Bonn |
| | Abfahrt 8.45 Uhr |
| | Rückkehr gegen 17.30 Uhr |
| Freitag 31.3.1997 | Phantasialand |
| | Abfahrt 9.00 Uhr |
| | Rückkehr gegen 18.00 Uhr |
| Samstag 1.4.1997 | Familientag |
| Sonntag 2.4.1997 | Familientag |
| Montag 3.4.1997 | Rückkehr unserer Gäste nach England |
| | Bitte pünktlich vor der Schule treffen |

Die Jugendlichen benötigen für <u>alle</u> Ausflüge Verpflegung und Getränke, ebenso für ihre Rückkehr nach England.
Wir wünschen Euch und Euren Gästen aus Castle Point eine super Woche.

## Reading

**Instructions to candidates:**
Foundation Tier: attempt questions 1–3
Higher Tier: attempt questions 2–5
You must answer *all* the questions.
Read the instructions and the questions carefully.
You may use a dictionary.

1    Lesen Sie den Artikel und füllen Sie die Tabelle aus.

### Hallo Niklas!

**Wem hilfst du?** Ich helfe meinen Eltern.
**Und wobei hilfst du?** Ich arbeite im Garten oder kümmere mich um unsere Hunde und Pferde. Im Haushalt helfe ich ab und zu. Ich sauge die Teppiche in meinem Zimmer oder im Wohnzimmer. Manchmal wische ich auch Staub von Möbeln oder den vielen Geweihen, die in unserem Wohnzimmer hängen.
**Bekommst du etwas für deine Hilfe?** Ab und zu. Meiner Mutter biete ich aber freiwillig Hilfe an.
**Gibt es Menschen oder besondere Organisationen, denen du gerne helfen würdest?** Ja, Umweltorganisationen. Umgekehrt würde ich Leuten, die ich nicht mag, nur sehr ungerne helfen.
**Warum hilfst du anderen Menschen?** Ich kann Ihnen helfen, Probleme zu lösen.
Das mache ich gern. Wenn ich Probleme habe, wünsche ich mir auch Hilfe.

### Hallo Katja und Julia!

**Wem helft ihr?** Unseren Bekannten und den Eltern.
**Wobei helft ihr?** Eigentlich bei allen möglichen Sachen: Wir kaufen ein, kochen, waschen, spülen, räumen auf, bringen den Müll weg oder decken den Tisch.
**Bekommt ihr etwas für eure Hilfe?** Nein, wir helfen freiwillig mit. Das geht auch nicht anders. Unsere Eltern sind beide berufstätig. Da muß jeder mithelfen. Wir bieten unsere Hilfe auch gerne an, etwa wenn wir auf Kinder von Bekannten aufpassen.
**Gibt es Menschen oder besondere Organisationen, denen ihr gerne helfen würdet?** Ja, Tierschutzorganisationen. Seltene Tiere sollte man besonders schützen. Außerdem sind Tierversuche unserer Ansicht nach überflüssig.
**Warum helft ihr anderen Menschen?** Unseren Großeltern erleichtern wir mit unserer Hilfe schwere Arbeiten. Das ist nur ein Beispiel. Es ist wichtig, hilfsbereit
zu sein und anderen Menschen dadurch eine Freude zu machen.

### Hallo Sven!

**Wem hilfst du?** Ich helfe meistens meinen Freunden.
**Und wobei hilfst du?** Eigentlich bei allem, was mit Schule zu tun hat. Meistens aber bei Hausaufgaben und Prüfungsvorbereitungen. Nachhilfestunden in Biologie oder Chemie gebe ich ziemlich regelmäßig, weil ich in diesen Fächern ganz gut bin.
**Bekommst du etwas für deine Hilfe?** Ja, manchmal. Ich bessere mein Taschengeld mit Nachhilfe auf.
**Gibt es Menschen oder besondere Organisationen, denen du gerne helfen würdest?** Allen netten Leuten helfe ich gerne.
**Warum hilfst du anderen Menschen?** Es ist schön, wenn sie sich über Mithilfe freuen.

| | Sven | Katja | Niklas | |
|---|---|---|---|---|
| muß manchmal zu Hause helfen | | | | (1) |
| schützt die Tiere | | | | (1) |
| arbeitet ab und zu, um Geld zu verdienen | | | | (1) |
| arbeitet gern mit anderen Menschen | | | | (1) |
| lernt gern Naturwissenschaft | | | | (1) |
| teilt die Hausarbeit, weil die Eltern oft beschäftigt sind | | | | (1) |
| ist umweltfreundlich | | | | (1) |
| geht von Zeit zu Zeit Babysitten | | | | (1) |
| füttert die Tiere | | | | (1) |

**2** Lesen Sie der Text durch und antworten Sie die Fragen.

## Hier geht's rund

Die Kirmes kommt. Karussells, Riesenräder und andere Attraktionen stehen mitten in der Stadt. Es riecht nach Würstchen und Süßigkeiten. Riesige Stofftiere warten am Losgeschäft auf Gewinner. Besonders beliebt sind die großen Karussells. Claudia war schon dreimal in der Schiffschaukel. 50 Menschen haben darin Platz. Ein Motor bewegt das riesige Schiff hin und her. Besonders beliebt sind die hinteren Plätze. Da fliegt man bis ganz oben. „Ein tolles Gefühl," findet Claudia. An der „Krake" stehen die meisten Jugendlichen. Hier fährt man zwar „nur" im Kreis. Doch aus den Lautsprechern kommen die neuesten Hits.

Thomas arbeitet in einer alten Schießbude. Er reist seit vier Jahren herum. „Eigentlich bin ich Maurer," erzählt Thomas, „aber dieser Job macht mehr Spaß. Ich reise gerne. Ich habe auch schon viele interessante Leute kennengelernt." Thomas lädt die Gewehre. Die Kunden schießen auf kleine Röhren aus Plastik. Man kann Blumen, bunte Federn und Postkarten gewinnen. An besonders langen Röhren hängen größere Gewinne. Da braucht man allerdings viele Schüsse. Die Kirmessaison dauert von Februar bis Oktober. Die Besitzer und Mitarbeiter von Karussells und Buden nennt man Schausteller. Sie fahren mit ihren Wohnwagen von Stadt zu Stadt. Ihre Kinder gehen meistens auf ein Internat. Nur in den Schulferien sind sie bei den Eltern.

„Wir haben einen anstrengenden Beruf," meint Albert Ritter, Besitzer mehrerer Karussells. „Alle vierzehn Tage sind wir in einer neuen Stadt. Manchmal müssen wir nachts aufbauen." Trotzdem wünscht er sich keinen anderen Beruf. „Fast alle unsere Kinder wollen auch Schausteller werden," erzählt Ritter. „Viele von ihnen machen eine Lehre oder studieren. Aber dann kommen sie zu uns zurück."

**(a)** Was kann man auf einem Jahrmarkt finden. (Mach eine Liste von 4 Dingen.)

....................................................................................

....................................................................................

**(b)** Was hat Thomas früher gemacht?

....................................................................................

....................................................................................

**(c)** Warum kann er im Winter nicht auf der Kirmes arbeiten?

....................................................................................

....................................................................................

**(d)** Warum gehen die Kinder auf ein Internat?

....................................................................................

....................................................................................

**(e)** Was machen die Schausteller?

....................................................................................

....................................................................................

**(f)** Wo wohnen die Schausteller und ihre Familien?

....................................................................................

....................................................................................

(6)

## 3 Ein Besuch in der Bibliothek

Viele Schulklassen besuchen geschlossen die Stadtbibliothek. Die Bibliothekarinnen freuen sich darüber und nehmen sich Zeit, den Kindern alles zu erklären. Geduldig beantworten sie die Fragen der Kinder.
Manche Kinder nutzen die Gelegenheit und lassen sich sogleich einen Bibliotheksausweis ausstellen. Mit diesem Ausweis können sie gleich bei ihrem ersten Besuch Bücher, Cassetten, Schallplatten oder Spiele und Bilder ausleihen.
Wie gut es einer Klasse in der Bibliothek gefallen hat, das könnt ihr an der folgenden Geschichte erkennen:

### Kennst du Elebib?

Am vergangenen Freitag fuhr ich mit meiner Klasse nach Gütersloh. Der Bus hielt an der großen, prächtigen Bibliothek. Schon beim Eintreten bekam ich vor Staunen ganz große Kulleraugen, denn das gesamte Gebäude beeindruckte mich sehr.
Nun ging ich eine Treppe hinunter in die Kinder- und Jugendbibliothek. Mir gefiel das Hexenhäuschen am besten. Es war ein kleines Haus, in dem man ungestört lesen konnte. Ich habe mir zwei Bücher mit hineingenommen. Dann habe ich mich auf den Boden gelegt und gelesen.
Nun will ich noch erklären, wer Elebib ist. Elebib ist ein großer Stoffelefant. Der Name ist eine Zusammensetzung von Ele = Elefant und bib = Bibliothek. Elebib ist das Markenzeichen der Bibliothek.

## Elebib's Ratschläge für Bücherwürmer

Die Gütersloher Stadtbibliothek wirbt auf vielfältige Art, um neue Besucher und Benutzer zu gewinnen. Das ist notwendig, denn manche Leute scheuen sich, die Bibliothek zum erstenmal zu betreten. Sie wissen nicht genau, wie es dort zugeht, wie man Bücher ausleiht und wer welche ausleihen darf. Sie haben Sorge, daß sie etwas falsch machen. Da hilft die Bibliothek mit einem Informationsblatt, das sich besonders an die Bücherwürmer unter den Kindern wendet.

### Wie melde ich mich an?
Um die Bücher, Schallplatten … auch mit nach Hause zu nehmen, brauchst du einen Ausweis. Du bekommst einen Vordruck für die Anmeldung. Du nimmst ihn mit nach Hause und bringst ihn ausgefüllt und von den Eltern unterschrieben zurück. Wenn du 12 Jahre alt bist, darfst du deinen Bibliotheksausweis selbst unterschreiben.

### Was kostet es?
NICHTS! Nur wenn du die Bücher zu spät zurückbringst, mußt du etwas bezahlen. Auch andere Kinder lesen gern deine Lieblingsbücher. Deshalb ist es wichtig, daß du sie pünktlich zurückbringst und gut behandelst!

### Wie lange kannst du die Bücher oder Spiele behalten?
4 Wochen. Wenn du einmal ein Buch, eine Cassette länger entleihen möchtest, mußt du damit rechtzeitig in die Bibliothek kommen und die Leihfrist verlängern lassen.

### Was findest du in der Bibliothek?
In der Kinderbibliothek gibt es viele Dinge, die bestimmt auch dich interessieren.
Auch die Sachbücher sind nach deinen Interessen aufgestellt. Du findest Hobby und Bastelbücher, Spiel- und Sportbücher, Biologiebücher, Sachkunde- und Erdkundebücher, Musikbücher, Mathematikbücher, Ratgeber und vieles mehr. Und wenn du ein ganz bestimmtes Buch suchst, so findest du es in einer langen Reihe von Büchern, die nach den Namen der Schriftsteller alphabetisch geordnet sind.
Wenn du beim Suchen nicht zurechtkommst, helfen dir gerne die Bibliothekarinnen.

---

Lesen Sie den Artikel über die neue Bibliotek in Gütersloh. Können Sie die zwei Hälfte zusammensetzen?

| | |
|---|---|
| **(a)** Wann können die Schulkinder die Bibliothek besuchen? | **(i)** Das Markenzeichen der Bibliothek: er hilft den Kindern in der Bibliothek. (1) |
| **(b)** Was kann man in der Bibliothek ausleihen? | **(ii)** Bücher, Cassetten und Schallplatten. (1) |
| **(c)** Wo ist die Kinderbibliothek? | **(iii)** Wenn die Bibliothek zu ist. (1) |
| **(d)** Wer ist Elebib? Was macht er? | **(iv)** Im Untergeschoß. (1) |

**4** Wenn Sie wirklich mit dem Rauchen aufhören wollen, haben Sie drei verschiedene Möglichkeiten: Sie hören sofort auf; Sie rauchen allmählich immer weniger, bis Sie Nichtraucher sind; Sie rauchen so wenig wie möglich, obwohl es sicher am besten ist, ganz aufzuhören. Um das Aufhören leichter zu machen, können Sie folgendes tun:
– Nehmen Sie nie Streichhölzer, Feuerzeug oder Zigaretten mit.
– Lehnen Sie jede angebotene Zigarette ab.
– Rauchen Sie in bestimmten Situationen nicht, z.B. wenn Sie telefonieren, Tee oder Kaffee trinken, usw.
– Rauchen Sie nur eine halbe Zigarette.

– Rauchen Sie leichte Zigaretten.
– Kaufen Sie erst wieder Zigaretten, wenn die alte Packung leer ist.
– Rauchen Sie nicht vor oder nach Mahlzeiten, denn das ist besonders ungesund.
– Rauchen Sie nicht, wenn Nichtraucher oder Kinder dabei sind.
– Stellen Sie keine Aschenbecher in Arbeits– und Wohnzimmer.
– Schränken Sie das Rauchen auf maximal 10 Zigaretten pro Tag ein.
– Wenn Sie den Wunsch nach einer Zigarette haben, gehen Sie an die frische Luft oder atmen Sie tief vor dem offenen Fenster durch.

**(a)** In what different ways can you stop smoking?

.............................................................................................................

............................................................................................................. (3)

**(b)** What can you do to help you give up?

.............................................................................................................

............................................................................................................. (3)

**5** *Fragen Sie Frau Martina ...*

*Liebe Frau Martina!*

*Seit langem habe ich Probleme mit meinem Vater. Er liest auch einfach meine Briefe. Können Sie bitte deshalb Ihren Rat abdrucken und mir nicht schreiben?*

*Obwohl ich schon 16 bin, besteht mein Vater immer darauf, daß ich ihm sage, wohin ich gehe, mit wem ich verkehre und was ich mache. Nun habe ich einen Freund. Meiner Mutter habe ich davon erzählt. Sie hat Verständnis für meine Situation; meinem Vater habe ich nichts darüber gesagt. Gestern hat er uns aber nach der Schule gesehen. Vater hat meine Mutter und mich angeschrien und gesagt, wir hätten ihn betrogen. Er sagt, er will mich jeden Tag von der Schule abholen und mir nicht mehr erlauben, abends auszugehen, damit ich meinen Freund nicht mehr treffen kann. Was soll ich nur machen? Was raten Sie mir?*

*Christina X*

**Liebe Christina!**

**Du tust mir leid, denn ich finde, Dein Vater zeigt wenig Verständnis für Dich. Ich bin aber sicher, er meint es gut und tut das alles nur, weil er Dich liebt, und sich Sorgen um Dich macht. Ich bin der Meinung, er sollte viel mehr Vertrauen zu Dir haben, denn Du bist kein kleines Kind mehr!**

**Wenn Dein Vater nicht will, daß Du ausgehst, könnten Du oder Deine Mutter ihm vorschlagen, daß Dein Freund Dich zu Hause besucht. Auf diese Weise kann Dein Vater ihn kennenlernen. Wer weiß, vielleicht findet er, daß er ganz in Ordnung ist!**

*Frau Martina*

**(a)** Warum soll Frau Martina Christina nicht nach Hause schreiben?

.............................................................................................................

............................................................................................................. (1)

**(b)** Was ist das Problem zwischen Christina und ihrem Vater?

.............................................................................................................

............................................................................................................. (1)

**(c)** Zu wem hat sie ein gutes Verhältnis, und warum?

.............................................................................................................

............................................................................................................. (1)

**(d)** Was will ihr Vater jetzt machen, und warum?

.............................................................................................................

............................................................................................................. (1)

**(e)** Was denkt Frau Martina über Christinas Vater?

.............................................................................................................

............................................................................................................. (1)

**(f)** Was für eine Lösung bietet sie an?

.................................................................................................................

................................................................................................... (1)

## Writing

**Instructions to candidates:**
Foundation Tier: attempt questions 1–5
Higher Tier: attempt questions 5–6
You must answer *all* the questions.
Read the instructions and the questions carefully.
You may use a dictionary.

**1** Schreiben Sie ganze Sätze.
   **(a)** Fünf Hobbys (Aber passen Sie gut auf: Sie treiben nicht gern Sport.)
      Zum Beispiel: Ich tanze gern.

      **(i)** ...................................................

      **(ii)** ...................................................

      **(iii)** ...................................................

      **(iv)** ...................................................

      **(v)** ...................................................

   **(b)** Fünf Schulfächer, die Sie gern mögen.
      Zum Beispiel: Ich lerne gern Englisch.

      **(i)** ...................................................

      **(ii)** ...................................................

      **(iii)** ...................................................

      **(iv)** ...................................................

      **(v)** ................................................... (10)

**2** Ihr Brieffreund/Ihre Brieffreundin aus Deutschland kommt bald nach England.
Welche Gebäude und Geschäfte gibt es in Ihrer Stadt zu sehen? Machen Sie eine Liste!

................................................     ................................................

................................................     ................................................

................................................     ................................................

................................................     ................................................

................................................     ................................................ (10)

**3** Sie machen Urlaub im Lake District. Schreiben Sie eine Postkarte an Ihren Brieffreund/Ihre Brieffreundin in Deutschland.
   Sagen Sie:   mit wem Sie Urlaub machen.   Beschreiben Sie: das Wetter.
                 wo Sie wohnen.                    die Umgebung.
                 was Sie machen.

(10)

**4** Hinterlaßen Sie eine Notiz für Ihren Brieffreund bzw. Ihre Brieffreundin.

Wer ist gekommen?     Wann?    

Warum?

Wo haben Sie es gelassen?    

Wohin sind Sie gegangen?

Machen Sie entweder Aufgabe **5 (a)** oder **5 (b)**.

**5** **(a)** Sie haben diesen Brief von Ihrer Brieffreundin bekommen. Lesen Sie den Brief und schreiben Sie eine passende Antwort darauf. Schreiben Sie 100 Wörter.

> *Hannover, den 14. Januar*
>
> *Hallo!*
>
> *Hier schreibt Liesel. Es geht mir im Moment echt gut. Und Dir?*
>
> *Letztes Wochenende habe ich viel Spaß gehabt. Am Samstagmorgen bin ich mit meinen Freundinnen in die Stadt gegangen. Wir sind in viele Geschäfte gegangen, und ich habe endlich etwas für die Party bei Peter gefunden. Ich habe einen schönen Minirock gekauft und ein hellgrünes T-Shirt.*
>
> *Zu Mittag haben wir in Macdonalds gegessen. Wie immer habe ich einen Cheeseburger mit Pommes frites gegessen. Ich habe auch ein großes Eis gegessen. Es hat mir gut geschmeckt.*
>
> *Gehst Du oft ins Restaurant?*
>
> *Am Nachmittag habe ich meine Oma besucht. Sie wohnt nicht weit von uns.*
>
> *Am Abend bin ich auf die Party bei Peter gegangen. Ich habe stundenlang getanzt.*
>
> *Und Du? Was hast Du letzten Samstag gemacht? Gehst Du gern ins Kino? Welchen Film hast Du neulich gesehen? Ich habe den neuen Film mit Michael Douglas gesehen. Toll!*
>
> *Bald fahre ich wieder auf Urlaub. Ich mache eine Klassenfahrt nach Österreich, um Ski zu laufen. Wir werden am 19. Februar abfahren. Wann fährst Du zum nächsten Mal in Ferien?*
>
> *Schreib bald wieder und vergiß nicht, die Fragen zu beantworten.*
>
> *Alles Gute.*
>
> *Deine Freundin*
>
> *Liesel*

(20)

**5** **(b)** Dein Brieffreund/deine Brieffreundin wird nächsten Sommer nach England kommen, um dich zu besuchen. Schreib an ihn/sie einen Brief von ungefähr 130 Wörtern.

Erzähl ihm/ihr: etwas über dein Haus

wo er/sie schlafen wird

was du vorhast – mindestens drei Dinge

(20)

**6** Sie haben einen Ferienjob gehabt. Schreiben Sie einen Bericht darüber für die Schülerzeitung Ihrer Brieffreundin/Ihres Brieffreundes! Sie sollen erklären, warum Sie diesen Job gewählt haben und was Sie davon halten.

(Schreiben Sie ungefähr 150 Wörter.)

(30)

---

## Listening transcripts

## Recording 22

**Mann**

Achtung, Achtung. Der Nahverkehrszug aus Ulm, planmäßige Ankunft 14.30, planmäßige Abfahrt 14.36, hat voraussichtlich 25 Minuten Verspätung. Ich wiederhole …

## Recording 23

**Frau**

Achtung bitte am Gleis acht ! Der verspätete Intercity Walküre läuft in wenigen Minuten ein. Die Wagen der ersten Klasse befinden sich im mittleren Teil des Zuges. Der Speisewagen befindet sich am Schluß des Zuges. Dieser Zug fährt nach kurzem Aufenthalt weiter nach Frankfurt am Main. Der Zug ist zuschlagpflichtig. Bitte Vorsicht bei der Einfahrt des Zuges. Ich wiederhole …

## Recording 24

| | |
|---|---|
| **Herbergsvater** | Guten Abend, kann ich Ihnen helfen? |
| **Peter** | Ja, wir haben reserviert. |
| **Herbergsvater** | Ihr Name? |
| **Peter** | Ich heiße Peter Schiller. |
| **Herbergsvater** | Ja, Sie wollen eine Woche hier bleiben. |
| **Peter** | Ja, das stimmt. Hier sind unsere Ausweise. |
| **Herbergsvater** | Gut, in Ordnung, wollen Sie sich hier bitte eintragen. |
| **Peter** | Um wieviel Uhr macht die Herberge abends zu? |
| **Herbergsvater** | Jeden Abend um elf Uhr. |
| **Peter** | Kann man hier warmes Essen zu Abend kriegen? |

| | |
|---|---|
| **Herbergsvater** | Normalerweise ja, aber am Mittwoch ist der Koch nicht hier. Am besten gehen Sie in die Stadt. Das Restaurant zum Roten Löwen am Bahnhofsplatz kann ich Ihnen empfehlen. |
| **Peter** | Ist es weit von hier? |
| **Herbergsvater** | Ungefähr zehn Minuten zu Fuß. |
| **Kellner** | Guten Abend, was darf es sein? |
| **Peter** | Haben Sie eine Speisekarte? |
| **Kellner** | Wir haben eine Tageskarte: zu fünfunddreißig Schilling, zu fünfundvierzig Schilling oder zu sechzig Schilling. Bedienung und Nachtisch sind inklusiv. Sie müssen die Getränke extra bezahlen. |

## Recording 25

**Frau**

Guten abend, liebe Zuschauer. Ich möchte Ihnen nun einen Überblick über unser Programm für den heutigen Sonntagabend geben: Wie immer werden wir um 20 Uhr mit der Tagesschau und dem Wetterbericht beginnen. Um 20.15 Uhr folgt dann eine weitere Folge der Tatortserie. Kommissar Müller wird heute abend einen besonderen Mord untersuchen. In den Hauptrollen sehen Sie Curd Jürgens und Maria Schell ... Um 21.45 Uhr werden wir einen Dokumentarfilm über Indien zeigen. Dieser Film hat deutsche Untertitel ... Danach können Sie um 22.30 Uhr die heutige Ausgabe der Sportschau mit den neuesten Fußballergebnissen sehen. Wir werden unser Programm mit den Nachrichten um 23.30 Uhr und anschließender Ziehung der Lottozahlen beenden. Sendeschluß wird voraussichtlich gegen 1 Uhr morgens sein. Ich wünsche Ihnen gute Unterhaltung.

## Recording 26

**Junge**

Letztes Jahr fuhren meine Familie und ich mit unserem Wohnwagen an den Bodensee auf der Schweizer Seite. Wir hatten Glück, das Wetter war so herrlich, daß wir jeden Tag mit unseren Kanus auf dem See paddeln konnten. Unser Campingplatz war nur fünf Minuten zu Fuß vom See entfernt, und das Wasser war immer ruhig.
Auf dem Weg nach Hause hatten wir einen kleinen Unfall. Wir fuhren in die falsche Richtung, und Vati mußte rückwärts in einen Parkplatz fahren. Leider bemerkte er nicht die kleine Mauer am Rand des Parkplatzes und fuhr auf sie drauf.

## Recording 27

**Mädchen**

Mein Job macht mir viel Spaß. Im Moment arbeite ich in einer Bäckerei, um Geld für meinen Urlaub zu verdienen. Ich hoffe nächsten Sommer nach Italien fahren zu können. Leider muß ich sehr früh aufstehen – oft um halb fünf morgens, aber ich gehe um zwölf Uhr wieder nach Hause. Aber das ist nicht so schlimm, besonders, da ich acht Mark pro Stunde bekomme. Nachmittags habe ich die Zeit, meine Ferienreise zu planen, Freundinnen anzurufen oder Einkäufe zu machen.

## Recording 28

| | |
|---|---|
| **Junge** | Heutzutage gibt's viele Probleme in den Großstädten in Deutschland. Die Verschmutzung durch die Abgase von PKWs, LKWs und Bussen ist enorm. Was meinst du dazu? |
| **Mädchen** | Ja, stimmt, wir haben zu viele Autos und andere Fahrzeuge in der Stadtmitte, sie verpesten die Luft und sind außerdem laut. Die Politiker sollten etwas machen. |
| **Junge** | Ja, aber wir sollten auch etwas tun, um die Umwelt zu schützen. Zum Beispiel sollten wir nicht immer mit dem Auto in die Schule fahren. Es wäre gesünder, mit dem Fahrrad oder zu Fuß in die Schule zu kommen. |
| **Mädchen** | Sicher, und wir sollten auch keine Abfälle auf die Straßen werfen. Altpapier, Dosen und Flaschen sollten wir recyceln. |
| **Junge** | Vielleicht könnten wir eine Altpapiersammlung in der Schule organisieren. Das wäre etwas Positives. |

# Suggested answers

### Listening
## Recording 22

1 aus Ulm
2 25 Minuten

## Recording 23

1 bald
2 in der Mitte des Zuges
3 nach Frankfurt am Main
4 man muß Zuschlag zahlen

## Recording 24

1 (c)
2 (d)
3 Am Mittwoch
4 am Bahnhofsplatz
5 35 Schilling
6 (c)

## Recording 25

| 20.00 | **Tagesschau/Wetterbericht** |
|---|---|
| **20.15** | eine Serie |
| 21.45 | **ein Dokumetarfilm über Indien** |
| **22.30** | **die Sportschau** |
| **23.30** | Nachrichten und ........................ |
| **01.00** | Sendeschluß |

## Recording 26

1 in der Schweiz
2 herrlich
3 jeden Tag
4 weil das Wasser immer ruhig war
5 Vati/Vater
6 die (kleine) Mauer

## Recording 27

1 in einer Bäckerei
2 um Geld für ihren Urlaub zu verdienen
3 nach Italien zu fahren
4 um halb fünf morgens aufzustehen
5 acht Mark pro Stunde
6 ihre Ferienreise planen, Freundinnen anrufen, Einkäufe machen (*two of these*), weil sie um zwölf Uhr wieder nach Hause geht

## Recording 28

1 die Verschmutzung durch die Abgase von PKWs, LKWs und Bussen
2 zu viele Autos und andere Fahrzeuge
3 Zum Beispiel sollten sie nicht immer mit dem Auto in die Schule fahren.
4 Es wäre gesünder, mit dem Fahrrad oder zu Fuß in die Schule zu kommen.
5 Altpapier, Dosen und Flaschen
6 eine Altpapiersammlung in der Schule zu organisieren

Speaking
# Role-play 1

| | |
|---|---|
| **Teacher** | Guten Tag. Was darf es sein? |
| **You** | Ich möchte eine Tasse Kaffee. |
| **Teacher** | Sonst noch etwas? |
| **You** | Ich möchte auch eine Tasse Schokolade. |
| **Teacher** | Etwas zu essen? |
| **You** | Ich möchte ein Stück Apfelkuchen mit Sahne. |
| **Teacher** | Ist das alles? |
| **You** | Was kostet das?/Wieviel macht das? |
| **Teacher** | Zusammen macht das neunzehn Schilling. |
| **You** | Wo sind die Toiletten? |
| **Teacher** | Dort hinten. |

# Role-play 2

| | |
|---|---|
| **Teacher** | Guten Abend. Kann ich Ihnen helfen? |
| **You** | Haben Sie noch Zimmer frei? |
| **Teacher** | Ja, wir haben noch Zimmer frei. |
| **You** | Was kostet ein Zimmer pro Nacht? |
| **Teacher** | Ein Einzelzimmer kostet vierzig Mark. |
| **You** | Ich möchte ein Doppelzimmer mit Dusche. |
| **Teacher** | Für wie lange? |
| **You** | Für drei Nächte. |
| **Teacher** | In Ordnung. Bitte tragen Sie sich hier ein. |
| **You** | Wann wird das Frühstück serviert? |

# Role-play 3

| | |
|---|---|
| **Teacher** | Was kann ich für Sie tun? |
| **You** | Ich habe die Hose zerrissen. |
| **Teacher** | So ein Pech! Wie kann ich Ihnen helfen? |
| **You** | Können Sie die Hose reparieren? |
| **Teacher** | Ja, aber es wird einige Tage dauern. |
| **You** | Wann kann ich die Hose wieder abholen? |
| **Teacher** | In vier oder fünf Tagen. Ist es Ihre Hose? |
| **You** | Nein, es ist die Hose meines Brieffreunds. |
| **Teacher** | Oh, ... |
| **You** | Vielen Dank. |

# Role-play 4

| | |
|---|---|
| **Teacher** | Guten Morgen. Wer ist am Apparat, bitte? |
| **You** | Hier spricht Keely. |
| **Teacher** | Was kann ich für Sie tun? |
| **You** | Haben Sie Ferienjobs für Studenten? |
| **Teacher** | Was für eine Stelle suchen Sie? |
| **You** | Ich möchte in einem Café arbeiten. |
| **Teacher** | Wann können Sie anfangen? |
| **You** | Am ersten August. |
| **Teacher** | Leider haben wir im August keine Stelle frei. |
| **You** | Ja, vielen Dank. Wiederhören. |

# Role-play 5

This is an example of the sort of thing you might say.

| | |
|---|---|
| **Teacher** | Kannst du mir etwas über deinen Aufenthalt in Köln erzählen? |
| **You** | Ja, letztes Jahr bin ich mit einer Gruppe nach Köln gefahren. Köln ist unsere Partnerstadt, und wir sollten einige Tage bei deutschen Familien bleiben, um unser Deutsch zu verbessern. Der Besuch wurde von meinem Tischtennisklub organisiert, und es gab auch ein Turnier während des Austausches. |
| | Wir sind direkt mit dem Reisebus von Benfleet über Calais gefahren. Die Reise hat acht Stunden gedauert, und wir waren ziemlich müde, als wir Köln erreicht |

hatten. Die deutschen Familien haben vor der Albert-Schweizer-Schule gewartet, und ich war ein bißchen nervös.

**Teacher** Wieso?

**You** Das war mein erster Besuch in Deutschland, und ich wollte nicht viele Fehler machen, und meine Sprachkenntnisse sind nicht so gut.

**Teacher** Doch, du sprichst gut Deutsch!

**You** Also, ich habe meine Gastfamilie getroffen: Sie heißen Müller und sie wohnen in einem Wohnblock nicht weit von der Schule. Wir sind zu Fuß zu ihnen gegangen, und nach dem Abendessen bin ich sofort ins Bett gegangen. Ich war todmüde.

Am folgenden Morgen gab es eine Stadtrundfahrt. Wir sind zuerst ins Rathaus gegangen, und der Bürgermeister hat etwas über die Partnerschaft gesagt, aber ich habe fast nichts verstanden. Danach sind wir in einen Reisebus eingestiegen, um die Stadt zu besichtigen. Wir haben den Dom und andere Gebäude gesehen.

**Teacher** Wo has du zu Mittag gegessen?

**You** Meine Gastfamilie hat für mich ein Picknick vorbereitet, und wegen des Regens mußten wir im Bus essen.

**Teacher** Und am Donnerstag?

**You** Dann sind wir nach Bonn gefahren. Wir haben den Bundestag besichtigt, das war langweilig. Wir haben auch eine Rheinfahrt gemacht. Das Wetter war herrlich, und wir haben uns gesonnt. An Bord haben wir eine andere Gruppe aus England kennengelernt. Wir haben viel Englisch geredet.

Und dann, am Freitag, sind wir mit unseren Partnern nach Phantasialand gefahren. Wir haben das Riesenrad gesehen und auch das Piratenschiff. Es gab viele Attraktionen wie in Alton Towers hier in England. Wir haben viel gelacht, und es hat Spaß gemacht. Auf der Rückfahrt bin ich im Bus eingeschlafen. Es war ein bißchen teuer, so wie in England.

**Teacher** Und am Wochenende?

**You** Naja wir haben die zwei Tage mit den Familien verbracht. Ich habe ihnen meine Fotos gezeigt und habe von meiner Familie erzählt. Wir haben über die Schule und das Leben in England diskutiert. Und ich habe mich ausgeruht.

Am Samstag fand das Turnier statt. Die Engländer haben gewonnen! Es gab Bier zu trinken und Würste zu essen.

**Teacher** Wann bist du wieder nach England gefahren?

**You** Am Montagmorgen. Der Besuch war kurz, aber wir haben viel Deutsch gesprochen, und ich freue mich auf den Besuch der Deutschen. Sie kommen im August nach England, und wir planen schon ihren Besuch. Wir hoffen, einen Tagesausflug nach London zu machen. Wir können auch nach Alton Towers fahren, aber das hängt vom Geld ab.

## Reading

1

| | Sven | Katja | Niklas |
|---|---|---|---|
| muß manchmal zu Hause helfen | | X | X |
| schützt die Tiere | | X | |
| arbeitet ab und zu, um Geld zu verdienen | X | | |
| arbeitet gern mit anderen Menschen | | | X |
| lernt gern Naturwissenschaft | X | | |
| teilt die Hausarbeit, weil die Eltern oft beschäftigt sind | | X | |
| ist umweltfreundlich | | | X |
| geht von Zeit zu Zeit Babysitten | | X | |
| füttert die Tiere | | X | |

2 **(a)** Karussells
Wurstbuden
Riesenräder
Schießbuden

**(b)** Er war Maurer.

    **(c)**  Es gibt keinen Jahrmarkt.

    **(d)**  weil sie die Qualifikationen brauchen/weil sie sonst zu viel Schule vermissen würden

    **(e)**  Sie arbeiten auf dem Jahrmarkt.

    **(f)**  in einem Wohnwagen

**3** **(a)** (iii)

    **(b)** (ii)

    **(c)** (iv)

    **(d)** (i)

**4** **(a)** stop immediately; smoke fewer cigarettes daily until confident enough to stop; smoke as few cigarettes as possible

    **(b)** do not take other things to do with smoking with you e.g. matches, lighter
- refuse cigarettes when offered
- avoid smoking at key times during the day; e.g. when you are on the telephone
- smoke half a cigarette
- smoke mild cigarettes
- only buy the next packet of cigarettes when the current one is empty
- do not smoke before and after meals
- do not keep an ashtray in the living-room or at work
- cut back to 10 cigarettes per day
- if you feel the craving to smoke, go for a walk or try relaxing breathing at an open window

**5** **(a)** Ihr Vater öffnet ihre Briefe.

    **(b)** Er versteht sie nicht. Er liest z.B. ihre Briefe.

    **(c)** Zu ihrer Mutter, weil sie alles mit ihr besprechen kann.

    **(d)** Er will sie von der Schule abholen, so daß sie ihren neuen Freund nicht mehr sehen kann.

    **(e)** Er sorgt sich um seine Tochter.

    **(f)** Ihr neuer Freund soll zu ihr kommen, um einen Abend mit ihr und ihrer Familie zu verbringen.

## Writing

**1** **(a)** Ich lese gern, ich höre gern Musik, ich sammle Briefmarken, ich sehe fern, ich gehe gern einkaufen, ich spiele gern Schach, ich bastele gern. *Choose any five from these – if you are not sure what they all mean, look them up.*

    **(b)** ich lerne gern Deutsch, ich mag Erdkunde, ich mag Mathe, ich mag Kunst, ich mag Technik, ich mag Informatik, ich lerne gern Geschichte. *Choose any five from these – if you are not sure what they all mean, look in Chapter 4.*

**2** *You were asked to provide a list of buildings and shops in your town. Take any ten from these, if you do not know what they are, look them up in your dictionary:*

Gebäude: die Bibliothek, die Burg, der Dom, die Kirche, das Museum, die Polizeiwache, das Postamt, das Rathaus, das Wirtshaus, der Zoo.

Geschäfte: der Buchladen, die Drogerie, das Kaufhaus, die Konditorei, der Supermarkt.

**3** Ich bin in Ullswater mit meiner Familie.

Ich wohne in einem Hotel.

Wir besuchen die Stadt/den Dom.

Das Wetter ist gut. Es ist sonnig.

Die Landschaft ist schön.

**4** Der Briefträger ist heute morgen um zehn Uhr gekommen. Er hat ein Paket gebracht. Das Paket ist im Wohnzimmer. Ich bin in die Stadt gegangen.

**5** **(a)** *Liebe Liesel,*

*Vielen Dank für Deinen netten Brief. Es geht mir auch gut. Im Moment muß ich viel für die Schule machen.*

*Letzten Samstag bin ich mit meiner Mutter nach York gefahren. Wir wollten einkaufen. Wir sind früh mit dem Zug von Newcastle abgefahren. Die Fahrt war nicht zu lang – etwa anderthalb Stunden. In York sind wir in viele Geschäfte gegangen, und schließlich habe ich eine Jeans und ein schönes T-Shirt gekauft. Meine Mutter hat einen neuen Badeanzug gekauft. Zu Mittag haben wir in einem Pizzarestaurant gegessen. Ißt du gern Pizzas?*

*Später sind wir ins Kino gegangen. Im Moment läuft der neue Film mit Brad Pitt. Er ist so schön. Kennst du ihn?*

*Wir sind um 10 Uhr abends wieder in Newcastle angekommen. Mein Vater hat uns abgeholt.*

*Ende Mai fahren wir nach Spanien. Wir werden zwei Wochen in unserer Villa am Strand verbringen. Ich freue mich schon auf die Ferien.*

*Wie war die Klassenfahrt? Bist du viel Ski gelaufen? Schreib bald.*

*Deine Freundin Lisa*

5 **(b)** **Lieber Karl!/Liebe Antje!**

**Wie geht's Dir? Vielen Dank für Deinen letzten Brief, den ich vor kurzem erhalten habe. Ich schreibe, um Dich einzuladen, nächsten Sommer zwei Wochen bei uns zu verbringen. Wir wohnen in einem ziemlich großen Haus, das vier Schlafzimmer hat und in einem Vorort von Chelmsford liegt.**

**Wenn Du nächsten Juli kommst, wirst Du im kleinsten Schlafzimmer schlafen müssen. Obwohl es sehr klein ist, hat es eine sehr gute Aussicht auf den Garten und die schönen Bäume im Park hinter unserem Haus.**

**Während Deines Aufenthalts werden wir sicher einen Ausflug mit dem Zug nach London machen. Wir könnten den ganzen Tag dort verbringen, wenn Dir die Idee gefiele. Wir können auch im modernen Hallenbad in Chelmsford schwimmen gehen und einen Tag am Meer in Southend verbringen. Schreib bitte bald!**

**Herzliche Grüße an Dich und Deine Familie,**

**Dein Peter/Deine Karen**

6  Zu Ostern habe ich mich um einen Ferienjob in einem Supermarkt beworben. Ich hatte Glück, sie haben mich als Verkäufer/Verkäuferin für zwei Wochen angestellt. Ich arbeitete nur Teilzeit, meistens drei Stunden pro Tag, aber das konnte entweder früh morgens ab halb sechs oder spät abends bis elf Uhr sein. Manchmal habe ich auch während des Tages gearbeitet, das hing von der Schicht ab.

Ich habe diesen Job gewählt, weil ich noch viel Arbeit für meine Prüfungen hatte. Ich wollte auch wissen, wie anstrengend so eine Stelle sein würde. Aber es war nicht zu anstrengend, und ich hatte viel Freizeit, Sport zu treiben und zu lernen.

Es war interessant, allerlei Menschen zu begegnen. Ich mußte auch schnell lernen, wo alles im Laden war, so daß ich den Kunden helfen konnte. Am Ende der zweiten Woche wußte ich genau, daß ich Verkäufer/Verkäuferin nie werden wollte. Die Arbeit war zu langweilig, und man verdient nicht genug Geld.

# Index

# GCSE German CD/Cassette

If you have purchased a copy of our Study Guide for GCSE German and would like to buy the accompanying CD or cassette, or if you have bought the CD and would like to swap it for a cassette, please tick the relevant box below, complete the order form and return it to:

**Letts Educational Ltd**
**Aldine Place**
**London W12 8AW**
**Telephone 020 8740 2266**

Forenames (Mr/Ms) _____

Surname _____

Address _____

_____

_____  Postcode _____

Please swap the enclosed CD for a cassette: ☐

Please send me:

| | | Quantity | Price (incl VAT) | Total |
|---|---|---|---|---|
| GCSE German CD | ☐ | _____ | £4.00 | _____ |
| GCSE German cassette | ☐ | _____ | £4.00 | _____ |
| Add postage – UK and ROI 75p for each CD/cassette | ☐ | | | _____ |

I enclose a cheque/postal order for £ _____
(made payable to Letts Educational Ltd)

Or charge to Access/Visa card No. ☐☐☐☐☐☐☐☐☐☐☐☐☐☐☐☐☐☐

Expiry date _____

Signature _____